Joseph L. Blau

COLUMBIA UNIVERSITY

MEN *and* MOVEMENTS
in
AMERICAN PHILOSOPHY

Prentice-Hall, Inc.

ENGLEWOOD CLIFFS, N. J.

PRENTICE-HALL PHILOSOPHY SERIES
Arthur E. Murphy, Ph.D., Editor

First Printing . . . . May, 1952
Second Printing . . . . June, 1953
Third Printing . . . . June, 1954
Fourth Printing . . . . . . February, 1955
Fifth Printing . . . . January, 1958
Sixth Printing . . . . June, 1961
Seventh Printing . . . . April, 1963
Eighth Printing . . . . January, 1965

L. C. Cat. Card No.: 52–8596

57486–C

For

HERBERT W. SCHNEIDER

FOREWORD

The story of American philosophic development is unknown to most Americans, and even to many students and teachers of philosophy in America. The neglect of this study may be partly the result of an excessive modesty about our own cultural achievements and partly the result of an excessive admiration for European cultural achievements. In the case of the "professional" philosopher, there is some excuse for both the modesty and the admiration: Until quite recently philosophy in America has not been pursued as a technical discipline. It is this very fact which should make it possible for many Americans to learn and to take pride in our philosophic history. There has been a "democratic" quality to American philosophizing; it has grown as much outside of academic circles as it has within the colleges and universities. Contributors to America's philosophic history have come from the farm and the factory as well as from the seats of government and of formal learning.

This book does not try to cover the full range of the story of American philosophy. It makes no pretense to being encyclopedic. What is attempted here is an introductory account, stressing the more formal side of our philosophic history, to provide a background for the general reader and the beginning student which will enable them to read further both in and about American philosophy. This history is treated in terms of the emergence, under various stimulations, of ten "movements," or "schools," of philosophy. No two philosophers, even of the same school, ever produce identical philosophic positions. To the general outlook which is characteristic of his school, each one contributes his own particular (and, often, peculiar) insights. A presentation of this history entirely in terms of movements would do violence to the individuality of philosophers. To avoid the impression of uniformity, each summary of the position of a movement in American philosophy is accompanied by a description of two or three distinctive individual philosophies within the school. Considerable selectivity has been exercised about the choice of philosophies to be presented. In some cases, better-known figures

v

have been omitted and relative "unknowns" included, for the sake of showing how very different may be the philosophies proposed by adherents of the same movement.

Again, as a matter of principle, after the time of the American Revolution, I have selected representatives whose training was largely American. This has been costly in three cases. In Chapter 2, it has led to the omission of Thomas Cooper as a spokesman of enlightenment. In Chapter 3 it has compelled the omission of a full discussion of the philosophy of James McCosh, who was brought over from Scotland in his maturity to head Princeton University. In more recent times, the policy of narrowly defining an American philosopher has excluded Alfred North Whitehead, whose American adventures of ideas began when he was sixty-three years of age. The advantage gained at the expense of this sacrifice is that there are American backgrounds and American cultural influences reflected in the philosophers discussed, and this volume becomes a case study in what Charles Jared Ingersoll, more than a century ago, called "the influence of America on the mind."

The writer of a book of this sort incurs many obligations, and it is but just that those who have helped to make it possible should be recorded, although the final responsibility for everything which is included or excluded is mine, not theirs. Preliminary studies leading toward this book were carried on with assistance provided by a grant extended by the American Council of Learned Societies in 1944. My friends Willis Moore, Harold A. Larrabee, Harold Hantz, and Willard Arnett have read and criticized drafts of parts of the manuscript. My wife, Eleanor W. Blau, has borne loyally with me every difficulty and, I hope, some joy in its composition, as well as repeatedly reading, criticizing, and retyping the work. Herbert W. Schneider, whose knowledge of the field of American philosophic history is unsurpassed, has given the final version the benefit of reading and suggestions, thus putting the seal on his earlier kindnesses to me as my teacher and my colleague. Finally, my exposition owes much to the discipline I have gained from my students at Columbia University, the University of Minnesota, and the University of Arkansas. I can only hope that what I have done is some recompense for what they have done for me.

JOSEPH L. BLAU

Columbia University

ACKNOWLEDGMENTS

Permission to use material quoted in this book has been granted by the following:

George Allen & Unwin, Ltd.: W. M. Urban, *The Intelligible World* (London, 1929); W. M. Urban, *Beyond Realism and Idealism* (London, 1949); G. P. Adams and W. P. Montague, *Contemporary American Philosophy* (London, 1930).

Felix S. Cohen: M. R. Cohen, *Reason and Nature* (Harcourt, Brace & Co., New York, 1931).

Columbia University Press: F. J. E. Woodbridge, *The Realm of Mind* (New York, 1926); Y. H. Krikorian, ed., *Naturalism and the Human Spirit* (New York, 1944).

Harcourt, Brace & Co.: J. Buchler, ed., *The Philosophy of Peirce: Selected Writings* (New York, 1940).

Harvard College, The President and Fellows of: R. B. Perry, *The Thought and Character of William James* (Little, Brown & Co., Boston, 1935).

D. C. Heath & Co.: John Dewey, *How We Think* (Boston, 1933).

Henry Holt & Co.: M. R. Cohen, *The Faith of a Liberal* (New York, 1946); M. R. Cohen, *A Preface to Logic* (New York, 1944); J. Dewey, *Human Nature and Conduct* (New York, 1922); J. Dewey and F. H. Tufts, *Ethics*, rev. ed. (New York, 1932); J. Dewey and others, *Creative Intelligence* (New York, 1917); J. Dewey, *Reconstruction in Philosophy* (New York, 1920).

Kappa Delta Pi: J. Dewey, *Experience and Education* (The Macmillan Co., New York, 1938).

Longmans, Green & Co.: W. James, *Collected Essays and Reviews* (New York, 1920); W. James, *Essays on Faith and Morals* (New York, 1943; copyright 1896, 1899, 1900, 1911, 1939); W. James, *Pragmatism, with Four Related Essays selected from The Meaning of Truth* (New York, 1943; copyright 1907, 1909); W. James, *A Pluralistic Universe* (New York, 1943; copyright 1909); R. B. Perry: *Present Philosophical Tendencies* (New York, 1925).

The Macmillan Company: J. E. Creighton, *Studies in Speculative Philosophy*, copyright 1925 by The Macmillan Company and used with their permission; Holt, Marvin, et al, *The New Realism*, copyright 1912 by The Macmillan Company and used with their permission; R. W. Sellars, *The Philosophy of Physical Realism*, copyright 1932 by The Macmillan Company and used with their permission; Adams and Montague, *Contemporary American Philosophy*, Vol. II, used with the permission of The Macmillan Company.

The Open Court Publishing Co.: J. Dewey, *Experience and Nature* (LaSalle, Illinois, 1925); G. H. Mead, *Philosophy of the Present* (La Salle, Illinois, 1932).

Prentice-Hall, Inc.: W. P. Montague, *The Ways of Things* (New York, 1940).

Charles Scribner's Sons.: R. B. Perry, *The Moral Economy* (New York, 1909); G. Santayana, *Dialogues in Limbo* (New York, 1926); G. Santayana, *The Genteel Tradition* (New York, 1931); G. Santayana, *The Middle Span* (New York, 1945); G. Santayana, *The Realm of Spirit* (New York, 1940); G. Santayana, *Reason in Common Sense* (New York, 1922); G. Santayana, *Reason in Science* (New York, 1933); G. Santayana, *Scepticism and Animal Faith* (New York, 1923).

The University of Chicago Press: G. H. Mead, *Mind, Self and Society* (Chicago, 1934).

Vanguard Press, Inc.: R. B. Perry, *Puritanism and Democracy* (New York, 1944).

Yale University Press: J. Dewey, *A Common Faith* (New Haven, Conn., 1934).

CONTENTS

PRELUDE

THE PURITAN BACKGROUND

The earliest permanent European settlers of New England brought with them little in the way of material goods. They had few skills to enable them to withstand the rugged conditions of life in the northeastern section of what is now the United States of America. To compensate for these deficiencies of goods and skills, they had a strong faith in the rightness of their beliefs, and a conviction that this rightness was of God. These views, so strongly authenticated to the settlers, made up the religion of the Puritans and their philosophy. We must take the philosophy of Puritan New England as our point of departure as we try to unravel the strands of thought which have gone into the making of the American mind.

At the very outset, we should emphasize the fact that most of what the Puritans thought and taught was in no way novel. The Puritans were the heirs of the whole Christian tradition. They were, it is true, Protestants; but the heritage of medieval Christian thought was as much a part of the background of Protestantism as it was of Catholicism. The differences were not in the fundamentals of faith but in the superstructure. Protestantism emphasized the idea that salvation was a matter lying directly between an individual and God, and therefore it placed less stress on the church as an intermediary in achieving salvation. Thus Protestantism heightened, though it did not invent, the sense of human dependence upon God.

Of the various patterns of Protestantism, the one which the Puritans accepted was that of the followers of Calvin. It was the special place of Calvinism in the Protestant movement to resist the tendencies to extreme individualism and sectarianism which were latent in the Protestant conception of salvation. By insisting that God alone had the power to elect those who were to be saved and that nothing that men could do contributed in any way to their election, the Calvinists made God the sole determiner of human destiny and the constant center of human concern. This Calvinist view further intensified the notion of human dependence upon God, the exclusive ruler of all the

1

universe; kings and princes, ministers and magistrates, were earthly agents and representatives of the divine government.

The Puritans, however, although they were Calvinists and insisted on the absolute supremacy of God, belonged to a group which modified somewhat the arbitrary character of Calvin's God. This group, adherents of the "Covenant" theology, thought of God as a constitutional ruler, whose actions were taken in accordance with covenants accepted by men. God's actions were considered predictable by human reason. The Covenant theologians, by eliminating the element of caprice from their idea of God, were able to take a view higher than other Calvinists of the possibilities of the human mind. This group believed, without taking anything away from the glory of God as the First Cause and Creator of the universe, that He exercised His dominion over the universe according to a regular pattern of law. In that part of the universe coming under man's observation, in the environing nature which man experiences, this regularity can be discovered in the operation of natural causes, called "secondary" in tribute to the primacy of causation by God.

The knowledge that men derived from the study of nature and its regularities was considered to be harmonious with the Divine Revelation. Both faith and knowledge were thought to lead men to a proper realization of the glory of God. To the Puritans, the study of natural science was, as Cotton Mather indicated in his *Christian Philosopher*, an acceptable and encouraged method of paying tribute to God.[1] From its earliest days Harvard, then the Puritan's college, was well-supplied with scientific instruments and equipment for the study of nature. The Puritan reason for studying science was not that of the scientist of today, but the contribution of Puritans to scientific progress in their own age was not negligible. A final point of difference between the Covenant theology and other varieties of Calvinism is that its lessened emphasis on the arbitrary character of God's rule over the universe led men to think of themselves as citizens of that universe rather than merely dwellers in it. In the strict Calvinistic view of unconditional predestination by an arbitrary God, it is difficult to argue for the moral responsibility of man. While predestination remained a central tenet of Covenant theology, the belief in the constitutional character of God's rule left more place for moral responsibility and the operations of the human conscience.

The Puritans, then, belonged in their theology to the Covenant twig of the Calvinist branch of the Protestant trunk growing out of the Christian root. And, in addition to their theology, the Puritans maintained a Congregationalist view of church government. This view required that individual churches should be small in size, completely independent of all other churches, self-constituted by a membership of "saints," and not established by any superior ecclesiastical authority. Some of the Puritans, among them those who settled Plymouth, thought it necessary to assert their complete separation from the Church of England in order to live according to their principles. Others, including the settlers of the Massachusetts Bay colony, thought that they could remain members of the English Church and work for its reformation and its purification from within. For all those who crossed the Atlantic, whether separatists or not, migration was a physical separation from the home church.

Migration to the American continent, which was at one and the same time their wilderness and their promised land, for a while led the Puritan settlers to take quite literally the parallel between themselves and the Hebrews of the Exodus. The Old Testament was more than a sacred history to the New England Puritans; it was guide and handbook in all aspects of their lives. When the need for civil government became clear to the Puritans it was only natural that they should establish a theocratic government after the Old Testament model, with close cooperation between church authorities and secular governors, and with church membership a prerequisite for citizenship. Even before the Plymouth settlers left Holland they heard from their pastor, John Robinson, that civil magistrates are ordained by God and that the Puritan, to be true to his faith, must consider his governors of God's ordination. Since, unfortunately, some of the civil authorities in England and Holland behaved in such a way that the conscientious Puritan found it difficult to believe in their Divine ordination, Robinson argued the necessity for migration: The Puritans should escape from the domination of corrupt rulers and be free to choose for themselves other rulers who would live up to the ideal Puritan conception of magistracy. Migration and the selection of proper governors were given as evidences of "wisdom and godliness." [2]

Beginning in 1631, by ordinance of the Massachusetts Bay colony, only church members were freemen of the civil society, which meant that only church members had a voice in the government of the colony. But church membership was not open to all, under the Congregationalist scheme. The saints — the elect of God — constitute the church; citizenship and the privileges of freemen could, therefore, be vested only in the elect. Because of this close tie between the political and the religious aspects of Puritan life, it is advisable to consider what the Puritans meant by a "saint," and how the community could judge which of its members were to be regarded as saints. For, after all, only God has infallible knowledge of who the saints are.

First, there was the whole body of God's elect. These were known in the Calvinist tradition as "saints by calling." In addition to members of this group living at any one time, the group included those whose lives had been completed, and those as yet unborn whom God had predestined for salvation. The "invisible church," of which Christ is the head, is constituted of the entire group of saints by calling. The members of the invisible church are united with Christ by spiritual ties, by faith, and by God's free grace.

But, in addition to this invisible church which is one and universal, there are visible churches, congregations of saints, united by the Church Covenant. In theory, every saint is obligated to join a church, and no one who is not a saint is to be permitted to join. For the purposes of covenanting, then, a working definition of the saint was necessary—a method within *human* competence for separating the sheep from the goats. A sorting device of this kind was described in the Cambridge Platform of 1649, which defined saints as those who have attained a knowledge of the principles of religion, whose lives are free from "gross and open scandals," who have made frank profession of their faith and repented of their sins, and, having done so, lead thereafter a blameless life. The judgment of the congregation of saints may be misled in some few cases by those who, while apparently spotless, are "unsound and hypocrites inwardly." By and large, however, the method, exercised with "charitable discretion," might be expected to work well.[3]

Since the saints, by covenanting together, created the church organization, in the final analysis it was up to the saints to decide whether any group action fell within the scope of the covenant. This is an apparently democratic aspect of Puritan church government. In practice, this worked out as an aristocratic rather than a democratic method, because, in most cases, the minister on behalf of the elders made clear to the congregation how it should exercise its powers. For very weighty reasons the congregation might question or contradict the directed verdict; too frequent opposition was regarded as "manifestly contrary unto order and government." [4] John Cotton, in a clever image, compared the congregation to a queen and the elders to sailors in the employ of the queen. She might summon her sailors and order them to carry her in her ship to some definite place but, having issued these orders, she must leave the actual navigation to them, "must submit herself to be ruled by them, till they have brought her to her desired Haven." [5] So the congregation, having once selected its minister and its elders, was thought to have surrendered to these officers the right to make decisions. The "Christian liberty" of the common man was no more or less than his liberty to enter into a church covenant if he could prove that he possessed faith. Small wonder it is to find the system described by Samuel Stone as "a speaking Aristocracy in the face of a silent Democracy." [6]

The fundamental philosophic doctrine of the Puritans, from which all the rest of their intellectual position can be derived, is an expression, in terms of the kind of God in whom they believed, of a view of the nature of the universe as old as Plato. It is, in fact, a Christian version, following that of Peter Ramus (1515?-1572), of a pre-Christian theory of cosmic order.[7] The Puritans believed that in the mind of God, prior to the material creation, there was a rational and well-structured scheme of ideas to serve as the ground plan or blueprint of the creation and of all subsequent events. God, said Samuel Willard, "contrives in his mind an Eternal Idea of all things that are to be." [8] Not only the beginnings of the universe and its operating principles, or natural laws, but the precise activity of everything in the universe, and the place of these multifarious activities in an overarching cosmic scheme, was thought to be included in God's master plan.

Thus history was sacred drama. It started as an idea in God's mind; its plot included the creation of the universe and of man, the revolt of the creatures against the creator, the subjects against the ruler, and the gracious offering of the possibility of redemption through Jesus Christ; its closing scene was to be the last judgment. God was throughout the drama not merely the dramatist, the director, and the audience, but at every moment the central figure. The Puritan universe was God-centered. Where every event in the universe was regarded as involving God, unusual, extraordinary, and noteworthy events were thought to have special meanings for those who could discover them. This is the explanation of the unremitting search of the Puritans for "remarkable providences."

The political expression of the Puritan view that man lived in a God-centered universe was theocracy. God was considered to be the *real* ruler of the civil society and to act through its *nominal* governors. The position of the human rulers in the state resembled closely that of the leaders in the churches. Popular rights, John Winthrop declared in 1639, extended only to the selection of magistrates; once these men were elected, their power was absolute. Any attempt to oppose an action of the magistrates, except on grounds of conscience, "savors of resisting an ordinance of God." [9] Civil liberty, the same Governor Winthrop told the Massachusetts General Court in 1645, "is maintained and exercised in a way of subjection to authority; it is of the same kind of liberty wherewith Christ hath made us free." [10] Winthrop, it is true, held an extreme view of the divine right of magistrates. At the same time John Cotton, who expressed himself more moderately on most matters, declared that democracy was not a fit form of government for church or state, and asked the crucial question, "If the people be governors, who shall be governed?" [11]

In a theocratic society which yet maintained some measure of distinction between church and state, the precise character of the relation between these equally divine institutions was a perennial theme for discussion. Much of this discussion is reminiscent of the medieval controversy about the mutual relations of the Roman church and the Holy Roman empire. It was John Davenport who gave the clearest and best statement in Puritan terms of the theory of the "two swords," which had been given its earliest formulation by Pope Gelasius I in A.D. 494. Davenport asserted

> that these two different Orders and States, *Ecclesiastical* and *Civil*, be not set in opposition as contraries that one should destroy the other, but as coordinate States, in the same place reaching forth help mutually to each other, for the welfare of both according to God: So that both Officers and Members of Churches be subject, in respect of the outward men, to the Civil Power, of those who bear Rule in the Civil State according to God, and teach others so to do: And that the Civil Magistrates and Officers, in regard of the inward man, subject themselves

Spiritually to the power of Christ in Church-Ordinances, and by their Civil Power preserve the same in outward Peace and Purity.[12]

The interpretation given by many Puritan writers to the mutual assistance pact called for by Davenport required that civil as well as religious punishment be meted out to those — heretics, blasphemers, or infidels — who violated religious principles. This view of the proper relation of church and state led directly to the many acts of spiritual intolerance and physical persecution visited by the Massachusetts colony upon Baptists, Quakers, and Roman Catholics. Many Puritans demanded, as the Boston Confession of Faith of 1680 attests, that resistance to the authority of the civil power "may lawfully be called to account and proceeded against by the censures of the church and by the power of the civil magistrate." [13] Thus, revolution, or even a mild rebellion, was declared a religious as well as a civil crime.

If liberty was in this fashion virtually denied, so too was the very possibility of equality. Any attempt to achieve social equality was regarded as subversive. In an election sermon of 1676, William Hubbard defined order as "such a disposition of things in themselves equall and unequall, as gives to every one their due and proper place." [14] Order, thus conceived, was the soul of the universe, and an attempt to maintain equality would break this order down into "an heap of confusion." In his further development of this view, Hubbard constructed an extended analogy between the political order and that of the human body — one of the earliest clear statements of organic political theory to be produced on the American continent.

From what has been said, it is apparent that the Puritan theocracy can not be called democratic in its political philosophy. The Puritans did, however, conceive of secular power and authority as stewardship — government *for* the people, if not *by* the people — and, furthermore, they believed in the limitation of the power of the secular magistrate by God if not by man. The good ruler was thought of as one whose course of action was invariably chosen for the good of the public, for, as Samuel Willard said in an election sermon in 1694, "A People are not made for Rulers, but Rulers for a People." [15] The happiness of a good governor is entirely dependent upon that of his subjects.

To the extent that a more truly democratic mood can be found, it is revealed in the scattered opposition to theocracy. The Baptists in Rhode Island — many of them, like Roger Williams, expelled from Massachusetts — the Quakers in Pennsylvania, and little groups of independent individuals like the recalcitrant fishermen of Maine who were able to maintain a small democracy from the death of Thomas Gorges in 1649 to the seizure of their territory by Massachusetts in 1652 — these are the heroic ancestors of American democratic theory. Not until the early eighteenth century, however, do we come to the formal expression of an American political philosophy that is akin to democracy as we know it and think of it. It is interesting that this discussion was still carried on in the context of problems of church government.

In 1717 a group of Boston and Cambridge ministers were attempting to break down the autonomy of the local churches, especially those in more rural sections of the colony. John Wise sprang to the defense of congregational self-determination in a tract called *A Vindication of the Government of the New England Churches.* In the first part of this controversial pamphlet, Wise uses traditional theological and scriptural arguments for Congregationalism. In the second part, however, he argues philosophically, from "the Light of Reason." Here he introduces what he called the "natural immunities" of men; nearly sixty years later Thomas Jefferson was to substitute the phrase "inalienable rights" for the liberty and equality to which Wise referred.

Wise also argued that secular society had been established by a social contract among men. Thus he completed the covenant theology of the earlier Puritans by supplementing the covenant of grace — leading to individual salvation, and the church covenant — based upon the congregational unity of the elect, with a political covenant — based upon the need of all men for "rule and order," asserting that the ultimate sovereignty, the right to establish "what species of government they please," resides in the people. Wise expresses some inclination toward democracy, but he does so with many reservations. Of all the Puritan writers, however, he is the nearest to a political democrat. We may well reckon him as one of the precursors of the later democratic mood that promoted revolution, proclaimed independence, and produced our federal system.[16]

1

COLONIAL MATERIALISM AND IMMATERIALISM

I. THE COLONIES DISCOVER LOCKE AND NEWTON

The Puritans were not indifferent to the study of nature and the natural sciences, even though they made no significant contribution to the advance of science in a period when British and European science was developing rapidly. The Puritan colonials were not creative scientists, but rather absorbers of science. The reason for this may well be that the Puritan clergy studied scientific materials not for their own sake, but for the sake of the moral and theological lessons to be drawn from nature. The Puritans mastered the "new" astronomy — the Copernican system. At Harvard, Copernican astronomy was certainly a subject of instruction by 1659 and may have been taught even earlier. The New England almanacs of the period contained essays on the new astronomy in popularized form. The interest which lay behind this study, however, was not an interest in the heavens as such: It was the heavens as the work of God, and astronomy as a repository of illustrations for sermons and tracts on the Providence of God, that interested the Puritans.

Though the scientific interests of the New England Puritans were those of amateurs, they were more than those of dilettantes. Within some twenty years after the formation of the Royal Society of London there were American colonials elected as fellows of that Society. These Americans, some of whom were bearers of the best-known of Puritan names, like Mather, Leverett, and Winthrop, sent communications to England reporting their observations of natural phenomena in the colonies. After 1672 astronomical observation in the true sense became a possibility for American students, when Harvard was given a telescope by the younger John Winthrop. This was the telescope used by Thomas Brattle in observing the comet of 1680. Brattle's reports of his observations were used and

9

acknowledged by Sir Isaac Newton (1642-1727) in his celebrated *Principia — The Mathematical Principles of Natural Philosophy*, published in 1687.[1]

Thus, although the primary concern of the Puritans was not for scientific materials in themselves, they were studying, teaching, and concerning themselves with science in a period when a radical reinterpretation of the nature of science and of scientific methods was taking place. Almost unwittingly the newer conception of science, with its mathematical and experimental foundation, its reliance upon sense experience rather than intuition, innate ideas, or authority, and its concentration upon explanation in terms of mechanical processes rather than ultimate purposes, replaced, in the minds of educated New Englanders, the older conception of science as a dogmatic subject matter. When the work of the two writers who represent the culmination of more than a century of the development of the new science — John Locke (1632-1704) and Sir Isaac Newton — reached the American colonies, the ground had been prepared for their reception and acceptance.

Locke's *Essay Concerning Human Understanding*, whatever else can be said about it, described the psychological theory which the thinkers of its age used to justify their reliance upon sense experience for the data of science. The treatise expressed a theory of the nature, the scope, and the limitations of human knowledge. Accepting this theory meant denying the attribute "scientific" to much of what had been called "scientific knowledge" in previous ages. Locke argued that the mind of man prior to experience was like a completely blank tablet of wax, able to receive impressions from the world outside itself only by way of the senses. There was no mental content with which men were born; there were no innate ideas. Man's mind could contain no idea of anything in the external world unless it entered through the avenue of perception.

Locke called the impressions thus received from the external world, "simple ideas." He asserted that, once these simple ideas had been impressed upon the mind, the mind had the capacity of combining them in various ways to make up its more complex ideas of external objects and of "enhancing" them to produce conceptions like that of infinity. The simple ideas were qualities of objects as perceived by human senses. But the sense perceptions of men can give erroneous impressions of some of the qualities; familiar optical illusions make this clear. To those qualities about which Locke thought that the senses might err he applied the name of "secondary" qualities, while the qualities with respect to which the senses were reliable he called "primary" qualities. For Locke, then, man's knowledge could be founded only on impressions received through the senses, and could not be relied on beyond the limits of the accuracy of the senses.

Newton concerned himself with the working out of a consistent scheme of natural causes to explain what men experience. His rules of scientific procedure dealt with the method of reasoning from particular phenomena of experience to general conclusions about the causes of these phenomena. We must, he says, assign to any natural event only its necessary natural causes, "for Nature is pleased with simplicity, and affects not the pomp of superfluous causes." [2] One method of avoiding superfluity is to insist on consistency, always ascribing the same natural cause to the same natural event, although it may feed our vanity or our orthodoxy to assign a different cause to a human effect than to a like effect among animals. In the third place, we may legitimately generalize that properties which are found to be common to all bodies within our experience and in respect to which our experiments reveal no difference of degree are common to all bodies. Fourthly, when we have thus obtained results by means of a full induction from the particular phenomena of our experience to legitimate generalizations, these generalizations are to be considered as highly probable until they are shown by later phenomena within our experience to be in need of correction.

Locke's view of knowledge and Newton's description of the method of the scientist seeking the natural causes of natural events were widely read and studied, though, perhaps, not widely understood, in eighteenth-century America. Because of the attention paid to Locke's individualistic theory of government as well as the study of his *Essay Concerning Human Understanding*, Merle Curti's estimate of Locke as "America's philosopher" is valid for the eighteenth century. There were fewer competent Newtonians than there were Lockeans in the colonies, because an advanced knowledge of mathematics was necessary for the full understanding of Newton's scientific work. Nevertheless, F. E. Brasch, an able historian, refers to the prerevolutionary period as "the Newtonian epoch in the American colonies." [3]

Until 1727, however, the only work by Newton which was studied at Harvard was the *Opticks;* Harvard's first copy of the *Principia* was a third edition which Professor John Winthrop, the fourth of his name to be of importance in Massachusetts and at Harvard, acquired and used in his teaching. Even before this, three Harvard teachers of natural philosophy, Thomas Robie, Nathan Prince, and Isaac Greenwood, were introducing Newtonian concepts through secondary sources. Yale was more fortunate. Newton himself gave J. Dummer, the colonial agent for Connecticut, a copy of the second edition (1713) of his *Principia* as well as a copy of the *Opticks.* Though Yale could have taught Newtonian science from 1714, there is no evidence of formal inclusion of Newton's work in the Yale curriculum before 1740. Prior to that time some interested students, like Samuel Johnson, who later became the first president of King's College (now Columbia University), Daniel Browne, and Jonathan Edwards, studied the work for themselves.

Edwards had already read Locke's *Essay Concerning Human Understanding* when he was only fourteen years old. This was in 1717, the year in which the *Essay* was introduced as a textbook in Yale. Edwards found much enjoyment in the reading — more, he said, "than the most greedy miser finds, when gathering up handfuls of silver and gold, from some newly discovered treasure." [4] Under the stimulus of this reading and study, he began a series of "Notes on the Mind," in which he attempted to develop the implications of his reading in Locke. The ideas which Edwards worked out were similar to those which George Berkeley (1685-1753) was to draw from his study of Locke, though Edwards, in his notes, left more room than did Berkeley for abstract ideas. Edwards realized, as did Berkeley, that Locke's argument against the objective reality of the secondary qualities applied to our experience of the primary qualities as well. What we can know as a result of our sensations is never the qualities as they exist "out there," but only the idea or impression which the sensations implant in our minds. The world as we know it can only be a world of ideas, which we can know, not of things, which we can not know.

The primary qualities of figure, motion, extension, and solidity, which Locke left outside the mind as qualities of material substance, Edwards reduced to resistance or modes of resistance. Solidity is itself resistance; figure is the ending of the resistance; extension is one aspect of figure; motion is the communication of resistance from space to space. If, then, Edwards could prove that resistance does not exist outside of the mind, he could establish his philosophic position as an immaterialism based upon a complete denial of our knowledge of matter.

Thus, when nothing is actually resisted, we would not assert that resistance exists outside the mind, but only that a *power* of resistance exists. "And as Resistance is nothing else but the actual exertion of God's power, so the Power [of resistance] can be nothing else, but the constant Law or Method of that actual exertion." [5] We can mean nothing by resistance except an idea in some mind; of this idea the law or power is the external manifestation. Otherwise we can not explain what is being resisted. Every quality that can possibly exist outside of the mind has been reduced to resistance; if so, what is resisted must itself be resistance. But this, Edwards pointed out, is ridiculous. "There must be something resisted before there can be Resistance; but to say Resistance is resisted, is ridiculously to suppose Resistance before there is anything to be resisted." [6] To this absurdity we come as long as we try to assert the existence of resistance outside of the mind.

If, on the other hand, we allow with Edwards that resistance is a mode of an idea, that resistance is mental, we have no such difficulty. For we have all the secondary qualities as ideas to be resisted. But if resistance is declared to be in the mind, then "the world is . . . an ideal one," and the idea in some mind is the only substance. The mind in which this idea is present cannot be a fallible, inexact, mortal, finite, human mind. Edwards therefore concludes that "That which truly is the substance of all is the infinitely exact, and precise, and perfectly stable Idea in God's mind." [7]

Edwards had manifested an early interest in the study of natural phenomena even before his entry into Yale, and wrote an essay "Of insects" at the age of eleven. Childish as this essay is in many respects, it was accurate and detailed in reporting young Edwards' observation of the flying spider. Some aspects of his description of this insect anticipated by a century and a half the first account in the work of professional entomologists. When Edwards read Newton, he attempted to pursue the implications of the Newtonian system in a series of "Notes on Natural Science." He was not as completely at sea in Newton as some of his fellow students might have been. From the time of his studies in Newton, he accepted as a fundamental premise the statement that "Nothing ever comes to pass without a cause." His "Notes on Natural Science" would, however, have been as unpalatable to Newton as the "Notes on the Mind" would have been to Locke. For Newton led Edwards to elaborate an immaterialism similar to that which he derived from Locke. For example, Edwards drew the conclusion that space is not a physical being, but rather that it is "necessary, eternal, infinite and omnipresent. But I had as good speak plain; I have already said as much as that Space is God." [8]

Whether Lockean or Newtonian language was used, Edwards reached a view in which all things were known as joined into one inclusive system, which he called the Divine Mind or God. We can, if we will, talk "as if the Material Universe were existent in the same manner as is vulgarly thought," [9] rather than speak in the strict and abstract terms which his immaterialism calls for; to Edwards it is all one as long as we recognize that "the corporeal world is to no advantage but to the spiritual." We can talk of systems of related ideas, or we can talk of atoms; in either case it is a spiritual system which is our subject. If our thinking were sufficiently comprehensive and perfect, he believed at this time, we could reconstruct the entire pattern, God's blueprint, from the present state of the world, just as we can determine from a study of part of the fall of a ball of lead what the rest of its motion must have been. Nature and history form a complete and potentially intelligible system of ideas in God's mind.

In his later life, Edwards largely abandoned this line of thought, though we do not know why. It may be that he recognized and was horrified by the incipient deism of his views. On the other hand, he may merely have become too preoccupied with the problems of pastoral life and theological discussion after his graduation from Yale to have time to continue his undergraduate speculations. Edwards' early nature essays and his "Notes" give teasing promise of a Lockean-Newtonian idealism that was never to be fulfilled. Locke remained a strong influence on Edwards, but all that remained of Newton in Edwards' thought was his insistence on the principle of causation and an occasional figure of speech in his sermons or sermon notes.

Some of these are not without interest. Edwards speaks, for example, in one "Image," edited by Perry Miller, of the preservation of the material universe by the force of gravitation, the mutual attraction of bodies. Thus the parts of the universe are mutually beneficial. For sermonic purposes, Edwards adds that this is the "type" or representation, in the material realm, of Christian love in the spiritual. Again, in his "Notes on the Scriptures," Edwards accepts the "wheels within wheels" of Ezekiel as a statement of a mechanical interpretation of the laws of nature. Similarly, he draws images from hydraulics, astronomy, physics, and even what we would call the social science of economics: "The changing of the course of trade and the supplying of the world with its treasures from America is a type and forerunner of what is approaching in spiritual things, when the world shall be supplied with spiritual treasures from America." [10]

Other eighteenth-century American colonials who read Locke and Newton were chiefly impressed by the regularity of natural law to which the works of the two British thinkers pointed. We have seen that Covenant theology reduced the elements of uncertainty, arbitrariness, and capriciousness in the Calvinist conception of God. Now we find a readiness on the part of those who accepted a constitutional regularity in the conception of God to accept the view that the universe, God's creation, is intelligible through and through because it is governed according to regular natural laws. "To find out the reasons of things, in Natural Philosophy," wrote the young Edwards, "is only to find out the proportion of God's acting." [11] For many, like Edwards, Newton's work expanded and made more definite the idea of a reign of law; scientific necessity and the doctrine of predestination seemed to supplement each other and between them tell the whole story.

This was the impression that Samuel Johnson of Yale and King's College gained from his study of theology and of Newton, and it did not satisfy him. He wondered how man could be considered a moral agent while we believe in "this necessitating doctrine." He insisted on a "self asserting power" in man, a freedom of man's will to choose or to refuse, to act or not to act. Although Johnson had been brought up a Congregationalist and trained at Yale for the Congregational ministry, he became a convert to the Church of England because of his dissatisfaction on this point and others. He asked, "What signify all laws and rules of action, all motives taken from praise or blame, hope or fear, reward or punishment, while everything we do is under a fatal necessity, and we can do no otherwise than we do?"[12] He asserted that it would be "the greatest injustice" to punish anyone for doing worse than we expect him to do, if we believe that all his actions are predestined.

After Johnson had eliminated Calvinistic predestination from his philosophic views, he remained in sympathy with Newtonian views of the regularity of nature. He was morally concerned to reinstate man's freedom of will, but saw no reason to grant a like concession to inanimate nature. In 1729, however, George Berkeley visited America. Johnson, as an outstanding colonial figure in the Church of England, paid his respects in person to Bishop Berkeley; the two men had philosophic discussions when they met and continued their exchange of views by letter. Berkeley convinced Johnson that consistent following of Newtonian ideas could lead to a denial of the existence of God. Johnson drew back from this possibility and gradually, after many doubts, arrived at an acceptance of the immaterialism of Berkeley as the only position which left spirit as the operating agent in the universe while not denying regularity in nature or free will in man.

Johnson's version of the philosophy of Berkeley stressed the existence of finite, human minds and emphasized the freedom and activity of these minds. In essence, Johnson claimed, finite minds are as free as God is; in practice, however, the freedom of the human mind is restricted by God's readiness to communicate Himself: God, by His self-revelation, furnishes the human mind with ideas, and each man is personally responsible for the use to which he puts these ideas. In this way Johnson found in Berkeley's philosophy a method of satisfying his theological doubts about Newtonianism and his moral doubts about Calvinism.

Johnson did not forget what he had learned from Newton; he tried, rather, to translate it into the language of his new philosophy. In his philosophic correspondence with Cadwallader Colden as well as in his treatise called *Noetica*, which Franklin published in 1752, Johnson repeatedly asserted that Newton's concept of inertia (*vis inertiae*), which Johnson preferred to call "resistance," must be a direct action of God upon the mind of man. Colden, as we shall see (this chapter, section III), disputed this point because he conceived of matter as an active force while Johnson insisted on the passivity of matter. In one of Johnson's letters there is a rather pathetic sentence which summarizes the issue between the two thinkers: "All the odds between you and me is that you make matter a self-exerting active principle, whereas I give that denomination [i.e., matter] only to what is merely passive and inert and give the name of spirit to that which is the principle of activity, pervading and agitating all things."[13]

Colden and Johnson, although both took their start from Newton, were worlds apart. Johnson's version, like that of Edwards, was immaterialistic, insisting on the exclusiveness of spiritual agency. Colden's was more materialistic, insisting on the activity of matter as well as of spirit. In the remainder of this chapter we shall examine in more detail the mature form of Jonathan Edwards' idealism, and the alternative as presented by Cadwallader Colden.

II. THE IDEALISM OF JONATHAN EDWARDS

The early speculative ideas of Jonathan Edwards developed from his reading in Locke and Newton. He was led in a direction parallel to that which his English contemporary, Bishop Berkeley, was following, to a recognition that perception is central to all human knowledge. The contents of the human mind are either simple ideas received from perception or complex ideas built up out of the simple ideas received from perception. We can not, therefore, assert our knowledge of the material character of the world; all we can know is our idea of the world. Edwards, in his teens, conceived but did not elaborate a very subtle immaterialism.

After his training had been completed, when he was engaged in his lifework as a minister of the gospel, he did not pursue these metaphysical speculations and amplify them into a philosophic system. He devoted himself, rather, to the creation of a philosophic defense of his religious views, of Puritanism as he understood it. It was neither the Puritanism of the first generation of Massachusetts colonists, nor the Puritanism of Cotton Mather which Edwards presented. The religious ideas proclaimed by Edwards were, rather, a translation of Puritan doctrines in terms of the religious experience of the individual. Edwards' version of Puritanism was a psychological version. His concern was to show why men should feel a sense of their "total dependence" upon God rather than to demonstrate that men are actually entirely dependent upon God. Where the earlier Puritans had tried to convert men by convincing their minds of the truth of the Puritan doctrines, Edwards wrote an intellectual justification for trying to convert men by persuading their emotions.

It is easy to see why Edwards, in whose congregation at Northampton the Great Awakening of 1740 to 1742 had one of its earliest manifestations, should have taken this course. His own sensitivity to personal religious experience is clear from the entries in his diary,[14] and it was natural for him to approach the conversion of others as he would himself have been most affected. Early in his ministry, in 1734 and 1735, an emotional revival, which swept through many towns in Massachusetts and Connecticut, had started in Northampton. The success of the emotional appeal seemed clear when more than three hundred persons were converted in his parish. The first work to spread the fame of Jonathan Edwards was his account of this revival and its effects, his *Narrative of Surprising Conversions* (London, 1736). Edwards was, however, cautious about the stimulation of the emotions as a good in itself. He refused to accept emotional hysteria accompanied by some of the external trappings of religion as the equivalent of true religious emotion. It was necessary, therefore, for him to make a careful theoretical statement of what he considered the proper place of emotion in the life of religion.

The psychological analysis of religion which Edwards developed is presented in most detail in his *Treatise Concerning Religious Affections*, published in 1746, but he had stated its central positions twelve years earlier in a sermon called "A Divine and Supernatural Light, Immediately Imparted to the Soul by the Spirit of God." The views expressed in the treatise and the sermon are an expansion of the psychology Edwards had learned from his study of Locke. The mind of man has two faculties, the understanding and the inclinations, which sometimes are called "heart" and sometimes "will." These are both natural faculties or powers of the mind and are served by the senses, the imagination, the memory, and the judgment. The senses are the primary servants of the mind. "There can never be any idea, thought, or act of the mind, unless the mind first received some idea from sensation." [15]

If we mean by the senses only the natural senses, the five avenues of sight, hearing, smell, taste, and touch — by means of which the passive mind receives its "simple ideas" or impressions of the external world — then there are difficulties for a religious world-view in sensationalism. On such a psychological basis it is impossible to account for our idea of God. For this must be a simple idea, since

God is One and uncompounded — yet we cannot see, hear, smell, taste, or touch God, and these are the ways by which we acquire our simple ideas. To escape this pitfall, Edwards suggested that we need not restrict ourselves to the five natural senses. Some of the British ethical theorists of that age accounted for our moral ideas, also a problem in a strict sensationalism, by saying that the five natural senses are supplemented by a moral sense, which "perceives" right and wrong. Edwards asserted that some men, by an act of divine grace, have a "supernatural sense" bestowed upon them. By their exercise of this additional sense, their minds have the simple ideas of divinity impressed upon them.

The chief end of man, "the great business for which God has created him," is religion.[16] Religion, Edwards insisted, is the product of the stimulation of man's "heart," that is, his inclinations and affections, by the supernatural sense. Edwards further averred that doctrinal and theological knowledge, the use of the understanding, without a deep engagement of the affections, is not the business of religion. A true conversion can not take place exclusively on the level of intellectual understanding. True repentance, true humility, true atonement — all require that the affections be moved. The affections, like man's other powers, are given him by God so that they may be religiously engaged.

Fallen man, however, exercises his affections and engages his heart far more on other business than on the business of religion. Not all stimulation of the affections leads man to religion. "In things which concern men's worldly interest, their outward delights, their honor and reputation, and their natural relations, they have their desires eager, their appetites vehement, their love warm and affectionate, their zeal ardent. . . . But how insensible and unmoved are most men about the great things of another world!" [17] What is lacking in most men is the supernatural sense which is God's gracious gift to the elect, the saints, whose affections are thereby made gracious.

For, evidently, the special kinds of experience which the saints possess are not natural; nor can they be caused by the operation of natural causes, explained on natural principles, or developed by the improvement or compounding of natural experience. The religious experience of the saints differs from natural experience not only in degree, but also in kind. The gracious affections of the saints have a supernatural source. There is some new idea in the minds of the saints, which was not in their minds before their sanctification, and which is not in the minds of the unsanctified. The new idea can not be identified with or explained by any natural sensation. There must, then, Edwards asserted, be "a new inward perception or sensation of their minds, entirely different in its nature and kind, from anything that ever their minds were the subjects of before they were sanctified." [18] The new power or sense which enables the saint to perceive the new supernatural idea must come from God.

Just as the Puritans of an earlier generation had to decide who were the elect, Edwards had to determine which of the members of his community had been chosen by God to be recipients of the supernatural sense. This was an especially important decision for him to make, because his congregation in Northampton, under the spiritual leadership of his predecessor and maternal grandfather, Solomon Stoddard, had fallen into the practice of what was called the "halfway covenant." This meant that all attendants at the church were accepted at the communion table whether it had been ascertained that they were of the elect or not. Edwards resolved to lead his congregation back to the more traditional practice of reserving communion for the saints. He needed, therefore, a practical test of regeneracy, and sought to find one by erecting the possession of gracious affections into a criterion of election.

On this issue Edwards was fighting against the trend not only of his own time but also of ours. But while his propositions would require a great deal of explanation for most of us today, the eighteenth-century climate of opinion could more willingly understand a flat statement of Edwards' views. He maintained in this controversy, as he maintained throughout his life, that natural goodness, which is the living of a moral life, and supernatural godliness, which is the living of a Christian life, are totally distinct. Godliness is different in kind from goodness; it is not simply a superlative degree of goodness. To Edwards, being religious meant being completely under the sway of the emotions induced by the perception of the glory of God. The morality of the natural man, at its best, is merely prudential and self-preservative. It has nothing to do with salvation or the living of a spiritual life. Not even the desire to affiliate with a Christian church, accompanied by a firm resolve to live as a Christian — accepted by advocates of the "half-way covenant" as sufficient indication of what they called moral sincerity — was enough to satisfy Edwards, who insisted that what was needed was "gracious sincerity," the sincere expression of those who possessed a gracious heart.

There are results, visible in the world, of the "gracious and holy affections." These affections lead their possessor to make a "business" of the Christian life. This meant for Edwards that the behavior of the saint on earth would conform entirely to the Christian rules by which it was directed, and that this "holy practice" would take precedence over every other activity of the saint's life. Somewhat more strikingly, and with unfortunate effect on any attempt to use the visible results as a practical criterion for church membership, Edwards also insisted that no final decision about the possession of gracious affections can be rendered unless the person believed to have affections of this sort persisted in evidencing Christian practice until the end of his life — "so that it may be said, not only to be his business at certain seasons, the business of Sabbath days, or certain extraordinary times . . . but the business of his life." [19]

This concern for the practical fruits of election leads us to a consideration of Edwards' ethical theory. It is well for us to recall that his ethical ideas developed out of a Calvinistic background, in which the doctrine of man's utter depravity was a vital belief and not a mere form of words. Men come into the world unable by their own efforts to do good or to avoid doing evil. This is the view that Edwards expounded in his tract called *The Great Christian Doctrine of Original Sin Defended.* He began this work with the assertion that evidence for the sinfulness of mankind is discoverable by the study of history and the observation of those about us. In all ages and in every place we find men sinning. Since sinful behavior in any situation evidences a tendency to sin, it follows that there is in men a sinful nature; the universality of sin leads us to conclude that this sinful nature is "inherent" in all men.

Edwards had, as we have seen, pondered Newton, and as a result maintained throughout his life the belief that everything finite must have a cause. The innate depravity of human nature must, then, have a cause. To attribute human depravity to God would be to make God the author of sin, an unthinkable position. Edwards, in line with the Christian tradition, explained that man's sinful nature is the effect of the sin of Adam. He did not, however, follow literally the traditional doctrine of the imputation of Adam's sin to all mankind. He was concerned to bolster up the doctrine of original sin against Dr. John Taylor, the English clergyman, and others who argued that sorrow, toil and death — in general, suffering — is the lot of men as a consequence of Adam's sin, but that men were not punished for Adam's sin by becoming totally depraved. Men were not guilty of Adam's sin because sin is a personal matter. Taylor went as far as to assert that the moral condition of men born after the Fall was no worse than that of Adam at his creation.

This argument was having great currency at the time that Edwards wrote his tract, so that he felt the need for developing a new theory of imputation which would nullify Taylor's position. This Edwards did by proposing an argument for a unity of the human race so closely-knit that Adam's sin *is* the sin of all men, and not merely another's sin imputed to them. The identity of any created object through time, its continued existence at different times, is directly dependent upon "God's sovereign constitution." Its present existence can not be the effect of its existence in the past; that existence, being "wholly a passive thing," could not be an "active cause." Each moment of existence must, then, be the effect of an exercise of God's "sovereign will and agency." By the same sort of "arbitrary constitution" by which God determines the perseverance of a created object, He has determined that the human race shall have an identity. Edwards speaks of humanity as a great tree, and asserts "that since Adam, the head of mankind, the root of that great tree with many branches springing from it, was deprived of original righteousness, the branches should come forth without it." Mankind is not many, sinful by imputation, but one, with Adam as its "federal head." All the descendants of Adam partake of his sin and its punishment.[20]

Again, attacks on the Calvinist doctrine of original sin were founded on the assertion that this doctrine makes God the author of sin. Edwards' reply to this view made an extremely clever theological translation of an ethical theory current at his time to serve as his solution of the perennial problem of evil. When God created Adam, Edwards said, He implanted in him two sets of principles, natural and supernatural. The natural principles, intended by the Creator to be inferior and subordinate, may be summed up as the principles of "self-love." The superior supernatural principles, "given to possess the throne, and maintain an absolute dominion in the heart," may be "summarily comprehended in divine love," or benevolence. Thus Adam's nature was one of "Original Righteousness." When Adam fell, God removed the supernatural principle of benevolence; Adam was left with only self-love as his motive principle. God, therefore, is not the author of sin; He merely took away from Adam the benevolent principle which prevented sin.[21] In effect, Edwards associated his view of human nature with that tradition in ethical theory which insists that men's moral choices have been motivated exclusively by self-interest since the Fall. At the same time, he indicated that he did not consider self-interest as a desirable spring of action; in fact, he identified self-interested action with sin. This was his description of the basis on which men *do* act; the basis on which men ideally *ought to* act is benevolence.

Disinterested benevolence — precisely the principle that God removed from Adam — is Edwards' definition of virtue. If men lack this principle, how is it possible for them to be virtuous? Edwards' resolution of the theological problem of evil left him with an ethical problem of good. This ethical problem was especially difficult for him because he could not accept a solution that based virtue upon right reason. Virtue is not founded upon the understanding, man's rational faculty, but upon the affections, man's emotional faculty. Both self-interest and benevolence are affections; self-interest leads to a disposition toward evil while benevolence leads to a disposition toward virtue. How can men, who lost the principle of benevolence in Adam's fall, overcome their disposition toward evil? This is the question that Edwards faced in his posthumously published dissertation on *The Nature of True Virtue*, where he offers a solution based upon an interesting doctrine of "love of being," which has close affinities with the "ladder of love" discussed by Plato in his *Symposium*.

The Nature of True Virtue begins by explaining that virtue is a kind of beauty. Not all beauty, of course, is called virtue, but only some beauty belonging to men, to "Beings that have perception and will." It is not the external beauty of men which is called virtue, but only a beauty of the mind. Not all beauty of the mind is called virtue; the beauty of speculative ideas and, in general, the beauty of understanding is not known by the name of virtue. Virtue is the beauty of those qualities and acts of the mind to which praise or blame are attached. "Things of this sort . . . are not any thing

belonging merely to speculation; but to the *disposition* and *will*, or
. . . the *heart*." [22] After this analysis, he is able to rephrase his question about the nature of true virtue thus: "What that is which renders
any habit, disposition or exercise of the heart truly beautiful." His
inclusion of the words "true" and "truly" was designed to exclude
any possibility of a utilitarian conception of virtue or beauty. True
virtue or true beauty he limits to that which is "agreeable *in itself*
and *immediately* pleasant" to the beholder, denying the title of
virtuous or beautiful to any thing agreeable only in the light of its
consequences.

Having carefully laid this foundation, Edwards defines true virtue
as "benevolence to Being in general," where benevolence means "that
consent, propensity and union of heart to Being in general, that is
immediately exercised in a general good will." Every individual
being in existence is related in some definite fashion to the totality
of being, Being in general. Being in general is, then, the universal
system of existence. The true virtue of the individual existent in
such a system is its union of heart, its benevolence toward the whole
system. In the Christian tradition, Edwards points out, virtue "most
essentially consists in love." We can now say that true virtue is the
union of the individual heart in love with the system of being. Love
which has an individual for its object is not the same as love for
Being in general; love of the particular is not true virtue, although
affection toward particular intelligent beings may arise readily in
those who have a generally benevolent disposition.

Benevolent love is not necessarily directed toward a beautiful
object; delight in beauty can not, therefore, be the essence of virtue
—especially since virtue has already been declared to be a kind of
beauty, and, if it were also a delight in beauty, it would be a delight
in itself, which is absurd. Nor can the essence of virtue be gratitude
to another for his benevolence, because the benevolence which
awakens our gratitude can not itself be gratitude. We are left, then,
with the conclusion that the primary object of benevolence is Being
itself, and, since benevolence is a desire for the highest good of its
object, true virtue will have an "ultimate propensity" to the highest
good of Being in general. This will include seeking the good of
every individual being so far as that good is consistent with the
highest good of Being in general.

Of all individual beings, that One who has "most of Being" will

have the greatest share of the benevolent affections of the virtuous heart. And, in general, each individual will be the object of
benevolence in proportion to the degree of existence which men
understand it to possess. Edwards justified his speaking of varying
degrees of being in this interesting note:

> I say, in proportion to the degree of *existence*, because one Being
> may have more *existence* than another, as he may be *greater* than
> another. That which is *great*, has more existence, and is further
> from nothing, than that which is *little*. One Being may have
> every thing positive belonging to it, or every thing which goes
> to its positive existence (in opposition to defect) in a higher
> degree than another; or a greater capacity and power, greater
> understanding, every faculty and every positive quality in a
> higher degree. An *archangel* must be supposed to have more
> existence, and to be every way further removed from *nonentity,*
> than a *worm*, or a *flea*.[23]

The primary object of a virtuous disposition is Being in general, and
this benevolence is reflected towards particular beings in proportion
to their degree of existence. Human virtue is manifested primarily in
love of man for God, and secondarily and in a reflected fashion in
the love of man for man.

But, we are told in Edwards' *Dissertation Concerning the End for
which God Created the World,* just as human excellence consists in
love of God, God's excellence consists in love of Himself. His end in
the creation of the world was to manifest, and thereby to communicate, his glory. The things of the world are but a "reflection of
the diffused beams of the glory of God." Most men are lost; God's
end in the creation could not conceivably be their happiness. Any
concern which God may show to His creatures is a mode of manifesting His glory. Man's only hope of salvation is to consent to his
Sovereign, and to pray to be incorporated into that divine excellence
in which those on whom the grace of God is bestowed may share.
Thus grace alone enables man's inherently sinful nature, motivated
exclusively by self-love, to achieve virtue. Nothing that man can do
will enable him to develop virtue in himself. Virtue must "take its
rise from creation or infusion by God." The benevolent disposition
which God removed from Adam He restores in His saints. "If ever
men are turned from sin, God must undertake it, and he must be the
doer of it." [24] God is glorified, Edwards explained in a sermon in
1731, by man's total dependence upon His grace for redemption.

Throughout his mature life Edwards devoted his acute mind and extraordinary talents to the building of a solid philosophic foundation for Calvinism. The work in which he was most successful in carrying out this intention was *A Careful and Strict Enquiry into the Modern Prevailing Notions of that Freedom of Will which is supposed to be Essential to Moral Agency, Vertue and Vice, Reward and Punishment, Praise and Blame* (1754). The Calvinistic doctrine which *The Freedom of the Will* was written to support was the doctrine of predestination. Edwards thought of this doctrine as the keystone of the Calvinist arch; without the principle of necessity, the entire structure would collapse. Again in this work, as in the others that we have discussed, Edwards brought to the support of his theology the psychological theories of Locke and the Newtonian principle that every event must have a cause.

Particular acts of will, then, particular volitions, must have a cause. Edwards asserted that this cause is that motive which seems to the mind to be strongest, even as Locke had asserted in his *Essay Concerning Human Understanding.* Then Edwards departed from Locke by arguing that will and desire, will and preference, and, in fact, all other terms expressing inclinations, are merely different names for volition. Under whichever of these names men refer to the act of willing, the will is a passive mechanism which is necessarily drawn toward the greatest apparent good in any situation. The will, therefore, is not free, but determined in what it wills. It is determined by the decision of the understanding concerning the greatest apparent good.

In another respect, however, a man *is* free, though he is not free to will as he pleases, when he is free to do as he wills. Like Locke, Edwards insisted that no higher liberty than this "could ever possibly enter in the heart of any man to conceive." [25] What Edwards did in the positive part of *The Freedom of the Will* was not to deny, but to limit this freedom. Morally, in terms of its making of choices, the will is determined by the strongest apparent motive; naturally, in terms of its acting on these choices, the will is free. This position he summarized in his definition of liberty as "the power, opportunity, or advantage, that any one has to do as he pleases, or conducting in any respect, according to his pleasure; without considering how his pleasure comes to be as it is." [26] The advantage that Calvinism gained from his position is that he made clear how, since men are free to act according to their desires or preferences, men may be held morally accountable even though their desires and preferences are determined. Men are accounted praiseworthy or blameworthy in that they may do what they choose, even though they do not choose their choices.

Jonathan Edwards labored to develop a philosophic justification of his belief in Calvinism. He, and many others in his time, felt that he had produced an impregnable theological position. European scholars found in him America's only metaphysical talent, and he was, indeed, the first American philosopher of stature. Despite his great ability and his influence in his own time, however, there is little vitality left in Edwards's thought. Strong as his system seemed, like the deacon's "one hoss shay" it fell to pieces all at once, leaving scarcely a trace behind. Yet Edwards' ingenious use of Locke and Newton set the pattern for nearly a century of American idealism, a pattern which was not dismissed until more sophisticated forms of idealistic philosophy were imported from Germany.

III. THE ACTIVITY OF MATTER: CADWALLADER COLDEN

We have seen how the legacy of Locke and Newton was combined with elements of Platonic thought and a basically Calvinistic orientation in the theological philosophy of Jonathan Edwards. Without relinquishing either the reliance on sense experience which he learned from Locke or the principle of causation which he drew from Newton, Edwards found himself able to develop a view of the universe in which matter was not a fact, but merely a manner of speaking about our experience of a reality which was mental and spiritual. To round out our picture of the influence of Locke and Newton on the pre-revolutionary eighteenth century in America we are to examine here the philosophic ideas of a scientific thinker of the same era — Cadwallader Colden.

It was an era, be it remembered, in which there was a widespread impulse to scientific speculation. Indeed, it is a tribute to the development of scientific habits of thought among many people during the seventeenth and eighteenth centuries that so much of the scientific speculation and subject matter of the age became obsolete so rapidly. The study of Newton's magnificent synthesis led many to believe that nature worked according to a completely regular pattern of natural law. This belief, in turn, led many to search out hitherto undiscovered regularities and to attempt to state the natural law which expressed these regularities. The resultant rapid changes in scientific beliefs made most works in science out-of-date almost as soon as they were published. Newton's success in stating systematically the valuable results of the preceding two centuries of thought becomes all the more remarkable when we consider the high mortality among scientific statements in the eighteenth century.

Cadwallader Colden, whose thought we are to discuss in these pages, was not American-born or educated. We can not, therefore, consider his competence as a Newtonian as an early triumph of American scientific education. We can not even compare his ability directly with that of American-trained Newtonians like Professor John Winthrop of Harvard. Of all those living in America in his time, Colden was the thinker most concerned with the philosophic outcomes of studies in both Newtonian mathematics (the theory of fluxions) and Newtonian physics (the theory of gravitation). Above all his other qualifications for these studies which he carried on, Colden, who had studied at the University of Edinburgh and received his Bachelor's degree there in 1705, had gained from the teachings of his alma mater a deep and abiding distrust of the method of authority in intellectual matters.

This method of authority, the common coin of medieval education, was known as scholasticism. In practice, it amounted to the posing of a question, followed by the marshalling of authorities on both sides of the question, which was followed, in turn, by a conclusion in which the practitioner determined to his own satisfaction which side of the argument was more strongly argued — thereby adding one more authority to be quoted by the next writer to consider the question. As a scientific method, scholasticism was essentially sterile; it placed a premium on what was read in books rather than on ever-renewed observations of natural phenomena. As a theological method, scholasticism was much more fruitful, and has continued in widespread use until the present. It was the predominantly scientific outlook of the University of Edinburgh in Colden's student days which resulted in the opposition to scholasticism there.

When Cadwallader Colden came to America, with his Edinburgh degree and a training in medicine, he settled first in Philadelphia and tried to establish medical practice there. He was not as rapidly successful as he wished, however, and he left Philadelphia for New

York and a career in public administration which was both successful and profitable. For the fifteen years before his death in 1776 he was Lieutenant-Governor of the province of New-York. He found time to continue all sorts of studies despite the demands of his career. His *History of the Five Indian Nations* (of New York) contains much valuable information and was the standard work in its field for many years. The study to which he gave most consideration, however, was Newton's physics.

Colden's work was an attempt to supplement Newton's by considering the cause of gravitation. In 1745, he published a first essay, entitled *An Explication of the First Causes of Action in Matter;* a revised version of this essay was published in 1751 under the title *The Principles of Action in Matter, the Gravitation of Bodies, and the Motion of the Planets Explained from these Principles.* His note-books from 1751 to his death a quarter of a century later contain paragraph after paragraph of emendation and revision, suggesting that he intended ultimately to publish still a third version. The germ of Colden's contribution is to be found in Newton's statement that gravitation is not a cause, but a name for a class of observed effects of some unknown cause. Newton had protected himself here against criticism; in the science of the middle ages, explanations were frequently given in terms of "occult causes" which were not physical causes at all. Thus, if a medieval scientist were asked what causes an airplane to leave the ground and fly, he might have answered that the "cause" was the "aviatory power" of the airplane. This phrase means, of course, no more than "the power of flight;" the entire explanation would reduce to the statement that an airplane flies because it has the power of flight. Newton realized that "gravitation" was a word meaning "the mutual attraction of bodies"; to say gravitation is the *cause* of the mutual attraction of bodies would be equivalent to saying that bodies are mutually attracted because they are mutually attracted.

Colden defined the causes of gravitation, or the attraction of bodies to one another, in terms of the actions, or, better, the active powers in matter. He distinguished three such powers in matter: The moving power, or principle of motion, which is light; the power of resistance or inertia, which is matter as the term is commonly understood, and ether, the elastic power, the medium which transmits movement and resistance, making possible action at a distance. The joint activity of these three powers he regarded as the cause of gravitation. For our purposes here, the scientific merits of Colden's solution need not be debated. Philosophically, what he did was to analyze gravitation into three activities and then assume these activities to form three independent sorts of matter. Thus he tried to follow out Newton's own rules of procedure. Having gotten this far, however, Colden exceeded his warrant by considering the powers which define gravitation as the causes of gravitation.

In doing this, Colden was led to some interesting speculations. In the first place, the prevailing theory in his period held that there were two forms of substance, spiritual or mental substance which was active, and material substance which was passive. Dissidents from this theory, like Berkeley or the young Edwards, denied the reality of material substance, making all reality spiritual and active. Colden's dissent fell on the opposite side; he admitted that if matter really is completely passive, there is no possible way of knowing it. He recognized, however, that an alternative line of argument is possible if we say that the ideas which we have of bodies "are excited in consequence of some action of matter." [27] Once this is our basis of argument, Berkeley's position is without force. Colden insisted that matter is not entirely inert and passive. Insofar as matter is knowable at all, it can not be passive. In order to be perceived, matter must be active and dynamic.

Colden believed, however, that the ultimate nature of things can be neither clearly conceived nor intelligibly discussed. The "matter" that man can know is material *action*, not some underlying material *substance*. Much of Colden's polemic against scholasticism consisted in ridiculing the scholastic claim that men can conceive substance by a process of abstraction. In his "Introduction to Phylosophy," Colden uses the candle before him to exemplify a scholastic method of conceiving of substance: The roundness of the candle is a *mode*, or quality of a substance necessarily depending on that substance and incapable of independent existence. The whiteness of the candle is a *quality*, or that by which our sense are affected; so, too, the greasiness and stiffness of the candle are qualities. The fact that the candle may be set on fire, after which it will burn and give light, is an *accident*, or inessential addition to the substance, "for it is as much a candle when it does not burn as when it does." Now, the substance of the candle is the idea that remains after stripping away modes, qualities and accidents — in short, nothing that can be conceived or known.[28]

Knowledge can not, then, be the cognition of inactive objects passively received by the senses. Our first notion of objects outside of ourselves must arise as a result of the actions of the objects on our senses. Colden took the position that all knowledge is limited to things in time and space; that these things, to be known, must be active; and that what we call "knowledge" is our perception of the actions of things. Thus, for Colden, matter is expressed and known as energy, as force. The energies, forces, or powers of resistance, motion, and elasticity distinguish the three basic activities of matter, or ways in which matter is known. Thinking, too, was regarded by Colden as a kind of action; he recognized a mental or spiritual agency as well as a material agency. Colden, although he insisted upon material agency, was not, in the ordinary use of the term, a materialist; he did not attempt to reduce everything to matter and material motion. In fact, he criticized, in one of his works, those writers who "have denied the existence of spirit or that there is any kind of being beside matter." [29]

The key to Colden's philosophic position lies, however, far less in the distinction between matter and spirit than is true for most of his contemporaries. Matter is his name for certain types of activity; spirit is his name for other types of activity. The activities of body and the activities of mind operating jointly produce our perceptions of objects. A passive object (assuming that there can be one) can never be known. All knowledge is of action and its effects. As far as our knowledge is concerned, passivity is the equivalent of nonexistence. "For if anything produce no alteration in our senses, it is impossible to know that any such thing exists; and every effect must be produced by some cause, or by some action." [30]

Although matter is active, however, its activities are such that we can not think of them as the product of an intelligence or a will in matter. Nor can we conceive of matter as possessing sense or perception. We do, nevertheless, recognize clearly and without any doubt the existence of sense, perception, intelligence and will. The fact that we recognize or know these indicates that they must be active powers. It follows that, besides matter, there must be another kind of being, to which Colden gives the name "intelligent being," known to us through these activities even as material being is known to us through motion, resistance and elasticity. Intelligent being is known through its actions and effects, even as material being. We can no more have a knowledge of the essence of intelligent being than we can of material being.

We can, however, establish the characteristic or essential distinction between the two sorts of being by applying Colden's principle that "The differences of things (so far at least as we can know) consists in their different actions, or manner of acting." [31]   Material agents always act uniformly, and the effects of their actions are exerted in all directions. They are not able in themselves to increase or diminish the force with which they act, nor to limit the directions in which their action will be exerted. Any such alteration, increase, or diminution in their action or its direction must be made by a power external to the material agents. Intelligent agents, on the other hand, determine their own actions in both force and direction, by purposes, designs, or ends which they have in view. The uniformity of action of material agents makes this type of action susceptible to mathematical, quantitative investigation. But, Colden says, the actions of intelligent beings can not be investigated mathematically because they are not uniform but depend upon design, intention and will — which are not quantitative.

The actions of intelligent beings are also called moral actions. Colden, in his as yet unpublished "First Principles of Morality," retained the principle of activity as the foundation of ethical knowledge, even as he considered it to be the basis of every other kind of knowledge. He wavered somewhat in discussing what was later to become an important area of contention in ethical theory — the question of whether morality resides in man's intentions or in the consequences of his actions. At one place he maintained that in all moral actions "the intention, purpose, or will, is principally to be considered." In other statements he avowed the utilitarian principle that man's purposes are determined by his view of the harmful or beneficial results of his actions. In general, since Colden makes happiness the chief end of the moral life, his sympathies seem far more with the utilitarian approach to ethics.

Morality he defined as "the art and science of living so as to be happy." Happiness he viewed as the enjoyment, during our existence, of the greatest pleasure with the least admixture of pain. Knowledge, therefore, is prerequisite to morality, because "the more knowledge a man has the more happy he may be and must be if he make proper use of his knowledge." Of course, one can point to many men who have great knowledge and yet show that they are not especially moral, and do not enjoy great pleasures. The reason for this is that their knowledge is of a particular field; they are specialists. The type of knowledge which Colden believed to be in intimate relation with morality is general knowledge, or, as he expressed it, such knowledge "as procures general happiness." If this relation between general knowledge, "of such things as are necessary to all men in all conditions of life," and happiness, and happiness and morality be admitted to hold, then the primary purpose of moral precepts must be to teach this kind of knowledge. For Colden, then, as for Socrates, virtue is knowledge. "The more knowledge a man has the more sensible he will be of the benefits of morality."

Colden, then, was a hedonist: Morality, to him, was the art of happiness. It is far more commonly believed that the pursuit of pleasure leads rather to immorality than to morality. Also, if virtue and knowledge are related, then vice must be connected with ignorance and error. Colden acknowledged both these points, but went on to say that it is the shortsighted, and hence ignorant and erroneous, pursuit of particular pleasures "in such manner as to deprive ourselves of more numerous and essential pleasures" which leads to vice and immorality. When we make one special pleasure the focus of all our concern, neglecting all others, we misjudge the requirements for our achievement of happiness. This is so, however worthy the single pleasure may be; any monomania is vicious and immoral. Even an exclusive devotion to religion is sinful. "Religion arises from that pleasure which we expect and are sure of enjoying in the favor of God, but if in the pursuit of this we neglect all other pleasures we fall into the most dangerous sin of enthusiasm."

It is only among "unthinking people" that there is a danger in making the pursuit of pleasure the general motive of all men's actions. Actually, Colden insisted, it is very useful to be able to show "men of pleasure" that on their own principles immorality is "an absurdity, a contradiction to pleasure and an egregious folly." Furthermore, he pointed out that the "inspired writers," those who composed the Scriptures, often used the motive of pleasure to urge people to the living of a moral and religious life. In fact, considering the emphasis on the pleasures of a moral life in the Scriptures, it is difficult to figure out why so many people work so hard at persuading others "that, in order to be religious we must deny ourselves most, if not all, of the pleasures of life."

Colden was, after the manner of his age, a deist. He felt himself able to prove, from the design and harmony of the universe, the existence of a designer or harmonizer. He conceived of the creator and designer of the universe as an infinitely wise and intelligent being. To this view he added, in conformity with his pleasure principle, that God is also the most benevolent being. In the wisdom and benevolence of God Colden found a warrant for the assertion that God must so have ordained the constitution of his creatures that the means of achieving present happiness also tend to future happiness. An all-wise and all-good God could not have ordained the laws of the universe in such a fashion that men had to choose between this-worldly and celestial joy. Whenever in his writings Colden touched on religion, he maintained this optimistic view of the rational character of God's government of the universe.

Although Colden always speaks with respect of the Scriptures or revelation, Colden's God retained no element of the arbitrariness of the God of the Puritans. There are no miraculous interventions or special providences in Colden's religion. The infinite intelligent being never violates the laws according to which material beings act. Were He to do so, a contradiction or absurdity would be introduced into the universal system. The infinite wisdom of God is a sufficient guarantee that the system was created so well as to be in no need of perpetual correction and amendment. In this respect, beings of lesser intelligence follow the lead of God. They achieve their ends by utilizing the regular, mechanical, and predictable character and disposition of material being to serve their intelligent ends; they do not try to oppose or contradict the action of matter. If this is true of human intelligence, it is certainly clear "that perfect intelligence, or wisdom, will not, and consequently never can act in contradiction to the action of matter, otherwise anything may be absurd, and there would be no distinction between truth and falsehood." [32]

The universe, as Colden in his Newtonian fashion conceived it, is like a machine functioning perfectly for the purposes for which its creator formed and established it. Nothing less than perfect functioning could be expected of the handiwork of a perfect being. This universal machine is a system; that is to say, all its parts are connected in some way with one single point, and it is with reference to this point that the parts can be regarded as a unity. We do not define a system in terms of the identity of its parts or in respect to its place in space, but solely in terms of the relation of all its parts to the same central point. As long as communication between this principal point and the parts remains regular, the system remains healthy; if this communication should be disordered, the system is "sick." If communication to one part is completely blocked, that part dies; and if communication is cut off altogether from the entire system, the system is dissolved, for, properly speaking, it can no longer be called a system once there can be no communication with the central point. The principal point to be considered with reference to the entire system of the material universe is God, the infinite intelligent being.

If this is so, then a time when no matter existed is inconceivable. If it is consistent with perfect wisdom that material systems should exist at any time, then Colden claims that it is impossible that we should conceive of any time when material systems were not consistent with perfect wisdom. That particular material systems, like our solar system, should come into being and perish seemed to him highly probable. But "Nature, or more properly speaking, the infinite intelligent *Archeus*" has ordered it so that the dissolution of one material system is followed by the generation of new material systems. Colden offered the hypothesis that the method of the infinite intelligent being in producing new solar systems is "an extraordinary fermentation." Again, his hypothesis need not be considered closely here. What is important to us is his insistence on the eternity of matter as a corollary of the infinite wisdom of God.

Here we have the clearest indication of the degree to which Colden's speculations, arising out of his studies in Newton, produced conclusions far more materialistic than any which Edwards or Johnson could have entertained. Locke and Newton were widely read by colonial students and awakened many from "dogmatic slumber." Those who were awakened by the new science and its methods, as presented by these two British thinkers, were forced to fundamental reconsideration of their views of nature, man and God. This thoughtful reformulation did not, however, lead the colonial thinkers to identical conclusions. It led, rather, in various directions — to the immaterialistic and psychologized theology of Jonathan Edwards as well as to the materialistic and deistic mechanism of Cadwallader Colden.

2

THE AMERICAN ENLIGHTENMENT

I. CHARACTERISTIC IDEAS
OF THE REVOLUTIONARY ERA

The second half of the eighteenth century not only brought the beginning of the development of an American nation and an American culture, but also gave expression to a complete, rounded, and reasonably consistent pattern of thought and action. The pattern is sufficiently like that of the corresponding period in Western European intellectual life to have led to a general use of the descriptive phrase "the American Enlightenment" as a characterization of the age. We are to be concerned here with the ideas of the American Enlightenment — the patterns of thought of the men who made our nation and gave direction to its heritage. We are to examine the philosophy which underlies our national existence, to try to see the pattern of enlightened ideas which forms the heart and core of the American mind.

This pattern was complete and rounded; it was applied in all the areas of human concern. Science, religion, politics, and economics in that age were all involved and interconnected in the thought of the men of the Enlightenment. The same methods were applicable to all; the same type of certainty was thought to be achievable in all. There was no conscious cleavage between philosophy and religion, religion and science, politics and economics, as there is for so many of us today. All the aspects of life and thought fell under one general pattern of understanding. Subject matters in these different areas might be discriminated from each other, but the same principles of analysis were thought to be applicable to all.

There are two qualifications to be expressed before we proceed to state the characteristic ideas of the Revolutionary era. The first

36

of these is that not all the men of the American Enlightenment, not even all the leaders of the American Enlightenment, held identical views in all of the fields of human thought and human effort which were mentioned above. Even where the thinking started from identical principles and used the same methods of reasoning, the resulting ideas were sometimes different. For the most part, there was even less agreement than this statement suggests, because it was rare for any two men to start from *identical* principles. However, the pattern as it has come down to us in our literary heritage was sufficiently widespread and influential to justify being called characteristic of the period. The second reservation is that we must be cautious in asserting extensive popularity for the ideas of which we talk. These ideas have come down to us by way of a written tradition. We can not know with any certainty what the opinions of the non-literate were; they have left no written trace. Any generalization we make must be limited to that relatively small segment of the population in the late colonial and early national periods for which the written word was a familiar, everyday tool of communication.

If these two reservations are granted, a thorough search of the literary remains of the second half of the eighteenth century in America would reveal a dominant pattern of thought combining several strains of European thought of previous periods. There was a reliance on the power and reach of the human mind, and a belief that by the use of mathematical method, reasoning deductively from secure principles to secure conclusions, men might expand their knowledge indefinitely without the need of supernatural aid. Together with the lessened sense of dependence upon divine assistance in establishing the basic principles on which all knowledge was thought to rest, there was a widespread shift from other-worldly to this-worldly concerns. Salvation was no longer the burning center of men's attention; human happiness had replaced it as the goal of human effort. The study of man and of his natural and political environment became important; the contributions to these fields of British secular thinkers and writers of the seventeenth and early eighteenth centuries were widely influential. Out of the ferment, Americans in the late colonial period and the first years of national existence developed an ethics of secular benevolence, a deistic theology, a faith in the perfectibility of man and in the progress of science, a democratic political theory, and a *laissez-faire* theory of economics, all culminating in a cosmopolitan ideal of world citizenship.

This pattern can be discovered only by a thorough search into the oddest corners of the archives. The leaders of thought in the American Enlightenment were men of action. They were too busy shaping the course of events to be able to spare the time for theoretical exposition of the ideas in which their actions were rooted. Philosophical treatises are not written in battlelines, and for half a century or more the makers and shapers of the culture of the American Enlightenment stood in the forefront of a battle which knew no truce. Occupied night and day with the problems of revolution, establishing a nation, developing security and stability, evolving the terms and conditions of representative government on an unprecedented scale, they failed — with notable exceptions in political theory — to set forth their speculative views systematically. The ideas of these men must be gathered from incidental comments in letters written at widely different periods of their lives, from occasional addresses, and from *obiter dicta* in state papers. The early years of the United States of America approximated Plato's ideal of a republic where the kings were philosophers, but an unsuspected weakness of the ideal came to light: The kings were so busy ruling that they had no time for expounding their philosophies.

When things had settled down a bit, however, there might well have been systematic exposition of the philosophy of the founders. If poetry is emotion recollected in tranquility, perhaps philosophy might not ineptly be described as thinking remembered in abstraction from the behavior in the course of which it arose. Unfortunately, however, for a variety of reasons chief among which was its failure to develop an adequate theory of human nature, the American Enlightenment halted rather abruptly. Its philosophy became obsolete before it had been systematically presented. Reaction against its ideas preceded their proper statement. Gaps appeared in the fabric before it could be stitched into garments. Neither in its heyday nor after did the philosophy of the American Enlightenment receive adequate expression.

Long before the beliefs of the Enlightenment were stated by its major prophets, there were faint signs of its coming. There was, for example, a gradual shift from pessimism to optimism in theology.

The first American Puritans, as we have seen, conceived of God as a strict ruler, intervening directly and arbitrarily in the affairs of this world. Much of what later generations ascribed to natural law and natural causation seemed to the Puritans to be evidence of the direct manifestation of God's eminent power. The Puritans thought of man as a vile creature, and of nature as a manifestation of God's judgment of mankind, not of His love of mankind. For the Enlightenment, in contrast, nature was beautiful, God was good, and natural law had replaced divine intervention as a principle of explanation. God was the great engineer who had created in nature, for the benefit of man, a perfect machine which functioned independently of its creator. Even Cotton Mather, in his later works, shows traces of enlightened ideas. In *The Christian Philosopher* (1721), he said that the world is well-planned, well-ordered, and beautiful, that to study nature is to realize God's goodness, and that man can appreciate God by the exercise of observation and reason.

Mather's *Essays to Do Good* (1710) suggested another of the themes of enlightened philosophy, the ethics of benevolence. For Mather, the Christian life consisted in doing good for others; the tone in which Mather wrote about his efforts to help others indicates that he derived a great deal of personal satisfaction and pleasure from his efforts. A man, he said, must "manage" his opportunity to do good "with a rapturous delight, as a most suitable business, as a most precious privilege."[1] But if, in Mather, there seems a smugly complacent sense of superiority at the root of benevolent activity, there is also to be noticed a shift toward humanitarianism. Man's love can be directed toward his fellowmen, and not exclusively toward God.

The English deistic writers of the eighteenth century developed an ethical position in which humanitarian behavior by men coincided with God's design in the creation of the universe. The providence of God did not, in their opinion, consist of a care and watchfulness over particular incidents and particular individuals; it was rather a general providence, a universal plan for the good of man. This argument, to be found in such British works as the *Analogy of Religion* by Bishop Joseph Butler (1692-1752), the *Natural Theology* by William Paley (1743-1805), and *The Religion of Nature Delineated* by William Wollaston (1659-1724), found many adherents in enlightened America. Thus Samuel Johnson, the first president of

Kings College, later to be known as Columbia College, made Wollaston's work the basis of his *Ethica*, asserting that man is created for eternal happiness. Man's good and happiness, Johnson said, "does necessarily coincide with, and even result from the truth and nature of things."[2] The universe is designed to provide a basis for human happiness. Moral standards are, then, implicit in the nature of things.

When the young Benjamin Franklin was in London working as a type-setter, the book on which he was engaged to work was, by one of those sublime coincidences which would be found unbelievable in a work of fiction, Wollaston's *Religion of Nature Delineated*. The young printer was annoyed by the complacent optimism of Wollaston's work, and, to ridicule it, he composed a little tract called *A Dissertation on Liberty and Necessity, Pleasure and Pain*.[3] In this highly critical pamphlet Franklin insisted that the criteria suggested by Wollaston did not really provide a standard for discriminating between good and evil in our actions. Later in life Franklin called this work of his youth an error, because it denied the distinction between virtue and vice.[4]

Franklin's developed morality of benevolence and service took the form of an inversion of the superior attitude of Cotton Mather. Even while Franklin was in his teens and apprenticed to his brother in Boston, he wrote and had printed his "Dogood papers" in which he pointed to the shortcomings of the wealthy, the well-born, the pretentious — those people, in brief, in whom Mather could find little or nothing to criticize. Later, in Philadelphia, Franklin continued his comment on the same class of people in his "Busybody papers." Franklin's idea of improving one's fellowmen by benevolence was far more inclusive than was Mather's, and his life shows him as the epitome of secular humanitarianism. It was a life full of plans and systems whereby groups of citizens could improve themselves and their community without the mediation of church, creed, or minister. He sought to provide a practical sanction for the virtues of truthfulness, sincerity and integrity in their importance to "the felicity of life," to happiness here, not hereafter.

The highest type of Christian benevolence in the period of Enlightenment was to be found among the Friends, or Quakers. Of the Friends, Anthony Benezet and John Woolman deserve particular mention for their devoted struggles against the evils of slavery.

Though not a philosophical document, Woolman's *Journal* is an excellent illustration of the practical fruits of enlightened benevolence. Not slavery alone, but all exploitation of labor aroused Woolman's opposition. In a little tract called *Remarks on Sundry Subjects,* Woolman presents the philosophic basis on which his opposition to economic exploitation rests. This is particularly interesting because of the way in which the doctrine of stewardship of wealth and love for one's fellowmen are tied together with approbation for a moderate capitalism, kept moderate by a religious self-control rather than by any form of social intervention.

Together with Woolman's growing sense of the undesirability of any form of exploitation of man by man, whether in slavery or in inadequately compensated "free" labor, he manifested the Quaker strains of passivism, quietism, and pietism. In the deep personal piety of the Quaker, Woolman waited constantly on the Lord for guidance; his way of living was based upon the "inner light." His quietism must be distinguished sharply from the active benevolence of Benjamin Franklin, even as the Quaker inner light is to be carefully distinguished from the supernatural sense, the "divine and supernatural light," of Jonathan Edwards. The Edwardean divine light (Chapter 1, section II) was a supplementary sense added to man's natural senses by divine Grace, as a foundation for man's ideas of divinity. The Quaker inner light was a specific and direct guidance from God to prompt man to particular actions in any situation, and therefore a foundation for man's humanity. Woolman resembles Emerson (Chapter 4, section II) in his teaching that God is an invisible spiritual being who speaks directly in man, and that man must wait for and follow the "inward drawings" which come from God's indwelling presence.

Franklin's ethics of benevolence was a secular version of Mather's Puritan ethics. Similarly, the secular theory of the American Revolution and, later, of American independence developed out of the discussion of church government which had been an important aspect of Puritan life and thought. An excellent example of the transition from a purely religious to a purely secular political theory in America is to be found in John Wise's *Vindication of the Government of New England Churches* (1717). In this treatise, as we have seen (see Prelude), Wise tried to justify the autonomy of local churches against the attempt of a group of Boston ministers to exert control over all the churches of New England. The first part of Wise's discussion uses traditional ecclesiastical arguments; in the second part, Wise turns to the argument from "the law and light of nature" and develops a theory of the "prime immunities of man in a state of natural being," that is, a doctrine of natural rights or what are called in the Declaration of Independence "inalienable rights." Wise does not follow these ideas to a democratic conclusion; his preference is for a limited monarchy. The importance of his work is its shift from a basis in theological sanctions to a basis in natural law.

Some of the Puritans followed the arguments of Jonathan Mayhew, whose theological orthodoxy was questionable, but whose political thought was well-liked. Mayhew's "Discourse on Unlimited Submission and Passive Obedience," delivered in celebration of the one hundredth anniversary of the execution of King Charles I of England, gave the right of revolution a footing in natural religion. Mayhew's sermon — John Adams called it "the opening gun of the Revolution" — was a loosely-reasoned, but very moving argument against political absolutism and the divine right theories which justify absolutism. Mayhew forged a combination of liberal political views, derived from John Locke (1632-1704), John Milton (1608-1674), and Algernon Sidney (1622-1683), with a religious liberalism drawn from Ralph Cudworth (1617-1688), Samuel Clarke (1675-1729), and Francis Hutcheson (1694-1747).

The essential contribution made by Mayhew to the development of political theory in America was to incorporate the right to revolution among the natural rights of man and to justify this inclusion in part on the basis of a reconsideration of the Scriptures. He questioned whether men are obliged to yield absolute submission to their rulers, or whether disobedience and resistance might not be justifiable in some cases. He argued for the latter alternative.

Mayhew shocked other ministers and many laymen by discussing political and moral issues from his pulpit instead of limiting himself to doctrinal controversy. It seems to have been his intention to transform the Puritan idea of the glory of God from a theological to a moral and social concept. To effect this shift, he placed emphasis on the goodness of God rather than on His glory and asserted salvation to be the result of moral struggle rather than of free grace. Because of this shift of theoretical perspective, he was able consistently to make of his pulpit a sounding-board for liberal views on specific political issues, for, as he said in 1763, he believed that true religion includes the love of liberty and of country and the hatred of all tyranny and oppression. It is in general worthy of remark that Mayhew's political thought, unlike that of most of his predecessors and contemporaries in the colonial ministry, was humanistic and secular in its tendency. In 1754, for example, he asserted that society has a human origin. The people, he said, grant authority to civil government to do whatever is necessary for the maintenance of peace and prosperity. When government fails to do that for which it is established, the people are within their rights in resisting and overthrowing it. This view, in greater detail, lies at the heart of his celebrated sermon of 1750.

Gradually the theory and spirit of the natural right to revolution was transformed into the specific theory of the American Revolution. The formulation of the theory of the American Revolution was the work of many men. Without attempting here to present in detail the views of Samuel Adams, John Adams, Thomas Jefferson, Alexander Hamilton, or even of Thomas Paine, whose *Common Sense* was the most influential statement of the theory, let us summarize the ideas on which these men and their fellow revolutionaries were in agreement.

The theory of the American Revolution began in the argument that the American colonies and the British homeland were united only through the duty each owed to the English king. The colonies, as Hamilton said in "The Farmer Refuted," held lands in America by charters from the British monarchs, not from Parliament, and therefore owed no duty of obedience to the decrees of Parliament. Jefferson echoed this theme in his "Summary View of the Rights of British America," referring to the colonists as "His Majesty's subjects in America," and arguing that no title can be given to "that authority which the British Parliament would arrogate over us."[5] Because colonial allegiance was the due of the Crown and not the Parliament, the action of the Parliament in attempting to tax the colonies was not only unwise and unfair, but also improper — actually a violation of the British constitution.

Furthermore, the colonists maintained that their charters gave them title to all the right of citizens in the homeland. One such right, the colonial leaders argued, was to be taxed only when they were represented in the taxing body. John Adams pointed out that the colonists do not have representation in Parliament, "unless it be by a fiction of law," and the conclusion drawn from the absence of representation was that American taxes might be levied only by the colonial legislatures.[6]

The colonists, asserted the bold declaration of the Congress of 1774, "are entitled to life, liberty and property, and they have never ceded to any sovereign power whatever a right to dispose of either without their consent."[7] In making this statement, the Congress was assuming the whole "social contract" theory of the origin of society. This theory maintained that before the establishment of civil government, men lived in a "state of nature," in which each man possessed a number of natural rights. The extent of these rights every man determined for himself and each enforced his own determination. The fruits of this primitive anarchy were unsatisfactory, so men, by means of a mutual agreement, a contract, yielded some of their natural rights to allow the establishment of a common authority or civil government. In the event that the government thus set up fails to create the security and stability for the sake of which it was established, or if it oversteps its functions and becomes oppressive, the people may exercise their right of revolution by overthrowing the government which is their own creation and returning to the original state of nature.

In the state of nature no man is the subject of any other man; each one is a completely independent sovereignty. Since each has the same jurisdiction and authority, all men are equal. No man is born with any special advantages. Political rights are not given by governments. All men have rights in the state of nature; while some of these rights are surrendered to make government possible, others cannot be surrendered. These "inalienable" rights are the true foundation of all political rights. Everyone is familiar with the description of these rights in the Declaration of Independence; perhaps their meaning will emerge more clearly if we report an alternative expression. The original provisional constitution of the State of New Hampshire (1776) called them "certain natural, essential and inherent rights, among which are the enjoying and defending life and liberty; acquiring, possessing, and protecting property; and in a word, of seeking and obtaining happiness."[8]

It seemed to the men of the Enlightenment necessarily true — "self-evident" — that the only possible foundation of political society must be the consent to government implied by the social contract theory. There was little attempt to specify the exact nature of the contract or even to assert that there was any specific historic occasion on which men met together to negotiate a contract of this type. The entire theory was regarded as axiomatic, as the only kind of explanation which made sense. Once the idea is accepted that there must have been consent to the establishment of government, the idea that there must be some form of consent to all legitimate legislation follows. The consent to legislation may be by proxy; there need be no direct assembly of the people if there is an adequate representation in government. "A freeman," said John Adams, "is one who is bound by no law to which he has not consented." [9]

Behind the political and moral views just discussed lay a view of human nature and the nature of God which made possible the assertion of the competence of each man to make political decisions wisely. The tremendous scientific advances of the sixteenth and seventeenth centuries, culminating in Newton's mechanical view of the universe, made many phenomena which had seemed miraculous to men of earlier days intelligible on natural grounds. The need to refer to God to explain natural events became rare, and, with this decreasing need, men's view of God changed. He become in men's mind less the personal Being of the theistic tradition and more the impersonal, remote ultimate principle of deism. Meantime, as men's explanations of the universe became more and more adequate and complete, faith in man's ability to know and to utilize his knowledge grew. Scientific knowledge was sure to advance, and scientific advance would provide the key to unlock all the mysteries of the universe. Progress toward complete understanding and complete control was regarded as certain and inevitable. The ordinary man no longer felt it necessary to rely upon the institution or the individual which had established a special relation to God; churches and states, prophets, priests and kings, were all unnecessary. Open eyes and an active mind — enlightenment — were available to every man, and were the guaranties of a good life.

The working-out in practice of this pattern of opposition to traditional institutions and reliance upon human reason is best seen in the early history of the United States of America. We shall describe its development in three of the spokesmen of the American

Revolution and the spirit of Enlightenment: Thomas Jefferson, Thomas Paine, and Benjamin Rush.

II. ENLIGHTENED POLITICS:
THOMAS JEFFERSON

The ideas and themes of the Enlightenment in America were nowhere more fully expressed than in the thought and life of Thomas Jefferson. In fact, the reading of a thorough and careful biography of Jefferson would be an excellent introduction to the study of the Enlightenment. His active career as a lawyer spanned nearly half a century, and his political activities occupied nearly forty years of that period. In addition, he was a man of many and varied interests and skills: He was a distinguished amateur in science, a member of the American Philosophic Society; he was a farmer, deeply interested in making of his Monticello estate, near Charlottesville, Virginia, a successful experiment in scientific agriculture; he was an inventor, and some of his inventions and skillful adaptations of the inventions of others are still to be seen at Monticello; he was an architect of ability, and some of his buildings still stand as monuments to his skill and taste; he held high appointive offices, attesting to the respect that other leaders of his time had for his capacities; and he held the highest elective offices in Virginia and in the federal government, testifying to the admiration which the people had for his abilities.

Jefferson himself, however, when he reviewed the achievements of his life in the light of choosing the inscription for his tombstone, named three contributions to the development of our country which he wished to have remembered. He asked, accordingly, that he be recorded as the writer of the Declaration of Independence, the author of the Bill Establishing Religious Freedom in Virginia, and the founder of the University of Virginia.

Jefferson was not a systematic philosopher; his views on the nature of man and of society, on ethics, politics and religion, must be built up from fragmentary comments in his public papers and his extensive correspondence. Part of our problem in selecting these fragments and constructing his philosophic outlook is to try to determine why Jefferson regarded these three as the most important of his many contributions to the growth of the United States of America. In order to do this we must ferret out the guiding principles of his life.

Jefferson, like many if not most of the intellectual leaders of his age, was profoundly influenced by the currents of thought which flowed from the work of Newton. He believed that there were regularities in nature and human nature which could be discovered by scientific study and applied for the benefit of mankind. He was preëminently practical in his interests and concerns. A beautiful and ingenious systematic theory interested him only insofar as he could see in it the possibility of application to human life for the betterment of human living. Jefferson's temper was experimental: He considered no theory valid until it had successfully passed the test of practice. Of the many attacks upon him, none were more unfair than those which criticized him for being overspeculative.

The purely speculative thinker, who is unconcerned about the practical applications of his thought, expresses his conclusions in absolute terms. Jefferson, the anti-dogmatist, was usually far more tentative in his expression, and relative in his conclusions. So he asserted that democracy might be a workable form of government in America, not the only form of government that a reasonable man can accept. He held to a view that we today would call cultural, namely, that the appropriate form of government for any group depends upon the conditions under which that group lives at the given time, and that a government is good to the extent that it is adapted to the condition of those whom it governs. Though Jefferson accepted this relative view with respect to immediate practical necessities, he was by no means a complete relativist; he believed that there were certain absolute and necessary truths ("self-evident truths") which serve as a moral beacon, a guide for mankind's strivings. He accepted the idea which was current in his time that progress toward these ideals is an inevitable consequence of the progress of science. Intelligence is innate in all men; restrictions of various sorts, imposed by various authorities, have prevented men from receiving the training which would enable them to utilize their intelligence. Once these restrictions are overcome, Jefferson felt that the rate of progress would increase in science, in the arts, in human relations, and in government, until, in the end, men are completely governed by reason.

This end, this state in which all men are completely reasonable, is a large part of what Jefferson meant by the word "happiness." He considered happiness to be the goal of the moral life, and believed that, since "virtue and interest are inseparable," man's self-interested pursuit of happiness would lead to social benefits. Jefferson thought, too, that every man is born with a moral sense or instinct, imperfections in which can be corrected "by appeals to reason and calculation." Thus the moral sense is not a conscience, giving us immediate and intuitive knowledge of virtue and vice, but is, rather, an aspect of the reasoning, mathematical intelligence, leading to a recognition of the utility or inutility of certain actions. "Nature," Jefferson continued, "has constituted *utility* to man the standard and test of virtue." Although Jefferson's term "moral sense" was that used by some of the British writers in ethical theory in his time, there is a difference in its use. For these British writers, the moral sense gave absolute laws of morality; for Jefferson the moral sense gave relative judgments of utility or expediency. "Men living in different countries, under different circumstances, different habits and regimens may have different utilities; the same act, therefore, may be useful, and consequently virtuous in one country which is injurious and vicious in another differently circumstanced."[10]

Jefferson believed that, for the most part, the promptings of reason would induce men to perform actions which lead to general happiness. He referred occasionally to a "future state of retribution for the evil as well as the good done while here," [11] but in general he did not stress religious beliefs about the future life as a sanction for morality. In part, at least, he was able to avoid emphasizing the influence of eternal rewards and punishments in man's moral behavior by the optimistic view he took of human nature. He wrote to Dupont de Nemours in 1816 testifying to his belief that "morality, compassion, generosity are innate elements of the human constitution." Human nature, then, is innately good, not sinful. Evil impulses are the exception, not the rule. If this is so, then education and the appeal to reason should suffice, without the introduction of supernatural terror to return evildoers to the natural path of goodness.

Jefferson's political theory is based on the asumption that man living in society is innately good and reasonable. Like many other political thinkers of his time, Jefferson regarded government as the handiwork of men. Men living without government had created it to meet their needs. The primary purpose, "the only orthodox object of the institution of government," is to make possible the happiness of the citizens. If governments do not fulfill the purpose for which they were created, it is the right of citizens to overthrow their creation and to substitute a government which does what they established it to do. In the Declaration of Independence, speaking for all his countrymen, Jefferson voiced a moderate, yet firm, espousal of revolution. Here he said that only for the most serious and long-continued abuses should men rebel and throw off the yoke of government. When he spoke for himself alone, his position was far more extreme. He thought of rebellion as a medicine necessary for maintaining the government in sound health. "God forbid we should ever be twenty years without . . . a rebellion," he wrote to William S. Smith in 1787, "The tree of liberty must be refreshed from time to time, with the blood of patriots and tyrants. It is its natural manure."[12]

The right to revolution is the consequence, in Jefferson's political theory, of the view that governments are created by men. Men establish government to protect their liberties and their happiness. "The freedom and happiness of man . . . are the sole objects of all legitimate government,"[13] he wrote, and insisted that in every measure he advocated it was his intention to strengthen the liberty of the people. In part, the liberty of men consists in their natural rights. These rights, as formulated in the Declaration of Independence, were life, liberty, and the pursuit of happiness. These three, without further specification, do not, however, exhaust Jefferson's thought on this theme. Included in his broadest conception of natural rights are freedom of thought, freedom of religion, freedom of speech, freedom of communication, freedom of the press, and freedom of trade, as well as the right of personal freedom. Even self-government he considers as a natural right, which men "receive . . . with their being from the hand of nature."[14]

In addition to these natural rights, Jefferson held that there are what might be called social or civil rights, such as the right to property. These are, in a sense, limited rights; men have them only to the extent that they can be had "without violating the similar rights of other sensible beings."[15] On the other hand, other writers had claimed certain rights which Jefferson could not accept. Conservative and reactionary thinkers in the eighteenth century had found the language of rights as easy to learn as had liberals. In opposition to the rights they asserted, Jefferson insisted that no man has a right to commit aggression on the rights of another; that no man has a right to be the judge in a case to which he is himself a party; that no man has a natural right to oppress others; and that no natural right to monopoly exists.

A special use of the doctrine of natural rights emerges in Jefferson's denial of the right of one generation to bind its successor. It is in this point that Jefferson's political theory most directly challenges the thought of influential conservatives like Edmund Burke (1729-1797). Such conservatives, usually lawyers, held that the being of a nation includes its duration through time, and that, as a consequence, actions taken or regulations enacted at any period in national history are binding by precedent or tradition on all subsequent generations. Jefferson argued that, if this position be taken, the earth belongs to the dead, not to the living. To this doctrine Jefferson opposed the view, equally legalistic, that "the generations of men may be considered as bodies or corporations. Each generation has the usufruct of the earth during the period of its continuance. When it ceases to exist, the usufruct passes on to the succeeding generation, free and unincumbered, and so on, successively, from one generation to another forever."[16] Thus each generation, as life tenant, may use all the fruits of its land for whatever purpose it desires, binding its own members in any way that they will accept. The next generation must, however, receive its life tenure in the estate free of all encumbrances. By 1823, this legal interpretation which Jefferson, even ten years earlier, had been willing to argue had taken on in his mind the character of self-evident truth. He no longer felt it to be a disputable position, but insisted rather that it needed no explanation or defense.[17]

On the one hand, in some statements, Jefferson includes the right of self-government among the natural rights of men, while on the other hand, in other contexts, Jefferson treats self-government as a hypothesis subject to processes of verification. Thus he wrote in 1787, "I have no fear, but that the result of our experiment will be that men may be trusted to govern themselves without a master."[18] That is to say, we can find in his writings one and the same idea, self-government, expressed in two different ways — as an eternal truth and as a tentative theory. The reason for this double type of statement seems to lie in the fact that Jefferson was trying to do two different things — to state an ideal for all government, and to develop a practical program for the government of the United States. Jefferson's two statements about self-government might be connected in this manner: "The ideal form of all government, in theory, is one in which the people govern themselves by right. It has been held that this ideal is unreachable, because the people are incapable of governing themselves. We, in the United States, instead of denying categorically that the ideal is realizable, are trying to prove that self-government is both realizable and practical."

If this is the meaning of Jefferson's experimentalism, then it is easy to understand why he dismisses so summarily the writings of earlier political theorists. "The introduction of this new principle of representative democracy has rendered useless almost everything written before on the structure of government."[19] The judgments of earlier writers on the possible success of a democracy were based on the assumption that the only possible democratic form of government involved the direct participation of the citizenry in the process of making decisions. Inasmuch as the American experiment denies this assumption by introducing *representative* democracy, the possible outcome of this experiment can not be predicted by a study of men who knew not representation.

It is easy, too, to see why, in this case, Jefferson wished for as thoroughgoing a test of the principle as could be made. "My most earnest wish is to see the republican element of popular control pushed to the maximum of its practicable exercise."[20] Only if this has been done, only if the last possible vestige of autocratic government has been eliminated, is the experiment of republicanism (or representative democracy) in America a conclusive one. In his anxiety to eradicate all the residue of autocracy, Jefferson maintained, in various forms, the view that that government is best which governs least.

He admitted that he was not "a friend to a very energetic government." Such a government, he felt, is always oppressive, favoring the governors at the expense of the people. In order to stabilize the government and to avoid the extreme of anarchy to which his own principle might lead — did not Henry Thoreau a quarter of a century after Jefferson's death paraphrase Jefferson by averring that government to be absolutely best which governs not at all? — Jefferson became a staunch advocate of popular education. Domestic peace, he maintained, is best preserved by giving information to the people rather than by giving additional police powers to the government. By educating and informing the whole mass of the people we will "enable them to see that it is their interest to preserve peace and order, and they will preserve them." [21]

The decision of the people is to prevail. But if the people do not know how to decide, we should not deny their right to self-government; instead we should give them enough training so that they will be capable of making decisions. Certainly the history of monarchies and the situation in Europe in Jefferson's time gave plenty of latitude and ample support to his contention that popular decisions could be no worse than monarchic or ministerial decisions. "No race of kings has ever presented above one man of common sense in twenty generations. The best they can do is to leave things to their ministers; and what are their ministers, but a committee, badly chosen? If the king ever meddles, it is to do harm."[22]

Jefferson's faith in human nature led, as we have seen, to his affirming the rights of individual liberty against the authority of monarchs and their ministers. It led, too, to his belief that any man, without the authority of church or clergy, is able to think through the questions of religion as well as those of politics and arrive at conclusions which, at least, satisfy his own conscientious needs, and may lead him to eternal truth. In 1800, when Jefferson was a candidate for the presidency and was under attack by conservative clergymen because of the liberality of his religious views, he wrote, "I have sworn upon the altar of God, eternal hostility against every form of tyranny over the mind of man."[23] Religiously, politically, and educationally this might serve as the motto summing up Jefferson's career on behalf of liberty.

The basic assumption from which Jefferson argued the case for religious freedom is stated in the first clause of his Act for Establishing Religious Freedom in Virginia: "Well aware that Almighty God hath created the mind free . . ." If this be assumed, then it can never be the right of any man or any group of men, church or state, to place bounds and limits upon man's use of his mind. Should the intellectual principles reached by any man "break out into overt acts against peace and good order," it is time for the agencies of government to intervene. "The legitimate powers of government extend to such acts only as are injurious to others. But it does me no injury for my neighbor to say there are twenty gods, or no God.

It neither picks my pocket nor breaks my leg."[24] Government, therefore, has no cause to compel the citizens to support any particular form of religious worship, nor to make any citizen suffer in any way whatsoever for his religious opinions. It is, rather, the obligation of government to see to it that "all men shall be free to profess, and by argument to maintain, their opinions in matters of religion" without in the least affecting their civil status thereby.[25]

Jefferson's concern for equality was never pressed by him to the same extent as this care for liberty. He was in no sense a pure egalitarian, but believed, rather, in equality of opportunity within each generation. In the State of Virginia he gave an example of his concern for equalizing opportunity within each generation by his campaign for the abolition of the legal traditions that the oldest son was to be the sole heir of landed property and that estates might not be disposed of piecemeal (primogeniture and entail). In the second place, his devotion to public education was, in part, a manifestation of his belief in equality of opportunity. Each child, he thought, deserved the chance to develop his intellectual capabilities to their fullest extent, regardless of the poverty of his family. Education ought not to be a benefit of the wealthier classes alone. In consequence of this belief, Jefferson drew up a plan whereby free public education from grade school to college could be made available to every child. The University of Virginia, which he founded, was the capstone of this educational structure. It was to provide even advanced education for those whose abilities were adequate to college work.

Jefferson never thought that every child in each generation is equally talented or equally virtuous. He did not oppose the idea of aristocracy as such, the idea that some men in any place and time are better qualified to lead their people than others. What he did oppose, most heartily, was the view that either heredity or wealth give one title to aristocracy. The only type of aristocracy which Jefferson would admit was a natural aristocracy. Even the Society of the Cincinnati, the post-Revolutionary organization of veterans of the revolution, seemed dangerous to Jefferson (as he wrote to Washington in 1784), because it would introduce into American life an hereditary difference between man and man, and might lead to the formation of a military caste. In 1786 he said, "In America no other distinction between man and man had ever been known, but that of persons in office, exercising powers by authority of the laws, and private individuals."[26] It was his hope and his faith that the wisdom of the people, operating through our free system of elections, would select the "really good and wise," the natural aristocrats, for office, rather than members of the "tinsel-aristocracy."

Although Jefferson did not make, and did not believe in making, class distinctions, he did frequently make occupational distinctions. He thought of the farmer, independently owning his small-holding, as the backbone of democracy in America. "Merchants, priests, and lawyers" were disloyal in their thinking, preferring England and monarchy to the American Constitution. Merchants, he said, are attached to profits, not to country; priests are always in alliance with despots; lawyers have not always been unsympathetic toward democracy, but the books they have been studying, notably Sir William Blackstone's commentaries, have made Tories out of all young lawyers. Farmers, unlike all these, "are the chosen people of God." Individual farmers may become morally corrupt, but never the mass of cultivators of the soil. They are dependent only upon their own land and their own labors, and not subject, therefore, to "subservience and venality."[27]

As long as agriculture should remain the principal occupation in America, Jefferson looked forward to continued virtue and sustained democracy. He believed, however, that "when we get piled upon one another in large cities, as in Europe, we shall become corrupt as in Europe, and go to eating one another as they do there." An urban population, "the mobs of great cities," seemed to Jefferson the diseased part of a society, even as the farmers are its healthy and uncorrupted part. City folk, he insisted, "add just so much to the support of pure government, as sores do to the strength of the human body."[28] He advocated a policy of limiting manufacturing in America, sending our raw materials to Europe to be manufactured there, and sending our surplus foodstuffs to Europe to feed its laboring population. Whatever the economic effects of such a policy might be, Jefferson felt sure that its moral effects would justify it. A society of farmers was Jefferson's ideal of a classless society.

With this background in Jefferson's ideas, it is easy to understand why he selected as the three greatest achievements of his life the Declaration of Independence, the Act Establishing Religious Freedom, and the founding of the University of Virginia. The first symbolized for Jefferson the devotion of his lifetime to the cause of political freedom, representing his contribution to the making of a world in which governmental oppression would be no more. The second, the basis for the separation of church and state, meant the liberation of the mind of man from the dead weight of clerical domination. The third laid the foundation for an education which would be an important instrument in preserving and maintaining the gains of political liberty and religious freedom. No civilized nation, he asserted, can be both ignorant and free. The elimination of ignorance, the diffusion of information, is the only foundation on which free government can rest.

III. ENLIGHTENED PUBLICIST: THOMAS PAINE

Thomas Jefferson, in trying to work out the implications of his belief in the power and reach of the human mind, was led to belief in political democracy, universal education, and religious freedom. God, said Jefferson, had created men with certain inalienable rights, leading to political freedom, and with free minds, leading to religious freedom. Political or religious authority, because it interfered with these divinely instituted freedoms, was not to be tolerated. The Jeffersonian ideal was that of free minds in a free society. Virtually all of the leaders of the American revolution believed as Jefferson did, though for the most part they were not as vocal and explicit in proclaiming their views.

One of those who went at least as far as Jefferson, and possibly even farther, in devotion to the cause of freedom thus broadly conceived was Thomas Paine. But whereas Jefferson's ideas were chiefly reserved for his private correspondence or expressed with great caution in state papers, Paine was a publicist, popularizer, and propagandist. It was Paine who had the vigor of style and simplicity of expression necessary to give the ideas of the enlightened revolutionaries widespread currency. Up to a point, this was considered a useful service to the new country, and Paine was regarded as one of the more valuable aids to the revolutionary party. In 1782 Washington, Robert Morris, and Livingston valued Paine's literary contribution to the revolution so highly that they arranged for him to receive a salary of eight hundred dollars a year, no trivial sum in those days, to write in the cause of liberty.

Paine's popularity and the high esteem in which he was held by such men as Washington faded fast, however, after the beginning of the French Revolution. At this time, when many other American revolutionary leaders were either maintaining a politic silence or turning themselves into conservatives, Paine remained the same outspoken exponent of radical and revolutionary views that he had always been. The loss of prestige which overtook Paine in the later years of his life was the result of changes in the environment, not in Paine. In fact, some of the frustrations and bewilderment of Paine's old age seem to have been the result of his dazed recognition that his old comrades were no longer in the revolutionary camp.

Yet there is one respect in which Paine should be considered with Alexander Hamilton as somewhat more conservative than the other leaders of the time. Whatever their differences on other matters, both Hamilton and Paine favored a strong, centralized national government for the United States. Neither believed in the many limitations on national power and the safeguards of state sovereignty which were written into the frame of the American government. It is readily understandable that this should have been so. Neither Hamilton nor Paine was born in the American colonies; neither felt the strong tie to a native state that Washington or Jefferson felt for the Old Dominion of Virginia, or John Adams for the Commonwealth of Massachusetts. They served the nation, for it was the nation which had enabled Hamilton to overcome the handicap of illegitimacy and Paine to rise above his lower middle class birth to association with America's leading spirits.

Like so many of the other American revolutionaries, Paine was interested in science, both pure and applied. As early as his twentieth year, in London, Paine heard and was much influenced by popular lectures on Newtonian astronomy. Seventeen years later, in 1774, when he met Benjamin Franklin in London, their point of contact was Paine's interest in electrical phenomena. Carrying a letter of recommendation from Franklin, Paine migrated to America and was employed by Robert Aitken, publisher of *The Pennsylvania Magazine*. One of the first of Paine's papers to be published was an account of a new electrical machine. After the revolution, with the encouragement of Benjamin Rush, Paine devoted his time to the development of technological applications of science, like a smokeless candle and a new type of iron bridge. It was partly in order to promote the sale of this new type of bridge that he went to Europe in 1787. His English patent for it was issued in 1790. Even this brief summary is enough to show that though Paine was largely self-educated he had enough background in the science of his time to share in its chief assumptions.

As we have seen, the most important of the consequences to flow from the Newtonian view of the system of the universe was the belief in order and regularity in nature. In Paine's writings the appeal to nature invariably involves a reference to the systematic and orderly harmony of the universe, and hence, by implication, its predictability. Nature is "no other than the laws the Creator has prescribed to matter." "It is the laws by which the universe is governed." Scientific investigation does not invent or introduce the pattern or regularity, the "unerring order and universal harmony," which it proclaims. Newton did not make "the ratio of gravitation." The pattern is divine; it was established by God in the creation of the universe. By using the methods of scientific study, men are able to discover the divinely-made harmonies. Furthermore, for Paine, nothing could be admitted to be of divine origin unless it manifested regularity, law, and order. It is for this reason that he rejected the claims of the so-called miracle, that is, "something contrary to the operation and effect of those laws" by which nature is supposed to act.[29]

Paine reproduced in abbreviated form the argument of David Hume (1711-1776) against the credibility of miracles. Our acceptance of an account of a miraculous occurrence is sought not on the basis of our having seen the event, but upon the report of others who claim to have seen it. "It requires a transfer of faith from God to man to believe a miracle upon man's report." If we read an account of an event occurring in contradiction to the laws of nature, we have, Paine said, to ask ourselves which is more probable — that nature should stray from her usual course or that man should stray from the truth. During our lives we have never seen nature go out of her course; in the same period, we have heard many lies. The probability that the reporter is false is far higher than the probability of the miracle's having occurred as reported.[30]

His belief in the regularity of nature and the unlikelihood of any significant breakdown of its orderly pattern reveal Paine as a typical representative of the Enlightenment. Furthermore, if nature operates according to rules which have been defined by a benevolent Creator, man, who participates in the divine benevolence, is himself a creature formed to behave in accordance with a definite set of rules, a pattern of conduct known as moral law. The moral law is the natural law for men. Even as the natural law is discoverable by the workings of human reason, the moral law can be discovered by reason. And even as our discovery of natural law reveals to us the physical harmonies of the universe, the moral law reveals the moral harmonies of the universe. The course of Paine's political and economic thought, as well as his religious, is the attempt to rediscover the moral harmony of the universe which has been distorted by centuries of clerical misinterpretation and bad government.

To understand Paine, then, we must return to "natural man," man as he issued from the hands of his Creator, unspoiled by governmental institutions. When, for example, in his pamphlet on "The Rights of Man," Paine criticizes Edmund Burke for his recourse to the argument from history and tradition, Paine's criticisms are not directed against the method itself, but against Burke's failure to carry the method back far enough. Why should we accept some arbitrary date like 1066, the date of the Norman Conquest of England, when William the Conqueror usurped the royal power in that land, as the beginning of the British tradition? Naturally, Burke's argument depends upon this arbitrary date, because the tradition he wishes to defend starts then. But Paine insists that "The error of those who reason by precedents drawn from antiquity, respecting the rights of man, is that they do not go far enough into antiquity."[31] He would go the whole way, not stop in any intermediate stage. To go the whole way means to return to man in the state of nature, when "Man was his high and only title," that is, before titles like King, Emperor, Lord or Esquire had been imposed upon him.[32]

When this ultimate antiquity has been reached we find that man and his rights were created together. We come to "the divine origin of the rights of man at the creation."[33] The account of the creation evidences to us that all men are born equal and with equal natural rights. The natural right of each infant born into the world today is exactly of the same degree as was that of "the first man that existed." In the scriptural account of the creation, the only distinction which is pointed out is that of the sexes. "The equality of man, so far from being a modern doctrine, is the oldest on record."[34]

These rights, then, in respect to which men are equal at creation are natural rights; each man is entitled to them simply and solely by virtue of his existence. Each man does not, however, have sufficient power, as an individual, to maintain all these rights. Paine follows closely Jefferson's discussion of rights: There are some which the individual is competent to maintain, like "the intellectual rights" and "those rights of acting as an individual for his own comfort and happiness, which are not injurious to the rights of others."[35] Other rights, especially those concerned with security and protection, though equally rights by nature, can not be perfectly maintained by the individual.

To protect their title to this second class of natural rights, "those in which, though the right is perfect in the individual, the power to execute them is defective,"[36] men unite into societies and transform these natural rights into civil rights. Thus every civil right is a natural right "exchanged." Civil power is the sum total of the rights surrendered to the common stock of society; this civil power may not invade the natural rights retained by the individual. Paine's picturesque account of the first founding of society is idyllic. There is here none of the compulsive urgency which breathes through the otherwise similar account in the *Leviathan* of Thomas Hobbes (1588-1679). Paine regarded society as a blessing, government as a necessary evil. The first thought of men in a state of nature, he argued, would be to form a society, which would for a time be guided exclusively by the moral law. Later, as the members of the society "begin to relax in their duty and attachment to each other," they are constrained to establish some form of government "to supply the defect of moral virtue." Then:

> Some convenient tree will afford them a statehouse, under the branches of which the whole colony may assemble to deliberate on public matters. It is more than probable that their first laws will have the title only of REGULATIONS and be enforced by no other penalty than public disesteem. In this first parliament every man by natural right will have a seat.[37]

This idyllic democracy does not last, of course. The group grows too large for its tree, and some form of government by the few is adopted — monarchy, aristocracy, or representative democracy. Of these only the last is an unperverted form, carrying out the original purpose of union into society, the achievement of security.

Monarchy and aristocracy are inevitably the result of some usurpation of power. Although such writers as Burke talk of the "right" of a ruler to continue in power, Paine denied that there is any such thing. A right, to be truly such, must be right in itself; it must be based on the moral law. The so-called rights of rulers are originally founded in wrong; they are based upon violations of the moral law, being established by conquest, power, or violence. Paine constantly stressed the connection that exists between legal or political right and moral right. He denied that an assumed right, or right founded in wrong, could be maintained, and insisted that principled action must have priority over political expediency. "Of more worth is one honest man to society . . . than all the crowned ruffians that ever lived."[38] It is perfectly true, of course, that a particular generation may make choice of a "crowned ruffian," a despotic ruler. But this choice by no means establishes an hereditary right in the ruler's descendants. Laws made in one generation may continue in force in succeeding generations, but this is so because they *are not* repealed, not because they *can not be* repealed.

The fact that some laws are not repealed though they might be is equivalent to the tacit consent of the living to these laws. Inasmuch as each new infant born into this world is born with a full set of rights equal to those of the first created man, no generation can bind its successors in any way which affects their rights. Like Jefferson, Paine insisted that "as government is for the living and not for the dead, it is the living only that has any right in it"[39] Each generation is as free to act for itself as any of its predecessors were, and for the same reason — the inalienable character of its rights. It must be understood, too, that to safeguard the rights of posterity is a duty. When Paine defended the French "Declaration of the Rights of Man and of Citizens," he pointed out that a declaration of rights is also reciprocally a declaration of duties. "Whatever is my right as a man, is also the right of another; and it becomes my duty to guarantee, as well as to possess."[40] This duty to guarantee to others the rights which one has as a man is a universal obligation, binding not only within an age but also through the ages.

The equality of rights which Paine so steadfastly maintained is not to be thought to imply any more general belief in equality. Talent and ability are widely and unequally distributed through the population of any country. Somewhere in the society there is always enough ability for all its purposes, but from generation to generation that ability changes its place. Talents and abilities, Paine asserts, can not descend by heredity; like Benjamin Rush and Jefferson, he recognized that to assume the hereditary descent of ability was to weaken the human basis for democracy and implicitly to justify aristocracy. Experience is called to witness that "it is impossible to control nature in her distribution of mental powers." Wisdom "has most probably visited in rotation every family of the earth." The order of government must follow the order of nature; though in each generation there are superior men, a "natural aristocracy" as Jefferson called them, their superiority gives no warrant to any form of hereditary system of government. On the contrary, the desirability of smoking out ability wherever it may be reenforces the argument for universal suffrage in his doctrine of rights.[41]

In his economic views Paine likewise believed in original equality as the birthright of every man, but did not believe in the stifling of individual initiative and ability. He was far more of a believer in commercial capitalism than Jefferson, or men like John Woolman who shared Jefferson's agrarian ideals. Paine held an elevated view of the ultimate possibilities of commerce, if it were permitted free development. He was an advocate of commerce because, as he put it, "I am a friend to its effects."[42] Trade leads to peaceful relations, among nations as well as among individuals, tending to unite men by making them useful to one another. If it were permitted "universal extent," there no longer would be any cause for wars. It is the "greatest approach towards universal civilization" made by men in any area except that of moral principles. There is mutual benefit and a spirit of participation as the inevitable result of commerce. No nation can flourish alone; "she cannot be the seller and the buyer of her own merchandise."[43] The most effective way for any nation to ruin her own commercial prosperity is to destroy the trade of other nations. There is no radicalism at this point in Paine's economic views.

He did, however, also insist on his principle of original equality, to which in the economic field, he gave the name of "agrarian justice." In a fashion characteristic of the advocates of capitalism in his age, he would make the landed proprietors pay the chief part of the cost of original equality by breaking down the right of inheritance. We have seen earlier that Paine argued that the only distinction at creation, and therefore the only distinction sanctioned by the Creator, was that between male and female. Just as there was no distinction with respects to rights, so there was no distinction of rich and poor. God gave the earth to men for their inheritance. In the natural state, as illustrated by the American Indians of Paine's time, land was not owned by the individual, but held in common for the use of all members of the group. This natural state is free from the extreme of poverty found in the civilized state, but it is deficient in "those advantages which flow from agriculture, arts, sciences, and manufactures."[44] Paine nowhere idealizes the state of nature as does Jean-Jacques Rousseau (1712-1778).

Paine insists, however, that "the first principle of civilization ought to have been, and ought still to be, that the condition of every person born into the world, after a state of civilization commences, ought not be worse than if he had been born before that period."[45] His argument here parallels exactly his argument for the universality of rights and the equality of each man with respect to these rights. It points to the conclusion that land — the earth — ought to remain the common property of all men, not to be appropriated in perpetuity by any purchaser. Each cultivator is a user of the land; he has a natural right to occupy it during his life and to support himself on its fruits. In exchange for this use, society is entitled to a ground rent from the agriculturalist. The right of the community is a right in unimproved land; the additional value created by the labor of the cultivator is the legitimate property of those who did the work which made the land productive. Paine does not advocate redistribution of the land in any commonly-accepted sense.

What he was concerned, and deeply so, to remedy is that large numbers of rightful owners of the earth have been dispossessed by the system without indemnification. To repair this omission he proposed that each person, rich or poor, be paid fifteen pounds sterling on reaching the age of twenty-one as partial compensation for what the introduction of the system of landed property has cost him, and that, after the age of fifty, each should be given an additional sum of ten pounds sterling annually. To finance this plan, Paine suggested the establishment of a national fund out of the ground rents paid for the life tenure of land. The ground rent of any piece of land, Paine argued, could be collected when an heir receives a bequest, "by subtracting from property a portion equal in value to the natural inheritance it has absorbed."[46] Further details of the plan have no relevance here; what is important is that Paine conceived this plan broadly as a social security program, designed for the sake of justice and humanity; it served also as a method of protecting the propertied classes from depredation. He was benevolent, just and humane, but also as he confessed, "a friend to riches."

Paine's stalwart defense of all the rights was especially vigorous when he was defending the "intellectual rights" — freedom of thought and utterance and the rights of conscience. When the British royal proclamation of 1792 against seditious writings led to Paine's indictment and the attempt to suppress his "Rights of Man," he castigated the British government in an open letter, accusing the British of following in the footsteps of the Spanish monarchy and the old regime in France. "It is a dangerous attempt in any government to say to a nation *'thou shalt not read.'* . . . *Thought* by some means or other is got abroad in the world, and cannot be restrained, though reading may."[47] He had no hesitation in his insistence on the rights of conscience. The use of the word "toleration" roused him to fury because it presupposed the right of the person who used it of another to withhold or grant liberty of conscience at his pleasure. So "Toleration is not the *opposite* of intoleration, but is the *counterfeit* of it. Both are despotisms."[48]

Tom Paine could have used the freedom of thought, speech, and conscience which he had advocated for others when in 1794 he published *The Age of Reason,* subtitled "An Investigation of True and of Fabulous Theology." He pleaded for the right to his opinion in the letter of dedication to his fellow-citizens of the United States. This plea was, however, rejected; Paine was vilified, abused, slandered, and misunderstood. He was called an atheist, though the chief aim of his work was to salvage "the theology that is true" from the general destruction of all theologies which accompanied the French Revolution. The pamphlet was anti-Christian, it is true, but not anti-religious. On the contrary, the position Paine took was that of many of the intellectual leaders of his age, the religion of Deism. The ferocity of the attack on Paine's *Age of Reason* can be understood only if we remember that he wrote for the masses, not for an intellectual elite. Church membership in the United States was at its lowest ebb when his pamphlet appeared. The forces of Christian clericalism had to attack vigorously to protect their own position.

Paine sought to go beyond an external freedom in religious matters which allows each man to choose a form of religious activity which, once chosen, has elements of compulsion internal to it. He sought to go beyond all superstition, and to found his religion on reason. He said, "My own mind is my own church," [49] and hoped to build on the freedom of his own mind a religion of minimum dogmatic content to which any other reasonable man would be constrained by reason and not by compulsion to agree. This minimum creed included the belief in one God and the moral law, and the hope of eternal happiness — no more than these and no less:

> I believe in one God, and no more; and I hope for happiness beyond this life.
> I believe in the equality of man, and I believe that religious duties consist in doing justice, loving mercy, and endeavoring to make our fellow-creatures happy.[50]

In defending this simple creed, Paine attacked all existing churches. Established churches in particular, "national institutions of churches," seemed to him deplorable agencies of enslavement and monopoly, terrifying men by the human inventions of priests. He indicated his disbelief in the claims of the various churches to possession of revealed truth, arguing that what comes to us at second hand can not be revelation, but is only hearsay. Moses and Jesus as men produced excellent moral precepts, as fine as any that lawgivers or philosophers of any age or clime had produced. The Christian church was created by men who built upon the simple life of Jesus, a "virtuous reformer and revolutionist,"[51] a tissue of mythology and fable. Paine dismissed much of both the Old Testament and the New because they embody a lower standard of morality and scientific understanding than Jesus or Moses could be charged with.

The true revelation of God Paine found in the visible creation, the world of nature and man, "which no human invention can counterfeit or alter." Man's only possible idea of God is that of first cause; but His power, wisdom, munificence, and mercy are revealed in the universal language spoken to man by the creation. Only by the exercise of his reason can man discover God; but not even human reason can gain a complete knowledge of God. The Christian introduction of a Redeemer between man's reason and God is described by Paine as "a sort of religious denial of God."[52]

It is characteristic of Christian theology to study the opinions and fancies of men with respect to God; natural philosophy is the true theology, for it is a direct study of the works of God, and an indirect study of God through his works. The discovery of scientific principles is made by a study of the structure of the universe. God is "the Almighty lecturer" [53] who displays the eternal principles of science in the structure of the universe so that men may study its laws and imitate nature's operations in human technology. Even the plurality of worlds known to the student of astronomy is an indication of God's beneficence toward his creatures. "The solitary idea of a solitary world, rolling or at rest in the immense ocean of space, gives place to the cheerful idea of a society of worlds so happily contrived as to administer, even by their motion, instruction to man." [54] What credence can be given to the Christian myth in such a universe? Man's moral duty is to imitate the benevolence which God's creation manifests. This would entail the abandonment of cruelty and persecution of man by man, of the imposition of despotic rule upon him, of the denial of his rights.

Paine's confessedly Deistic view provides a religious basis for the social, political, and economic ideas which we have sketched in this section. The reputation of Thomas Paine has suffered because of the attacks which were made on *The Age of Reason*, and his very real services to the formation of the American nation have been too frequently overlooked. But we should remember that these were not particularly radical views in Paine's time. He was by no means the only leader of the era of the American Revolution to be a Deist. These were religious views that were prevalent among the better educated men of the eighteenth century, men familiar with the natural science and political theory of their age. These are not the views of an isolated individual; they are typical of enlightened religion.

IV. ENVIRONMENTALISM AND
DEMOCRACY: BENJAMIN RUSH

We have had occasion to mention, in connection with Franklin, Jefferson, Hamilton, and Paine, the widespread interest in natural science which was characteristic of the era of enlightenment in America. The Newtonian vision of a world-machine, operating in orderly fashion according to principles or laws introduced by the Creator and accessible to men through the exercise of reason, had great appeal to the eighteenth-century mind. Almost every man of any education followed closely the new developments in science; accounts of the work of scientists were published even in the popular gazettes and journals. Poets sang of scientists as national heroes, who would rescue the world (in the words of Joel Barlow) from ignorance, bigotry, and superstition. Man's expected progress from strength to strength was thought to be closely linked to the advance of science.

Outstanding among the scientists whose work was done in this age was Benjamin Rush. His work in chemistry and physiology helped to push back frontiers in these sciences. Medical education was one of his major concerns, and many of the physicians of the early nineteenth century acknowledged their debt to his training. He was a practical philanthropist and practising humanitarian who carried forward Benjamin Franklin's projects for the welfare of Philadelphians in the medical school of the University of Pennsylvania and in the construction of the first public dispensary in America. Rush was also an ardent republican and an advocate of American independence who served his country well both in the Revolution and after its end. Beyond these achievements, Rush was a "natural philosopher" who held, more or less explicitly, both a philosophy of science and a scientific philosophy. His philosophy of science appears chiefly in his discussion of scientific method and in his theory of excitability. His scientifically grounded philosophy is revealed especially in his speculations on the political, social, and ethical questions of his day.

In Rush's time debate between advocates of rational and empirical methods was still prevalent, especially in the medical field. The rationalists believed that a complete system of medical practice could be worked out by deductively reasoning from first principles supplied by medical authorities. The empirics maintained that observation alone, without deduction from established principles, was the only way to establish medical science upon a firm basis. Rush carried over into medicine from his other scientific studies the principles of method which had proved so fruitful there. He insisted that neither observation nor reasoning is by itself adequate to the formulation of any scientific position. The schools of rationalism and empiricism he regarded as barriers to progress in medical science. Each, by its refusal to consider the justice in the position of the other, was helping to keep medicine from making the advances that physics, astronomy, and chemistry had made by joining empirical and rational procedures.

The discussion of "Observation and Reasoning in Medicine" which Rush presented to his students in a lecture in 1791 is especially interesting for its revelation of the extent to which the ideas of Deism had entered into Rush's thought. The Creator, according to the Deists, had ordained for the universe a benevolent plan designed, as we have seen in Paine, for the instruction of mankind. Rush maintained that to divide reason from sensation is to make "a breach in the symmetry of the divine government." A benevolent God would not have given man these two avenues of knowledge unless they were intended to supplement each other. God must have intended experience and reasoning to be united. Men must preserve and cultivate the union of mind and sensation in order that science may develop, and that, through its development "extensive and lasting blessings" may accrue to mankind.[55]

The result of Rush's application of his own principles of method was the statement of his theory of excitability. This theory is based upon observation, developed by reasoning, and extended by a broad speculative hypothesis. Although Rush elaborated his theory as one aspect of his work in physiology and presented it in his "Lectures on Animal Life," its chief influence came in the field of psychology, and it was also of some importance in the ill-advised attempts which led to the pseudo-science of phrenology. The observation with which Rush began his theory was that every part of the human body, both internal and external, is endowed either with the power of having sensations aroused in it by the action of impressions from outside itself, or with the property of moving in response to impressions from outside itself, or with both powers. The power of having sensations he called "sensibility," that of being excited to motion he called "excitability." By reasoning from this observation and the general nature of an organism or living body, Rush reached the conclusion that the stimulus of sensibility or excitability in any part of the body need not be directly applied to that part; when the body is in a healthy state, an impression made upon any part will cause sensation or movement, or both, in every other part of the body. When the fingertips are burned, the whole body feels the pain and withdraws from the contact. Thus far, save for the fact that there is no reference to any spiritual agency, but solely to material causes, Rush's view could be widely accepted.

The speculative hypothesis which he derived from this view is, however, far less generally acceptable. For he asserted that life itself "is the effect of certain stimuli acting upon the sensibility, and excitability which are extended in different degrees, over every external, and internal part of the body."[56] Life was to be considered, then, not as the product of some divine influx into inert matter, but as the purely mechanical effect of material causes. The functions of the body and the operations of the senses were included in this account of the cause of life. But Rush did not limit his theory to explaining physical life. He also regarded the action of the brain, the power of thought which had traditionally been proclaimed to be God's special gift to men, as the effect of physical stimulation.[57] Despite the care with which Rush disavowed the charge of materialism, there is no other description which can be given to this theory.

In Rush's own work there is an extension of this general hypothesis into psychology and ethics. This is his belief that the physical environment is a major element in determining man's capacity for distinguishing between good and evil and for choosing good rather than evil. He believed that men's moral choices were influenced by physical causes. Rush had no intention here of trespassing on theological grounds. He declined to discuss the conscience, whose invisibility placed it beyond investigation. Virtuous and vicious are terms applied to actions, not to opinions. Whatever conscience may lead men to think, it is their will, manifested in actions which affect social welfare, which can be investigated. It is this will which Rush, borrowing from the Scottish tradition, calls the "moral faculty," that is in his view stimulated by external physical causes.

There are two points to observe here: The first is that Rush, by using the terms "virtuous" and "vicious" to describe actions of consequence to the well-being of society, was leaning heavily toward a utilitarian ethical theory equating humanitarian benevolence with virtue. There is practically no trace of the theological virtues left in his thought. Although Rush was like Jonathan Edwards (see Chapter 1, section II) in adopting from the Scottish philosophers of his time the idea of virtue as benevolence, for Rush benevolence meant love of humanity while for Edwards it meant love of being in general. In the second place, when Rush limits the moral faculty by insisting on considering "virtue and vice to consist in action, and not in opinion,"[58] he is maintaining in ethical discourse the metaphysical principle of "Occam's razor" — that unnecessary entities are not to be assumed — which lies behind Newton's principle of the limitation of postulated causes. Rush's position is that virtue and vice are not entities, but attributes of actions. Similarly, conscience is a superfluous hypothesis; we already have will to account for virtuous and vicious behavior and physical causes to determine will. It is unnecessary, in Rush's view, to add the further explanatory entity of conscience with no real job to do.

When Rush discussed the possibility that his theory would be regarded as materialistic, he took a position less detailed than that of Cadwallader Colden (Chapter 1, section III) but similar in essentials. Like Colden, Rush held that matter was eternal. His view, he maintained, was entirely neutral on the question of materialism. He did not deny the possibility that there is a soul, or that the soul is immortal, but he insisted that the soul is not necessarily immaterial. If in fact "matter is in its own nature as immortal as spirit,"[59] as Rush argued, then it is indeed possible to talk of an immortal soul without committing oneself either to materialism or to immaterialism. What Rush committed himself to was the principle that the moral world and the realm of nature are to be interpreted in similar fashion, that we are not to use one type of explanation for moral, and another for natural, phenomena. In typical Deistic fashion, he regarded the phenomena of both worlds as parts of "the operation of the divine government." In the natural realm, divine government is carried on through the agency of secondary, physical causes. Consistency leads him to maintain that secondary, physical causes are the divine instruments in the moral realm as well.

The ultimate conclusion of Rush's philosophy of science was, then, that there is a complete dependence of the mental and moral aspects of human life on physical stimulation. On this foundation Rush built his social philosophy. The influence of physical causes on man's moral behavior became the central theme of an environmentalist and democratic view of the possibilities of man in society. The proper management of the external physical environment can produce revolutionary changes in man's moral choices and in his actions. Human nature is not fixed, but plastic. It can be modified and altered. Men are slavishly prepared to accede to authority because they have lived so long under despotisms, not because obedience is a permanent characteristic of human nature. Under conditions of freedom men will develop free minds and the morals of free men. It is from this general position that Rush's belief in republican forms of government, his views on education, his opposition to slavery, and his ideas on the rehabilitation of criminals fall together into a consistent and well-knit system.

So, for example, if we accept the basic principle that physical causes affect the moral faculty, the physical conditions under which education takes place become matters of vital importance. Rush did discuss educational questions frequently in his works. In 1786 he proposed a plan for the establishment of public schools in Pennsylvania, carrying out in that state the program advocated in Virginia by Jefferson.[60] Rush's plan went beyond the mere creation of schools. He was interested in assuring that the education provided in these schools should be conducted "agreeably to a republican form of government." What he meant by this was that the physical environment of the educational process, the physical discipline of the school, was to be such that it would forward the cause of republicanism. Rush's educational theory and his practical program centered on the control of physical stimuli.

Again, if we really believe that physical causes influence the moral faculty, we can not maintain that there is such a thing as a criminal type. Every criminal can be regenerated. He became a criminal because the physical conditions of his environment led him into vicious behavior. He will stop being a criminal when he is placed in an environment which leads him to virtuous behavior. Criminality can be wiped out by the elimination of the physical conditions which produce crime and the substitution of physical conditions which produce benevolence. Now if this is true, the theory of punishment must be considerably modified. We may still place persons guilty of criminal behavior in jails, but the character of the jails will be entirely different from what they would be under another theory. If, for example, we believe that there are men who are criminal by nature, punishment by imprisonment will be quite literally the revenge society takes against these criminals. A prison will be a house of detention. But if we believe, with Rush, that criminal behavior is environmentally caused, imprisonment will be the period during which society provides the proper regenerating physical environment. A prison will be primarily an educational institution, a house of correction. The period of detention will be valuable as a time when control over the environment can be maintained.

Although some aspects of Rush's thought might be well-received today, his system as a whole was evidently characteristic of its age — the age of enlightenment and of the American Revolution. A brave, new world was thought to be on its way. The American Revolution was far more than merely a political movement to its supporters. For men like Rush, ardent republicans, it also was cultural, marking the overthrow of all opposition to progress, the beginning of a progressive era that was expected to produce ever-increasing happiness for all mankind. Like Paine and Jefferson, Rush believed that the ideas of the revolutionary generation contained the specific remedies for all the ills with which society is afflicted. He talked with optimism and boundless apostolic zeal of the effects of the Revolution.

> Human misery of every kind is evidently on the decline. Happiness, like truth, is a unit. . . . The world, from the progress of intellectual, moral and political truth, is becoming a more safe and agreeable abode for man. . . . All the doors and windows of the temple of nature have been thrown open by the convulsions of the late American Revolution. This is the time, therefore, to press upon her altars. We have already drawn from them discoveries in morals, philosophy and government, all of which have human happiness for their object.[61]

This exhortation to further progress was spoken by Rush at the climax of a lecture on the duties of a physician. A man of science himself, he was encouraging other men of science to give wholehearted allegiance to a program which went beyond their interests as scientists to include their concerns as men.

A similar combination of a mechanistic science, dependent largely on the Newtonian concept of a world-machine, with democratic political and social views and a Deistic religion can be found in other natural scientists of the age. Men like Benjamin Franklin, Joseph Priestley, Thomas Cooper, and Joseph Buchanan were thinking along the same lines as Rush and reaching conclusions like his. Others, like Thomas Jefferson, Thomas Paine, and John Adams began with political considerations and found that their thoughts were led to religious conclusions and scientific ideas like those of the scientists. The thought of the men of the Enlightenment in America lacked the sense that science, politics, and religion might be separate compartments of thought. It was their faith that human reason might be applied in like fashion to all areas of human concern, and that there could be no inconsistency or conflict between the results reached by reason in these various areas. This was a comforting faith, and to it we owe our existence as a nation.

3

PHILOSOPHICAL ORTHODOXY

I. THE REACTION AGAINST ENLIGHTENMENT

The era of the American Revolution was a period of radical changes in men's ways of thinking about religion and science as well as a period of political upheaval and of new directions in political theory. The thought of the men of the revolutionary period was hostile to traditional institutions, whether political or religious. It was opposed to authoritarianism, whether that of kings or that of priests. The revolutionary generation had faith in the dignity of each and every individual, and based its ethical and social thinking on the radically humanistic view that each man, sheerly and simply because he is a man, is free and is equal in rights to any other man.

After the changes of the revolutionary period, an era of consolidation set in. The values of stability and permanence were again placed above those of novelty and change. The country became more prosperous; it began to settle down. Mild evidences of unrest were magnified in the telling into major upheavals. There was a widespread fear that the anarchy of the French Revolution might hurtle across the Atlantic and destroy the hard-won security of the young American republic. A period of reaction set in, during which the ideals of the revolutionary generation were critically reconsidered and, in many cases, restricted in their application or discarded completely. Several features of the reaction were given philosophic expression. There was a failure of nerve, manifested in the reaction against the ideas of the Declaration of Independence. There was increasing tension because the Jeffersonian tradition in the South did not meet the problem of slavery adequately. There was a return to religious orthodoxy, even among liberals, which led to a closing of the ranks against any scientific view which could not be reconciled with Christian belief. Finally, there was the beginning of an academic

73

tradition in philosophy, grounded on the intuitionist "common sense" philosophy which had developed in Scotland and was sympathetic to a protestant Christian faith. In this section we shall discuss these features of the post-revolutionary reaction.

With the exception of a relative handful of Tory-Loyalists, like Jonathan Boucher in Maryland, there was little outspoken intellectual opposition to the American Revolution. Even so, it has been estimated that one-third of the nation — the best housed, best fed, and best clothed, for the most part — favored the British cause. When the Revolution was successfully concluded, there was a revulsion of feeling against its ideology as expressed in the Declaration of Independence. This revulsion was especially pronounced among members of the commercial upper class. Alexander Hamilton, for one, had supported the Declaration in 1776. As early as 1781, however, in his *Continentalist* papers, he expressed the conviction that not tyranny but anarchy was the real danger. He ascribed his earlier sympathies to a lack of experience and a failure to understand "the practical business of government." With the gaining of experience came Hamilton's recognition of "many chimerical projects and utopian speculations" in the earliest management of military and civil affairs in our nation.[1]

At the time he wrote these papers, Hamilton was advocating a stronger central government. He realized that the loose federation of the earliest days was, as he put it, "dictated by our situation," and felt that this loose type of union was no longer either necessary or expedient. It was not until much later, in bitterness at the general lack of appreciation of his contributions to the American nation, when he came to feel that our real disease was democracy [2] that he gave vent to his unfortunate exclamation, "The people! Your people, sir, is a great beast." His primary interest was in a more stable government. This cause he served early and late. We have seen his interest in stability illustrated even before the end of the Revolution. It is prominent in his advocacy of the new Constitution in the *Federalist* papers; into the writing of his contributions he poured his best talents, even though he felt sure that the Constitution was an insufficiently forceful compromise, a "frail and worthless fabric." Again, as Secretary of the Treasury in the cabinet of President Washington, he toiled unceasingly to stabilize the government as well as the finances of the infant country. His search for stability was not merely part of his thought; it had a very practical external reference. It arose out of his concern for the international standing of the United States, its public credit in the world, because he was deeply interested in the commercial development of the country.

John Adams, too, was at one time a supporter of the Declaration of Independence. He was a member of the committee which drafted the Declaration; while the actual formulation was Jefferson's work, Adams approved it. That was in 1776. By 1787, Adams had moved toward a different theory, still claiming roots in nature, but relying on experience rather than on reason. Near the end of his *Defense of the Constitutions of Government of the United States* he criticized Montesquieu's theory of democracy: He proclaimed that self-interest is the mainspring of human activity and that democracy can therefore only issue in anarchy.[3] As early as the time at which this work appeared the seeds of Adams' belief in a natural aristocracy were already present.

In Adams' *Discourses on Davila* (1790) and other works of his middle years, he began to be preoccupied with the discussion of inequalities, which he found everywhere. Inequalities were implanted in the structure of the universe by God and nature; these "no human legislator ever can eradicate." [4] Among men these inequalities result in the appearance of a natural aristocracy of "the rich, the well-born, and the able." This natural aristocracy flourishes everywhere, despite the abolition of titles of rank in democracies. In the later years of his life, Adams retained his belief in natural aristocracy, but modified it, somewhat paradoxically, into a democratic concept by defining it simply as the possession of influence over others, however this influence may be achieved. An aristocrat is described in Adams' *Letters to John Taylor of Caroline* (1814) as "a citizen who can command or govern two votes or more in society." [5] By this description even a ward heeler might be considered a natural aristocrat.

Others in whose writings may be seen a rejection of the ideas of the Declaration of Independence include such long-standing conservatives as David Daggett of Connecticut and Fisher Ames of Massachusetts. An Independence Day address of 1799 delivered by Daggett has the astonishing and ingenious title "Sunbeams may be extracted from cucumbers, but the process is tedious." This is, throughout, a satiric attack on the Jeffersonian group in American politics as the American representatives of an experimental attitude toward government. The key to Daggett's position lies in his statement that the political theorists of the French Revolution, and, by extension, the Jeffersonians, their American sympathizers, "have made an open and violent war upon all the valuable interests of society." [6] Daggett was afraid that Jefferson and his followers would destroy property rights. He was concerned to see that propertied interests were adequately represented in the American government. Fisher Ames was also interested in keeping the ruling power in the hands of property owners; however, he maintained a Puritan ideal of stewardship of wealth which somewhat mitigated his insistence that property and property alone should be represented in government. He approved of republican institutions provided that they were not based upon popular sovereignty; his most characteristic work was titled "On the Dangers of American Liberty."

The previously described turning back from the high ideals of the Declaration of Independence was reinforced in the 1830's, when Alexis de Tocqueville visited America and wrote his justly-praised book, *Democracy in America*. DeTocqueville, writing as an aristocrat, feared that American democracy was foredoomed to failure because of its belief in the sovereignty of the people. His work became the political gospel of many Americans who shared the French author's fear of the masses. The politics of the Whig party was shot through and through with a distrust of liberty and of equality and a poorly-concealed scorn for popular sovereignty and public opinion.

While the more conservative of America's early political leaders were experiencing this failure of nerve and retreating from the principle of equality, the Jeffersonian group, especially in the South, was having difficulties in reconciling the principle of liberty with the maintenance of chattel slavery. The slavery question arose even in the Constitutional Convention, but it was put off by a double compromise. Instead of abolishing slavery, the delegates agreed to abolish the slave trade. Instead of abolishing this monstrous trade immediately, the delegates permitted its continuance for twenty years, until 1808, and authorized Congress to prohibit it thereafter. This dual compromise bred one of the touchiest intellectual and social problems of American life.

Thomas Jefferson had violently opposed slavery, although he was himself the owner of slaves. But even John Taylor of Caroline, whose work is in so many respects a systematic version of Jefferson's ideas, initiated the movement of the Jeffersonian Democrats away from the views of Jefferson on the subject of slavery. In Taylor's *Arator* (1813), a series of essays on agricultural subjects, he argued that slave-owning nations of the past, like Greece and Rome, had produced great citizens, and that Jefferson himself was evidence that slavery in the United States would do as well. He maintained that slavery improved the character of the masters both by a direct stimulation of their benevolent feelings and by establishing a clear-cut contrast between vice and virtue; slaves are by nature morally inferior. Taylor, however, never could bring himself to call slavery an unqualified good, as did Thomas Dew and John C. Calhoun.

Dew had been educated in Germany; when he returned to the United States he attended sessions of the Virginia legislature in the course of which there was discussion of the abolition of slavery in that state. Horrified by this possibility, Dew wrote and published a *Review of the Debate in the Virginia Legislature of 1831 and 1832,* which defended the South's "peculiar institution" by moving from the individualistic terms in which earlier discussion had been carried on to an organic view of the commonwealth. Dew showed a way to escape conceding rights to slaves by denying the theory of the rights of man. He was rewarded for this contribution to the pro-slavery argument by being given the presidency of William and Mary College.

Calhoun worked out a philosophy of politics chiefly to provide a consistent and systematic defense of slavery. To do this, he, like Dew, found it necessary to reject the enlightened views of the Declaration of Independence. He did not believe that there had been an early "state of nature," after which governments were formed by agreement, by "social contract." He thought of government as the natural medium for the expression of man as a social being. If there has been no prior state of nature, man has no natural or inalienable rights; whatever rights he may now have are social rights, granted to him by virtue of his participation in government. Security is the basic objective of government and the prerequisite to liberty, which can be achieved only in society and only by virtue of security. He recognized equality before the law, but declared that with this exception a belief in equality was untenable. Inequality he thought to be the only possible basis for progress. Out of this general view he developed his principle of concurrent majorities to prevent the tyranny of a numerical majority over a sectional interest. He led the legislative fights for states' rights and the sectional interests of the South during the last fifteen years of his political career. He had an important part in the pro-slavery cause.

There were many facets to the pro-slavery argument; every type of approach can be found in the voluminous literature of the movement. Our special concern here, the philosophic defense of slavery, is represented at its best in the *Essay on Liberty and Slavery* of Albert Taylor Bledsoe, who taught mathematics at the University of Virginia. Bledsoe argued against the definition of civil liberty as that part of man's natural liberty which is left after his entrance into the social state. Such a definition, he said, could arise only where natural liberty is anarchistically interpreted as the right to do as one pleases. To the contrary, Bledsoe insisted that natural liberty means action in conformity with the will of God, and is, therefore, unabridged by man's entrance into society. There is no surrender of rights when societies are formed. Civil society is the agent which secures to men the liberty to enjoy their rights. Public order is the basis of security; slavery is justifiable as in accord with the necessities of public order.

Without further details of Bledsoe's interesting argument, we can now see that the degeneration of the Jeffersonian tradition in the South, from John Taylor of Caroline, through Thomas Dew and John C. Calhoun, to Albert Taylor Bledsoe, reduces to an attack on the principles of the Declaration of Independence similar to that which we have found among the Federalists and Whigs of the North. The reaction against the ideals of the revolutionary era was not sectional but national.

A resurgence of religious orthodoxy paralleled the turning from democratic ideals which has just been described. There had been a widespread disregard of organized religion and an emergence of untraditional forms of belief in the period of the revolution; by the turn of the century the tide had turned. For the first time, national denominational organizations were formed during the first decade of the nineteenth century. A strong trend to revivalism and highly emotional conversions appeared, especially on the frontier. Colleges which had been secular in spirit, like Transylvania University in Kentucky, developed a religious tone. Those which had been established under denominational auspices intensified the religious life of their students. Abortive attempts were made to break down the separation of religion and politics. All in all, the first half of the nineteenth century reveals a strengthening of the position of religion in American life.

During this period preliminary skirmishes were fought which give a preview of the later conflict between religion and science over the evolutionary hypothesis. The keynote of the period of orthodox reaction was that the doctrines of religion were higher in sanction and superior in certainty to the discoveries of science. Wherever any apparent contradiction appeared, science could be adjusted to the basic truths of religion. In general, the favorite approach of such spokesmen as Mark Hopkins of Williams College, Edward Hitchcock of Amherst, and Andrew Preston Peabody of Harvard was to make a judicious selection from the mass of scientific material of those facts which could be brought into accord with religion. So Hitchcock claimed that there is scientific evidence to prove that God intervenes at His pleasure in the operations of nature. In a sermon preached before the Massachusetts Home Missionary Society in 1852, he applied the chemical theory of catalytic agents to religion. He talked of "the blended rays of knowledge and religion," [7] and in all his work he exploited science in the service of religion.

Even more extreme was the position taken by Tayler Lewis of New York University in 1838, in an address at Union College on "Faith, the Life of Science." In this talk Lewis, whose *Six Days of Creation* a few years later made religious capital out of geology, asserted that "Science commits suicide when it separates itself from religious beliefs." [8] Science in the nineteenth century, he thought, was not, on the whole, hostile to faith, but its spirit was somewhat alien. This was, first, because the motive of practical utility was held out as the reason for studying science rather than the true motive, cultivation of the mind; second, because physical science was exalted over moral science; and, third, because the method of study, emphasizing observation, experiment, and inductive reasoning, leads science away from faith. Science glorifies the sense, and "The 'great contest between sense and faith' must go on, until the latter hath put its last enemy under its feet, and reigns supreme, not as the suspected foe, or barely tolerated ally, but the rightful lord of philosophy, science and politics." [9]

Politically, then, the trend of reaction was away from those "self-evident" truths asserted in the Declaration of Independence and toward the "self-evident" need for authority. Religiously, reaction led to opposition to natural religion and the scientific spirit. Philosophically, the intellectual reaction took the form of decrying speculative freedom in thinking. The course of academic philosophy in nineteenth-century America strengthened the appeal to authority while weakening intellectual independence. The change was engineered largely by the development of systematic instruction in philosophy in the American colleges. Academic orthodoxy in philosophy depended on two things: Widespread acceptance of a system, and a concern for teaching. Both of these were developed early in the nineteenth century.

The system which was widely accepted as a basis for the teaching of philosophy in the colleges was that of the Scottish school. As the century moved along, elements drawn from German philosophy were introduced into the prevailing system, as far as this could be done without destroying its consistency. The choice of Scottish "common sense" realism for American colleges was dictated primarily by the need for a system which did not conflict with the teachings of a Protestant, chiefly Calvinist, religion. A majority of the post-revolutionary colleges in the country were organized and supported by religious groups. While they were interdenominational in their student body and invited financial aid from all sects, there was no attempt to be nonsectarian. Scottish philosophy, although not dominated by theology, was generally acceptable to America's Protestant colleges. After all, it had been worked out in a country of Presbyterian orthodoxy and came into conflict with none of the tenets of any Calvinistic group.

Systematic instruction, again, requires that in addition to concern for system there must be concern for teaching. The materials had to be organized and reduced to teachable form. Textbooks of philosophy were produced in great numbers, chiefly by the minister-presidents of the colleges, aptly called by one writer "bearers of the old tradition." These textbooks were responsible for a major change in the perspective of the study of philosophy. Under their sway, philosophy was considered as a body of material to be learned by the students and recited to the teachers. Consider this revealing statement from the preface to Francis Wayland's *Elements of Intellectual*

Philosophy (1854): "I have, therefore attempted to present and illustrate the important truths in intellectual philosophy rather than the inferences which may be drawn from them." [10] Wayland, who was by no means the most conservative of the college presidents, was teaching a dogmatic orthodoxy, in which there were "truths" to be presented and illustrated, not the search for and love of wisdom, which would require emphasis on the "inferences."

Before this time, philosophy had been a search for wisdom, not a subject matter; it was a method of approach to problems, not a study of conclusions. Samuel Stanhope Smith, when president of Princeton, had declared that "Philosophy is an investigation of the constitution and laws of Nature, both in the physical and moral world, so far as the powers of the human mind, unaided by the light of revelation, are competent to discover them." [11] Eliphalet Nott, the remarkably long-lived president of Union College, who made no claim to being a teacher of philosophy, developed an informal course, remotely based upon Lord Kames' *Elements of Criticism.* Frederick W. Seward, later Assistant Secretary of State under his father during Lincoln's administration, remembered Nott's course as "a comprehensive study of human nature, ranging over the whole field of physical, moral and intellectual philosophy, and applied to practical use in business, politics, and religion." [12] How entirely different this is from the formality and didactic tone revealed in the preface to Wayland's early and very popular textbook, *Elements of Moral Science,* where the author says, "I have rarely gone into extended discussion, but have contented myself with the attempt to state the moral law, and the reason of it, in as few and as comprehensive terms as possible." [13] Yet Wayland was one of Nott's protégés. The shift to formality arose out of the demands of the cultural situation.

The approach to the teaching of Scottish philosophy as a doctrinal system led to the division of philosophy into subject matters of elementary courses. At first it was a simple division into Moral Philosophy, sometimes called Moral Science, and Mental Philosophy, or Mental Science. The latter included sections devoted to how men know, partly concerned with the nature of the mind itself, or psychology, and partly concerned with the philosophic questions about the relation between the mind and the external world, called "theory of knowledge" or epistemology; sections devoted to the methods of the mind in thinking, or logic; and sections concerned with the first principles and basic truths, which men discovered by intuition and which furnished the groundwork for all their thinking, or metaphysics. Gradually each of these branches of Mental Philosophy came to include a sufficiently large body of information to be taught as a separate course and to require its special textbooks. Some of the teachers, like Noah Porter of Yale, wrote highly specialized works; Porter's *The Human Intellect* was an important milestone in the development of psychology in America. Others, like James McCosh of Princeton and Laurens Perseus Hickok of Union College, covered the whole range of philosophic studies in their texts. McCosh developed his thought in strict accord with his Scottish forebears. Hickok, at the other extreme, shows more German influences in his thinking than any of the other system builders and textbook writers in American colleges.

The number of books produced in this generally unoriginal and conservative movement is staggering. Texts were written for every sort of special purpose. Leicester A. Sawyer, of Central College in Ohio, wrote his *Elements of Mental Philosophy* to serve as a philosophic foundation for millennialism and evangelicism. One textbook on Moral Philosophy was written expressly for use in the United States Military Academy at West Point. There was a wide variety of minor differences between works whose fundamental outlook was similar. Of this large output, we will here concern ourselves in detail with Francis Wayland's ethical views and his philosophy of science, Laurens Perseus Hickok's rational system, and Noah Porter's psychologized theory of knowledge. Each of these teachers went beyond a strict and literal restatement of the Scottish philosophy, although its naive realism gave their work its basic orientation. The chief interest of what they did lies in these modifications and adaptations.

II. *FRANCIS WAYLAND: TEACHER OF PHILOSOPHY*

When, in 1827, Brown University, a Baptist institution in Providence, Rhode Island, was looking for a man to become its fourth president, Francis Wayland was elected to the office without a dissenting voice. He was a young man, barely thirty-one at the time of his election, with small academic achievement to his credit. What earned him favorable consideration for the presidency of Brown was a sermon he had preached three years earlier on "The Moral Dignity of the Missionary Enterprise." It was not the delivery of this sermon which created a sensation and enhanced its author's reputation. Quite the contrary; the morning after he had spoken, Wayland disconsolately told a friend, "It was a complete failure, — it fell perfectly dead." One of the auditors, however, a printer, was shrewd enough to recognize that the young preacher had made a common mistake, that he had preached an essay instead of a sermon. This printer induced Wayland to let him publish the manuscript. What had been a failure as a sermon became a success as an essay; three editions were exhausted rapidly in the United States and other editions were called for in England. The influence of Wayland's discourse was felt beyond his own sect. It was praised highly in informed circles in other denominations.

The young preacher was a graduate of Union College in Schenectady, where he had learned the elements of Scottish "common sense" philosophy. Wayland stood high in the esteem of Eliphalet Nott, Union's president. When young Wayland received his Union degree, he resolved to study medicine, and did, in fact, enter upon his studies. His call to the ministry, however, proved too much for him to resist; he abandoned his medical studies and entered Andover Theological Seminary. This was, in itself, an unusual step for him to have taken, for the Baptists of that period had few ministers with any formal education. In the year that Wayland spent at Andover, he won the friendly interest of Professor Moses Stuart, one of America's most distinguished theologians. At the end of the year, Wayland was offered the pastorate of the First Baptist Church in Boston. Stuart advised him to accept the offer on the ground that this group in Boston was a good place to begin to break down the Baptist distrust of ministers with schooling, "to begin the cure of that malady that reigned among his brethren on the subject of educating preachers." Wayland was to represent learning among the evangelicals. His effectiveness as a preacher was in part the result of his attempt to combine emotional fervor with rationality. Not only his sermon on the missionary enterprise but also others from the same period of his life, like his two 1825 "fast-day" addresses on "The Duties of an American Citizen," won far more acclaim from readers than from hearers.

In 1826 Wayland left his pastorate to become a tutor at Union

College; his chief responsibilities were to have been for the teaching of mathematics and natural philosophy. Before he could settle into this position, his election to the presidency of Brown called him to larger duties. To this position he devoted the next twenty-eight years of his life. When he took over, Brown was in bad shape, torn by internal dissension and poor student morale. Wayland quickly restored a better atmosphere at Brown and made it one of the finest colleges of New England. He stood out among the college presidents of his time because of his interest in reformulating educational policy on the higher academic level. Before his time, the program of nearly all the colleges was one designed for the training of Christian ministers. Despite the fact that more and more of the students had secular careers in view, the pattern of instruction was slow to change. Wayland was the first of the college presidents to advocate extensive changes designed for the training of Christian laymen. Chief among these suggested reforms and revisions was the proposal for a far more extensive elective choice among subjects for the students. Years after Wayland began his advocacy of these changes, other colleges and universities followed his example.

His earliest proposals for educational changes at Brown were made shortly after his appointment to the presidency in 1829. In 1840 Wayland went to Europe and studied collegiate education in Germany, France, and England. His recommendations, formulated on the basis of this comparative study, were set down in a book in 1842, under the title *Thoughts on the Present Collegiate System in the United States.* He felt that this book was disregarded, and a few years later he submitted his resignation from the presidency of Brown. He was persuaded to remain, his stipulation being that more attention should be paid to his theories of the nature of collegiate education. In 1850 he submitted his specific suggestions for the reconstruction of Brown in a "Report on the Condition of the University." The trustees of Brown carried out the suggestions made in the report as far as their available funds would allow. Wayland's conception of a university as it was presented in this "report" was that it was to be a social agency. He asserted that the services and the facilities of the university should not be for the benefit of students only, but that they should be extended and made widely available to the entire society. Here is the germ of what has today matured into the "extension" services which, under one name or another, many of the colleges and universities of the United States maintain. Wayland was firmly convinced that higher education had to contribute directly to the needs of society.

In addition to these concerns for higher education, Wayland was deeply interested in public affairs. Some part of this interest was in elementary education. He was one of the organizers of the Providence public schools and the author of a plan for the extension of free public education throughout the state of Rhode Island. Furthermore, when the American Institute of Instruction was formed, he was elected its first president. Other concerns were more general. He was interested in prison reform, and was a member of the State Prison Board; in that capacity he was instrumental in a thorough housecleaning and reform in Rhode Island's state prison. He served on the Board of Trustees of Butler Hospital. He founded a free public library in the town of Wayland, Massachusetts. The influence of the Dorr Revolution on his social thinking appears in his 1847 tract on *The Duty of Obedience to the Civil Magistrate*. Wayland wrote a textbook on *The Elements of Political Economy*, in 1837, in order to expound the doctrines of free trade in opposition to the Whig party's espousal of the protective tariff. His statement in favor of free trade makes it clear that he considered it not merely practically better than protection but also philosophically sound and true, because it was based upon a proper interpretation of the nature of freedom. Wayland's economic ideas were drawn from his study of Adam Smith.

On the great slavery controversy which was rending the United States in his time, Wayland's position was sufficiently ambiguous to be described as both anti-slavery and anti-abolitionist. In his textbook of 1835 on *The Elements of Moral Science*, he maintained that slavery "violates the personal liberty of man as a *physical, intellectual, and moral being*." [14] The effects of the institution of slavery on the morals of both master and slave and on national wealth are harmful. The moral precepts of the Bible are uniformly opposed to slavery, and, furthermore, some of the moral duties which the Scriptures demand, while they do not mention slavery directly, yet can not be fulfilled where the slave system exists. Under a slave economy, then, the duty of a master would seem to be the immediate emancipation of his own slaves. However, it might be fact, as it was claimed, that "immediate abolition would be the greatest possible injury to the slaves themselves. They are not competent to self-government." [15] This, Wayland insisted, is a question which moral philosophy can not determine. Just in case it is true, he proposed the following suggestions: Inasmuch as the slave is a slave by his master's act and on his master's responsibility, it is his master's care to see to it that the obstacle to emancipation is removed; meantime the master continues to own the slave, but not "*on the ground of right over* him, but of *obligation to him* . . . for the *purpose of accomplishing a particular and specified good.*" [16] Thus in form, the master holds the slave in bondage, but is, in fact, guiltless of the sin of slavery. The slaves, of course, have no option save "obedience, fidelity, submission, and respect to their masters." [17] Wayland softened the blow a little by basing these obligations of the slaves on their "duty to God" not their duty to man. His statement, however, satisfied no one.

Spokesmen for the Southern slaveholding interests resented Wayland's insistence that slavery is anti-Scriptural. He was forced into a controversy to defend his position; the letters which he exchanged with his Southern opponent, Richard Fuller, were published in *Domestic Slavery Considered as a Scriptural Institution*. Wayland's failure to satisfy the South led, only two years after the publication of his otherwise satisfactory text, to the writing of *The Elements of Moral Philosophy* by Jasper Adams of South Carolina. On the other hand, Wayland's insistence that the abolition of slavery was a matter for the individual conscience of the slaveholder, and not a matter of political concern, led to great dissatisfaction in the North. In 1837 Wayland was led to defend his position in an *Essay on the Limitations of Human Responsibility*. In this work he maintained that man's moral responsibility extends only to his own acts and not to the acts of the society of which he is a part. Thus he attempted to cut the ground out from under the Abolitionist position, which involved the assertion that each American citizen, as a member of his country, bore the moral guilt for the institution of slavery. Despite the dissatisfaction with its stand on slavery, which was felt on both sides of the Mason-Dixon line, Wayland's *Elements of Moral Science* was one of the most phenomenally successful of the textbooks of its period, selling more than two hundred thousand copies in the sixty years after its publication.

This success attended Wayland's work because, without departing radically from the American values of liberty and equality, he was able to abandon completely the enlightened base on which the eighteenth century had grounded these values and to substitute a more orthodox foundation. Wayland was not a thoroughgoing conservative, although he did insist on a denial of the continuing right of revolution and on the religious duty to obey the civil magistrate as well as the master of slaves. He emphasized with equal stress the duty (rather than the right) of granting other men personal liberty and of "reciprocity" or equality. He founded his moral system on a specifically Christian consideration of the Scriptures and belief in a personal God. The eighteenth-century ethical system of William Paley had been popular in America and was in use at Brown University when Wayland came there. Wayland rejected Paley's system because it was founded on utilitarianism and natural religion. Throughout his work, he transformed the concept of the rights of man which had been central to the thought of the Founding Fathers into a concept of the threefold duties of man — to God, to his fellow men, and to civil society.

Wayland's *Moral Science* suited the temper of his time, again, because of its denial of the utilitarian criterion in ethics. In the *Atlantic Monthly*, two years after Wayland's death, it was noted that Wayland himself sometimes regretted that he had moved from the pulpit to the college; the writer commented "We reconcile ourselves to the loss of a few sermons on the evils of infant baptism, for the sake of the most vigorous assault upon utilitarian ethics that has appeared in the present century." [18] Wayland insisted that it is not the consequences, but the intention of an act in which its moral quality resides. Whatever the results of an action may be, a man's guilt or innocence is judged by what he intended, "without any respect to the happiness or misery actually produced." [19] If a man intends harm to his fellow man, the fact that his plan backfires does not remove his guilt; if a man intends good to his fellow man, the fact that good does not occur does not lead us to call him guilty. We may cause pain to another person without incurring guilt. Thus, if we pain another in the interest of justice, "we inflict pain which he deserves," and to which he has been properly adjudged.[20] There is, in this case, pain inflicted, but no intent to injure. On the other hand, we may cause pain to another person and incur great guilt thereby, if in inflicting the pain we intended to injure him, "as in cruelty, malice, revenge, deliberate slander." [21] Intent may also be wrong when it is not directed against another person, but toward ourselves —as in the gratification of our own desires without consideration of the good of our neighbor. Kant, whose work Wayland had never read, urged that man exists as an end in himself, not as a means to be used by other men. Wayland expressed the same idea in a more conventional fashion by saying "The Creator never conferred on man the right to destroy another's happiness for his own gratification." [22]

Wayland's strict and formal insistence upon the importance of intention led him into some difficult positions, as we have seen in terms of the question of slavery, and some extreme positions. When an action is intended, even though it is not performed, praise or blame attaches to the intention even though it was in no way carried out. The person who thinks with pleasure of a wicked act is as guilty as if the act were performed. "He who meditates, with pleasure, upon fictions of pollution and crime, whether originating with himself or with others, renders it evident that nothing but opposing circumstances prevents him from being himself an actor in the crime which he loves." [23] Nor does this extreme formalism apply to negative cases only; it is as true of virtue as of vice. The performance of an act usually regarded as virtuous, if it be without the particular intention essential to it, is "destitute of the element of virtue." [24] A child is to obey his parents with the intention of manifesting his love and gratitude to them. Obedience with any other intention is not to be considered as the virtue of filial obedience, but solely as the result of passion or self-interest.

In its general tenor, then, as we have seen, Wayland's ethical text attempted to reinstate a supernatural sanction for morality and thus to return from the eighteenth-century grounding of morality in nature to a more orthodox view akin to that of Bishop Butler. Although he spoke of moral science, Wayland did not mean to suggest that ethics could become, like physics or chemistry, one of the natural sciences. Quite the reverse; he would have liked to bring the natural sciences themselves into the orbit of religion. Indeed, he tried to do this in his one published venture into the philosophy of science, his Phi Beta Kappa address of 1831, entitled *A Discourse on the Philosophy of Analogy*. The point of the address was to show that the scientist who is a Christian will of necessity be more successful in predicting future areas of discovery than the scientist who is an infidel. Wayland allowed to the infidel scientist distinction

in using the results of these novel discoveries, while reserving to the
Christian distinction in pure science. His development of this theme
is of considerable interest because it reveals, in addition to his
thoughts on science, the general pattern of his theory of knowledge.

The "Discourse" opens by asserting the Lockean view that human
beings are born without innate ideas; their minds are blank tablets,
"entirely destitute of knowledge."[25] Wayland follows this by upholding the naive view of the Scottish philosophers that, despite this initial
handicap, man is constituted in such a fashion that knowledge inevitably comes to him because it is the nature of his mind to know,
and the nature of his external environment to be known. Man has a
"universal appetite for knowledge"[26] which, like other appetites, in-
creases as it is fed. Meantime the universe which surrounds him
corresponds to his mental character by being adapted at once "both
to gratify and stimulate inquiry."[27] It is, however, neither the
appetite for knowledge nor the relation between this appetite and
the universe by means of which he acquires knowledge. This
acquisition comes about because man is by nature endowed with
certain inborn faculties whose exercise leads to the discovery of
truth. Knowledge is not innate, but the mechanism for gaining it is
— and the surrounding universe lies ready and waiting to be probed.

Wayland's views on method emphasized induction, as did those of
all followers of the Scottish school. In getting knowledge, the first
step is the observation of facts, learning by means of the senses that
certain things exist and that certain changes are taking place in them.
As these facts of existence and change accumulate in man's observation, it becomes evident to him that the facts are not merely
haphazard, but that there is an order, a constant succession among
them. At first the order is only dimly seen, but this faint realization
leads man to a more careful inspection which brings out the order
far more clearly. When this order is noted, man has achieved his
first conception of a law of nature. Later, by refined observation and
accurate experiment, accidental features which seemed part of the
law are seen for what they really are, and other changes which at
first glance seemed unrelated to the law are brought under its operation. By a constant process of refining experimental results, our
statement of the natural law becomes a closer approximation to "pure
and unchangeable truth."[28] The function of this knowledge is
practical. "By knowing the laws which govern any particular class

of objects, we preclude the necessity of innumerable experiments, and are able to predict, under given circumstances, what, throughout the material universe, will be the certain results." [29]

The natural laws thus discovered are found, after a time, to overlap under certain conditions; the laws, though they are general with respect to the particular phenomena for which they account, are themselves particulars with respect to a more general and overarching law. A general law of attraction would comprehend the particular laws of gravitation, magnetism, certain other electrical attractions, and so forth. We can not assume that we have reached a point at which the most general of laws have been discovered. There is still scope for the progress of human knowledge. Wayland maintained that not only is human knowledge extending itself continually in this way, but also that "a tendency to universal extension has been impressed upon it by its Creator." [30] The tendency of intellect is ever upward toward the Creator Himself.

Knowledge, however, does not come without labor; the desire to know, without the effort to know, never leads to the discovery of truth. There are two laborious methods by which knowledge may be acquired. The first of these, demonstration or deduction, has as its sphere, wherein its dominion is absolute, the science of quantity, or mathematics. Demonstration proceeds from self-evident principles to the necessary results of these principles. The second instrument is induction, which begins with individual instances, and works its way to laws of a more and more general character. Induction proceeds from known effects to a discovery of their antecedents. It is the method of all the non-mathematical sciences. These two methods are the only methods by means of which we can extend our knowledge. They are the only aids by means of which we can construe nature's answers to the questions we ask.

Skill in interpreting nature's answers is important, but far more important for the progress of knowledge is skill in asking proper questions. For nature answers only the question which is asked, and gives as answer only a simple "yes" or "no," both of which are equally difficult to interpret. When proper questions are asked, nature's answers are more readily interpreted. It becomes important, then, for a study of proper questioning to be undertaken. This is what Wayland meant by a science of analogy, "a science, which, standing on the confines of what is known, shall point out the direction in which truth probably lies, in the region that is unknown." [31] This would be the science of sciences in that it would serve as the direction-finder for all the other sciences. Wayland insisted that, although there is no such science, its laws, when discovered, will rest upon two "self-evident" principles.

> First. A part of any system which is the work of an intelligent agent, is similar, so far as the principles which it involves are concerned, to the whole of that system.
> And, secondly. The work of an intelligent and moral being must bear, in all its lineaments, the traces of the character of its Author. [32]

Now, if these are the underlying principles of the science of analogy, it follows that the most skillful scientist in that field will be the one who most thoroughly understands "the spirit of the system" and who is most deeply aware of "the attributes of the first Cause of all things." [33] Here obviously the Christian has an advantage over his infidel fellow-scientist. He has both qualifications in full measure; it is for this reason that, even in the absence of a science of analogy, Christians have made the most significant contributions to scientific advance. Furthermore, each application of the new science will lead to increased understanding of the system, and thereby to increased knowledge of God; the increase in man's knowledge of God, whether thus indirectly achieved, or more directly gained from the written revelation, will lead to improvements in the science of analogy.

Wayland made in this essay a striking attempt to remarry natural science and revealed religion, which had become estranged during the Enlightenment. From time to time during his life, we are told by various biographers, the veneer of college president and teacher of philosophy would fall away as Wayland talked, and the evangelical fervor of his pulpit days would return. Something like this must have happened as he approached the end of his talk on the science of analogy, and in a few words he characterized not merely the purpose of his own life in philosophy but that of his colleagues, the minister-presidents of American colleges. For after speaking of the way in which various recent discoveries in science were testifying to the accuracy of Scriptures, he insisted that this testimony was only the beginning: "Who can foresee the glory of the result, when the full blaze of every science shall be concentrated upon the page of everlasting Truth, and thence reflected, with undiminished effulgence, upon the upward path of baptized philosophy." [34] This pious and worthy but essentially unspeculative goal was the aim of academic orthodoxy.

III. LAURENS P. HICKOK:
THE ORTHODOXY OF REASON

The philosophy of Immanuel Kant (1724-1804) had little influence on the academic teaching of philosophy in America in the first half of the nineteenth century. Some aspects of Kantian thought affected the New England transcendentalists (see Chapter 4) after 1830, but these ideas entered into American thought indirectly and in modified form through the study of the philosophic works of Samuel Taylor Coleridge (1772-1834), whose direct dependence was not upon Kant, and Victor Cousin (1792-1867), who combined Kantian and Scottish ideas into an eclectic system. It was not until about mid-century that teachers of philosophy like Noah Porter of Yale and Francis Bowen of Harvard began to be concerned with the newer ideas which were being developed in Germany. Bowen devoted his earlier years in academic life to editing abridged versions of the classics of Scottish philosophy and to reproducing Scottish themes in his more original productions. When he finally began to study German thought he wrote a book on "modern" philosophy which concerned itself almost entirely with the German thinkers he had so long overlooked.

After 1850 almost all of the academic philosophers lost their exclusively Scottish orientation. They began, especially in the field of ethics, to mix some German elements into their thought. The best that Scottish ethical theory had been able to produce in this field was the thin and unconvincing assumption of a "moral sense" by means of which men perceived the laws of morality. The moral sanctions they recognized were self-interest and benevolence, on one or the other of which they founded their ethical systems. Kant's doctrine of the practical reason as the source of moral ideas and his tremendous "categorical imperative," the unqualified demand that morality be founded on a single universal principle, seemed to furnish a far more satisfactory basis for American ethical thought. More and more, however, it became necessary for those who were attempting to write in the tradition of Kantian thought to face the whole tradition. Kant's ethical theory was based upon his theory of knowledge. As American thinkers became more sophisticated, they realized that a Kantian ethic could not rest on their naive view that the mind was made to know reality and reality was made to be known by the mind. American writers found it impossible to accept Kant's practical reason without coming to grips with his analysis of the "pure" reason.

One of the first American thinkers to approach the study of German philosophy energetically and thoroughly and to attempt a systematic formulation of his results was Laurens Perseus Hickok. Today Hickok can be classed as a forgotten man, although at one time his disciples saw in him the only hope of an American philosophy and his adversaries thought him a most dangerous heretic, full of German ideas. Hickok lived ninety years; after an early career in the ministry, he became a professor of philosophy at the age of about forty. Later he served Union College in Schenectady, New York, as its vice-president under Eliphalet Nott, and for two years as president. From the time he left the ministry, books and articles on philosophic themes rolled off the presses in fairly rapid succession until his system was complete. He wrote on psychology, philosophic anthropology, ethics, esthetics, cosmology, theology, and logic. Toward the end of his long life, while he was living in retirement, Hickok helped his nephew, President Julius H. Seelye of Amherst College, to write abridgements of two of his works for use as textbooks. With Hickok, then, we come to the earliest — and one of a very few — system builder in American philosophy. It is worth our while to trace the structure and interrelationship of various aspects of his thought so that we can learn how a philosophic system is organized.

Hickok divided all human knowledge into two broad areas, the empirical and the rational. His distinction between the two areas was based upon the test which is used to validate the knowledge falling into that area. In the empirical area, we test our ideas by their consequences in our experience. In the rational area validity is tested by means of the principle of sufficient reason, that is to say, the principle that every idea is connected in determinate ways with definite other ideas, so that we do not know the full nature of any idea until we know its position and relations within a system. Broadly speaking, truth in the empirical area is the correspondence of our ideas with fact; in the rational area, truth is the coherence of any one of our ideas with all our other ideas.

The empirical area is limited in the types of knowledge to which it can give the sanction of validation. There is the realm of physical science; in physical science we can study and attain knowledge of mechanical relations between objects, organic connections within living structures, and emotional connections among conscious beings. To test our knowledge in these areas, no special arrangements are necessary. If our future experience is uniform with our previous experience we consider our knowledge to have been validated. The second realm of knowledge within the empirical area is that of psychical science. In this realm, we mean by knowledge a recollection of our former perceptions, with logical conclusions from these past experiences, and an experimental testing of these conclusions. That is to say, what Hickok calls "physical science" is the common sense knowledge that we gain without conscious effort or any deliberate method, simply by our awareness of the world in which we live; what he called "psychical science" is the whole area of the natural sciences, in which a conscious activity on our part is necessary to select, to classify, and to utilize relevant aspects of our experience. There is an important recognition here by Hickok that natural science is not something that takes place in nature, but rather something that takes place in the human mind.

The method of "psychical" empirical science, as Hickok describes it, is a process characterized by consciousness and "spontaneity" or self-motivation. Remembering is conceived literally as re-collection, or bringing together again, impressions which one has gained in the past. The conscious and spontaneous activity involved in recollection is the "arrangement of the old facts together in their relative places and periods and interconnections." [35] When we remember, we reconstruct old scenes. The first step in the method of psychical science is, then, a regrouping of old data into a significant order from which logical deductions can be made.

Again, consciousness and spontaneity enter into the logical process. The process is conscious because it takes place in accordance with definite rules. The spontaneity is evident in the construction of the syllogism, an activity of mind which is certainly self-motivated, and in the deduction of conclusions. Finally the process of verification is not merely the casual and unsought experience of uniformity, but rather a conscious and spontaneous movement to recapitulate one's conclusions and one's data, and to set up conditions whereby one can verify the old by means of the new.

Although Hickok explained the nature of the empirical area in his philosophy, he did not believe that philosophy is concerned with the empirical. The entire area of the rational is the proper interest and concern of philosophy. There is in all men a type of spontaneous intelligence which is absorbed in sensory experience. Most men never go beyond this into the rational area. "They perceive that which appears in the light of the common consciousness, and deduce more or less practical conclusions from experience." Only a few in any generation can "rise into the higher light of a purely philosophical consciousness," turning their reflections back upon consciousness itself, studying patiently the necessary conditions of all experience.[36] Within the rational area are two sciences: Rational science and theistic science.

The function of philosophy in the realm of rational science is to attest to the absolute and necessary principle in the reason under which the particular facts of experience are intelligible. Rational science comprises three branches, esthetics, cosmology, and ethics. Esthetics is the development of the "aesthetic Standard of Taste." There are indications of the standard of taste in the successive instances of pleasure and pain in the senses, particularly those of vision and hearing. These empirical indications can be brought together into a formulation of the standard of taste. But only in the reason can it be demonstrated that this standard of taste is necessary and eternal. In cosmology, the outcome is the formulation of the "Philosophic Law of Truth." Again, the experience of the senses and the understanding must be examined, and ultimately, by purely rational techniques, the entire content of experience can be accounted for under this one universal and necessary law of truth. Similarly, ethics is concerned to find the universal and necessary "Ethical Rule of the Right." Each of these three ultimate laws must include in its coverage all of our experience. It is the rule of the right which is the ultimate test of both truth and beauty; moreover, we cannot attribute beauty to any experience which does not fall under the law of truth as well. "Empirical connections must be beautiful, accordant with an ultimate standard of taste, nor can they be so except as also they conform to the Ultimate Law of the True; and now we can see moreover that they can be neither beautiful nor true except as they conform to an Ultimate Rule of the Right." [37] Each of the three, beauty, truth, and right, is in one sense an independent standard. Yet in ultimate terms these three are one.

Theistic science, which also falls within the rational area, is concerned with the ultimate validation of the experience of all humanity. Experience which is common to all humanity cannot be validated by reference to a standard which can be appropriated by any individual. The appeal must be to a common source. We must postulate this common source, or God, to meet the demands of reason. Within theistic science, God is known not by revelation or by authority, but by the needs of reason. "The Reason which shall fulfil the ends of a testing appeal for the verity of all common experience must be ultimate authority for entire humanity, and as such it is the God of humanity." [38] The second realm of theistic science is concerned with knowledge of the Divine authority for human history. Here reason establishes the necessity for revelation and for God's moral government by a consideration of the nature of God as a rational personality. The final aspect of Hickok's view of theistic science, which served for him as the necessary condition of rationality throughout his entire system, was the knowledge of tripersonality in the activity of God. "The first and last truths of human experience can be put into its history and the whole be combined in completed system through no other agency than that of a Deity before and beyond the experience, and yet interfering in experience at his pleasure. . . . Nor can the finite human reason recognize God's agency in creation and redemption otherwise than through his tripersonality." [39]

This summary of the structure of Hickok's system, showing the place of each type of knowledge, from the obvious generalizations of everyday, common sense existence to the rational justification of the doctrine of the Trinity, accounts for most of his philosophic writings. There are, however, two major works whose contents are not included in the rational structure. The reason for the exclusion is that these two books concern not the rational system of the universe but the nature of the human mind which is capable of knowing the system of the universe. Each of these two books is called a "psychology," but they really serve to present Hickok's theory of knowledge. *Empirical Psychology* occupies the position of an introduction to the entire system of both empirical and rational science.

Rational Psychology is introductory only to rational science. More specifically, *Rational Psychology* provides the bridge between the empirical and rational areas, enabling us to cross "the otherwise impassable chasm between empirical deduction from tested fact, and rational induction of efficient causes for the facts." [40]

The justification which Hickok proposed for making empirical psychology, or the study of the mind as it is found active in our experience, the foundation of his philosophic system is an interesting one. All our sciences are mental products. They are formed and shaped by the human mind. They are, therefore, no more reliable than the agent which forms them — no more trustworthy than is the human mind. Until we know the laws of mind and the reliability and trustworthiness of their operations, we can be sure of nothing whatever in science. In discussing either philosophy or science the only logical point of departure is the mind, which thinks and knows. Empirical psychology, the study of the thinking and knowing mind and its powers, must be the basis for the study of philosophy or science. We must begin any but the most elementary of studies by a careful consideration of man as he exists today; we must test and retest his mental powers; only by doing so can we define man's mental endowments and determine their reliability.

How do we know that there is a mind? We know it, says Hickok, from the fact that there is an agent which makes and records scientific experiments. An experiment differs from an experience in being a conscious retrial, carefully performed and accurately recorded. The conscious care and accuracy of the scientific experiment is evidence for the existence of a mental agent, or mind. That is to say, at the very least we can define mind as the agent which makes and records experiments. "Wherever, in any and every age the works of nature or of man have been subjected to close experiment, there mind has evinced its presence and its power." [41] Now, if this is taken to be the meaning of mind, there are certain comments on the nature of mind which we can make. These comments lead us into the heart of empirical psychology.

In the first place, the mind is motivated to scientific experiment by the desire to satisfy its own curiosity, and not by any possible external motivation. Since the mind's actions are internally motivated, we are justified in speaking of the mind as a spontaneous agent. Its activity is self-activity. In the second place, the mind distinguishes itself from its objects. We may call the mind, for this reason, a self-conscious agent. Thirdly, the mind can and does make its own actions the object of its investigations. It can, by looking into its own operations (or introspection), be both thinker and subject matter. Hickok asserted that an introspective investigation is more satisfactory and secure in its results than any experiment that can be made upon external nature, because the subject matter of introspection is more immediate than that of external experimentation. Fourthly, mental activity does not take place in a void; we do not just think, but we think about something. That we have something to think about is a precondition of thought. The whole psychological process we call thought is a series of mental activities which occur in an invariable order: Sensation, the content of consciousness as a result of sensation, knowing, feeling, and willing. As in Locke, Hickok believed that we can have no content in the mind which has not previously been in sensation; the successive operations of knowing, feeling, and willing are performed by the mind on the content which has entered by the avenue of sensation.

The mind (again as in Locke) is passive in sensation. Sensation is not conscious, yet it is the precondition of the awakening of the mind to consciousness. The mind's capacity for knowing is called intellect; intellect includes three faculties which are not three distinct organs or parts of mind, but three different capacities for action in the one mind. The three faculties are called sense, understanding, and reason. Sense is not to be confused with sensation; sensation is the invasion of the mind by an external agent, while sense is an internal power whose function is to construct our ideas of things in the outside world out of impressions in our consciousness. Hickok called our ideas of things in the outside world "concrete objects of experience." These "concrete objects" are not things but ideas or mental states. Sense, by acts of defining, distinguishing, and connecting, transforms impressions into objects of experience. Understanding, the second faculty comprised in intellect, includes two kinds of mental activity, memory and reflective thought. Memory recalls the objects of sense, but in reverse order, as a mirror reflects the objects of vision. Reflective thought treats the objects of sense, as recalled by memory, as data for further investigation, comparison, and classification. In order to do this, reflective thought (and, therefore, understanding) must be capable of abstraction, that is to say, of separating in thought what cannot be separated in sense. The faculty of reason will be considered later.

The faculties of the mind up to and including reflective use of the understanding, if carelessly and casually used, lead to the knowledge of everyday and commonplace relations — what we called earlier "physical science." When these faculties are used with care, and their operations tested over and over again, the results of this repeated process of re-testing make up the content of the natural sciences. No power of the mind beyond understanding is ever used in working out the natural sciences. We can now see Hickok's answer to one of the questions with which his study of empirical psychology was introduced. The sciences are trustworthy and objectively valid only to the extent that the powers of the mind used in their creation are. One of the powers of the mind used in creating the sciences is the understanding. Understanding, since it is but reflective, can lead to results no more secure than that which it reflects. But understanding reflects sensory data; we can never test and re-test the objects represented to us in the sense-data. We can be conscious of the mental states produced in us by external agents, but never of the agents themselves. We can, to use Kant's terms, know "phenomena" but we can not know "noumena," or "things-in-themselves."

Our mental states, however, the content of natural science — hence called "psychical" science by Hickok — are not objective but subjective. They are in us, and not in the external world. The objects of science are mental images. It is conceivable that these images may be exact copies of objectively existing things, though we can not prove that they are, without going beyond sense data as reflectively used in the understanding. We can not prove the objective validity of science without going beyond science. Only if the laws of thought are shown to be the laws of things can mental image and external object be shown to be necessarily the same and skepticism be overcome.

It is the faculty of reason on which Hickok relies to establish the postulate that the laws of thought are the laws of things. That we have such a faculty Hickok attempts to prove from the general consciousness of something beyond the limits of understanding. It is one of his principles that this type of proof is valid in an empirical system. "When, between any number of minds there is an alleged contradiction of consciousness, the umpire is found in the general consciousness of mankind." [42] An appeal of this sort, he suggests, "may properly be termed the tribunal of Common Sense." Men are conscious that empirical science does not include the whole sphere of mental action, because, as Hume demonstrated, empirical science can not prove causation; yet the mind is confident that there are efficient causes. Nor can we move from the particular places and particular periods of empirical science to space and time; yet we have ideas of space and time without which our experience would not be meaningful. Empirical science can not give us the concepts of pure mathematics; yet we have these perfect ideas. Pure mathematics is not the product of sense and understanding, nor are our ideas of causation, space, and time. They are the product of reason, without which man could never reach a knowledge of necessary and eternal truth.

We have already seen that Hickok accepted the general principle of John Locke's theory of knowledge, that the mind can have communication with the world outside itself only through the senses. He also accepted the criticism presented so sharply by Hume and Kant that universal and necessary truths such as the postulates of reason can in no way be derived from the information given to the mind by the senses. He had to explain in some way, therefore, how the postulates of reason could be given by the mind itself. The road he chose, while similar to that taken by Kant, differed from Kant's in the way it was expressed. The postulates of reason, Hickok said, are the laws or facts of its existence; they are the capabilities of reason as the principles of geometry are the capabilities or laws of space. Kant had called the postulates of reason "forms of thought." To this Hickok objected, because, he maintained, Kant's term leads us to infer that these forms are subjective. Hickok insisted that the mind must be endowed with the power of absolute knowledge at least of itself. As a minimum the mind must know itself not as a phenomenon, but as a thing-in-itself. This is very much like the view of Noah Porter (see the next section). These postulates, principles, ideas, are the self-affirmations of reason. They are the insights reason has into its own capabilities.

If we grant, with Hickok, that reason has an absolute self-knowledge, then, he argued, we must grant that its postulates are unquestionable realities. This concession does not itself prove his contention that the laws of thought are the laws of things, but it does provide the basis from which he argued to that conclusion. The mind can be immediately conscious only of itself. It does really exist and is, therefore, one of the entities in the universe. The self-knowledge of mind is knowledge of one thing-in-itself. Knowledge of even one thing-in-itself is a valid ground for generalizing our conclusions to include all things. Since the one thing-in-itself which we do know is mind, we may legitimately generalize that all existence is either minds or their products. If this is so, then the laws of thought are the laws of things.

Reason possesses not only this absolute self-knowledge, but also self-direction. That is to say, reason includes will, and is therefore a personal agent or first cause. Just as the self-knowledge of reason is proved in the general consciousness of its possession, the self-direction of reason is proved in the general consciousness of personal responsibility. Part of the self-knowledge of reason is knowledge of its own finiteness and dependency; human reason affirms that its existence is not independent, but is derived from a higher reason, or God. Human reason in knowing itself knows that it is made in the image of the Higher Reason; since it knows itself to be a personal agent, it knows that God is a Person. Human reason, in knowing itself as a first cause, knows God as First Cause. Reason, knowing itself as a thing-in-itself, knows that its laws of thought are also laws of Divine thought. Since things are Divine thoughts to which reality has been given by Divine will, just as human thoughts may be realized by human will, knowledge of the laws of Divine thought is knowledge of things-in-themselves. Again we see that the laws of thought are the laws of things.

Thus far we have moved with Hickok through an empirical psychology, the elements of which are the facts of mind as given in experience. As an empirical psychology, it is subject to the same questionings and doubts that we may have of any empirical study. Though, as we have said, Hickok maintained that an introspective investigation is more certain than any external experiment, the certainty is, in his own terms, subjective. Even as it is the function of the rational sciences to ground our knowledge of beauty, truth, and goodness in eternal and necessary laws, so it is the place of rational psychology to base "an exposition of the human mind not merely in the facts of experience, but in the more adequate and comprehensive manner, according to the necessary laws of its being and action as a free intelligence." It is the science of sciences, because it expounds the principles which must be true about Intelligence itself. It is, like pure mathematics and pure physics, a demonstrative science, completely transcending experience, which is only "facts which appear to be," and sustaining itself among "those necessary sources from which all possible experience must originate." An empirical system may defend itself against any challenge from within, but it can not defend "the stability of its very foundation," should this be called in question. Should this challenge arise, knowledge can be defended only by showing that it must be so. We can do nothing about a thoroughgoing skepticism, which casts doubts on experience, "except as we also go back of experience, and by a rigid transcendental demonstration determine from the conditioning principles of all intelligence how experience in the senses is possible to be." [43]

On this foundation Hickok built his systematic philosophy. Its presuppositions were those of orthodoxy; its philosophic foundations were laid in both Scottish and German thought. Hickok's work, in terms of the knowledge of his own day, was a substantial achievement. Even today there are many who could rest content in such a philosophy, which translates the "old-time religion" into a rational system of knowledge. That its influence did not persist may well be due as much to the tortuous and difficult style in which Hickok wrote as to the loss of interest in the order of problems with which he dealt.

IV. THE PSYCHOLOGIZING OF PHILOSOPHY: NOAH PORTER

Noah Porter was the son-in-law and disciple of Nathaniel W. Taylor, the Yale professor, and founder of the New Haven school of liberalized Calvinistic theology. After Porter's student years, he indulged in a brief intellectual flirtation with the philosophic ideas of Samuel Taylor Coleridge, which also had considerable influence in the shaping of the Transcendentalist movement. In 1846, when he was thirty-five years of age, Porter was named professor of moral philosophy and metaphysics at Yale, a chair he held for a quarter of a century. In 1853 and 1854, he traveled in Europe and studied with Adolf Trendelenburg (1802-1872), professor of philosophy at the University of Berlin. His work with Trendelenburg reinforced and made explicit the interests which had in the first instance drawn him into philosophical study. He came back to Yale sure of himself, his philosophic views, and his importance in the history of philosophy. From this time on, he concentrated his attention on taking his place in what he thought to be the main current of modern thought, the development out of René Descartes (1596-1650), John Locke (1632-1704), and Immanuel Kant (1724-1804).

Porter insisted that the German followers of Kant had branched away from the central tradition by their failure to realize the importance of the problem of knowing. Unlike the founders of the tradition, they had sought a theory of the nature of being without basing it upon a theory of knowledge. Porter sought to correct this misdirection by his insistence on considering the problem of knowledge, the epistemological problem, as a necessary prelude to the problem of being, the ontological problem. He argued that the best approach to the problem of knowledge is psychological, that the first obligation of the student is to understand the instrument of knowledge.

Porter maintained that a scientific study of the mind is the only proper introduction to questions concerning the origin and destiny of man, the metaphysics of nature, the existence and character of God. No matter where an inquiry in these metaphysical and ontological areas seeks to arrive, it is constantly being led back to questions about the knower himself and about the nature, the reach, and the certainty of the act of knowing. There can be no security in our statements about the objects of knowledge while there remains any insecurity about the knowing subject or about the process of knowing. In his monumental work, *The Human Intellect*, Porter insisted that "The man who seeks to enter the temple of Philosophy by any other approach than the vestibule of psychology, can never penetrate into its inner sanctuary." [44]

The Human Intellect is printed in three different sizes of type. In the largest type, Porter presents the views of various British and German psychological theorists who were seriously considered in his time. In intermediate type he gives a critical examination of these theories. In small type are Porter's own views, his original contributions to the field of psychology. This odd arrangement evolved less from Porter's modesty than from his concern for the usefulness of his work as a textbook. In using the book, a student might read only the largest type and gain therefrom a knowledge of current psychological theories. A second reading, adding the material in intermediate type, would make the student aware of the weak spots in these theories. A third reading, including the smallest type, would set the students on the road to truth.

Porter's relation to the Scottish philosophy and to Thomas Reid (1710-1796) in particular is evident in his treatment of psychology as one of the inductive sciences. For Porter psychology could not possibly be a rational, deductive science because this type of science must proceed from first principles to conclusions. First principles are the subject matter of metaphysics, and it has already been shown that for Porter there could be no sound metaphysics prior to psychology. Psychology, then, must precede metaphysics, and can not depend upon it. It must be an inductive science, building up generalized conclusions out of particular observations. In analyzing the power of knowing we first discover what it is to know, and then we discover what objects and relations are essential to knowledge.

Although this account of "mental science" seems very close to Porter's view of what he called "material science," there is a difference. The observations on which we base our generalizations in material science are observations of the external world, of things outside of ourselves. The observations on which psychological generalizations are formed are introspective. We gain the data for psychology not by the observation of others, but by turning our attention inward to the phenomena of our own consciousness. The only method for the study of psychology of which Porter approved required that we watch our own minds at work. Any other method, he felt, might result in great harm; the student could not and should not carry over methods, laws, and analogies from the physical to the psychical sciences.

The greatest harm which had come to British psychology was the result of John Locke's "one-sided sympathy with the awakening physics of his time." This sympathy, "which was feebly counterpoised by his positive recognition of spiritual phenomena and relations," [45] led Locke to describe the mind as passive in the receptive phase of the knowing act. Later British thinkers without Locke's "counterpoise," like David Hume (1711-1776), David Hartley (1705-1757), James Mill (1773-1836), and John Stuart Mill (1806-1873), "never ceased to regard and treat the human soul as in all its processes entirely passive." [46] Locke had thought of the mind as passive only in receiving impressions from the external world; these others had insisted that the mind was entirely passive. Reasoning processes which Locke had regarded as active powers of the mind were considered by Hartley and the Mills as passive results of the association of ideas. In thus making a mechanical association their substitute for "generalization and reasoning," these philosophers had, Porter said, transferred physical law to the psychical realm. They had accepted as one of their dogmas "that the law of necessity holds good of the phenomena of spirit as truly as of the phenomena of matter." [47]

Against this associationist view which was widely held in his day, Porter argued that the mind of man is active throughout the knowing and thinking process. Even in the first stage, the receiving of impressions of the external world, "we do not merely submit." In all stages of knowledge, the "soul" has faculties by virtue of which it is enabled to act in the appropriate fashion.

Furthermore, Locke and his followers had argued that what the mind receives passively by way of the senses are "simple ideas" which then must be built up and combined into complex representations of things and events or situations. Porter stressed the point that knowledge does not begin with simple ideas; it begins with wholes, with patterns, which the mind breaks down by analysis into ideas and expresses in language. By this insistence Porter escaped one of the problems which had developed in the Lockean tradition; instead of having to account separately for things and the relations between things, Porter finds things and their relations invariably given together in experience. Things "are known to exist, and not only are known to exist, but to exist in relation to one another. They are necessarily and uniformly given in combination." [48] The relation of cause and effect, which had been explained by Hume as a contribution of the mind to the knowing act, and spatial and temporal relations, which Kant had accounted forms of thought, subjective contributions to the knowing act, became in Porter's theory as objective as the things which were causally or spatially or temporally related.

Thing related to thing is the pattern in which the mind actively grasps the world outside itself, and knows it. Things, relation, thing — subject, verb, object — is not only the form of the sentence we speak to express our knowledge, but also the pattern of knowledge itself. Grammatical relationship of words in a sentence is not an arbitrary convention but is a representation of the first step in the knowing act. As we can analyze a sentence, breaking it down into grammatical units, only after it is stated as a whole, so we can analyze experience, breaking it down into its components, only after it has been experienced as a whole.

Porter's interest in language was intimately bound up with his whole philosophic perspective. Of American writings on the subject, he was familiar with the "Essay on Language" of Rowland Gibson Hazard, Rhode Island's businessman-philosopher, and with the incidental comments of the theologian Horace Bushnell. But his views were given polish in Germany by his contact with the ideas of Karl Ferdinand Becker (1775-1849), who had been Trendelenburg's friend, and whose linguistic theories Trendelenburg expounded. When Porter accepted the editorship of a revision of the Webster dictionary for the Merriam company, he looked upon the job as more than a routine piece of hack work. He felt it to be a meaningful contribution to the understanding of the pattern of the English language.

It is, thought Porter, the self — "that masterful entity, the *ego*" [49] — which actively grasps things and their relations in perception, is actively conscious of its own operations, actively remembers, reasons, invents, and interprets. The self is an "individual agent," an individual which acts. In no way is the self merely passive or dependent upon the things outside itself which the self discerns. Unlike Locke, but again in agreement with Reid, Porter held that we have an immediate knowledge of the self; we are, he said, directly conscious of the ego itself as well as of its states and conditions. Each individual agent is not only conscious of his mental states, but also knows these states as belonging to himself. He is conscious of the states as changing, variable, and transitory, unable to exist independently. Mental states must be states of some psyche. "A mental state which is not produced or felt by an individual self, is as inconceivable as a triangle without three angles, or a square without four sides." [50] In the very moment of being conscious of our changing mental states, we are directly and immediately conscious of our selves as the permanent and unchanging ground to which the mental state belongs.

Kant was, therefore, in error when he asserted that we cannot know "things-in-themselves," things as they really are apart from our knowledge of them. There is at least one "thing-in-itself" that we can know immediately; the thinking agent is known to itself as a permanent reality. Porter also insisted that the not-self is knowable by the self, at least in certain respects. This partial knowledge is none the less knowledge. We do not need to know completely in order to know anything at all. To say that our knowledge is partial is only another way of saying that human beings are finite. But to say that we know the not-self involves two further statements for Porter. Viewed from the standpoint of the knower, knowledge carries with it an assurance of certainty. Of that which is known, knowledge requires reality. In saying that we know the not-self, Porter is claiming certainty for our knowledge of the not-self and objective reality for the not-self as the object of our certain knowledge. Derivatively, then, and indirectly, we know the not-self as an independently existing reality, a thing-in-itself.

Porter's discussion of perception shows a marked affinity with the discussions of this theme in members of the Scottish school, especially Reid and Sir William Hamilton (1788-1856). The mind, immediately and by an inexplicable act of its own, perceives one object, the body with which it is associated. There is this one situation in which spirit perceives and knows matter directly. In this one case there is no "problem" of knowledge. All other perceptions of matter by mind are derivative from this one basic and unproblematic perception. We start with a real agent, the active individual self, which has certain faculties, certain innate powers and capacities. This real agent has an intuitive, underived knowledge of that which is external to it and is extended, in the form of its own body as a seat of sensation. Porter suggests that all perceptive knowledge beyond this is the result of processes of observation and induction carried on from the human being's earliest years. This inductively derived knowledge gradually advances from the infant's barely conceivable minimum of distinct perception through discriminations of constantly increasing range and power to the adult's distinct perception and cognition of the visible realities which surround him.

There is other intuitive knowledge, in Porter's view, besides man's knowledge of his own body, but it is not knowledge of objects of perception. Certain fundamental laws and necessary truths which are presupposed by inductive thinking can not themselves be derived inductively. They must, therefore, be known by intuition. The fundamental ideas which men acquire prior to any experience include what philosophers have traditionally called "categories," that is, the most general classes under which everything that can be asserted about any subject can be arranged, like "cause," "substance," "time," and "space." Immanuel Kant had considered these categories to be merely organizing principles which the mind imposed upon its disorderly and chaotic perceptions to produce some kind of rational pattern. We can not know, Kant thought, whether there is anything in the world of real objects which corresponds to the mind's organizing principles. Porter, on the contrary, insisted that the categories are valid for describing the objective world.

He argued, further, that the axioms of mathematics and the basic laws of thought were intuitively known before experience, and that these axioms and laws are necessarily true, their negation being inconceivable to the human mind. Finally, he believed that we need, as a basis for our thinking, an intuitive knowledge that particular events and processes are not merely random, haphazard affairs, but rather reveal an internal design, arrangement, and purpose, and also that all the things, events, and processes in the universe have their place in an all-inclusive, overarching, universal purposive pattern, pervading all existence. Purposiveness and design are indispensable "as the ground of the scientific explanations of the facts and phenomena of the universe." [51]

We have seen that Porter approached philosophy by way of psychology, that he paid particular attention to the structure of language, because he believed that this structure represents the pattern in which the mind receives its impressions of the outside world, that he believed that the human mind is altogether active in perception and in knowledge, and that he thought that there were certain ideas that were apprehended intuitively by the mind, after which the method of reasoning was inductive. It remains for us to show what place the belief in God had in Porter's thought, and thus to point to the orthodoxy of his philosophic position. Here it is necessary for us to refer back to Porter's view that men need not know completely in order to know at all. For it is clearly impossible for the finite human mind completely to know the Infinite, the Absolute, the Unconditioned. Yet, because knowledge does not have to be complete, Porter could maintain that the finite mind of man could know God.

He did not mean that our knowledge of God was reached by faith or emotion. Man's knowledge of God is to be gained by the same cognitive processes as man's other knowledge. Faith is not altogether different from knowledge, for every act of faith must include an element of knowledge. On the other hand, we do not come to our knowledge of God by either inductive or deductive reasoning. God's existence is axiomatic; the Absolute and Infinite must necessarily be assumed to explain and account for the finite universe. The Infinite and Absolute is the correlative of the finite and relative not merely as an aspect of the structure of language, but also as an aspect of real existence. Furthermore, if the Infinite is the "correlate" of the finite, then there must be some relation between the Infinite and the finite. The precise nature of the relationship is less important than the assertion that the existence of the Absolute in relationship to us makes possible our knowledge of its nature. The existence of the Absolute is axiomatic; we know *that* it is. Its relations to our minds lead us to a partial knowledge of *what* it is.

And what is it? The Absolute is a thinking agent. The universe is a thought as well as a thing; the design of the universe reveals thought as well as force. The thought revealed in the design of the universe includes the idea of the origin of forces, their laws of operation, their combinations and their uses. This thought must include the whole universe. The controlling thought, the design of the universe, must be a single thought, the thought of an individual mind. If gravitation prevails everywhere and is a thought as well as a force, then the universe, insofar as it depends on and is affected by gravitation, is a single thought. But a thought implies a thinking agent; if the universe is a single thought, it was thought by one thinking agent. To say that an Absolute of this sort exists is to provide a basis for our own thought and our own knowledge.

> We do not demonstrate that God exists, but that every man must assume that He is. We analyze the several processes of knowledge into their underlying assumptions, and we find that the assumption which underlies them all is a self-existent intelligence, who not only can be known by man, but must be known by man in order that man may know anything besides.[52]

Porter's orthodoxy consisted in regarding the existence of God as psychologically necessary, not in order that man's emotional life might reach a culmination and fruition, but in order that man's intellectual life might have a basis and foundation.

4

NEW ENGLAND'S WILD OATS

I. TRANSCENDENTALISM

The first half of the nineteenth century was marked by a revolt against the enlightened ideals of the Revolutionary era. This revolt took the form of a return to orthodox and somewhat dogmatic ideas in many fields, including academic philosophy. In this chapter we are to consider another reaction against the age of Enlightenment — occurring in the same period as the orthodox reaction, but centering largely in New England, and stemming from the romantic movement in Germany and England. The sources of this American romanticism were various — New England's wild oats were drawn from many a foreign clime. Even Oriental, and particularly Hindu, writings were drawn upon by the transcendentalists to feed their ranging imaginations. But their chief sources were the ideas of the post-Kantian German philosophers, especially Friedrich W. J. Schelling (1775-1854), as these ideas were interpreted by the English poet, theologian, and philosopher, Samuel Taylor Coleridge (1772-1834).

There is a certain sense in which transcendentalism should not be considered as a movement at all. There was a great deal of disparity among the transcendentalists. James Freeman Clarke, who was one of the group, is reported to have said "We called ourselves the club of the like-minded, I suppose because no two of us thought alike."[1] This is certainly an exaggeration, but there were differences of opinion sufficient to justify the criticism that the only agreement among the transcendentalists was an agreement to disagree. If, then, we consider the criterion of a movement the adherence of its members to any set of common beliefs, it is difficult to find a basis for calling transcendentalism a movement. In another sense, however, the transcendentalists had much in common. They shared certain antagonisms — and no better bond of union than a common enemy has ever been discovered. They shared a characteristic mood or temper, a common method or philosophic habit of mind. It is in this latter sense that we here consider transcendentalism as a movement.

Transcendentalism was, in the first instance, a religious philosophy. It was born in dissatisfaction with the then-current opinions in liberal theology and the philosophic views on which these theological opinions were based. Its earliest advocate were convinced that Unitarian theology was unsatisfactory because of its dependence on the "reigning sensuous philosophy, dating from Locke"[2] — that is, its dependence on the empirical tradition. What the transcendentalists wanted to achieve and thought that they could achieve by a discipline of their intuitions was a direct relationship between the soul and God. This direct relationship was to "transcend," to pass beyond, all the conventional avenues of communication — not only to transcend the senses, but also to transcend churches, clergy, and Scriptures. Transcendentalism was the assertion that man has an intuitive capacity for grasping ultimate truth, and thus achieving a sure knowledge of a supernatural order, beyond the reach of the senses.

In the transcendentalist theory of knowledge, men were not limited as they were in the Lockean theory to the phenomena of sensory experience. Transcendentalist intuition was similar in effect to the "supernatural sense" of Jonathan Edwards (see Chapter 1, section II); it led to the immediate grasp of supernatural reality. But where Edwards had maintained that the supernatural sense comes only to the elect, and is the fruit of God's grace, the transcendentalists held the more democratic view that intuition, the ability to know Divine reality directly, is the birthright of every human being. Because of their common possession of the faculty of reaching God, all men have inalienable worth. All men are spiritually equal and of equal dignity in that all men are able to communicate with God. It is through this principle that transcendentalism affected deeply the development of democratic ideas in America.

Theodore Parker, who of all the transcendentalists was the least affected by the romantic aspects of German thought and most influenced by German critical philosophy, considered transcendentalism an intellectual challenge or problem. "The problem of transcendental philosophy is no less than this, to revise the experience of mankind and try its teachings by the nature of mankind; to test ethics by conscience, science by reason; to try the creeds of the churches, the constitutions of the states, by the constitution of the universe."[3] Each clause of this statement is interesting for what it reveals about the beliefs of the transcendentalists. Parker makes certain assumptions throughout. In proposing as one aspect of his problem "to revise the experience of mankind and try its teachings by the nature of mankind" he suggests that there is a knowledge about human nature which is accessible to the human mind and which does not come through the experience of men. The background of this assertion lies in the long-standing philosophic distinction between appearance and reality. Experience can yield only opinion; it can reach only the phenomena or appearances. Some superior philosophic method is required to learn about the real nature of things which lies behind experience. For the transcendentalists this superior method was intuition. "To test ethics by conscience" suggests the belief that conscience is the form taken by the moral intuitions of individuals. Ethics is a man-made, conventional pattern of moral choice; conscience, which is the intuitive apprehension of the moral law as it is established in the transcendental realm, is clearly superior. "To try the creeds of the churches, the constitutions of the states, by the constitution of the universe" assumes that the constitution of the universe, its transcendental law, can be known by men, again intuitively, so that it can be used as a measuring-rod to test the human institutions of church and state.

Of all the clauses in Parker's statement, however, the most revealing is the call to test "science by reason." The science of the seventeenth and eighteenth centuries, including the Newtonian system, had been erected upon a foundation of observation and experiment supplemented by the rational techniques of mathematics and deductive logic. The results of the application of this method had inspired the faith of the Enlightenment that science would lead men along the road of indefinite progress toward perfection. But Immanuel Kant's careful *Critique of Pure Reason* had made clear the limitations of scientific method. Scientific results could never be more than probable, because the understanding is restricted to phenomena, to its own ideas of things, and is forever shut away from the things-in-themselves, or reality. The great religious and moral concepts of God, freedom, and immortality, which are not phenomenal, can not be reached by any exercise of discursive scientific thinking. Yet Kant recognized that these concepts must have a foundation. Man's consciousness of the moral situation, the necessities of which imply God, freedom, and immortality, led him to the realization that there must be another form of pure reason, to which he gave the name "pure practical reason." Some of Kant's followers, and to an even greater degree the followers of his followers in England, gave this intuitive "practical reason" supreme eminence, and in some cases restricted the use of the term Reason to this meaning. In their thought science was reduced to a subordinate status to which Kant himself had never assigned it. They used the term Understanding to describe the inferior type of discursive empirical thought on which natural science is based. Their distinction between Reason and Understanding parallels the distinction drawn by Laurens Perseus Hickok (see Chapter 3, section III). Theodore Parker was the heir of this romantic use of the term Reason. He, too, considered natural science as the product of an inferior faculty of Understanding. Thus he might with justice call for a trial of the product of the Understanding at the bar of Reason.

In these various ways, transcendentalism was a reaction against the excessive emphasis on science and rationalism which was characteristic of the Enlightenment. There are, however, other transcendental themes which are continuous with the earlier period. Thus, for example, the enlightened faith in progress reappears in the later group as a transcendentalist faith in progress. In the Enlightenment this faith had been based upon a belief in the inevitable advance of science. Among the transcendentalists, faith in progress was founded on the doctrine of self-reliance — the doctrine that an individual who steadfastly and honestly explored his inmost thoughts would find in them truths of universal import. In the increasing number of truths thus dredged up lay the hope for indefinite human advance. Again, although the transcendentalists no longer held the enlightened Newtonian faith that the order of nature could be understood and used by men, they substituted a belief in a different type of order, a supernatural order, which they thought intuition could reveal. Thus, while transcendentalism does not reproduce exactly the themes of the Enlightenment, in some ways there is a similarity of tone in the two movements.

Transcendentalism, because it held that intuition was the method for reaching truth, distrusted and resented every human institution which restricted in any way the free functioning of intuition. Science, in tying the inquiring mind down to orderly and systematic processes of observation and experiment, limited the mind's freedom to range through nature in search of insights. Tradition and history likewise seemed to them to place limits on the movement of mind; so, too, did the conventional morality and manners of the vulgar. For all of these, the transcendentalists repeatedly expressed their scorn. Even the discipline of regular work was too much of a burden for the more extreme members of the group. They organized the Brook Farm community to get away from the common herd; the community failed in part because the transcendental members would not organize their free spirits to get the chores done. Of all the organizations and institutions invented by man, the churches — even the comparatively mild Unitarian church from which most of them came — aroused their greatest resentment, because any church was an attempt to organize and institutionalize spirit itself.

Many of the transcendentalists left their church, feeling that only by doing so could they become free spirits. "It is necessary," said Thoreau, "not to be Christian to appreciate the beauty and significance of the life of Christ."[4] Others stayed within and tried to spiritualize the church, in line with William Ellery Channing's liberal and non-dogmatic assertion of man's "growing likeness to the Supreme Being." Because men are like God, Channing asserted, they can understand and enjoy the world He created. Channing was essentially transcendental in his insistence that we do not know God, as natural theology claims, through his works; we know God because "in ourselves are the elements of the Divinity" — because of our likeness to God. God becomes real to us as the Divine nature within us is unfolded. When a man grows in God-likeness, he develops a power of vision which enables him to see the Divine in everything, "from the frail flower to the everlasting stars."[5] There can be no question that, although Channing was not of the group, he was closely akin to the transcendentalists and was a great influence upon them.

It is fair to say that American religious liberals who thought like Channing had discovered that the rationalistic deism of the Enlightenment failed to satisfy their religious needs; yet they had become too enlightened to return to the superstitious creeds and sentimental piety of orthodoxy. They could neither run with the hare nor hunt with the hounds. At this point they discovered what Coleridge had done in England in the way of developing "spiritual religion," an intuitive philosophical Christianity, as a third way — neither as coldly rational as natural religion nor as much of a strain on the credulity as revealed religion. Intuition was the Coleridgean substitute for grace, and reflection his replacement for revelation. The Reverend James Marsh, president of the University of Vermont, was one of the first of the Americans to discover Coleridgean spirituality, and it was through Marsh that Coleridge's *Aids to Reflection* was given American publication in 1829.

Marsh wrote a lengthy introductory essay to this edition, an essay so searching that it has been included in the chief editions of Coleridge's works since that time. He also supplied very full notes making clear the application of Coleridge's method to the needs of religion in America. Marsh did not consider the *Aids to Reflection* as a dogmatic work presenting conclusions to be accepted. He insisted, rather, that what was important in it was the use of transcendental reflection, which he declared to be a self-correcting method. The particular conclusions reached by Coleridge might be in error, Marsh said, but this should be regarded as comparatively unimportant as long as the book teaches us to reflect well enough to detect the author's errors, and to go beyond these erroneous views to a more correct view. Over and above the interest of Coleridge's own opinions, Marsh thought that the *Aids to Reflection* had great value because of the themes toward which it directed men's attention. These themes are the constituent principles of human nature and the eternal laws of truth, as revealed in the reason, and duty, as revealed in the conscience.

Because Coleridge's book treated topics of theological controversy, Marsh felt constrained to enter a defense of its theological bearings. His chief contention and basic line of defense was that the work of Coleridge brought philosophy and theology together again after years of the Enlightenment during which philosophy and reason were conceived to be at war with religion. In the *Aids to Reflection* Coleridge had presented a philosophic position supporting religion instead of opposing it. This in itself, if the book had no other merits whatsoever, Marsh considered a sufficient warrant for the publication of a new edition making it available to American readers. Against the Lockean empirical tradition, Coleridge's view makes it possible to reinstate the distinction between the natural and the spiritual. It thus furnishes a rational ground for the belief in moral obligation, justifying the belief on the basis of a "higher law," higher, that is, than natural law.

It did not bother Marsh in the least that the position he took over from Coleridge might involve him in complete subjectivism. He insisted that the laws of spirit are "facts" of a sort which can neither be made a subject of instruction nor accepted on the authority of any person other than oneself. Each man must ascertain these laws for himself, "by reflection upon the processes and laws of his own inward being,"[6] else they can not be truly learned. Here Marsh, out of Coleridge, presented the heart of the transcendentalist method — that which was common to all the transcendentalists — the belief that it is possible for us to gain a true self-knowledge by reflecting upon "the objects of our inward consciousness," and that, when we have so reflected, our findings will necessarily agree with those of other men who follow the same course. Transcendentalist method is declared valid on the ground that universal truth is present in the inmost heart of each human being.

Another important figure in the transcendentalist movement who, like James Marsh, remained in the Christian fold was Frederick Henry Hedge. Hedge was the son of Levi Hedge, who taught philosophy at Harvard and who published a brief and conventional manual of elementary logic. The son, who spent several years studying in Germany, became a Unitarian minister and only in his later years succumbed to family tradition by joining the Harvard faculty to teach German literature. Of all the transcendentalists, with the possible exception of Theodore Parker, Frederick Henry Hedge was by far the most widely-read and well-informed on German philosophy and literature of the romantic movement. His studies included the reading of works by Kant, Fichte, and Schelling, but his knowledge of their philosophies was that of the student of literature, not that of the student of philosophy. His insights into the thought of these three important figures in German philosophy were occasionally penetrating, but neither systematic nor profound.

What has been called the Transcendental Club was inaugurated in

1836 as a consequence of a chance conversation between Hedge, Ralph Waldo Emerson, and George Ripley, in the presence of George Putnam, who apparently was less concerned than these three with the state of philosophy and theology. This group decided to hold a more extended discussion, a week or so later, and to invite other interested young clergymen to attend. Nearly a dozen came together on this occasion. From time to time during the next seven or eight years, whenever Hedge visited Boston, his transcendentalist friends met together. Because their meeting-times coincided with Hedge's visits, members of the group spoke of it as the "Hedge Club."

In addition to his services to the transcendentalist cause by his talks with his friends about Kant, Fichte, and Schelling among the Germans and Coleridge and Carlyle among the English, Hedge contributed an interesting evolutionary account of man's spiritual growth into a religion of love. Man, he said, develops in continuous fashion through three realms. The first of these is the realm of nature; while man is in the natural stage of development his motives to action are derived from the needs and interests of his physical organism. Man's second stage is the realm of morals, in which the governing motive of his actions is the law of duty. The final stage Hedge called the realm of spirit; when man has reached this stage in his development, he is moved by love.

Hedge gave an explicitly transcendentalist interpretation to many of the traditional concepts of Christianity, resembling Channing not only in the spirit of his religious writings but also in his ability to make an old doctrine serve a new purpose. Thus he rejected the traditional trinitarian theology of Christianity. But he found that there was an idea to be salvaged from the rejection; it was not the idea of divinity made incarnate in a single individual, but the idea of "divine humanity" which seemed to him worth holding on to. He believed, he said, "in the ever-proceeding incarnation of the spirit of God in human life."[7] Giving the term Incarnation this wholly untraditional meaning, Hedge was able to use it honestly and without embarrassment. Similarly, he reinterpreted the term Transubstantiation to mean the gradual transformation of the world into the likeness of the divine idea. Interpretations of this sort made it possible for Hedge to use traditional terms without accepting what he called "the obsolete dogmas of the church."[8] In doing so, he maintained, he was being faithful to the spirit of Christianity.

Brief mention should be made here of Caleb Sprague Henry, professor of philosophy at New York University, who, unlike the others who have been discussed, held an Episcopalian pulpit. Henry had no direct connections with the New England transcendentalists, yet he helped the movement by his translation and sponsorship of the works of Victor Cousin (1792-1867), a French philosopher. Cousin had found it possible to combine post-Kantian German romanticism with Scottish philosophy by emphasizing the intuitions of fundamental truths which the Scottish thinkers asserted. Without making an explicit distinction between Reason and Understanding, Cousin — and Henry after him — stressed the contrast between the use of reason in moral and spiritual thinking and its use in science.

Caleb Henry himself was most important as a popular interpreter of moral themes, both as preacher and as writer. In his moral essays there appears a consistent opposition to utilitarian ethics with its appeal to happiness as the goal of human life. He attacked any ethical system which made self-interest a fundamental principle. An interesting illustration of his approach is to be seen in his essay on "Satan as a Moral Philosopher." At the beginning of the Book of Job, he pointed out, God called the attention of Satan to His servant Job, and praised Job's faithfulness. Satan asked, "Doth Job serve God for nought?" and suggested that if the benefits Job had received from God were to be taken away, Job would lose his faith. Satan's accusation, then, was that Job was a utilitarian, that he served God for a profit. Henry pointed out that Satan's reasoning was based upon the principle, which both God and Satan recognized, that goodness for a profit "was no genuine goodness at all. Now herein Satan appears as a sounder moral philosopher than the ethical system-makers — in the long succession from Epicurus and Horace to Hobbes, Locke, Helvetius, Paley, and down to our own day — who make self interest the sole ultimate principle of human conduct; who lay it down that the supreme motive which leads good men to be good is the advantage they expect to gain; who say there can be no higher motive and need be none."[9]

In many respects Theodore Parker, although he was by no means a typical transcendentalist, belongs with Marsh, Hedge, and Henry as a Christian minister with transcendentalist sympathies. Parker, too, never left the church. He thought of his lifework as a purification of Christianity and a spiritual or "philosophical" reconsideration of the basic principles of Christian belief. Parker held an evolutionary view of human institutions, asserting that these human creations not only developed but also improved through history. Christianity he did not conceive as the ultimate religion; it was, he thought, the furthest development up to his time of the spiritual ideal of direct experience of divine reality by each individual. The Christian religion, however, was in need of a new theology which would base itself upon the immanence of God in nature and in man, that is, a transcendentalist theology.

Parker distinguished between the "transient" and the "permanent" elements in religions. The essence of his view of Christianity was than its truths derive their value from their permanent intrinsic and inherent merit, rather than from their transient and temporary connection with Jesus. He believed that a true theology ought to be a science of religion in which the authority of a founder or a revealer of moral and religious truth would be of no more moment than the authority of the first proclaimer of scientific truths. The sanction of religious and moral principles is to be sought in human experience and reason, not in authority or tradition. The Christian religion is of human construction, like all other religions; it is neither unique nor divinely revealed. The chief standard of judgment which we apply to other man-made institutions must be applied to Christianity, too. This standard is the approximation of Christianity ("the creeds of the churches") to universal truth and reason ("the constitution of the universe"). This is as much as to say that whatever has permanent value in Christianity possesses it independent of its specifically Christian transient form. Toward the end of his life, Parker said, "There is only one religion in the world. . . . There are various helps to the acquisition of this one religion, and various hindrances with the name of helps."[10]

Early in his career in the ministry, Parker made up his mind that the only religion he would preach would be one which was both intuitive and reasonable. Following the advice of Emerson's "Divinity School Address" (see this chapter, section II), Parker "determined to preach nothing as religion which I had not experienced inwardly and made my own."[11] From this transcendentalist standpoint he attacked not only the Trinitarian Christians of his time, but also the false liberalism of his Unitarian brethren who insisted on clinging to old formulas while modifying their interpretation — precisely what Frederick Henry Hedge was doing. Parker's views were not popular with his fellow ministers, but they were warmly welcomed by his audiences.

Parker was also one of the more prominent social reformers of his day. Like William Ellery Channing, he became an outspoken abolitionist, and was in the forefront of other liberal social movements of the 1840's. Despite the impression to the contrary, most of the transcendentalists were politically and socially concerned. Their spirituality was not of the sort that runs away from unpleasant social facts, but rather of the sort that pitches in and tries to change the facts. Much of the inspiration of transcendentalist social thinking can be traced to their interest in the Utopian socialism of Charles Fourier (1772-1837). But we should not forget that there were reform tendencies in Coleridge's work and that Christian Socialism in England was developed, in part, by such Coleridgeans as Frederick Denison Maurice (1805-1872).

Not all of the transcendentalist reformers thought that it was possible to reform society directly. Many of them believed that the reforming process had to be undertaken indirectly, by the creation of isolated Utopian communities. When these communities had demonstrated how well the principles their founders espoused would work in practice, the enthusiastic founders thought they would become centers from which the new ideas would spread throughout the land. Brook Farm and Fruitlands were the chief examples of ideal communities undertaken under transcendentalist auspices. Neither was as successful as its founders hoped, perhaps because the colonists were far better at talking than at working, perhaps because their very separation from the world that needed reforming dulled the edge of their zeal. Whatever the reason may be, the record of the failure of Brook Farm may be read, etched in vitriol, in the *American Notes* of Charles Dickens, and that of Fruitlands in the heart blood of Bronson Alcott, as well as in the lighter vein of his daughter, Louisa May Alcott.[12]

Thus we have seen that although the transcendentalists differed from each other in many respects, there were some common attitudes that make it possible to call transcendentalism a movement. Chief among these was the belief that the individual thinker can intuitively reach universal truth. In the light of this belief, although some of the transcendentalists remained Christian and others left the Christian churches, the transcendentalist movement made important contributions to the spiritualizing of liberal religion in America. Transcendentalism also involved a general spirit of unrest and hostility to convention which led, at its highest, to a zeal for humanitarian causes, and in other cases to a too-easy acceptance of the newest panacea for all the ills of mankind. Philosophically, transcendentalism was a form of idealism which asserted that there are supernatural attributes present in the natural constitution of mankind. In the remainder of this chapter we shall examine the working-out of this idealism in the transcendental individualism of Ralph Waldo Emerson, the anarchism of Henry David Thoreau, and the religio-political social democracy of Henry James the Elder.

II. RALPH WALDO EMERSON: INDIVIDUALIST

When Ralph Waldo Emerson joined with Hedge and Ripley in inviting other young ministers to a discussion of the state of theology and philosophy, his action was the climax of a series of events that went back several years. In 1829, he had accepted a Unitarian pulpit, shortly after his graduation from Harvard Divinity School, with every hope of carrying on the high tradition of his family in a long career of service. Just three years later, in 1832, he found that his thinking and that of his congregation were no longer in tune, and he resigned his pulpit. At this time he had already read some of Coleridge's works, and his thinking had begun to be affected by what he had read. He had ideas and he had sincerity; but after his sincerity and his ideas had led him to break with Unitarianism, he found that he had neither purpose nor direction. Until that time his life had been concentrated toward what seemed his natural course; when it became apparent to him that he could not keep both his self-respect and his pulpit, he felt rudderless and confused.

In this state he left for a European trip in the hope of coming to himself again and rethinking his life pattern. He was to meet his heroes, Coleridge and Carlyle, to see new places and new faces, and perhaps to return, with the help of those he met, a new man. Actually, the new Emerson was born before any of these European contacts could be of much help. It may have been while he was still on shipboard that he found himself. Transoceanic voyages were longer in those days and allowed plenty of time for solitary communion.

As early as 1833 Emerson had come to this firm resolution, which he expressed in a poem called "Self Reliance:"

> Henceforth, please God, forever I forego
> The yoke of men's opinions. I will be
> Light-hearted as a bird, and live with God.[13]

What is more, he had made the important discovery, which converted him into a transcendentalist, that God could be found in the depths of his own heart, that with attentive ear he could hear the voice of God speak from his heart. Emerson had discovered the transcendental method. Had he turned back then and there, and never visited Europe, the remainder of his life would have been essentially the same as it was. He had found his own salvation, and for the rest of his life, he never stopped believing and leading others to believe that they could find salvation as he had.

By 1835 when Emerson returned to America, he had matured and strengthened in his resolution to follow the leadings of God within himself. In 1836, in his pamphlet called *Nature*, he set forth the first fruits of his self-discovery, and in the two succeeding years, in two addresses, he advocated a similar method of self-discovery for all leaders of thought, in his Phi Beta Kappa address on "The American Scholar," and for ministers, in his "Address to the Graduating Class of the Divinity School at Cambridge." For the most part, during the rest of his life, Emerson's writings were a reiteration of themes he had discussed in these three works. In them he defined the strategy of the transcendentalist life; in his later writings and speeches he made tactical additions without any alteration in the strategic pattern. Thus, when he joined in forming the Transcendentalist Club he was carrying forward in a new activity a career as transcendentalist spokesman to which he had already given his allegiance.

Now, transcendental method, as Emerson conceived it and used it, was wholly and entirely intuitive. It had no element whatever of logic or understanding. Each act of transcendentalist reflection was an individual, immediate raid on universal truth. It stood by itself; it had no connection with what came after it or what had gone before. There was room in the transcendental method for every inconsistency. The wind of the spirit did not always blow from the same quarter nor with the same intensity. Emerson cared not at all that the vagaries and willfulness of his spirit might lead him into self-contradictory views. "A foolish consistency is the hobgoblin of little minds."[14] There was simple honesty, too, in his reply to Henry Ware, Jr., one of the champions of a more conservative Unitarianism. Ware asked Emerson for his arguments in support of the views expressed in the "Divinity School Address." Emerson gave the thoroughly transcendentalist answer that he had no arguments and that he did not know "what arguments mean in reference to any expression of a thought."[15]

Nor would Emerson have admitted that his method led to insights which were valid only for the single thinker. It was introspection, of course. In his view, however, and that of the other transcendentalists, introspection leads not to subjective conclusions, valid only as a practical guide for the life of the individual, but to universally valid results. Emerson held a deep faith that a man who examines into the leadings of his own spirit honestly and searchingly comes to knowledge which transcends his own finite limits — knowledge which is universal. He was firmly convinced that what he found within himself by the use of the transcendental method was true for all other men. "Every man's nature is a sufficient advertisement to him of the character of his fellows."[16]

This is the foundation on which Emerson erected the belief that each sincere user of the method of transcendental introspection is a "representative man," the spiritual representative of the entire human race. The truly representative men are not chosen by the voice and suffrage of the people; they are self-chosen by virtue of their devoted following of the universal voice within their breasts. Arrogant as this sounds at first, and arrogantly as it might be applied by one who thought of individuality as egotism, Emerson meant it as a doctrine of true humility. Although the voice to be followed was within the individual, it was not of the individual. It was of God. The introspection of the transcendentalist was to go beyond the inner and unimportant self to the inmost core of being which is God. Only in this perspective was it possible for Emerson to say, "Nothing is of us. All is of God. The individual is always mistaken."[17] There is a universal mind, or God, which is the common property of all men; "of the universal mind each individual man is one more incarnation."[18] The representative man lives the life and thinks the thoughts of this universal mind rather than of his particular self.

Emerson expressed this central theme in various ways. Sometimes it became mystical, as in *Nature*: "Standing on the bare ground, my head bathed by the blithe air, and uplifted into infinite space — all mean egotism vanishes. I become a transparent eye-ball; I am nothing; I see all; the currents of the Universal Being circulate through me."[19] At other times the idea of humanity as the "greater man," as it appears in the thought of the Swedish mystic, Emanuel Swedenborg (1688-1772), provided Emerson with a framework on which to build his idea. In "The American Scholar," for instance, he uses this Swedenborgian idea as the basis of a myth which distinguishes between part men and whole men. Part men are farmers or lawyers or pedants — men who view their active careers solely as a means of earning a living. Whole men are representative men; they conceive of their activities as responsible service to all mankind. The farmer becomes Man sent out into the fields to gather food, not for himself but for humanity. He is the delegated food-gatherer of the race, and his agricultural activities have dignity and he has worth because of his representative service. The scholar, in this view, is not the pedant, but the delegated intellect of humanity. His thought is representative thought in the sense that it is thought for the best interests of mankind, not in the sense that it is typical, normal, or average thinking.

Sometimes, as in the essay on "Self-Reliance," Emerson tried to express his view simply enough so that it could be understood by everybody, only to fall into the pit of being misunderstood by everybody — or almost everybody. It is only as there is a transcendental and universal self underlying the individual that self-reliance can be translated as individualism. Emerson's ideal of self-reliance has been consistently misrepresented as sanctioning *laissez-faire*. What we want, he said, is "men of original perception and original action, who can open their eyes wider than to a nationality."[20] Certainly if they can open their eyes wider than to a nationality, it is true that they can open them wider than to an individuality. What Emerson demands of the self-reliant man is that his eyes shall open wide enough to include universality. True, Emerson recognized that the *natural* outcome of individualism is egotism. He insisted, however, that "the pest of society is egotists."[21] There is no need to follow individualism to its natural outcome. It is the function of culture to lead away from this natural outcome, to correct the egotistic, narrowly and selfishly individualistic theory of success, to lead men to proper standards and to the search for the *ideal* outcome of individualism.

Emerson built his new career as "the sage of Concord" around his role as self-consecrated thinker for the American people. In an era when mass communication as we know it did not exist, Emerson created a national audience for an unorganized religion of spiritual idealism of which he was the major prophet. He called his contemporaries to follow him in the development of "an original relation to the universe,"[22] in which tradition and history were to be disregarded. In the era of the great New England historians, Bancroft and Hildreth, Prescott, Motley, and Parkman, Emerson insisted that we need not rely on the past for answers to the questions that we would put to the universe. He held the view that nature was so constituted as to furnish the answers; "whatever curiosity the order of things has awakened in our minds, the order of things can satisfy."[23] Believing this, he was able to urge that poetry and philosophy in his day should be based upon fresh insight rather than tradition, and that religion should be founded on the ever-renewed revelation of God in the human heart rather than on the history of other, earlier revelations.

The Nature — the order of things — on which Emerson counted is not that of the scientist, but rather that of the nature-mystic. "The kingdom of man over nature" is not the product of the precise observations of the man of science. It is, rather, the dominion of the poet or artist who is the master of nature because he can take its separate forms, its trees and flowers and clouds, and integrate them into one landscape. It is, too, the power of the mystic to use nature as the focus of spirit, to develop the ability to become so completely absorbed in nature that he loses his sense of separateness and is aware only of his abiding kinship with all creation. Only to the man who goes out to meet nature in the mood of the nature-lover does nature reveal her secrets. The unchanging and objective face of nature which is the concern of the scientist did not interest Emerson. It was, rather, that varied and ever-changing face of nature which reflects and mirrors man's changing moods, the aspect of nature which "always wears the colors of the spirit"[24] in which he delighted. And his delight in it was more for what it meant to man, and how it served man's needs, than for what it was in itself.

Emerson found an order of increasing spirituality in the four classes of service rendered to man by nature. From the mere "commodity" or practical usefulness of nature, her value to man rises through "beauty," "language," and, finally, "discipline." Commodity is the only one of these uses which every man understands. It is the immediate and direct service of nature in helping to nourish man. Herein nature illustrates the "endless circulation" of divine love, for all the parts of nature must work together if man is to be benefited. Not sun, nor wind, nor ice, nor rain, nor plant, nor animal by itself can profit man, but only the combination of all these in the divine economy. "The wind sows the seed; the sun evaporates the sea; the wind blows the vapor to the field; the ice, on the other side of the planet, condenses rain on this; the rain feeds the plant; the plant feeds the animal."[25] And all this is requisite for the nourishment of man.

On the borderline between commodity and beauty lies the almost universal appreciation of the simple perfection of natural forms. Man's delight in the forms of nature must, however, be supplemented by a higher, more spiritual element if he is to gain a realization of the perfection of the beauty of nature. This spiritual element is introduced in the insight that virtue and beauty go hand in hand, that "Beauty is the mark God sets upon virtue."[26] A man of virtue is attuned to nature; she reaches out to take him in and to make him "the central figure of the visible sphere." Finally, the beauty of nature becomes an object to man's intellect. Beauty is related to thought as well as to virtue. This relation is one of creative use, or art. "The beauty of nature reforms itself in the mind, and not for barren contemplation, but for new creation."[27]

The third level of nature's service to man brings us to some of Emerson's most characteristic beliefs. Again, as in the case of beauty, there are three stages to Emerson's account of the relation between nature and language. In the first of these stages, we come to appreciate the fact that all words are signs of natural facts. This is obviously true not only of the words we use to describe the natural facts themselves, but also of the abstract words in which we express moral or intellectual facts. Our more abstract words are rooted in the concrete words which describe nature. Language which is abstract is the metaphoric use of concrete language. "The use of natural history is to give us aid in supernatural history."[28] Next, we recognize that this relationship between thoughts, words, and things is more than a vague, general connection. There is a definite and precise correspondence between particular natural facts and particular spiritual facts. This has been called Emerson's "doctrine of correspondence." There is a particular spiritual fact which is symbolized by each and every natural fact. "Every appearance in nature corresponds to some state of the mind."[29] For the man of powerful mind who recognizes these correspondences, country living, facing nature day after day, is far more stimulating than living in cities, which tend to magnify trifles and degrade men. Finally, beyond the part to part correspondence of nature and mind, there comes the realization that nature as a whole symbolizes spirit as a whole. "The world is emblematic. Parts of speech are metaphors, because the whole of nature is a metaphor of the human mind."[30] There is a perfect parallelism between the laws of nature and the laws of thought; "the axioms of physics translate the laws of ethics."[31] That this should be so argues that behind mind lies Universal Mind, behind soul lies the Universal Creative Soul, the "Oversoul." It is this Oversoul which has life in itself and is therefore able to create life in other beings. "And man in all ages and countries embodies it in his language as the Father."[32]

The relation between the mind and nature is not the fancy of some poet. It is part of the creative pattern in the mind and will of God and is, therefore, open to all men's knowledge. It is the nature of spirit to take on material forms. Every material event and every material thing "preexist in necessary Ideas in the mind of God."[33] The nature of every material thing is prefigured in some configuration of ideas. "Nature [is] always the effect, mind the flowing cause."[34] Ultimately we emerge with Emerson into an idealism in which the laws of thought are the laws of things, and matter — perhaps by some process of emanation — is derived from spirit. "Every natural fact is an emanation, and that from which it emanates is an emanation also, and from every emanation is a new emanation." But whether or not natural facts develop by a process of emanation — and Emerson in his later years used this explanation more sparingly than in his earlier life — "a fact is the end or last issue of spirit."[35] The virtuous man, cognizant of this relationship, can gradually come to a knowledge of the hidden significance and purpose of the world.

The final stage of nature's service to man is its capacity to discipline his understanding. Meantime his reason — we have already met the distinction between understanding and reason — is able to avail itself of the lessons in which nature schools the understanding by gaining an appreciation of the principle which makes the discipline possible — "by perceiving the analogy that marries Matter and Mind."[36] Nature disciplines the understanding in intellectual truths; thus space and time teach the importance of differentiation and gradation, and that men are individual. Nature disciplines the understanding in moral truths. The objects of sensible experience reflect the judgments of conscience. "Every animal function from the sponge up to Hercules shall hint or thunder to man the laws of right and wrong, and echo the Ten Commandments."[37] Natural objects when they have fulfilled their natural purposes are still new for this moral purpose, which is public and universal. Finally the mind is disciplined to recognize the unity of nature despite its variety of content. Each thing in the universe is a reflection in miniature of the universe itself. The basic law underlying all creation is one and the same throughout. "Each creature is only a modification of the other; the likeness in them is more than the difference." There is a unity in nature which is so intimate that it must have its source in Universal Spirit. This unity is discoverable in thoughts as well as things. It is the systematic coherence of truth. "Every universal truth which we express in words, implies or supposes every other truth."[38]

The discipline of nature leads us to idealism, for we soon realize that while we can doubt the evidence of our senses, we can not doubt the permanence of universal laws. We can never assert definitely that nature has a substantial existence outside of our minds. We can not test the truth of what our senses tell us. It is only the untutored who can be led by sensory evidence to believe that nature certainly exists. Our first serious effort to think breaks down "this despotism of the senses."[39] We are led away from empiricism toward idealism, and gradually develop the ability to use the eye of reason in place of the eye of sense. Under the promptings of nature, in the four classes of commodity, beauty, language, and discipline we have made a beginning of culture.

The very first effect of this culture is to make us aware of a duality of observer and spectacle, man and nature, mind and matter. This is the dualism on which poets base their symbolism. To the man of common sense, thoughts must conform to things, mind to matter. The observer is limited by the spectacle. The poet makes things conform to his thoughts about them. Matter seems to him to be flexible under the impact of mind. The spectacle is ordered and created by the observer. It is the play of imagination which enables the poet to convert the objects of sense into the words of the reason. Imagination may be defined as "the use which the Reason makes of the material world." [40] The purpose of the poet's activity is the pursuit of beauty; the philosopher's end is truth — otherwise they are at one. For both poet and philosopher the "empire of thought" precedes and determines "the apparent order and relations of things."[41] Both poet and philosopher are able to dissolve apparently solid matter by their thought, thus imparting a spiritual life to all of nature. They are able to grasp by intuition the inner law which permeates nature. Philosophy invariably produces a doubt that matter really exists by concentrating attention on ideas. Religion and ethics supplement philosophy by suggesting that matter is inferior to spirit.

In all these ways culture leads men to idealism, to an inversion of the vulgar views of common sense. The advantage which idealism has over common sense is that "it presents the world in precisely that view which is most desirable to the mind."[42] Idealism sees the world as a huge picture painted by God for the soul to contemplate; as an instantaneous creation, not a slow accumulation. But though it is an invaluable beginning, idealism is not enough. There are three questions to which the mind seeks an answer — What is matter? What is its ultimate origin? And what is its destiny? Of these, idealism answers only the first.

The principle which is needed to supplement idealism is Spirit. Spirit leads us to solutions of the two questions which idealism fails to answer. "We learn that the highest is present to the soul of man, that the dread universal essence which is not wisdom, or love, or beauty, or power, but all in one, and each entirely, is that for which all things exist, and that by which they are; that spirit creates; that behind nature, throughout nature, spirit is present; one and not compound, it does not act upon us from without, that is, in space and time, but spiritually, or through ourselves: therefore, that spirit, that is, the Supreme Being, does not build up nature around us, but puts it forth through us, as the life of the tree puts forth new branches and leaves through the pores of the old."[43] This spiritualistic idealism is the philosophic foundation which Emerson built with the aid of the transcendental method.

To measure the full impact of Emerson's philosophic imagination, to determine all the outcomes of his work would be, in effect, to write the history of American culture since his time. This we can not do here. What we can do, and perhaps what we should do, is to see where his ideas led Emerson on some of the issues of his time. It is certainly well to start with a controversy that Emerson himself began by his "Divinity School Address." In this address he advised the young men just entering into the Christian ministry to forget about the traditions of Christianity, to forego preaching out of the gospels or the ecclesiastical records, and to preach out of their own hearts. Each man, he proclaimed, should consider himself "a newborn bard of the Holy Ghost."[44] In this way a generation of spiritual religious leaders might have been built up. Instead, the more conservative leaders of Unitarianism attacked Emerson's position, and succeeded in having him barred from speaking at Harvard for thirty years. There were a few who took Emerson's call to religious self-reliance as their guide, but for the most part his religious ideas had more strength among non-ministers and the unchurched than among ministers and church members.

Politically and socially, Emerson was no ivory-tower dweller. He had, indeed, some of the fire and passion of the Jacksonian reformers. His regard for the worth of all men as the vehicles of universal spirit made him an intense democrat in theory, although in practice he was somewhat averse to contact with people *en masse*. He was devoted to mankind as a whole, but there were few men he liked. He was socially aware, but not socially at ease. Although, in general, he felt that the party of the Jacksonians had the better cause, he saw that their opponents, the Whigs, had the better men. Yet until the slavery controversy stirred the conscience of New England he could not decide where he stood. Sometimes he talked like the wildest of radicals; he thought of himself as a member of the "movement party," of those opposed to the *status quo*. At other times he let his respect for such men as Daniel Webster and Edward Everett sway him to a more conservative stand. On the question of slavery, however, Emerson stood foursquare for the right. On this issue he was willing to be counted definitely among the anti-slavery forces.

In general, however, he did not let his reformist temper carry him too far. He did not approve of the conscientious stand which his younger friend, Henry David Thoreau, took at the time of the Mexican War. Earlier than this incident, in 1841, Emerson had said, "I do not wish to push my criticism on the state of things around me to that extravagant mark that shall compel me to suicide, or to an absolute isolation from the advantage of civil society."[45] He was less of an extremist than many of the other transcendentalists. He retained a sense of proportion and a sense of humor which many of his fellow transcendentalists were unable to keep. His life was far more conventional than his thought. To wear his heart on his sleeve, as Alcott and Thoreau and Margaret Fuller did, would have embarrassed him. "The leaders of society don't wear their hearts on their sleeves,"[46] he wrote in his later years. The caution and shrewdness which led him to this realization tamed considerably his expressions of New England's wild oats. Yet it should not be forgotten that, with all his "gentility," Emerson became an American institution, an example to his fellow-citizens, as the more volatile transcendentalists did not.

III. HENRY DAVID THOREAU: ANARCHIST

The opposition of the transcendentalists to history and science, to tradition and authority, gave increased importance in their thought to the transcendental method which was their substitute for all earlier ways of knowing. The transcendentalists could question the efficacy of all these other methods only because they believed in self-culture. And self-culture for most of them turned into a very solemn business. They rejected the Puritanical searching of the conscience which was their ancestral heritage, but they replaced it with a transcendental searching of the conscience which was every bit as demanding. They did not free themselves from rule, but gave up one rule in exchange for another no less galling. The transcendentalists were completely self-conscious in their conscientious search for self-culture. They read the books that ought to be read; not, perhaps, those which the general educated public kept on its library tables, but those which other transcendentalists were reading. They would have scorned keeping up with the Joneses, but they made frantic attempts to keep up with the Emersons. They formed a coterie; they talked the same oracular language, read the same recondite books, kept the same heart-searching journals, and gloried together that they were not as other men.

Into this circle there strayed a young man of Concord who had heard Emerson talk at Harvard and who had found in what Emerson said a program for living. The other transcendentalists, even Emerson and Alcott who were his nearest friends, never felt completely at ease when Henry David Thoreau was among the company. There was something a little odd about the young man. He wrote and talked interestingly, but roughly, with some scorn. One might almost think that he — this young man who tended Emerson's garden — was condescending to them. Thoreau had an unconscious arrogance about him, a true independence of mind which put their pallid pretense of independence to shame. It was not that he did not share their rejections. He did. Like them, he rebelled against the domination of the Puritan conscience, insisting that Puritanism allowed the conscience a monopoly over the whole life, a monopoly as unwarranted as that of the heart or the head. Just as there might be deranged emotions or distorted minds, Thoreau suggested, there might be diseased consciences. And a conscience which had grown over-large or over-irritable, giving its owner no peace, is a diseased conscience. A perpetually disturbed conscience leads to a fruitless life. Of men like the Puritans he said "They did not know when to swallow their cud, and their lives of course yielded no milk."[47] The thought was one familiar to the other transcendentalists, though the image was, perhaps, somewhat coarser than they liked.

The shoe began to pinch when Thoreau rebelled against the demands of the transcendental conscience as well. He pointed out that too much self-culture was as much a tyrannical monopoly over the whole man as too much head, too much heart, or too much conscience. "There may be an excess of cultivation as well as of anything else, until civilization becomes pathetic."[48] Thoreau accused his fellows of over-gentility, anticipating George Santayana by three quarters of a century. Thoreau himself was quite aware of his pagan leanings. He regarded the divinities of Greece as more liberal than the God of Americans. He thought of Jehovah as something of a Johnny-come-lately among the gods — an "almighty mortal hardly as yet apotheosized" — no more divine, though somewhat more despotic than the Greek Jove. Jehovah, said Thoreau, "is not so much of a gentleman, not so gracious and catholic, he does not exert so intimate and genial an influence on nature, as many a god of the Greeks." The Greek gods are unquestionably divine, and it is comforting to think of them as having the vices of men, as "youthful and erring and fallen gods," unlike the "infinite power and inflexible justice" which characterizes Jehovah. Pan was Thoreau's favorite divinity, "with his ruddy face, his flowing beard, and his shaggy body, his pipe and his crook, his nymph Echo, and his chosen daughter, Iambe; for the great god Pan is not dead, as was rumored. No god ever dies."[49] One can imagine the shock of horror with which words like these were received by the transcendentalists to whom the Jehovah worshipped in their time and place was all-too unspiritual, too crude. The transcendental method ought to produce a refinement of the God-idea, not this reversion to paganism.

Thoreau had little patience with such overscrupulousness. The god of civilized countries seemed to him to be divine in name, but not in essence. This essence he thought to be "the overwhelming authority and respectability of mankind combined."[50] The conscience of civilized countries seemed to him to be sickly, a hothouse product, "instinct bred in the house." What the civilized conscience needs, he said, is to be turned out of doors. Then it will develop a concern for large, basic problems, not for minute and transitory events. The plot of a man's life should be simple, so that he "lives one tragedy and not seventy." The transcendental antagonism to the traditional doctrines of Calvinism comes out with special force, and some venom, in Thoreau's verse:

> I love a soul not all of wood,
> Predestinated to be good,
> But true to the backbone
> Unto itself alone,
> And false to none.[51]

He scorned the "conscientious cowards" who were constantly worried about each trivial action of their lives. He preferred the carefree laboring man whose only concern with virtue is with the virtue of cheerfulness. There is no point to an incessant preoccupation with salvation; "Live your life," he recommended, "do your work, then take your hat." The conventional standards of society had no significance for him. He rejected them in practice in his Walden pond retreat, and gave his rejection theoretical statement in his doctrine of civil disobedience.

The immediate occasion for Thoreau's writing of his "Essay on Civil Disobedience" was the series of events preceding the Mexican War of 1848. As the unjust and aggressive acts of the United States unfolded, and the relation of the pattern of aggression to the expansion of slavery became clear, Thoreau conscientiously refused to pay his local taxes in order to register his protest. He was jailed for his refusal; his friends paid his taxes and he was released. The theoretical issue of whether refusal to pay taxes could be established as a right of conscience remained undetermined. An interesting sidelight on the divergent standards of respectability held by Thoreau and the other transcendentalists stems from this episode. It is reported that, when Thoreau was in jail, Emerson came to visit him, stood outside the cell and said, in a shocked tone, "Henry, what are you doing in there?" Thoreau, true to himself and not to any artificial social standards, replied, "Waldo, what are *you* doing out there?" He felt that it was a matter of vital importance to him to avoid supporting, and thereby appearing to sanction, injustice and he could not understand how Emerson could feel any less involved than he did. "Under a government which imprisons any unjustly," he wrote, "the true place for a just man is also a prison." [52] His reflections on the relation of the individual to civil government finally led him to the writing of the "Essay on Civil Disobedience," which is, to this day, regarded as a classic in the literature of non-violence. It was, for example, one of the works by which Mahatma Gandhi was deeply influenced.

Thoreau's "Essay" brings to sharp focus an anarchistic element which had been latent in American political thought since the time of the founding fathers. Many of them would have agreed with Jefferson that government is a necessary evil, and that the best government is that which governs least, and thereby reduces the evil to a minimum. As practical men of affairs, however, these early leaders made no attempt to go beyond this statement; they recognized the necessity for some government, but tried to keep the amount as low as possible. Thoreau, unhampered by any practical considerations, was prepared to accept the full implications of this latent anarchism. If, he said, that government is *relatively* best which governs least, then that government is *absolutely* best which does not govern at all. He was prepared to concede that all men are not yet ready for such a non-governing government, but added that when they were ready, that would be the kind of government they would have. In describing government as a *necessary* evil, the men of the Enlightenment had suggested that government was merely a matter of expediency. Thoreau picked up this suggestion and announced that "Government is at best but an expedient; but most governments are usually and all governments are sometimes inexpedient."[53]

The American people had rejected the traditional European standing army, on the ground that it was an unnecessary expense and that it permitted the institution of a despotism of the military caste. Thoreau insisted that all the objections against a standing army held with equal force against a "standing government" and that, ultimately, these objections would come to expression. Thoreau referred to the government of the United States as "a recent tradition trying to perpetuate itself."[54] The American government is somewhat better than other governments in the world because it is less restrictive. Its contribution to American progress has, however, been a negative, not a positive, contribution. Its only advantage has been that it has failed to impede progress. Whatever has been accomplished in America has been the product of the character of the American people. Indeed, if the government had not sometimes stood in the way, this progressive character "inherent in the American people" would have brought about somewhat more progress than it actually had.

Of course, Thoreau had a certain amount of practical sense and was aware that his proposal for no government at all was not for immediate realization. The immediate program for which he called was better government. Better government essentially meant to him government in which right and wrong are determined by the conscience of the citizen, not by majorities. There is, he recognized, a practical reason for majority rule in the physical strength a majority is able to muster, not in the likelihood that a majority decision is right. There are some matters taken up by government which do not involve questions of right and wrong, of justice or injustice. On matters of this sort, Thoreau was perfectly willing that the decision of the majority should prevail. "But a government in which the majority rule in all cases cannot be based on justice, even as far as men understand it." Where moral questions are involved no citizen ought to be asked to "resign his conscience to the legislator." The citizen is a man first, and a citizen afterwards; it is as a man that he must judge questions of right and wrong, for each man has a conscience. "The only obligation which I have a right to assume is to do at any time what I think right."[55] It is plain to see what direction transcendental individualism took in Thoreau.

To produce in each man a respect for the right as his conscience interprets the right seemed to Thoreau far more vital than to emphasize respect for law. There has never been a law which made men more just than they are. Quite the contrary; many laws lead men to the performance of actions of which they can not conscientiously approve, and thus result in injustice. Because of undue respect for law, "even the well-disposed are daily made the agents of injustice."[56] One of the more common results of respect for law is that wars are waged by armies of men who do not believe in war, who recognize it as "a damnable business." And Thoreau echoed Emerson's address on "The American Scholar" by asking whether these soldiers are really men at all. Are they not, rather, he demanded, "small movable forts and magazines, at the service of some unscrupulous man in power?"[57] It was the Fugitive Slave Law and the Mexican War and the shockingly unjust treatment meted out to the American Indians that had aroused Thoreau to this disdain for law. Because of these he felt that the place for an honorable man was in jail, "the only house in a slave State in which a free man can abide with honor."[58]

Thoreau felt that the right of revolution was still a living and practical right in his time. Many of his contemporaries still admitted a theoretical right of revolution, but denied that any occasion for revolution had existed in the United States since the American Revolution. Thoreau, however, pointed out that the right was to be exercised whenever the actions of a government were tyrannical beyond endurance. "All machines have their friction; and possibly this does enough good to counterbalance the evil. At any rate, it is a great evil to make a stir about it. But when the friction comes to have its machine, and oppression and robbery are organized, I say, let us not have such a machine any longer."[59] What makes

Thoreau's protest interesting and different is that he himself was affected only in conscience by the oppression against which he protested. He felt, if anything, that resistance was even more important when it was another country which his country was invading, and another group over which it was tyrannizing. He took the right of revolution to mean the right to refuse allegiance to a government as well as the right to resist it by force. The Abolitionists of Massachusetts were, he felt, wrong in their procedure of trying to win over a numerical majority to their side on a conscientious question. A better program he thought was to do as a body what he had done, withdraw support from the government of Massachusetts and, therefore, from the government of the United States, because these governments condoned injustice in the matter of slavery. Why wait for a majority when God is on their side? Besides, "any man more right than his neighbors constitutes a majority of one already."[60]

Any governmental authority is impure, and it requires the consent of the governed if it is to be strictly just. The increasing recognition of this importance of the individual is to be seen in the progress of our forms of government from absolute monarchy to limited monarchy and thence to democracy. But Thoreau was unwilling to admit that democracy, as practiced in the United States, is the final form of government. There is, to his mind, a higher type of state, the only kind for which he could have real respect, which would recognize in the individual a power higher than that of the state and independent of it — a power which is the source of the power of the state and must, therefore, be treated with respect by the state. A state which treated the individual with respect would be worthy of the respect of the individual. If there were to be such a state, it would recognize the right of dissenters like Thoreau to live within its borders but not to be its citizens, "not meddling with it, nor embraced by it,"[61] provided that these dissident individual sovereignties behave like good neighbors. This would mark a step of advance from the democratic state because it would eliminate more elements of compulsion. With the gradual increase in truly independent, truly self-reliant individuals, which would be the result of this policy, the ground would be prepared for the no-government state, the anarchism, which Thoreau envisaged as the government which would be absolutely best.

The "Essay on Civil Disobedience" was Thoreau's only attempt to write a systematic account of his ideas. For the most part, he was content just to write and let the ideas happen, as insights, without any pretense at rational exposition. If there are fewer inconsistencies in Thoreau's work than there are in Emerson's, the reason is that Thoreau was a less complicated person than Emerson. In Thoreau's writings the reader can trace the course of the theme of self-reliant independence as it is applied in new contexts, but the theme itself, the basic idea, remains unchanged. When he proposed independence as his personal standard, Thoreau suggested that this independence meant living up to his own self-image, and disappointing those of his friends who set up their standards as an ideal for him to live by.

> Great God, I ask thee for no meaner pelf
> Than that I may not disappoint myself. . . .
> And next in value, which thy kindness lends,
> That I may greatly disappoint my friends.[62]

As we have seen, this independence was to extend to his political life. The state can give the independent man nothing which he does not already have without its aid, and since the truly independent man owns nothing except his own spirit, the state can take nothing from him. The man who is in no danger needs no protection from danger. A free soul, one who is truly independent, has no wants which the state can satisfy. He can describe his life as both more civil and more free than any civil society.

> The life that I aspire to live
> No man proposeth me —
> No trade upon the street
> Wears its emblazonry.[63]

Thoreau even believed that this free life included the assertion of his independence from God.

Freedom of this sort must start within each individual. It can not be the product of legislative enactments or of collective action. Thoreau's fervent admiration for John Brown was based on Brown's recognition of this principle. Men who remain loyal to an unjust state are themselves slaves. They are slaves because they sell themselves for some fancied commercial advantage. The legislators in the nation's capital are slaves; they sell themselves for position and office. Why wait until one group of slaves orders the liberation of

another? Rather follow the path of John Brown and assert that
freedom exists by your own action.

> Wait not till slaves pronounce the word
>   To set the captive free,
> Be free yourselves, be not deferred,
>   And farewell slavery. . . .
>
> Think not the tyrant sits afar.
>   In your own breasts ye have
> The District of Columbia
>   And power to free the Slave. . . .
>
> Make haste and set the captive free —
>   Are ye so free that cry? . . .
>
> He's governed well who rules himself,
>   No despot vetoes him. . . .
>
> 'Tis neither silver rags nor gold
>   'S the better currency,
> The only specie that will hold
>   Is current honesty. . . .
>
> There's but the party of the great,
>   And party of the mean,
> And if there is an Empire State
>   'Tis the upright, I ween.[64]

The extreme point of Thoreau's passion for independence is revealed, however, not in any of these, but in his demand that, in a
certain sense, he should be independent of himself. He wanted to
be, as he said in *Walden*, beside himself "in a sane sense."[65] The
mind which is truly free is beyond its own involvement with nature.
It is spectator not merely of all time and all existence in general, but
of the particular time and particular existence which it shares with
a body. The detachment of mind which is the ultimate independence
is like the Hindu and Buddhist concept of Nirvana, a release from
physical concern. Thoreau, however, was in the Western tradition,
and thought of this release from involvement as the result of "a
conscious effort of the mind" in thinking. It is possible to become
as much the spectator of one's own experience as if one were wit-
nessing a theatrical exhibition, to be as far from one's own experience as from that of another person. "However intense my experience, I am conscious of the presence and criticism of a part of me,
which, as it were, is not a part of me, sharing no experience, but

taking note of it; and that is no more I than it is you. When the play, it may be the tragedy, of life is over, the spectator goes his way. It was a kind of fiction, a work of the imagination only, so far as he was concerned."[66]

This "doubleness" was the route Thoreau hoped to take in order to arrive at a set of values truer than those of his society, and to achieve the character of a philosopher. Not through the exercise of hands and feet, but by using his head as a cleaver he hoped to "mine and burrow" his way into the secret of things. The thin current of time slides away; eternity remains to be explored. In this exploration even the wisest of men is but a beginner; "I cannot count one. I know not the first letter of the alphabet. I have always been regretting that I was not as wise as the day I was born."[67] Yet a true set of values demands that this eternity which we are so backward in exploring should be the concern of our studies, not the panorama of passing events. It demands the perspective of a philosopher, which is "not merely to have subtle thoughts, nor even to found a school, but so to love wisdom as to live according to its dictates, a life of simplicity, independence, magnanimity, and trust."[68] This kind of living philosophy Thoreau tried to practice in his Walden Pond retreat.

Although we have seen evidence in Thoreau's ideas of a deeply spiritual and religious nature, and although there is a Christ-like quality to his life and his thought, none of the transcendentalists went farther than Thoreau in opposition to organized Christianity. He seems, even more than his fellows, to have been aware of the strangulation that overtakes the life of the spirit when it is organized and institutionalized. In the section titled "Sunday" in his *A Week on the Concord and Merrimac Rivers*, Thoreau gave expression to as lofty a brand of Christian freethought as has been heard in America. His Christianity was a pure appreciation of the beauty of the life of Christ. It was anticlerical and antiecclesiastical. "What are time and space to Christianity, eighteen hundred years, and a new world? — that the humble life of a Jewish peasant should have force to make a New York bishop so bigoted?"[69] It was completely non-dogmatic, insisting that if we would see clearly into the things of heaven, we must interpose no doctrinal scheme between our minds and their object. It was in the highest sense Scriptural, based upon a careful and sympathetic reading of the New Testament in order to find out what is said therein, not to seek proof-texts for some prior dogma. It was open-minded study of the New Testament, leading to the harsh conclusion that "It is remarkable that, notwithstanding the universal favor with which the New Testament is outwardly received, and even the bigotry with which it is defended, there is no hospitality shown to, there is no appreciation of, the order of truth with which it deals. I know of no book that has so few readers. There is none so truly strange, and heretical, and unpopular. To Christians, no less than Greeks and Jews, it is foolishness and a stumbling-block." The reason is that the truths of the New Testament are opposed to institutions; Thoreau's Christ was an anarchist like Thoreau himself. Some of the sayings of Jesus are so severe that "Let but one of these sentences be rightly read, from any pulpit in the land, and there would not be left one stone of that meeting-house upon another."[70]

The Christianity of the churches seemed to Thoreau to be without value for the healthy. "The church is a sort of hospital for men's souls, and as full of quackery as the hospital for their bodies."[71] Those who entered into the churches reminded him of the old sailors to be seen in sunny weather sitting outside their Sailor's Snug Harbor. Even so, the "religious cripples" find a sort of retirement from the active business of living in their churches. In the literal sense, there is no "infidelity," no lack of faith, "so great as that which prays, and keeps the Sabbath, and rebuilds the churches."[72] It is lack of faith because it is a retreat from life, a falling back, rather than falling forward with joyous recklessness onto whatever the future may hold in store.

When the final accounting of Thoreau's position is made it is apparent that the central principle and central value of all transcendentalism, reliance upon the inner spirit of each individual, became for him a principle of opposition to all rule. To follow the leadings of one's own spirit meant for him necessarily to be opposed to all rule, to all law, to all external restraints or discipline. His vision of man at the highest was of man unorganized. His philosophical anarchism transcended even the Golden Rule: "Absolutely speaking, Do unto others as you would that they should do unto you is by no means a golden rule, but the best of current silver. An honest man would have but little occasion for it. It is golden not to have any rule at all in such a case."[73]

IV. HENRY JAMES, THE
ELDER: SOCIAL DEMOCRAT

Emerson had said "Whenever a man comes, there comes revolution."[74] Thoreau had had the courage to follow his rebel temperament and to deny the conscientious standards of his fellow transcendentalists as well as those of the Puritan ancestors the transcendentalists were trying so hard to transcend. In the educational field Bronson Alcott had introduced a radically new and inverted emphasis with his belief that the younger a child, the more he knew of what had taken place in the realm of souls, before birth drew the veil. Margaret Fuller typified the revolt of the transcendentalists against the conventional place assigned to women in American life. Each of the transcendentalists was in active rebellion against one or another aspect of American life, and each carried on his personal crusade with whatever ability, vigor, and originality he was able to cultivate.

Of them all, perhaps the most able, and certainly the most vigorous, challenging, and original view was that of Henry James the Elder. James' achievement in producing two distinguished sons, the novelist Henry James and the philosopher William James (see Chapter 7, section III), has tended to distract attention from the real and daring intellectual formulation which was his own rebellion against conventional religious and social thought in America. He had no great following; his thought was too profoundly conceived and too obscurely presented for extensive popularity. Yet his ideas were a leavening influence in the thought of those whom he did reach and he is still regarded with respect by those who read his works today. Even those who can not sympathize with his views find in his works insights which arouse their interest and admiration. His philosophy has a rich fullness that defies summary. Even to attempt a brief statement of his major ideas is to meet a sharp challenge. But it is a challenge which must be met if we are to recognize that there was more to transcendentalism in America than the "genteel" tradition.

The major concern of James' thought was the exploration of the true relation between mankind and the Creator of mankind. At the core of his philosophy lay an intense conception of God as a personal Creator. He assumed the existence of God without any question or doubt. Thus, although his thought was deeply and profoundly religious, it was unconventionally so. The usual problem of religious philosophers is that of proving the existence of God from an accepted and admitted creation. The world is here and now; our problem is to learn about its Maker by the study of its nature. James' transcendental mind inverted the problem. It was the Creator whose reality James never doubted; what he sought to find was the creation. In his search for the meaning of creation James wandered from the orthodox Presbyterianism of his earlier years through Robert Sandeman's communalistic version of a Calvinistic primitive Christianity, to a highly personal interpretation of the teachings of Emanuel Swedenborg.

It is important to recognize that James did himself less than justice when he claimed Swedenborg as his intellectual parent. This was pointed out by J. J. Garth Wilkinson, the leading English follower of Swedenborg in the nineteenth century, who was responsible for James' introduction to the ideas of the great Swede. Wilkinson insisted that the ideas of James had been suggested by the collision of his mind with Swedenborg's. The collision was, said Wilkinson, a meeting of opposition, not of friendship; but that James had misunderstood — "He has struck you hard; and in the tenderness and generosity of your constitution, you have accepted his heavy blow as polite intercourse."[75] We need not, however, deny in as cavalier a fashion as did Wilkinson that there was a kinship of thought. Wilkinson, with all his generosity and friendship, was a rival interpreter of Swedenborg who, not unnaturally, believed that his own interpretation clarified Swedenborg's message along lines of which Swedenborg himself would have approved. That James did not regard Wilkinson's interpretation as final was enough to convince Wilkinson that James never really understood Swedenborg. It is perhaps best and most moderate to say that James' originality was fed by his reading of Swedenborg and that he expressed himself with most felicity when he used the language of Swedenborg.

Emerson, too, had some familiarity with Swedenborg; in his collection of sketches of thoroughly unrepresentative men, published under the title *Representative Men*, Emerson used Swedenborg to represent the mystical type. Although Emerson had a sensitive appreciation of Swedenborg's insights — the respect of one master of intuition for another — he felt that Swedenborg lacked a proper appreciation of the place of the individual in the cosmic scheme. It was precisely this aspect of Swedenborg's thought which was most appealing to James. The primary premise of James' philosophy is that the individual is, in himself, nothing. All that the individual seems to be he owes to the nature he inherits from the human race and to the culture of the particular society into which he chances to be born. That there is a lack of true selfhood, true individuality, in the human creature is an important factor in James' thought because this lack is an aspect of the problem of creation which defies further analysis.

Yet — the second basic premise of James' thought — although men lack real individuality, a great and good and loving Creator who has brought men as far along the road to salvation as they are will surely lead them the rest of the way, through all negativity and discord and out into harmony with themselves and their neighbors. False selfhood, which does not come from God, is "a showy and fallacious one . . . which is wholly inadequate to guarantee us against calamity."[76] When we shall have acquired real selfhood, which comes from God alone, we shall have in salvation that guarantee which is the quest of the ages. James accounts for both the dearth and the later plenitude by his theory of creation. Creation of real being out of nothingness, out of non-being, can not, as James explains the process, take place in one step. Real non-being can not be transformed immediately into real being. He postulates an intermediate stage in the creative process.

In this intermediate stage there is the production of an illusion of being. The Creator finds himself faced by the nothingness with which he has to deal, and sees that it is not merely the negation of being; it has a positive character of gaping emptiness which is the opposite of His fullness. In order to do anything at all with the great void, He is forced to introduce the illusory stage. This stage may ultimately become not the foundation, but the jumping-off place, or "surface of rebound," for a second movement of creation whose result is real being. Thus, in the first place, creation is a process compounded of two movements, the first of which is formation and the second of which is redemption. Formation, the stage of illusory being, the first quickening of the void unto itself, is Nature. Redemption, the stage of real being, the finished spiritual work of God, is Society.

Nature and Society do not differ in material; there is but one substance in the universe, and that is the Creator himself. In this pantheistic view God must be the matter of both Nature and Society. But Nature and Society do differ in form. Nature is the Creator swallowed up in the void of non-being. Society is the same Creator — but the void has found salvation. It is now shot through and through with the life, the being, of the Creator. All of humanity and the whole universe of phenomena experienced by men, making up humanity's total environment, are included in both Nature and Society. The great difference between the unredeemed and the redeemed form, the stage of illusory being and the stage of real being, Nature and Society, is a difference in direction. Nature points toward and culminates in the moral and religious consciousness of man. Society starts at and points away from this moral and religious consciousness.

In moving out of the formative and into the redemptive phase of its process, creation pivots on the consciousness of self, which is morality, and on the conscience, which is religion. God's first product, the stage of illusory being, is a Nature which is subject to self-consciousness. This self-consciousness is an awareness of our private and individual, our "showy and fallacious" selves; it is equivalent to selfhood (which Swedenborg called "proprium"). Nature must be essentially good because it is divine. Under the influence of selfhood, individuals selfishly and egoistically seize the goodness of Nature for their private ends. Selfhood is essentially atheistic, because it is unaccompanied by a sense of the participation of the Creator in the individual. It is "the feeling I have of life in myself, absolute and underived from any other save in a natural way." [77] God's energy, which is pure altruistic love, unmixed with any self-interest, is negated by selfhood which inverts altruism into selfishness. When this self-consciousness becomes the moral consciousness of self and the religious conscience, they form the reflecting surface from which the new creative movement of redemption takes its start. Morality and religion have no positive worth, no place in the redemptive process. They are agents to wean men away from the false selfhood of the formative process.

Morality and religion are not ends; they must be transcended. They are means, merely. They permit the old content of Nature to be rearranged into a new and truer form, that of Society or real being. In Society the illusion of self, with its acknowledgment only of a natural parentage, will be undermined; men will acknowledge that their life comes from God and will love each other as God loves, with a pure and altruistic love. They will recognize that God's real creature is not individual man but "aggregate humanity." Thus the regenerate social order, the kingdom of heaven on earth, will arrive. Nature is the unredeemed form of man; Society is the redeemed form of man. In Society God will be fully incarnated, not in any individual, but as "the Divine-Natural Humanity." The significant, perhaps the only true, difference between the unregenerate social form which is Nature and the regenerate social form which is Society is that in Nature the individual units will not establish relations with each other in accordance with the truth that aggregate humanity is God's real creature and that He can not show partiality to one fractional unit of mankind rather than to another, whereas in Society this is a pattern and an attitude which needs no enforcing. James had no patience with any educated person whose view of God was so simple that he could conceive of no better occupation for God than "literally to bestow divine and immortal life upon that dead, corrupt, and stinking thing" [78] — his selfhood.

In a somewhat more conventionally expressed, but basically no less radical treatment of the nature of man, James supplements and clarifies his notions of creation. James asserts that the life of man is composed of three realms: The first of these is exterior and physical, the realm of body; the second realm is interior or psychical, the realm of mind or soul; finally, there is the realm which is inmost or spiritual, the realm of spirit. In the realm of body the organization of life is based upon sensation; the sun is the light by which the life of sense is supported and strengthened; the light of the sun is essential to the health of the body. Life is organized scientifically in the realm of mind; its light is reason, which is necessary for mental health. The life of the realm of spirit is organized philosophically; revelation is its light, and is essential to spiritual health. These three realms are not continuous with one another; we can not move from the realm of body to that of mind, and from mind to spirit, because these realms are related by correspondence, not by direct agreement. The sun in the realm of body corresponds to reason in the realm of mind, but the sun casts no light in reason's domain, any more than reason does in that of the sun. To each realm its own light. Any attempt to make one light serve for another leads either to emptiness or to madness.

"If, accordingly, I use the light of one realm to illumine the objects of another one, I shall only be able to see things upside down, and hence hopelessly falsify my own understanding." [79]

The object of knowledge in each realm is a type of existence, but each leads to knowledge of a completely different type of existence. Through the senses, by the light of the sun, man becomes acquainted with finite existence, in the realm of body. Science leads to a knowledge of relative existence, and the purer and finer light of reason must replace that of sense. Finally, philosophy leads us to an acquaintance with infinite and absolute existence. To this end it requires a light more subtle than the light of nature, more penetrating and steadier than that of reason — "the serene and steadfast ray of Revelation." [80] Had it not been for this light men would forever have been completely shut away from the spiritual realm, which is "the true realm of the Divine creation," for this realm can neither be perceived by sense nor analyzed by science. Here, then, is the point at which we can clarify James' doctrine of creation. The creation of which he talks, with its dual movement of formation and redemption, is *philosophical* creation; it takes place within the realm of spirit. It is in this realm that revelation points out the truth of the Divine Incarnation — that the Divine Love is present in all mankind, that God makes no distinctions among persons, though men do measure their fellows "by mere ecclesiastical and political necessities." Revelation "declares that, in spite of all appearances to the contrary, our true life is an immortal one, not derived from our natural progenitors, standing in no natural gifts of any sort, whether of beauty or wit or intellect or temper, much less in any purely personal accomplishments, such as wealth or learning or manners or station, but flowing exclusively from the living acknowledgment of the Divine name, which means the hearty practical recognition of human fellowship. In short, Revelation ascribes to the whole human race the unity of a man before God, having but one body and one spirit, one Lord, one faith and one baptism, one God and Father of all, who is above all and through all and in all: this man being evidently social, as implying such a unity of all the members with each individual member and of each with all as will finally obliterate the iniquities of caste upon earth, or do away with all that arbitrary and enforced inequality among men which is the pregnant source of our existing vice and crime." [81]

The greatest tribute that can be paid to the sun is not, as the superstitious sun-worshippers believe, to stare into its fiery disk until one is blinded and unable to see anything. It is, rather, to turn one's back upon the sun itself, and to look at those objects which the sun illuminates. "Surely no light is designed to attract attention to itself, but only to dissipate surrounding darkness." [82] So, too, with the light of revelation. We do not pay it true honor by concentrating our attention on its "body," or letter, its sphere of existence. The existence of any light is subservient to its use. It is the power and use of revelation, the light which it casts upon human nature, which should occupy our attention. Not revelation itself, but what we see by the light of revelation, should be our concern. And, as we have noted, what we see by the light of revelation is the incarnation of God in aggregate humanity, or the "Divine-Natural Humanity." Whether our approach to James is by way of his theory of creation or of his theory of human nature, we find the climax of his thought in Society, the redeemed form of man.

The organizing principle of Society thus conceived is the pure, altruistic love of man for man. This is, of course, the principle of ideal, or regenerate, Society. We are not to expect to find any actual society thus organized. In varying degrees each actual society falls short of this ideal. Government and law are the measures of the degree in which natural societies fail to become redeemed Society. But the government and the laws, the coercion and the restraint of natural societies are, like the formative movement of Nature, part of the Divine Providence. Even as the stage of illusory being is a necessary prelude to true being, the stage of illusory society is a necessary prelude to true Society. The era during which men are forced by compulsion to do unto others as they would have others do unto them will yield to the time in which no compulsion is necessary because every man will *freely* observe this golden rule. "The use of all law or government among men has not been final but mediatory." [83]

In James' social thought, democracy — by which he meant social democracy rather than political democracy — occupies a position like that of morality and religion in his theory of creation. Democracy is the pivot, the focal point from which the new movement of redeemed Society takes its start. The universal law of spiritual evolution, in James' view, is that spirit can only grow and flourish by the shattering of old restrictions, the death of old forms and institutions. Democracy seemed to him to illustrate the working of this spiritual law, for he regarded democracy as "not so much a new form of political life, as a dissolution or disorganization of the old forms." [84] Democracy makes the assertion that man is more important than traditional institutions. It may well be that these institutions, like those of kingship and priesthood, had originally a merely symbolic meaning. Kings and priests represent, in natural society, the sacredness of "that divine or perfect man whose life descends to him from within, or from God, [85] that is, of the Divine-Natural Humanity. Such a symbolic representation had, in the past, great worth. But democracy has no respect for a worth that is merely past, unless it also reflects the present interests and needs of humanity. Neither tradition nor statute nor custom has in itself any binding obligation save as it is derived "from the instincts of the universal human heart." [86]

The positive results of democracy, James thought, are to be sought not in any increase of national wealth, honor, and glory, but in the increase of truly human (and, hence, truly divine) relations among the members of society. This is basic to his view that democracy is social and moral rather than political. Government has always represented the interests of a society conceived as a unit over against the individual and selfish interests of its members. It has always served to foreshadow an ultimate destiny in which individual and societal interests will be in complete harmony. The necessity for governments to exist has been the immaturity of society, the imperfect realization of the true fellowship of man with man. "No one can doubt that if human life had been perfect in the infancy of the race, that is to say, if just social relations had existed from the beginning, government would never have been thought of as a necessity of human society." [87] Laws can not declare what men are, only what they are not. Law describes man negatively, on the basis of the imperfections of unregenerate natural man; it can not speak positively on the basis of the perfections of redeemed man. Law, therefore, does not and can not establish absolute distinctions among men or classes. It only shows the relative and finite character of existing distinctions, which are not distinctions at all in the sight of God. This office of law and government becomes less essential, less necessary, as man is able to govern his life by "a wisdom proportioned to his needs." [88]

This wisdom democracy implicitly attributes to men when it pronounces them capable of self-government. In this respect democracy is a herald of the moral perfection of man. Democracy can, therefore, break down old traditions, laws, and precedents, and dares to remove "every obstacle to the exact public equality of man with man."[89] Democracy is the forerunner of redeemed Society. "It supposes that men are capable of so adjusting their relations to each other, as that they will need no police or external force to control them, but will spontaneously do the right thing in all places and at all times." [90] In this interesting fashion, James combined the themes he drew from Robert Sandeman and Emanuel Swedenborg with social ideas derived from Charles Fourier (1772-1837) to develop a theory which made social democracy the precursor of the spiritual solidarity of the kingdom of God on earth.

Unique and individual as was the philosophy of Henry James the Elder, it betrays throughout its transcendental character. Like Emerson and Thoreau, but more profoundly than either, James tried to account for man's spiritual development in terms of an indwelling divinity. His greater depth as well as his greater radicalism lay in his realization that the opulent fullness of divinity could be contained in nothing less than mankind. Emerson, Thoreau, and James all sought the meaning of true selfhood. Thoreau found a meaning in being "beside himself" — in the independence of his true self from the chances of the world. Emerson found a meaning of true selfhood in "self-reliance" — in the universality of the spiritual ideals a man found in his inmost soul. James found a meaning of true selfhood in otherhood — in the principle of "sociality" which represents among regenerate men in redeemed Society the principle of pure, altruistic love which is the principle of Divine creativity. Whatever their differences, however, these three and the other transcendentalists were at one in their search for a spiritual interpretation of American life.

5

THE BIOLOGIZING OF PHILOSOPHY

---

1. THE IMPACT OF EVOLUTIONARY IDEAS

The publication of Charles Darwin's *Origin of Species*, in 1859, and *The Descent of Man*, in 1871, called forth a great deal of controversy in American intellectual life. In some respects it is correct to say that the controversy has not yet subsided entirely. Our purpose here is to examine the effects of the introduction of Darwinian ideas and the cognate ideas of Herbert Spencer upon the course of philosophic thought in America. We shall find that even among those philosophers who accepted the Darwinian hypothesis as warranted there was little uniformity about the inferences which were drawn from Darwin's work in the fields of ethics, social philosophy, or metaphysics. But before we look at the effects of the stimulus that Darwin gave to American philosophy, we must recognize that evolutionary ideas of various sorts had been current in America for about a century before Darwin's time.

Some of these pre-Darwinian ideas of evolution were, like Darwin's own theory, developed in the context of biology. Thus, in the middle of the eighteenth century, the French naturalist Buffon (Georges Louis Leclerc, Comte de Buffon, 1707-1788) had maintained the theory that animal species were not fixed, but varied according to the influence of the physical environment upon their external forms. He asserted without adequate evidence that the New World environment led to the development of animals smaller than those which developed in the Old World. Thomas Jefferson was so aggrieved that he engaged men to hunt bison to send to Buffon as visible proof that the American climate had no such dwarfing influence as Buffon had claimed. Another French naturalist, Jean Baptiste Pierre Antoine de Monet de Lamarck (1744-1829), suggested the biological theory, known after him as Lamarckism, that evolutionary changes in animal

species may take place through the inheritance of acquired characteristics. Among the Americans who accepted early theories such as
these, Benjamin Rush and Samuel Stanhope Smith should certainly
be mentioned. Rush's environmentalism, shown especially in his
address on "The Influence of Physical Causes on the Moral Faculty,"
has been discussed earlier (Chapter 2, section III). Smith, who was
professor of philosophy and later president of the College of New
Jersey (Princeton), indicated his acceptance of the theory that
species are not fixed in a discussion of "The Causes of the Variety of
Complexion and Figure in the Human Species." In this essay Smith
maintained that all men, regardless of their differences in appearance,
were descended from a single pair of ancestors, and that, therefore,
external variations are the result of environmental modifications, not
of special creation. Although these theories were evolutionary, it
should be said that the development which their authors claimed was
always within a species. One form of horse might develop out of
another form of horse, but the line between horse and cow species
was never broken.

In the same period, the mid-eighteenth century, there developed in
America as well as in Europe an interest in fossil remains. This interest was stimulated in America by the American Philosophical
Society. The early records of this organization contain notes on
many fossil discoveries by eminent citizens of our infant nation.
Political opponents like Jefferson and Hamilton were at one in their
study of fossils. There were two sciences, both evolutionary in
character, which arose out of the study of fossils. One was paleontology; the fossil remains themselves could be readily arranged in an
evolutionary series, showing clear evidence of specific changes in
anatomical structure. The second new science, geology, arose incidentally in the attempt to define the time relationships between
different orders of fossils. It became evident very quickly that the
crust of the earth bore testimony to prehistoric floods and volcanic
eruptions, to shiftings of the face of the earth, and to a rough time
order which exceeded by millions of years the conservative estimates
based on the Bible. The English clergyman, Gilbert White (1720-
1793), stirred the minds of many by his book *The Natural History of
Selbourne.* The more nearly orthodox Hugh Miller (1807-1856) had
an even wider influence with his popular versions of the reconciliation of Genesis with geology.

In the United States, Edward Hitchcock of Amherst was responsible for the diffusion of geological information in his widely-circulated book, *The Religion of Geology*, and in many essays and lectures. Hitchcock's purpose was, of course, to demonstrate that there was really no contradiction between the Scriptural and the geological accounts of the beginnings of the earth. The two versions of the story supported each other. Not only in this respect, but also in every other, the relation between the theologian and the "philosopher," that is to say, the scientist, he once told the student body at Andover Theological Seminary, should be one of mutual helpfulness and respect. Speaking before an audience of scientists in 1856, he repeated these sentiments and added that, when there was any dispute or contradiction, the opinion of the theologian is to be accepted. As late as 1886, Alexander Winchell, professor of geology and paleontology in the University of Michigan, was maintaining similar views. Geological investigations reveal the presence of deliberate intention, design, and plan in our world:

> How admirably the constitution of the Drift is suited to human wants! To us it looks as if it had been an intentional preparation for man. There are persons, however, who prefer to say it is not so; but man is here only because the situation is one which permits him to be here. But we are sure, at least, that a happy coördination exists between our necessities and our surroundings; and the constitution of things which brings enjoyment out of the coördination is a beneficient constitution.[1]

From the evidence which the geologist brings to our attention, then, we are able to assert that things fall into a pattern, a design. A design, however, is an idea, Winchell points out. A plan is not a thing but a "mental concept." It is a product of thought. If there is evidence of thought in the universe, then there is reason to conclude that there is mind at work, and this implies a personal being. A plan revealed implies the existence of a planner. "Intelligence is an attribute; it belongs to being; it does not act abstracted from being."[2] If we find evidence of many plans, we may assert the existence of many minds. If, underlying all the diverse aspects in which nature is presented to us, we find a single plan, "if the material world is underlaid and pervaded and operated by plan, method, law, then the world is a constant revelation of a present intelligence, an omnipresent and omniscient Being."[3] The underlying plan, the method of creation, revealed to us in both organic life and the geological study of the "formation of worlds" is evolution. This is Winchell's version of the testimony of the rocks; it is clear that it does not leave much room for disagreement between theology and geology.

These scientific theories of development were not the only sources of evolutionary ideas before Darwin. In the eighteenth century, there had been a widespread belief that, as human reason grasped more and more, there would be an inevitable improvement of man's life on earth. The romantic philosophies of nineteenth-century German thinkers like Hegel (1770-1831), Schelling (1775-1854), and Oken (1779-1851) transformed this faith in human reason into a somewhat evolutionary metaphysics in which progressive development was the Absolute manifesting itself through nature. These ideas were diffused in America in various ways. Johann Bernard Stallo, a German political emigrant to the United States, published a book, *General Principles of the Philosophy of Nature,* in which he summarized these theories. Echoes of German philosophy of nature came into the thought of the transcendentalists through their reading of Coleridge, and into the American mind because of the influence of the transcendentalists. From 1825 on, an increasing number of American students completed their education by spending a year or more in Germany, exposed to these ideas at their source. With increased respect for the method of German university instruction there went hand-in-hand increased attention to the content of German university instruction, especially in philosophy and theology. Even the German evolutionary theories of religion, based upon studies of the development of language and of literary types, were imported into the United States. Theodore Parker translated for the American audience the work of one member of this German critical school, Wilhelm Martin De Wette (1780-1849), and also expounded, especially in his later sermons and addresses, an evolutionary account of the development of religious ideas.

One of the most influential books in popularizing the new theories of nature and their developmental consequences was the *Kosmos* of Friedrich Alexander von Humboldt (1769-1859). This conspectus of the sciences was published between 1845 and 1858. Astronomy, meteorology, geology, botany, biology, zoology, anthropology — all the sciences of the time, were brought together into a systematic portrait of the cosmic order by a scientist of varied attainments who had won the respect of all Europe by his specialized studies. The stimulation Humboldt's *Kosmos* gave to the imagination of European and American thinkers led many to attempt the outlining of a speculative interpretation of its themes. The period is rich in attempts to formulate cosmic philosophies.

There was, finally, some acquaintance in the United States with such early historical-evolutionary theories as that of the French founder of sociology, Auguste Comte (1798-1857). Comte thought of society itself as passing through an evolutionary development which, he said, had three stages. The first of these was the theological stage in which explanations were given in terms of superstitious myths; this was followed by a metaphysical stage, in which explanations were couched in terms of entities of a transcendent and unknowable character; the final stage he called the "positive" or scientific. Here superstition and transcendental speculation gave way to a religion of humanity based upon the supremacy of science and the methods of science in all areas of human life. In the mid-nineteenth century, when utopian communities were being set up in America under many auspices, the Comtean religion of humanity was the impelling force behind the establishment of various communities, including the village of Modern Times, now called Brentwood, on Long Island.

We may grant that no one of these pre-evolutionary theories had a large circle of adherents. Yet if all be taken together as parts of the cultural pattern into which Spencerian and Darwinian evolution came at the time of the Civil War, we see that the seed of scientific evolution did not fall among stony places. It fell, rather, into well-prepared and fertile ground. Furthermore, when Darwin's *Origin of Species* appeared in the United States, it came with the best of scientific credentials. Spencer's early works were already known, and, at least in some quarters, approved. Asa Gray, Harvard's professor of botany, one of America's most respected scientists, gave Darwin's *Origin of Species* a careful and thoroughly critical, but none-the-less favorable review in 1860. James McCosh, the respectable Presbyterian president of Princeton, accepted Darwin's ideas and incorporated them into his philosophic position. McCosh insisted that, when errors had been sifted out of the evolutionary hypothesis, "this, like every other part of God's work, would illustrate his existence and his wisdom." [4] Because he believed that there was harmony between religion and evolutionary geology, he "let it be known to the upper classes of the college" that with certain limitations, and subject to certain explanations, he favored the theory of evolution.[5]

Yet we know that despite these favorable auspices, Darwin's theory and Spencer's extension of it did not receive widespread acceptance in the United States for about a quarter of a century. To account for the adverse response to the work of Darwin and Spencer, despite the apparently receptive climate of opinion, is our next problem. In order to do so, we must consider what modifications the evolutionary theory made in various non-biological fields.

Since most controversy arose over the relations between evolution and theology, it is with this question that we should begin our survey. Acceptance of the evolutionary hypothesis seemed to make a change in men's way of thinking about God. Evolutionary science explained the appearance of different varieties of living beings as a result of the regular operation of the laws of nature. Men who accepted this view had far less reason than their ancestors for regarding God as a personal Being who constantly and miraculously intervened in the governing of the world. In the tradition of Christian theology, God was Creator, Ruler, and Redeemer. For evolutionists a pattern of regularities replaced God the Ruler; and for many of them the gradual processes of development were tending to be thought of as a substitute for Divine Grace in Redemption. God was still thought of as Creator, but the character of His creation was changed. Acceptance of the developmental hypothesis reduced the omnipotent, omniscient, and omnipresent personal God of the theological tradition to a remote First Cause, who set the universe in motion and then left it severely alone, in the grip of a multitude of secondary causes. This was not a denial of God, and many people have come to see that evolutionary belief may be held side by side with a very high and noble form of belief in God. But the immediate impact of the theories of Darwin and Spencer, on dogmatic theologians especially, suggested that evolutionary thought was atheistic. Charles Hodge, professor of systematic theology at Princeton, entitled an attack on evolution *What is Darwinism?* which arrived at the answer that Darwinism was atheism! For, said Hodge, "An absent God who does nothing is, to us, no God." [6]

There were other less serious effects of the acceptance of evolutionary ideas on religious thinking. The Scriptural account of a series of special creations conflicted directly with the principle of the developmental continuity of different species. Biblical chronology, painstakingly worked out in the seventeenth century by James Ussher, Archbishop of Armagh, so that the very children knew not only the date, but also the exact hour of the creation, bore no relation to the eras of evolutionary time, and even less to the preceding eons of geological time. The religious doctrine of man as a being created a little lower than the angels fell before the impact of Darwin's *Descent of Man,* which showed him to be but little higher than the beasts, and that little only after countless millennia of development. On the whole it is not to be wondered at that members of the orthodox clergy and their parishioners distrusted evolution.

Religious liberals could accept evolutionary ideas with less difficulty than their conservative fellows because their beliefs were more flexible, and less rigid and doctrinaire. For liberals the Scriptures were not divinely revealed truth, but inspiring records of human achievement set in a framework of mythology and primitive cosmic hypotheses, and these men welcomed contradictions between geological or evolutional accounts of beginnings and the biblical account as evidence of the advances of man's understanding of nature. Moreover, liberals in religion found the new sciences a useful ally in the struggle against orthodoxy. There was, the Unitarian Minot J. Savage insisted, an "irrepressible conflict between two world-theories,"[7] orthodox Christianity and evolutionary thought. "The inevitable surrender of orthodoxy" was the outcome he envisaged. Any attempt to harmonize Genesis and geology, evangelism and evolution, is futile. "The earnest world is getting tired of this business of reconciliation."[8] Religious liberals felt comfortable and at home with the Spencerian view of evolution as inevitable moral and social progress. They found in this position a substitute for the doctrine of the fall of man from which he could be saved only by the arbitrary and unpredictable grace of God.

It was among religious liberals that attempts to develop an evolutionary ethics were made. They were most ready to permit the extension of the theory beyond the limits of the science of biology and to allow it to rank as a universal method. Evolution, a biological hypothesis, was transformed in the minds of many liberals into evolutionism, a cosmic doctrine. When thus extended in its application, evolutionism became the dominant factor in the interpretation of any organic change. By a still greater extension, it was used as a basis for the interpretation of human history and the history of human ideas. George Harris, first a professor at Andover Theological Seminary in its liberal period, and later president of Amherst College, remarked quietly in his book on *Moral Evolution* that "It has become an important interest, both in the extent of its application and as readjusting and even revolutionizing long-accepted theories of man and society." [9] From Harris' book and others like it we learn that codes of moral behavior were no longer regarded as having been established by Divine decree, but rather as having developed over a long period of time out of some animal instinct. Each moral practice enshrined in a code reached that status by having "established itself as an advantage in the long struggle of the human species for existence and supremacy." [10] Thinkers sympathetic to this view did not regard evolution as morality, but rather as a method of approach which would enable us to understand morality. Man's moral ideals evolve out of the instincts of animal species as man's physical structure has evolved out of the structures of animal species. Darwin had maintained that natural selection operates to insure the survival of those physical variations which are most advantageous to the species in its struggle for existence. Liberal evolutionary moralists held that a similar principle assures the survival of advantageous ethical variations.

There was less uniformity and less optimism in the interpretations of what Darwin's views meant to social theory. Catch phrases of evolutionism like "the struggle for survival" and "survival of the fittest" were susceptible to various interpretations, each leading to a different social theory. If the struggle is understood as a contest between individuals within a species, as it was by the sociologist William Graham Sumner of Yale, then altruism, any concern whatever for the welfare of others, is a handicap to the man who might otherwise be one of "the fittest" and therefore entitled to survive. Social organization has an essentially unsocial purpose, the protection of the property already acquired by those who are fit to survive. This sort of police power is for Sumner the only legitimate function of government. The struggle for survival, whatever it may have been in earlier periods, is in our age an economic struggle, and fitness to survive is measured by financial success. Thus, in Sumner's theory of "social Darwinism" evolutionary biology is used as the rationale for a predatory and completely competitive capitalism. If, however, the struggle for survival is taken to be a contest among different species, if each species is thought to be vying with every other species for its foothold on earth, as Lester Frank Ward believed, then the identical evolutionary theory can become the justification for a welfare state. Social organization would have as its primary purpose the improvement of the human species by raising the quality of its inferior members, thus giving it a better chance to win out over other species, and to become the fittest to survive of all species.

Metaphysically, the most significant effect of the evolutionary theory on philosophic thought was the increased importance given to the idea of change. Plato had suggested the view, which over the centuries had become the common coin of the philosophic realm, that only the permanent, fixed, and unchanging was worthy to be dignified with the title of Reality. The changing, the impermanent, and the temporary was only apparent. To understand the fixed principles of Being was the only goal worthy of the philosopher. Concern with Becoming, with change, was an unworthy occupation. Human experience was experience of Becoming; it was impossible, Heraclitus had pointed out, to step into the same river twice. Philosophy was the art of getting beyond the flux of human experience to the underlying structure of Reality. With the widespread acceptance of evolutionary ideas, it began to be said that perhaps change and not permanence was the pattern of reality. For evolution, growth and Becoming were more vital than structure and Being, and the more important question was not what anything was, but how it had evolved. Under the spell of evolution, James Mark Baldwin wrote of the "genetic theory of reality," and Charles Sanders Peirce developed his theory of "evolutionary love" as an ultimate cosmic category.

Other consequences of the impact of Darwin on American philosophy will emerge in later chapters. These few suggestions are put forward here as a prelude to the examination of three major attempts to formulate philosophical systems on an evolutionary basis — the "cosmic philosophy" of John Fiske, the positivistic "psychozoölogy" of Chauncey Wright, and the "scientific realism" of Francis Ellingwood Abbot.

II. COSMIC PHILOSOPHY: JOHN FISKE

When the early works of Herbert Spencer, interpreting the evolution of society and its institutions in terms drawn from biology, reached America, they came into a climate of opinion which was favorably disposed toward evolutionary ideas. Yet they did not meet with the warm and immediate acceptance which might have seemed likely. It was not so much their evolutionary content which led American thinkers to hesitate about adopting Spencer's ideas as it was their agnosticism, which many Americans felt to be a thin disguise for secularism. Yet there were some who were not bothered by Spencer's "Unknowable," but felt that his position could be made consistent with an acceptable theistic belief. Chief among these American followers of Spencer was John Fiske (1842-1901), who was convinced in early youth, even before his twentieth birthday, that Spencer was the greatest of thinkers. Before he became much older, however, Fiske came to the view that his interpretation of Spencer was better Spencerianism than Spencer's own. Thus, while Fiske remained a disciple, there were many points on which he differed from his master.

In 1860, when Fiske was eighteen, he reviewed the *History of Civilization in England* of Henry Thomas Buckle (1821-1861). In the course of this early review he found occasion to explain his general outlook, to express his admiration for Spencer, and to indicate the place which, to his mind, Spencer held in the history of thought. Fiske believed, he said, that there are "fixed and ascertainable" laws to which social changes conform, just as there are such laws for physical process. The opposite view, that social changes are unpredictable, he describes as an illusion, induced partly by the insistence on supernatural and miraculous intervention in the affairs of the material world, partly by the insistence on the ultimate inexplicability of human agency, and partly because men persist in looking upon social facts as isolated individual cases rather than as related patterns of events which are subject to scientific explanation. The late development of social science is the result of its inherent difficulty and of the dependence of social science on the relatively simpler physical sciences. As long as the physical sciences were "metaphysical," they could not develop fully, and the social sciences were retarded. When physical science was "purified" of its metaphysical taint, "the conception of a universal and undeviating regularity in the succession of historic events was rendered possible." [11] There was, said Fiske, no science of society until modern times; Machiavelli, Vico, and Montesquieu began the work, Condorcet, and especially Voltaire, carried it on in the eighteenth century. But he insisted that not until the *Positive Philosophy* of Auguste Comte was there a true social science, in which social changes were shown to conform to invariable laws. Comte failed, however, to grasp the all-embracing law of evolution, the fundamental law under which human history and natural history can both be explained. This step was reserved for Herbert Spencer. Fiske enthusiastically proclaimed:

> This sublime discovery, — that the Universe is in a continuous process of evolution from the homogeneous to the heterogeneous, — with which only Newton's discovery of the law of gravitation is at all worthy to be compared, underlies not only physics, but also history. It reveals the law to which social changes conform.[12]

As these sentences suggest, Fiske threw all caution to the winds in his readiness to accept the principle of evolution as the overarching, transcendent explanation of everything in the universe; he was prepared to use the principle as the basis of a "cosmic" philosophy. Originally his intention in the work which came to be called *Outlines of Cosmic Philosophy* was merely to compose a series of essays illustrating, elucidating, and amplifying Spencer's "Synthetic philosophy." Fiske thought that "cosmic" was a better term for what Spencer meant than Spencer's own phrasing. Spencer disagreed, urging upon Fiske the consideration that in a certain sense every philosophic system, since it attempts an explanation of the universe (or Cosmos), can be called "cosmic." Fiske replied, in the same vein, that every philosophy, inasmuch as it attempts to formulate a synthesis of our knowledge about various aspects of the universe, can be called "synthetic." On the other hand, he defended his use of "cosmic" by a series of three arguments, each of which had as its purpose to show how one current philosophy with which Fiske disagreed was excluded by the term. First, cosmos means not only the totality of phenomena but also their order, pattern, and regularity; no theological system which admits of miracles, supernatural interpositions, or special creations can be cosmic, because it permits the violation of order. Second, no "ontological" or metaphysical system can be cosmic, because it discusses ideal entities which are not of the cosmos, or phenomenal universe. Third, no "positivistic" philosophy can be cosmic, because all such systems deny the possibility of a unified account of the universe. Thus Fiske defended his use of "cosmic" against Spencer's criticism. It may seem that so minor and merely verbal a difference as this between Fiske and his master was trivial and scarcely worthy of being remembered. But it is important as an indication that Fiske never carried his idolatry to the point of considering Spencer infallible and beyond criticism. This minor deviation was symptomatic of real differences in the views of the two men, which led to important divergences in the positions they took on more important questions.

One of these major differences between Fiske's outlook and that of Spencer was a matter of perspective. Spencer was a liberal social reformer, within the meaning of the word "liberal" in the nineteenth century, and had studied the natural sciences; he was not expert in any one science, but familiar with all, and his interest in them was comparative. He attempted to apply the methods of the natural sciences, and even, on some occasions, their results, to the formulation of social science as a program of social reform. Fiske, on the other hand, had very little knowledge of the natural sciences and very little concern for them, and was not interested in social reform. He was most ardently devoted to the study of history and to humanistic literature, and, indeed, he achieved his chief fame as a historian. Despite his recognition of the need for a scientific structure in the social studies, he never really achieved the view of social science as a natural science which is so characteristic of Spencer. Because of this major difference between his interests and Spencer's, Fiske gives far greater prominence in his discussions to the problem of human development, such as the laws of human history, the evolution of belief, religion, and (his point of chief originality and major contribution to evolutionary philosophy) the role of prolonged human infancy in the inauguration of the process of the evolution of society. Because of such differences it may fairly be said that Fiske's philosophy marks a growth beyond Spencer.

In its beginnings Fiske's theory of knowledge follows Spencer's closely to reach the conclusion that we can know only that which is caused, which is finite, and which is relative. By the nature of the knowing process, we are forever barred from knowledge of the Absolute, the Infinite, and the Uncaused. Because the ultimate nature of matter and mind must transcend the finite, we can affirm nothing whatever concerning this question. All that we can mean by knowledge is the classification of the states of consciousness produced in us by unknown external agencies. These external agencies must remain unknown in their essence; we can know only the appearances of things, not things-in-themselves. Our knowledge is forever limited by our own human limitations. What we know, then, under these restricted conditions, is not things as they really are apart from our knowing of them, but only things as they appear to us in the process of knowing. Thus, truth is never about things but always about our relation to things. For humans, a true proposition is one whose negation is inconceivable to the human mind. Thus far, Fiske has traveled with Spencer, but here, where Spencer stops, Fiske allows for the possibility that there might exist some other being who can conceive what is humanly inconceivable; the knowledge had by such a being would, of course, be superhuman knowledge and that being's truth would be superhuman truth. Thus, although Fiske's basic position is like that of Spencer and is rooted in human experience in a way that is usual in the tradition of British empiricism, Fiske's acknowledgment of the possibility of superhuman knowledge by a superhuman being brings him far closer to conventional theistic idealism.

Again, Fiske's discussion of causation, although its foundations were in general agreement with Spencer's views, illustrates excellently how minor differences in initial perspective led to major differences in outcome. Spencer, out of his background in the natural sciences, treated questions of causal sequence in terms of the persistence of force, a physical view. Fiske, because of his historical and literary bent, discussed the nature of causation in the context of the relativity of human knowledge. He emphasized especially the impossibility of our discovering what the true nature of causal connection is, since, according to his theory of knowledge, discussed above, we can know only the state of our consciousness produced by causal connection, and not the causal connection itself. But although the nature of causation is inscrutable because of our human limitations, a denial of the existence of objective causal connection is inconceivable to us; we must therefore hold the law of causation, that every finite event must have a cause, as a necessary truth. Reflection on this law had long ago led to the realization that insofar as these causes of finite events were themselves finite, they too must have causes. The process of discovering the finite causes of finite causes might be indefinitely prolonged without getting any closer to a real beginning, unless, somewhere along the line, the process is halted by the postulation of a First Cause, or Uncaused Cause. This First Cause could not conceivably be finite, else it, too, would have to be caused. The First Cause, therefore, came to be regarded as God, and, in the course of time, the various personal attributes of the Deity became attached to the pure philosophic concept of First Cause. Fiske maintained that if anthropomorphic attributes were gradually eliminated from the idea of a First Cause, we would be left with a conception which might be the object of worship. He himself expressed his thought thus: The First Cause is that which "is the proper object of religious feeling, but concerning the nature of which — in itself, and apart from its phenomenal manifestations — the human mind can form no varifiable hypothesis."[13]

This belief amounts to the same thing as Spencer's "Unknowable," but is far less harsh in its wording. By making judicious changes in the form in which the idea is expressed, Fiske has turned Spencer's agnostic concept into one which is more available for purposes of worship. Fiske was suggesting that his Cosmic Theism could replace Anthropomorphic Theism, but that with this change the churches could function as before. It was not part of the effect of science to lead us away from religion, but rather, as Fiske suggests in the title of one of his books, we are led *Through Nature to God*. "The hostility between Science and Religion, about which so much is talked and written, is purely a chimera of the imagination."[14] Indeed, for Fiske it could scarcely be otherwise; science is human knowledge and religion is human aspiration. No evolutionist like Fiske, with the optimistic faith which Spencer induced, could be led to argue for a "radical hostility" between our knowledge and our aspirations, for this would imply "a fundamental viciousness in the constitution of things."[15] Fiske discussed religious themes in many of his philosophical writings, and, as his life moved toward its close, he became more and more concerned with asserting the theistic outcomes of his cosmic philosophy. An interesting and excellent example of this direction in his thought is to be found in the address he delivered at the Concord Summer School of Philosophy in 1885.

This address was Fiske's contribution to a noteworthy symposium. Each year, in addition to its lectures in course, the Concord Summer School, which had been started by Bronson Alcott to acquaint philosophical circles in New England with the work being done by William Torrey Harris and his group of Hegelians in St. Louis, held a symposium on some outstanding issue of the day. In 1885 the topic was "Does Modern Science Lead to Pantheism?" In addition to Fiske, other of the participants included Francis E. Abbot, whose ideas will be discussed in Section IV of this chapter, George Holmes Howison, then active in the St. Louis group (see Chapter 6, section I), and Edmund Montgomery, the philosopher-biologist of Liendo plantation in Texas, whose researches on protoplasm and studies in Kantian theory of knowledge were combined strikingly into his *Philosophical Problems in the Light of Vital Organization.*

Fiske's address was intended to show that science has not asserted any distinction between natural law and divine law. "That distinction is historically derived from a loose habit of philosophizing characteristic of ignorant ages, and was bequeathed to modern times by the theology of the Latin church." [16] If one accepted the distinction as given by the theologians, the idea that divine activity is expressed by miraculous violation of the orderliness of nature, it might be possible to be an atheist. But if, instead, one grounds his thought in "the higher theism of Clement and Athanasius," if one really believes in "an ever-present God, without whom not a sparrow falls to the ground," [17] the false distinction between divine and natural law disappears. Warranted and attested natural law describes various orderly modes in which God acts. "The thinker in whose mind divine action is thus identified with orderly action, and to whom a really irregular phenomenon would seem like a manifestation of sheer diabolism, foresees in every possible extension of knowledge a fresh confirmation of his faith in God." [18] Scientific inquiry leads man to worship the God he finds everywhere in evidence in the natural order. "Each act of scientific explanation but reveals an opening through which shines the glory of the Eternal Majesty." [19] This is a far cry from Spencer's "Unknowable," yet, in its beginnings, Fiske's view seemed to differ only verbally from Spencer's.

An interesting difference between Spencer and Fiske comes out in the course of their writings when they discuss the sources of energy on earth. One question in this area concerns the relation between energy as known to us in physical phenomena and energy as manifested in mental or nervous phenomena. Spencer, as we have pointed out earlier, tended toward a physicalist view and, as far as possible, tried to reduce his discussion of non-physical phenomena to physical terms. This reductive tendency in his thought led him to maintain that physical energies are transformed into mental processes. His work is one of a long series of attempts to assimilate the operations of mind to those of matter. Fiske, on the other hand, never asserted such a transformation of energies as Spencer outlined. He believed, rather, that there is a correspondence or correlation between physical and psychical energies, that there is a "psychophysical parallelism." He went so far as to say "There is no such thing as a change in consciousness which has not for its correlative a chemical change in nervous tissue," [20] but he would not say either that the chemical change causes the change in consciousness, or that the chemical change becomes or is transformed into a change of consciousness. He went as far as he could when he accepted psychophysical parallelism; he insisted that "the gulf between the phenomena of consciousness and all other phenomena is an impassable gulf," [21] and that, therefore, there could be correspondence, but never transformation.

Thus far, in suggesting the chief aspects of Fiske's thought, we have been able to show his growing divergence from the ideas of Herbert Spencer and to explain this divergence by temperamental differences between the two men and by fundamental dissimilarities in their interests. We have seen Fiske achieve independence from the man he still named as his master. This independence led him to formulate his chief original idea, one without a source in Spencer's philosophy. Fiske expressed this new idea briefly in his *Outlines of Cosmic Philosophy*, and gave it fuller treatment in an essay on "The Meaning of Infancy." In this essay he undertook to trace the natural roots of the moral and social feelings of the human species to man's relatively prolonged period of infancy.

The human brain, he asserted, unlike the brain of other animals, passes through the most important stages of its development after birth. Compared with the young of any other species, the newborn human infant has very few fully developed capacities; yet in his dependent years, his years of infancy, he must learn a far wider range of behavior patterns than any other animal. There is no way in which so complex a brain as that of man can be given full opportunity to develop except by lengthening the period of dependence. Those members of the pre-human stock whose parents took good care of them would be most likely to survive; thus, natural selection would operate to preserve those individuals who were most likely to extend to their own offspring a care comparable with that which they had received. In this evolutionary fashion there must have come about a gradual growth of parental interest in and concern for the young. A relatively stable, if simple, family organization and ultimately clan groupings and civil society itself developed, he thought, out of the impulse to see the human young through their prolonged infancy. Paralleling this social development, Fiske believed that there was an evolution of moral qualities. This, too, he explained in terms of a process of natural selection. Those offspring would be most likely to survive whose parents took care of them best and longest; such parents, however, would be those in whom the virtues of sympathy were present in embryonic form. Their offspring, too, would be most likely to have the sympathetic virtues, and to pass them on to their children. It was by this process, he thought, that humane sentiment ultimately extended to the entire human race.

With the aid of this theory, Fiske made an evolutionary pattern of thought the basis of both morality and sociality, including both of these areas of human concern under his one "cosmic" principle of evolutionism. In his extension of the evolutionary principle from the biological science in which it had originated into a fundamental law of the structure of the universe, Fiske presents us with an extreme case of the philosopher overwhelmed by a scientific concept.

III. POSITIVISTIC PSYCHOZOÖLOGY: CHAUNCEY WRIGHT

Chauncey Wright died in 1875 at the age of forty-five. He was an obscure mathematician who supported himself by making computations for a nautical almanac. By working night and day, putting himself under tremendous strain, he finished each year's assigned work in two months, thus freeing himself in the remaining ten months for the reading and thinking and conversation with friends which made up his real life. For a short time he taught philosophy in a girls' school owned by Louis Agassiz. Twice in his life he taught at Harvard; the first time he had a temporary, one-year appointment to teach psychology. The second appointment, to teach mathematical physics, was to have been permanent, but it came less than a year before his untimely death. His writings, mostly reviews in *The Nation* and *The North American Review*, lack stylistic grace and are frequently difficult to read. His one extended article,

"The Evolution of Self-Consciousness," seems to be a preparatory study for a systematic work which he never started.

Yet, after the lapse of three quarters of a century, this dim figure emerges as one of the thinkers whose activity was central to the development of evolutionary naturalism in America. He helped Charles Peirce, William James, Oliver Wendell Holmes, Jr., and other friends to bring the seeds of their own thought to maturity. For a time his own few writings were almost forgotten and his name remembered only because of his relation to his better known friends. Today, however, Wright is regarded less and less as an adjunct to Peirce or James or Holmes, and more as a thinker in his own right, even though his contributions were more largely critical than constructive. In part, at least, the increased respect given to Wright in recent times is the result of a present-day shift, to some extent, to a view like his — that philosophic thought must be carried on with a precision and rigor comparable to that of the exact sciences. Wright believed that no statement, however widely it might be accepted or by whatever authority it might be sanctioned, should be taken as true without examination. It is conceivable that his earnest attempt to carry this principle out in his philosophic activity was responsible for his failure to leave a systematic work. His thought must be worked out from scattered suggestions embodied chiefly in critical works; it does not form an organized whole.

His sceptical temper led him to be especially dubious about those broad and poetic generalizations which have no foundation in verifiable human experience. He distrusted any explanation of our universe which introduced elements from beyond the universe. The dominant tendency of Wright's philosophic as well as of his scientific thought was opposition to making any one principle of explanation into the explanation of everything. Thus, although Chauncey Wright was one of the first American thinkers to accept Darwinian evolution as a biological hypothesis, unlike John Fiske, he refused to transform evolution into a cosmic hypothesis. Here, as in moral and religious matters, too, he opposed the "transcendental" tendency to make the propositions of any one discipline the basic principles of all. His anti-transcendental view came out very clearly in a letter to one of his regular correspondents, Miss Grace Norton, who had asked him "Why do *we* exist?" Wright replied by denying the relevance to our lives of any ulterior spiritual ends. "All the ends of life are, I am persuaded, within the sphere of life, and are in the last analysis, or highest generalization, to be found in the preservation, continuance, and increase of life itself." [22]

The key to Wright's opposition to transcendentalism was, then, his belief that there was no single, inclusive, metaphysical system which would serve as the foundation for discussion of matters of fact and evaluations. The position which he maintained involved a Baconian distrust and abandonment of traditional metaphysical thinking based upon eternal and immutable principles known to the human "Reason" prior to experience. For this type of thinking Wright substituted an emphasis on particular observations and experiments, leading to a step-by-step advancement of knowledge. He thought of scientific research as the best example of the search for factual knowledge, un-affected by any bias of the scientist or pressure from the social environment within which the scientist functioned, and subject at all stages to processes of verification by sense experience. This verification he considered an important part of scientific method. He ascribed the superiority of modern science over that of any previous era to the incessant insistence by the modern scientist on the empirical verification of all proposed hypotheses. Like Auguste Comte, the founder of Positivism, he proposed to rescue the pursuit of truth from the by-paths into which it was led by the emotional attachment of truth-seekers to the traditions of theology or metaphysics.

He demanded the freedom of the scientific investigator from all forms of external controls such as might be imposed by metaphysical, theological, or ethical systems. Although he found much in the thought of Comte with which he was in accord, he was too much of a sceptic to accept Positivism as a doctrinal position. He was con-sistent in including this in his rejection of all cosmic generalizations, even that derived from the Darwinian theory of evolution. To main-tain his position, he argued that philosophy is primarily concerned with method, and should not be characterized either as a positive doctrine or as a peculiar mode of intuitive knowledge. Wright took over Comte's classification of thought into theological, metaphysical, and scientific stages and agreed with Comte that these stages ap-peared successively. He maintained, however, that later in the history of any mature civilization all three stages exist at the same time; men have all three patterns of thought available to them. Of the three coexistent methods, Wright tried to limit himself to the third, scientific method. In his thought, the relation between philosophy and science was very close.

What he attacked as "metaphysical" thinking was the tendency to transform the words used in the explanation of observed phenomena into independently existing powers operating in the universe. He regarded the tendency to change names into powers by this sort of "personification" as a survival of a "savage and semi-barbarous mind" [23] and applied to it Professor Masson's phrase "ontological faith." Wright insisted that "Names are directly the designations of things, not of hidden powers, or wills, in things." [24] The frequently-offered defense that both theology and metaphysics keep alive the sense of mystery and devotion which science's attention to brute fact destroys he considered a poor argument. He felt that metaphysical (and, even more, theological) thinking nourishes a passive sentiment of mystery and devotion, symbolized in religious worship, and leading to the obedience of absolute submissiveness. The scientific mode of thought, on the other hand, fosters both mystery and devotion in active forms — mystery as the more sober and responsible ally of inquisitiveness, "inciting and guiding it, giving it steadiness and seriousness, opposing only its waywardness and idleness," [25] while devotion takes the active forms of usefulness and duty, and is allied to freedom. The passivity of the metaphysical mode leads it to stand in awe before the unknown; the activity of the scientific mode leads it to explore the unknown. Science develops abstract principles, it is true, but it develops them not as "summaries of truth" but as useful aids in enlarging "our concrete knowledge of nature." General principles in science are "working ideas," not finalities, but "finders." [26]

William James summed up the positivistic quality of Wright's thought in an obituary notice in *The Nation*. After taking note that Wright's way of looking at the universe did not allow for either pessimism or optimism, but was entirely neutral, and after pointing out that, unlike other men, Wright seemed most interested in an idea when it had least relation to human destiny, James went on to say that "when the mere actuality of phenomena will suffice to describe them, he held it pure excess and superstition to speak of a metaphysical whence or whither, of a substance, a meaning, or an end." James continued by saying that Wright condemned especially, "as a metaphysical idol," the concept of substance. Then, when his questioners would insist that there must be "some glue" to hold together the diverse phenomena of experience, Wright would reply "that there is no need of a glue to join things unless we apprehend some reason why they should fall asunder. Phenomena *are* grouped — more we cannot say of them." [27]

It is worth noting that Wright rejected not only the cosmic generalizations of Positivism and Evolutionism which were current in his day, but also the more traditional patterns of Idealism and Materialism. Either of these positions, if it were accepted to the exclusion of the other, would be unsatisfactory and partial. His devotion to science never led him to make extravagant claims for it; science remained for him "metaphysically neutral." He did not seek the confounding of religion by his advocacy of science. On the other hand, he did not believe religion and ethics to be necessarily linked. The domination of morality by theology aroused his special resentment because one historical result of making ethics dependent upon theology had been to distort and decry the values of the present human life. Wright attacked the view expressed by some believers that theological doubts imply moral disintegration and carry with them "contempt for all that is noble and worthy in human character." [28] For himself, he preferred to invert the usual linkage and to discuss the relation between ethics and religion in terms of the historical interpretation that moral views developed before religious ideas, and that, therefore, theological beliefs are accepted largely because of their traditional association with humanly satisfactory moral ideas. Science, ethics, and religion are related but independent aspects of man's life in the universe.

In a series of discussions with Charles Darwin, while Wright was visiting England in 1872, he agreed, as he explained in a letter to one of his friends, "some time to write an essay on matters covering the ground of certain common interests and studies . . . for which the learned title is adopted of *Psychozoölogy* . . . in order to give the requisite subordination of consciousness in men and animals to their development and general relations to nature." [29] As far as one can judge from the fragmentary evidence of his letters, this essay, had it ever been written, would have been a final statement of Wright's philosophic position, a combination of the utilitarianism of John Stuart Mill and a Darwinian evolutionary approach with whatever insights of his own had managed to survive the application of his rigorous standards of criticism. There are hints in various letters of what the position might have been. And, in his article of 1873 on "The Evolution of Self-Consciousness," there seems to be a preliminary statement, a clearing of the ground and building a foundation for the unwritten system.

In beginning his account of "The Evolution of Self-Consciousness," Wright asserts that men have come to recognize that the hypothesis of organic evolution as applied to the human race fits the facts more simply and with fewer difficulties than any other theory. Yet there is great reluctance to admit that self-consciousness can also be accounted for as of natural origin and evolutionary development. This is, in part, the result of a misunderstanding of the theory of evolution. Wright suggests that the outcome can differ only in degree, not in kind, from its source. New powers do not arise where nothing was before. New uses for old powers do appear, and although there is a gradual increase in the strength and serviceableness of these new uses, their characters are distinct from the outset. Thus each new use of an old power first appears as an incidental or accidental addition to old functions. Many of the powers of the human being have such multiple functions. Thus, even though the self-consciousness of man may never have been anticipated in pre-human acts, yet it "may have been involved potentially in pre-existing powers or causes." [30] Novelty in appearance may be explainable on natural grounds; it is idle to rush in with a miraculous or supernatural explanation. That self-consciousness is distinctively human does not eliminate the possibility that it is a development of latent or potential characteristics of simpler biological powers. There are "manifestations of mind" in animals. It is characteristic of "mysticism," which still is dominant in the science of mind, to attempt to enlarge the "really profound distinction" between human and animal consciousness in order to feed man's "feeling of absolute worthiness." This provides a simple, if unsatisfactory, answer to the question of the origin of self-consciousness. Less simple, but more in accord with the facts, is a scientific explanation of the phenomena of human self-consciousness in terms of the psychological antecedents in animal life. Man's reflective use of consciousness arises in the course of development of new functions for the mental powers of animals.

Much of the mental action of animals has hitherto been classified as instinctive and sharply contrasted with the intelligence of man's mental action. Wright thinks that this contrast has been made too much of; "the distinction of instinct and intelligence, though not less real and important in the classification of actions in psycho-zoölogy, and as important even as that of animal and vegetable is in general zoölogy, or the distinctions of organic and inorganic, living and dead, in the general science of life, is yet, like these, in its applications a vague and ill-defined distinction." [31] All these distinctions, vital as they may seem to a static account of the universe and its phenomena, become merely rough classifications for some momentary or special purpose when we turn to the sort of dynamic and functional analysis to which we are led by the evolutionary mode of thought. Each of these contrasts opposes crudely two extreme terms in a series; the contrast may be clear at the extremities, but it is difficult to define the point of division.

Wright's point might be expressed thus: Consciousness is found not only in man, but also, in elementary forms, in animals; the novel use of consciousness which arises in the human species is its reflective use. This reflective use leads the user to distinguish in memory "the phenomena of signification from those of outward perception," [32] that is, to distinguish between objects or events and the signs, whether vocal, gestural or graphic, by which men recall objects or events. Outward objects themselves can not be brought altogether under the control of the will; the inward signs can be. The signs, then, are seen to form "a little representative world arising to thought at will." [33] Aspects of human experience are classified as belonging to the object world of things or to the subject world of signs. The distinction of subject and object is not a foundational intuition, but an analytic discrimination within experience. It is not so much the *use* of signs that marks the distinction between man and animal; it is the fact that man *recognizes* his own use of signs. He is able to focus his attention on the sign, to think about thoughts, as well as to think about things. "Reflection would thus be, not what most metaphysicians appear to regard it, a fundamentally new faculty in man, as elementary and primordial as memory itself, or the power of abstractive attention, or the function of signs and representative images in generalization; but it would be determined in its contrasts with other mental faculties by the nature of its objects." [34] Out of consciousness, by reflection, comes self-consciousness. "The consummate self-consciousness expressed by 'I think,' needed for its genesis only the power of attending to the phenomena of thought as signs of other thoughts, or of images received from memory, with a reference of them to a subject." [35]

Wright sketched incidentally, in the course of this discussion, a parallel account of the genesis of language. Pre-language consists of the instinctive gestural use, not necessarily purposeful, of the voice, and the bodily organs; animals and men share this activity. Out of random sounds and movements, language was invented by men for social ends, in order to communicate with each other. The choice of sound or gesture in any particular instance might be in terms of some arbitrary association of the sign with what it signified. In this stage, language cannot be construed as determined by conscious invention; it *serves* a purpose, but its inventors can scarcely be said to *have* a purpose. Language becomes a conscious invention when the "secondary motives" are connected with "making our thoughts clearer to ourselves, and not merely of communicating them to others." [36] In its first, or social stage, and in its second, or mnemonic and meditative stage, language appears clearly as a system of inventions. This aspect of language is less apparent in the third, or traditional, stage of language functioning. Customs of linguistic usage develop, and it becomes less easily possible for the will of an individual to make changes in language. Once this point had been reached, the development of dialectal varieties, distinct languages, and linguistic families "present[s] precise parallels to the developments and relations in the organic world which the theory of natural selection supposes." [37] However arbitrary and subject to the will of the individual language development may have been in its inception, in later stages it becomes subject to natural law, rather than human caprice.

Even these briefly suggested themes indicate that, had Chauncey Wright lived, and had he overcome his preference for talking rather than writing, the systematic psychozoölogy of which this was the foundation might well have made an important and original contribution to American philosophy. For our present purposes, however, these fragmentary insights can serve to reveal to us that neither the transcendental nor the cosmic philosophies had altogether clear sailing in late nineteenth-century America. To survive they would have had to overcome philosophies like Wright's positivistic psychozoölogy. This, it seems from our retrospective position, they had neither the vigor nor the rigor to do.

IV. SCIENTIFIC REALISM:
FRANCIS ELLINGWOOD ABBOT

One of the more interesting philosophic developments on an evolutionary base was the complex and subtle realism of Francis Ellingwood Abbot. It was Abbot's distinction, only recently recognized, to have anticipated in the nineteenth century some of the more characteristic themes of twentieth-century American philosophy. He had a bold mind and considerable analytic ability. As a result of his conscientious following of the paths his thought discovered, however, his professional and intellectual life was not too happy. Though personally mild in temperament, he became a stormy petrel of American intellectual life, never quite accepted in the academic world, yet always too preoccupied with abstract and theoretical considerations to be completely at ease outside college walls. As early as 1866, when Abbot was thirty, he was considered for a teaching position at Harvard; his unconventional religious views were unquestionably a factor in his failure to receive this unsought nomination. In 1888, he replaced Josiah Royce (see Chapter 6, section III) at Harvard for one year; all that this led to was an unpleasant situation in which not only Abbot and Royce, but also William James and Charles Sanders Peirce became involved. Charges and countercharges were aired in open letters, some published as pamphlets and some in the correspondence columns of *The Nation*. In 1893, after the death of his wife, Abbot went into semi-retirement and spent ten years in the writing of a statement in two volumes of the elements of his philosophic position. When this book was completed, he added a brief preface setting down some of the main purposes of his life, and then, in October 1903, he went to the cemetery and killed himself on his wife's grave.

Abbot's philosophic awakening came about as a result of his dissatisfaction with the Law of the Conditioned, as stated by Sir William Hamilton (1788-1856), the last major philosopher in the Scottish tradition. Hamilton held that men can conceive only that which is conditioned, limited, or finite. The unconditioned, absolute, or infinite is inconceivable. The conditioned, that which is thinkable, lies between two extremes, each of which is unconditioned and, therefore, inconceivable. These two extremes are polar opposites; they are mutually exclusive or contradictory. One of these extremes is that of Absolute Limitation, the other that of Infinite Illimitation. Human knowledge, then, extends over part of a scale whose lower end, the zero, is unknowable, and whose upper end, the infinite, is also unknowable. When Abbot first read this, soon after his graduation from Harvard, he made a note recording his opposition to it. In this early note, he tells us, he maintained that space *is known* to be infinite, because it *is* infinite, and can not be otherwise; that is, that in at least this one case, something infinite and unconditioned is known. It is the infinity, the being infinite, of space which determines its being known as infinite. In knowledge, he said, the object (in this case, space), determines the subject or knower, rather than the reverse. Even before his first published articles, he had come to one of his central positions, one which he developed and matured throughout his career, the principle of philosophical objectivism.

In Abbot's first articles, both published in the *North American Review* in 1864, "The Philosophy of Space and Time" and "The Conditioned and the Unconditioned," this comment on Hamilton was amplified into a careful criticism of the views of Kant and Spencer as well as those of Hamilton. In the first of these articles Abbot deduced the germ of two important principles from his objectivism. First, he maintained that there is a perceptive understanding which immediately apprehends relations. Second, he suggested, without any amplification, that these relations are objective, and not introduced by the mind. "If we really *know* the objective relations of things, there must be some pure and immediate cognition of relations." [38] For the most part, however, these early articles did not develop Abbot's constructive position, but only made it clear that he was heartily opposed to any view which drew matter or motion, space or time into the mind of the thinker, as subjective ideas without any objective reference. At about the same time, however, he began to work out the consequences of his view that relations are objective. In a later statement Abbot claimed that, in 1864, he had formulated a three-fold division of existences — into existent things, existent relations, and existent conditions with a consequent division of perception into three classes — sensuous perception of existent things, intellectual perception of existent relations, and rational perception of existent conditions. It is his own claim that his entire philosophic position is a necessary outgrowth of these distinctions, derived from them by the principle of absolute logic, and serving as a solid and permanent foundation for objectivism and realism.

The principle of absolute logic means for Abbot the identity in difference of opposites, and represents in his thought the survival of Hegel's dialectic method. Abbot repeatedly expressed his distaste for the philosophic conclusions which Hegel derived by the application of his method, yet Abbot's own ideas march along in dialectical triads as evidently as do Hegel's. Surely Royce was not completely wrong in asserting that Abbot's philosophy was Hegel, warmed-over but unacknowledged. The protest of Abbot was no less justified than Royce's criticism. For, though there is a taste of Hegelianism in Abbot's language and logic, the consequences of his use of this language and logic are very different from those Hegel reached. Both Abbot's dependence and his independence are clearly revealed in his discussion of the relation of the syllogism to evolution. Here his fundamental statement is that "Whatever is evolved as consequent must be involved as antecedent." [39] The statement seems to mean that the evolutionary process does not produce complete novelty; it leads rather, to novel rearrangement of elements which are already "involved." The philosophical development which men like Spencer had given to evolutionary theory did not recognize this involvement, or "involution," as Abbot calls it. Spencer thought of evolution as a merely mechanical process, as "evolution without involution."

Evolution conceived thus mechanically seemed to Abbot to be but a half-truth, "more dangerous than a lie." [40] As early as 1868, Abbot, in reviewing Spencer's *Principles of Biology,* pointed out that unless the evolutionary principle itself were intrinsic to and inherent in life itself, the only change that was made by the philosophy of evolution was to shift from belief in a multiplicity of creative miracles to a belief in one creative miracle. Spencer's mechanism made it necessary to consider the evolutionary force as something outside of that which was evolving. Abbot, to express his disagreement with Spencer, accepted the hypothesis of "vitalism," namely, that the evolutionary force is a vital drive in that which is evolving. However, even this mechanical conception could be used as a stepping stone toward an organic philosophy of evolution, which would come with the recognition that evolution comes through involution, or "Whatever is evolved as consequent must be involved as antecedent." Evolution and involution are, of course, different; yet once Abbot's principle of the organic philosophy of evolution has been stated, it is clear that in some sense evolution and involution are identical. When, finally, it is understood that the sense in which they are one is as the continuity of being (that is, when it is understood that there is no leap from the involved to the evolved, but a gradual unfolding, so that at no point can one say that everything potential has been actualized, everything involved has been evolved), we have moved to "the spiritual philosophy of the identity in difference of evolution and involution." [41]   In the mechanical philosophy, evolution is stressed; in the organic, its opposite, involution, is maintained; in the spiritual, evolution and involution are seen to be a particular case of the identity in difference of opposites.

The syllogism of traditional logic consists of (1) a statement about a class of things, (2) an identification of a particular thing or another lesser class as a member of that class, and (3) a conclusion asserting that what is true of the more inclusive class is true of the lesser class or of the particular member of the class. Abbot, however, interpreted the process of reaching conclusions by the use of the syllogism as the discovery of the identity in difference of evolution and involution. The syllogism was for him the "necessary relational equation of the involved and the evolved in the world-process." [42]   There are several points to be commented on in this. In the first place, the conclusion in a syllogism is necessary; not necessarily *true,* or necessarily *real,* but logically compelled by the other two statements (the premises). Abbot saw this logical relation as more than merely logical. He thought it pointed to a relation of that which is involved and that which is evolved in being. His logic was not only a representation of the process of *thought;* it was also a representation of the process of *existence.* But where Hegel (and, as we have seen, Laurens Perseus Hickok after him) insisted on the primacy of thought, so that the laws of thought are the laws of being, Abbot inverted this objective idealism into an objective realism, making the laws of being the laws of thought as well. For Hegel, it was Reason or thought that was realizing itself through history. Abbot, to the contrary, believed that Being realized itself "through Knowing in Doing." [43]   This process of the universal and eternal self-realization of Being was what he called "world-process." Secondly, the pattern of relations in the world (its "relational constitution") was not imposed from without by any transcendent and non-natural force; it was internal to ("immanent in") the world. The world, then, has an "immanent relational constitution." [44] It is this internal pattern of relations which is determined by world-process. Since, in discussing the syllogism, we have seen that Abbot considered the relations it expressed to be necessary in existence as well as in thought, we are ready to see that the immanent relational constitution of the world must be made up of relations which are themselves necessary for thought as well as for existence. Thus the laws of being and the laws of thought are another case of identity in difference.

Again, we have noted that Abbot believed that Being realizes itself through Knowing in Doing. In our exposition, it has not yet been shown what Abbot meant by "Doing," or what place it had in his system of thought. Abbot seems to have included in this term the entire area of moral behavior, which constituted for him an absolute religion, or "free and intelligent obedience to an absolute moral law." [45] Only a philosophy grounded in what Abbot thought of as absolute logic could be the foundation on which such an absolute religion might be based. The person whose religion was absolute would be one who recognized the absolute moral law and followed it of his own free will because his intellect directed him to follow it. Such a person would be an ethical person. The world conceived as the environment of the ethical person is referred to by Abbot as "the Absolute Ethical I" or the "Ethical All-Person." This "Absolute Ethical I" is the immanent and necessary relational constitution of the world. "Doing," or moral action, since it arises in free will and yet is determined by a necessary ethical environment, is, then, another case of identity in difference — the identity in difference of freedom and necessity.

Although by far the largest part of Abbot's two volumes on *The Syllogistic Philosophy* is devoted to discussions of Being or of Knowing, the motivation of his work is clearly moral, concerned with Doing. In the sense in which he used the term, "absolute religion" or, as he calls it in other contexts, "scientific theism," was the goal toward which all of Abbot's thinking was directed. He believed that only absolute religion could "redeem the world from the imperialism, militarism, commercialism, and generally reviving barbarism" [46] which he saw (even in his time; how much more so in ours), evidently on the increase. Abbot wrote of his youthful ambition to interpret reflectively and to justify philosophically the "blazing ubiquities" of the Declaration of Independence. In his youth he thought that he could hold up to the world a proud example of the truth of these doctrines (as well as of his own philosophy) in the Constitution of the United States, and in the free obedience of his fellow-citizens to the Constitution and to the principles enshrined in the Declaration of Independence. His hope of doing this was shattered and he himself disillusioned by the course of events in the latter years of the nineteenth century, and, in particular, some of the immoral national attitudes during and after the Spanish-American War. In some ways he felt called upon to atone for whatever share he, as an American, had in the injustices of American policy. It was (he said) as partial atonement that he gave his final work to the world. "All that I can do to lighten the sense of my own unwilling complicity as a citizen in these national wrongs is to leave this work as my solemn protest against them, and to hope that reviving wisdom and virtue may yet lead my country to a better mind and better deeds." [47] National morality was as important to Abbot as individual morality. Doing was the climactic outcome and the purpose of his philosophic enterprise.

Abbot conceived of philosophy as a search for knowledge. He recognized however, that the type of knowledge which was sought differed in different eras. Among the ancient, classical philosophers the search was for knowledge of Being; the modern philosophers, he said, were seeking knowledge of Thought. Reformed modern philosophy, by which we may presume he meant his own philosophy, has as its object knowledge of Knowledge. The Knowledge which is his object is the indissoluble union of Being and Thought. Philosophy itself is much more than a record of the systems of individual philosophers; it can not be, as members of the historical school maintained, that "the history of philosophy is philosophy itself." Philosophy must be, by Abbot's reckoning, a "unitary and universal system of the Knowledge of Knowledge." [48] All the principles of discovered truth must be included within it. It must be capable of perpetual growth as a living whole, since the principles of newly-discovered truth must be incorporated into philosophy as integral parts, and not as excrescences, and, therefore, it must have an organic life-principle of its own by which it is animated. Philosophy itself, then, can not be the history of philosophy, nor can it be any mere aggregation or collection of individual philosophies. It can be nothing less than the philosophy of philosophy, "an all-inclusive and perfectly rational system, absorbing whatever is true in all prior and partial systems, . . . substantiating whatever truths it thus absorbs by a rigorous deduction of them from its own all-permeating principle." [49]

Philosophy historically has taken the form of a series of necessarily connected affirmations. The series must start somewhere; there must be a first affirmation. In most philosophies, this first affirmation is imported from some other aspect of human life; it is a physical affirmation, a religious affirmation, a biological affirmation, used as the starting-point for philosophic development, but not itself philosophical. It is a presupposition which can not be justified by the criteria of philosophy. Abbot declared that the obligation of philosophy is to find a beginning which is "presuppositionless," and is, therefore, a really philosophical beginning. The first principle of philosophy must be a necessary truth; it must be of universal scope; it must be objectively valid, and not produced out of any subjective sense of certainty; and, finally, it must depend on no other truth, whether explicitly or implicitly — that is, it must be rationally first as well as first in a series. If it is merely first in the series, but not rationally first, then it is grounded in another affirmation which is logically prior to it. Philosophy must find out a "beginning" which truly is a beginning. This beginning, moreover, must be rationally justified, not merely asserted. Yet, if it is rationally justified it would seem evident that it is not a beginning at all, but the affirmation which justifies it is the true beginning. We are caught in a demand which seems impossible of fulfillment.

The way out of this dilemma for Abbot is that the affirmation and its ground must be identical and simultaneous. If philosophy is to have a presuppositionless and philosophical beginning it must begin in a "self-grounded affirmation." [50] What this means is that what the affirmation asserts, its content, and the rational justification of this assertion, its ground, must be identical. It will affirm its universal ground as its particular content. The presuppositionless beginning will, then, be an intrinsic truth. In an earlier time, as we know from the Declaration of Independence, philosophers had maintained that there might be statements which were "self-evident," that is, statements which required no proof because of the certainty which they aroused in their reader or hearer. This theory, said Abbot, was on the right track, but erred in accepting a subjective criterion, the sense of certainty. He sought a statement which is self-evidently true because its proof is intrinsic to the statement itself. There is, he maintained, one and only one such affirmation, and it is the necessary starting-point of philosophy: "Human knowledge exists." [51] Considered as content, this is an empirical judgment; considered as ground, it is a rational judgment. Considered as content and ground in one, it is empirical as a particular judgment, rational as the universal ground not only of itself but of all particular judgments. It takes "the one universal ground of all philosophical or rational affirmation as its own particular content." [52] Although his statement is similar to the primary affirmation, "I think, therefore I exist" which Descartes had found satisfactory, Abbot's defense of his own version rests upon the fact that Descartes' affirmation is individual, while his own is universal.

Again, the proposition "Human knowledge exists" as content, that is, as an empirical judgment, is subjective as all statements based upon experience were considered subjective by the tradition in which Abbot was rooted. As ground, however, as a rational judgment, the proposition is objective. Thus the statement is in itself both objective and subjective. It is the exemplary case of identity in difference. We have seen that it unites content and ground, subjectivity and objectivity, experience and reason, individuality and universality, actuality (as content) and necessity (as ground). Because these opposites are indissolubly united yet without contradiction in the affirmation that "Human knowledge exists," Abbot called it a "momentous" assertion, and proposed to deduce from it his whole system of philosophy. It was to be a philosophical position which would provide a "way out of agnosticism," a deterrent to any rational system based on universal doubt. Abbot's "scientific realism" had no sympathy with the agnosticism which Herbert Spencer drew out of evolutionary theory. The ultimate affirmation of any absolute scepticism could not be self-grounded, according to Abbot, for it would have to presuppose the known existence of something to doubt.

There are two kinds of identity which Abbot distinguished. The first, like "A = A," he called identity without essential difference. The second, like "A = B × C," he called identity in essential difference. "Human knowledge exists" (content) = "Human knowledge exists" (ground) he regarded as an identity of the second sort, an identity in difference. There is an interpenetration of content and ground, like the interpenetration of color and form in an object of vision. Now, unless experience and reason can themselves be identical in difference there can not be any purely empirical content which is identical with a purely rational ground. If, then, he argues, we can actually produce an affirmation in which content and ground are identical, that affirmation must be "the *necessary consequence*, in that particular case, of a *necessary and universal condition:* namely, the identity of experience and reason in human knowledge itself." [53] But, as we have seen, Abbot considered that he had produced just such an affirmation; he concluded, therefore, that in opposition to the "fashionable metaphysic" of idealism, which is based upon the separation of experience and reason, he had provided the basis for a realistic philosophy, recognizing the "necessary inseparability," or identity in difference, of experience and reason in all human knowledge. Beyond this Abbot argued (though we shall not follow the course of the argument in detail), that the inseparable union of experience and reason in every act of knowledge implies the inseparable union of existence and knowledge in the knower, that is, in human self-consciousness. For this to be so means ultimately (leaping over sections of Abbot's argument) that in Nature, or unconditioned universal Being, there is an identity in difference of Existence and Knowledge, Being and Thought. Thus, a consideration of the affirmation "Human knowledge exists," shows that it rests on a "ground of all grounds," which is the "absolute rational series of the world." This is not an extrinsic ground for the affirmation of the existence of human knowledge, but is its immanent or intrinsic ground. "Human knowledge exists" and "Human existence knows" are equivalent statements. "Man is both the knowledge of his own existence and the existence of his own knowledge." [54]

Abbot accepted the long-standing philosophic distinction that by experience we can gain knowledge of particulars only, whereas reason gives us knowledge of universals, or general ideas. The distinctive difference between experience and reason is fixed by the essential difference between their objects. Abbot, as has already been pointed out, was one of the first thinkers to insist upon the objectivity of relations. We can expect, then, that in his discussion of the relations between the unit and the universal, the specimen and the species, he is not satisfied with any account which makes that relationship a creation of the mind. Units have real and objective existence; universals have real and objective existence; and the relations between them have real and objective existence. No unit can exist without, at a very minimum, two kinds of relations — particular relations to others of its kind, and universal relations to the whole of its kind. To be completely out of relation would be to be completely out of existence. If we can show that every thing and every kind must be at once both particular and universal — that units and universals are identical in difference in existence — we shall have a satisfactory basis for maintaining the identity in difference of experience and reason in knowledge. In bridging the gap between experience and reason, we make it possible to get away from the alternatives of reason without experience, which Abbot calls the principle of idealism, and experience without reason, which he calls the principle of materialism, to a rational empiricism (or "scientific method"), which he calls the principle of scientific realism.

Here Abbot believed the chief philosophic importance of the work of Darwin to lie. For philosophy, following the lead of Aristotle, had thought of individuals, of particulars, as concrete and changing representatives of abstract and unchanging universals, classes or species. Although the particulars were accessible to human experience, they were inaccessible to human knowledge. Although the universals were accessible to human reason, they were inaccessible to human experience. Only specimens were experienceable; only species were knowable. One tradition in philosophy granted the reality of the particulars and had difficulty in accounting for the universals; another tradition granted the reality of the universals and had difficulty in accounting for the particulars. Aristotle and all those who followed him in this paradoxical account made their error by insisting on the unchanging, immutable character of the species and by their failure to recognize the importance of individual differences. It was not until Darwin had propounded his hypothesis that "advantageous variations," or individual differences, were seen as essential rather than accidental, and it was the Darwinian "revolution" which led to the abandonment of belief in eternally fixed species. Abbot, by way of Darwin, thought that he had found "the truth which Aristotle failed to discover: namely, that *the individual difference is essential to the whole individual, and the whole in-*

dividual is essential to the whole species." [55]

This is to say, however, that the individual or specimen stands in the same relation to its individual differences as the species stands to the specimen. The particular, although it is a unit with respect to the species, is a universal with respect to individual differences. The individual is, then, a "unit-universal." As a unit, it can be perceived; as a universal it can be conceived. A unit-universal is a "percept-concept." It is the object of both experience and reason. "The identity in difference of experience and reason in all human knowledge is made luminously manifest in the necessary constitution of its ultimate molecule, the percept-concept." [56] The influence of Darwin on Abbot's philosophy was to make possible the realistic assertion that "existence and knowableness are of necessity one and the same; the unknowable is simply the non-existent." [57]

Without entering any more deeply than this into the details of Abbot's philosophy, enough has been said to make clear that he was working out, independently of any "schools" of thought, a careful statement of a realistic and scientific theory of being, knowing, and doing. His criticisms were directed with fine impartiality against the subjective idealism developed out of Kant in Germany, England, and America, and against the subjective empiricism developed out of Locke, Berkeley, and Hume in England and America. The key-note of his scientific realism was objectivity. In its final form, Abbot called his philosophy syllogistic. In addition to what has already been said about his use of this term, he meant that his ideas about being, knowing, and doing could each be summarized in a syllogism:

The Syllogism of Being

i. Species, or Kinds in Themselves, are evolved from Genera, or Higher Kinds in Themselves.
ii. Specimens, or Things in Themselves, are evolved from Species, or Kinds in Themselves. Therefore —
iii. Specimens are evolved from Genera, as New Individual Things in Universal Kinds.[58]

The Syllogism of Knowing

i. Concepts, or Comprehensions of Species, are evolved from Ideas, or Comprehensions of Genera.
ii. Percepts, or Apprehensions of Specimens, are evolved from Concepts, or Comprehensions of Species. Therefore —
iii. Percepts are evolved from Ideas, as Percept-Concepts or New Cognitions of Things and Kinds in Themselves.[59]

The Syllogism of Doing

    i. Good purposes, or Free Formation of Right Means are evolved from Good Ideals, or Cognitions of Right Ends.

   ii. Good Deeds, or Realized Right Ends, are evolved from Good Purposes, or Free Formations of Right Means. Therefore —

  iii. Good Deeds are evolved from Good Ideas, as New Individual Things in Universal Kinds.[60]

In the end, these three syllogisms are brought together into a Syllogism of Syllogisms which is the culmination of Abbott's philosophy:

    i. Knowing is Being: that is, true judgments are real specimens.

   ii. Doing is Knowing: that is, ethical deeds are true judgments.

  iii. Therefore, Doing is Being: that is, ethical deeds are real specimens.[61]

Thus the Philosophy of Philosophy, which is to say the Knowledge of Knowledge, becomes in the end, as Abbott promised, "a unitary and universal system" uniting existence, knowledge, and action into one comprehensive syllogism.

    Certainly it would be difficult to find three more divergent philosophic positions developed in the light of a single scientific hypothesis than those of John Fiske, Chauncey Wright, and Francis Ellingwood Abbot which have been presented here. For each of the three, Darwin's evolutionary theory provided a primary insight which was developed into a philosophy. For Fiske, acceptance of the theory that biological species develop led to the view that the moral and social life of man develops in parallel fashion. For Wright, no such overarching generalization was acceptable; what he drew from evolutionary theory was the belief that human self-consciousness had a natural rather than a supernatural origin, and that it had developed out of earlier animal functions of a biological cast. For Abbot, as we have just seen, Darwin's influence was felt especially in the formulation of a new theory of universals which enabled Abbot to reconstruct his philosophy on a realistic base in opposition to the idealisms and materialisms which were current in his day. Cosmic theism, evolutionary naturalism, and scientific realism in these three exponents tried each in its own way to interpret to its age the broader speculative significance of evolution; so, too, did other philosophies of that age. Beyond their dissimilarities, all these philosophies inspired by evolution are aspects of the same enterprise, the attempt to make philosophy take account of the facts of life as they were known to life-scientists. They all represent aspects of the attempt to naturalize and biologize philosophy.

6

VARIETIES OF IDEALISM

I. IDEALIST PROBLEMS AND PERSPECTIVES

By the second half of the nineteenth century, it had become a hazardous occupation for a philosopher to talk about our knowledge of the external world. Early in modern thought, mind and matter had become separated by the widely-accepted division of all substances into two classes, one called, broadly, thinking substance, mind, soul or spirit; the other called extended substance, body or matter. Important as it may have been to make this distinction in its day, it soon became evident that the making of it led to the posing of a significant problem of knowledge, which has become the central problem of modern philosophy. For if thinking substance and extended substance are different in kind, the question is bound to be asked how thinking substance, which is mind, can know extended substance, which is matter. Some of the proposed resolutions of the difficulty accepted the dualism of mind and matter, consciousness and the external world, at its face value. They proposed the simple answer that it is the nature of consciousness to know the external world, the nature of the external world to be known by consciousness. This naive answer does not, of course, solve anything; it leaves the problem where it was but provides a statement on the basis of which speculation can be carried on despite the unsolved problem at its base.

Other solutions took reductive forms; without breaking down the mind-matter dualism as it was originally stated, these thinkers evaded its implications for human knowledge either by the assertion that what we call mind is not really mind or that what we refer to as matter is not really matter. In the first case, mind is thought to be material action of one sort or another, and thus mind is reduced to a state of matter; that is materialistic reductionism. In the second case, it is asserted that what we call matter is merely our own states of consciousness or mental states, and thus matter is reduced to a state of mind; this is mentalistic reductionism. The mentalistic alternative is one of the forms which has been taken in the history of philosophy by the general world-view which is called Idealism, a philosophy which has been extremely influential and pervasive. It should be pointed out that this type of idealism does not deny that the world as we experience it really exists; it maintains only that everything that really exists is a mind or a state of mind. Mentalism denies that the world *is material*, but not that the world *is*. It is an attempt to resolve a problem of knowledge, not to answer questions about the fundamental nature of existence.

Other types of idealism, older in the history of philosophy than mentalism, do make the attempt to answer metaphysical questions. It is as a metaphysical position that idealism has made its greatest impression upon philosophic thought. In part we must assign this prominence of idealism to the similarity between its world-view and that of religion. A scientific world-view is but a recent arrival for most people in Western culture, and the naturalistic philosophy which supports and is supported by science has, therefore, found but little acceptance in most eras. Again, there are many varieties of metaphysical idealism, and any attempt to characterize them in a blanket fashion is bound to overlook important differences. For our purposes here, it is perhaps enough to say that the metaphysical idealisms agree in the belief that what men experience, the constant flux of becoming, the confusion of sensation, instability, and change, is not real existence, not Reality. These are but appearance, the shadow of the real. A knowledge of Reality can not be derived from consideration of its counterpart in experience. Our only instrument for gaining a knowledge of Reality is the mind, man's spiritual part, for Reality is spiritual in its fundamental character. The real universe is rational; it has an orderly, stable, permanent nature. Ultimately, in the real universe, existence, meaning, truth, and value are one. To the idealist, Reality is intelligible and valuable through and through, and it is man's system of meanings and man's system of values with which Reality is imbued. Undoubtedly much of the appeal of idealism lies in the fact that it assigns so important a place to man. Ralph Waldo Emerson, in *Nature*, was surely right in de-

claring that the advantage of idealism over a common sense acceptance of the reality of things as they are experienced is "that it
presents the world in precisely that view which is most desirable
to the mind."[1]

Although the transcendentalists in America had some acquaintance, mostly indirect (as we have seen in Chapter 4), with the impos-
ing systematic formulations of idealism of the German philosophers,
Kant, Fichte, Schelling, and Hegel, there was little careful study
of these masters until after mid-century. As time went on and the
demands of academic life increased, the number of American students who completed their formal education by a year or two of
study in Germany grew. There were a few who went to Germany
in the 1820's; by the 1850's the trickle had grown to a mighty stream.
By the end of the century it was rare to find a teacher of philosophy
in the major colleges who had not studied in Germany. It could
scarcely be expected that when they returned they would teach
their students the old Scottish orthodoxy in which they no longer
rested. They expounded an idealistic philosophy not so much as a
support for traditional religion, but as a spiritual substitute for it.
Meantime there was another source of interest in German ideas
which was felt increasingly after the mid-century. Johann Bernard
Stallo, an earlier immigrant, attempted to popularize the philosophy
of nature of the German romantics. After the revolution of 1848,
many disappointed liberals left their German homeland and migrated
to the United States. Many of these were well-educated men who
were able to play an important role in the lives of their new communities, and among other things, brought with them a knowledge
of the philosophical tradition of their homeland. They were an
important link in the chain of German-American intellectual relations.

At approximately the time when the influence of German idealistic
philosophy was first beginning to be felt in the colleges, the first
group of non-academic American students of idealism was born in
St. Louis. Here, under the inspiration of a German immigrant named
Henry Brokmeyer, a miscellaneous group of lawyers, teachers, and
others without special professional training met, at first informally,
for the study of Hegel. Among the members of this group were
such notables as William Torrey Harris, who later became the
United States Commissioner of Education, Denton J. Snider, whose

philosophic criticism of literature attracted a wide audience in later years, Thomas Davidson, a dour Scot who taught classical languages in the St. Louis schools, and George Holmes Howison, for many years a beloved member of the faculty of the University of California. After their informal meetings had continued for a time, this group undertook to work over Brokmeyer's translation of one of Hegel's works. From this time on their meetings became more firmly purposive, and the members of the group made great strides in attempting to acclimate Hegel to America. Their achievement includes the publication, for about twenty-five years, of the first exclusively philosophic journal to be published in the United States, *The Journal of Speculative Philosophy*. The St. Louis group entered upon this venture in a mood of pique and arrogance. An article by Harris was rejected by the *Atlantic Monthly* (on the advice of Chauncey Wright, who thought it was muddy in its thinking). The rejection was attributed by the St. Louisans to the New England scorn of "western" intellectual developments. In order to guarantee themselves an outlet and to show up the "easterners," the *Journal* was started. Throughout its existence, its editors published a high percentage of original articles, as well as some valuable translations from the German. There was some criticism of the space that was given to materials on the arts, but, on the whole, *The Journal of Speculative Philosophy* was a valiant and courageous (though financially unrewarding), venture.

On one of his lecture tours, Bronson Alcott, who had developed a considerable reputation as a transcendentalist, in part because the obscurity of his remarks was taken for profundity, stopped off in St. Louis and appeared at a session with the St. Louis Hegelians. He dropped his "orphic sayings" before them like pearls; but they had faced obscurity before, so they were able to argue with him and dispute his points. He had come to make transcendentalists out of them; he left resolved to make their Hegelianism known in the east. In order to fulfill this resolution, he sponsored the Concord Summer School of Philosophy, in which, for a number of years, lecturers from the west as well as from New England participated. Among the western lecturers was Dr. Hiram K. Jones of Jacksonville, Illinois. Dr. Jones was the founder and leader of a small group in his town which met together for the study of Plato. While this group can not be regarded as contributing directly to the development of idealism in American philosophy, its existence should not be forgotten. That such a group should have come together testifies to the yearning for speculative thought which can be found in all strata of the American people. When both Jones and Harris took part in the Concord Summer School, as they did in 1879 and 1882, the contrast between Platonism and Hegelianism was clearly revealed.

Thomas Davidson, although he met with the St. Louis group for a time, was never an Hegelian; he thought he had no sympathy for idealism and insisted that he had devoted his life to combatting it. He had actually worked out, on an Aristotelian basis, a dynamic and objective ethical idealism in which thought and action were regarded as inseparable aspects of life. He had hopes of reforming society by means of adult education, and in his later years he conducted a summer school for philosophical studies at Glenmore in the Adirondacks in upper New York State. He founded the Fellowship of the New Life, a reformist group with branches in England and in the United States. Out of the English group developed the Fabian Society; thus, paradoxically, a confirmed individualist became the parent of a mild form of socialism. For a time, Davidson was educational director of a settlement house in New York City's lower East Side; it was here that he discovered Morris Raphael Cohen (see Chapter 9, section III) and encouraged Cohen to continue his philosophic studies.

George Holmes Howison was another philosophic figure who began his career in the group of St. Louis Hegelians but did not remain satisfied with Hegel for very long. He distrusted the "Absolute" in Hegel's thought because he considered it to lead to pantheism and because he could not see what place was left for the individual once an Absolute was acknowledged. He took great delight in referring to the Hegelian Absolute as "that night in which all cows are black," although the phrase was originally used by Hegel as a comment on the Absolute in Schelling's philosophy. Howison set for himself the philosophic task of preserving a place for the finite individual; he attempted to do this by means of an idealism in which ultimate reality was conceived of as a plurality of persons, a pluralistic personal idealism. We shall see that Borden Parker Bowne of Boston University, whose philosophy was also a personal idealism, differed from Howison by insisting that the plurality of finite persons were all manifestations of one Infinite Person.

Howison, however, regarded the individual mind as an elementary, ultimate, and indestructible reality. Persons were the irreducible spiritual atoms of a world that has structure. In Howison we find a consciously close approach to the position of G. W. Leibniz (1646-1716). Leibniz's "monads" are represented by the indestructible spiritual units of Howison's thought.

We meet in Howison, too, a conception of the rational order as a social order. He thought of social communication as the realm in which knowledge occurs. It was this view which made it possible for Howison to retain the independence of the individual and yet to avoid subjectivism by making provision for interaction among independent individuals. Time, space, and all that we regard as the "contents" of time and space exist in the coexistence of minds, where this coexistence is neither spatial nor temporal (for space and time are derived from it), but means simply that each mind, in defining itself as a self-determining being, logically implies the existence of other self-determining beings. To this community of coexistent minds Howison applies metaphorically the names "City of God" and the "Eternal Republic." Within this community, God is "the living Bond of their union . . . the impersonated Ideal of every mind."[2] Not God alone, but the entire City of God, including God as its connective bond, is the "prime mover" of the philosophic tradition, "the genuine *Unmoved One that moves all Things.*"[3] The unity of the Eternal Republic is not a freedom-destroying absolute, but is the moral unity of harmonizing activity, of "spontaneous coöperation," of movement toward a common goal. It is this process to which the name of "evolution" is properly given. Howison, like Kant, believed that behind the structure of experience there lie principles which are prior to experience. These principles he referred to as signs that the mind is a purposive spiritual being. He could not, however, follow Kant in believing that behind experience there lies a realm of things-in-themselves; he did not agree that there is an objective world shut off from human experience. It might, he thought, lie beyond the reach of the individual, but it can not lie beyond experience because the objective world is implied by a society of minds and must be conceived as a rational structure.

For Davidson and Howison and, as we shall see later, Bowne and Royce, as well as many other American idealists of the late nineteenth and early twentieth centuries, the ethical motivation was a strong force leading to their acceptance of idealism, and a major influence on their formulations. In their philosophies the passage back and forth from "idea" to "ideal" was made without hesitation, almost without the realization that the idea of thought and the ideal of conduct are not necessarily interchangeable. One philosopher who made an attempt to avoid this easy identification was Felix Adler. Adler taught his ethical idealism for many years at Columbia University, and preached and practiced it for even longer as founder of the Ethical Culture movement. His thought began in a careful critique of the Kantian and other philosophical systems of ethics. All these systems, he pointed out, have started from an interest in science, logic, or esthetics. When they come to the problems of ethics, their approach is conditioned by concepts derived from these other areas. These systems all try "to fit the data of ethics into a scheme derived from data outside the field of ethics."[4] Thus, as Adler put it, "In Kant, the Newtonian physics shines through the categorical imperative, however sublimely proclaimed."[5] The object of his ethical philosophy, then, became the development of an ethical ideal based upon ethical data, and aimed at the solution of the ethical problem — "that of reconciling the individual sacred as an end per se to other individuals no less sacred than himself."[6] In the course of attempting to achieve this objective, Adler tried to eliminate metaphysics from its central place in the Kantian moral system and yet to preserve as much of this system as supported the Kantian ideal of an ethical religion.

In practice, Adler's version of the universal religion of right and duty was conceived in a more explicitly democratic frame of reference than Kant's. Thus, his most interesting position is that of the "ethical manifold," a non-temporal, non-spatial universe, which, considered under its aspect of unity, is the ideal of the whole, but, viewed under the aspect of plurality, is and must remain a manifold within which each member, an ethical unit, differs uniquely from the rest, preserving and maintaining his irreducible singularity. Since each ethical unit is intrinsically unlike every other, each is indispensable to the whole. But the uniqueness of each, in Adler's view, lies in his unique ability to bring out the uniqueness in the others. In this case, the unity of this infinite assembly of unlike units is "that the unique difference of each shall be such as to render possible the correlated unique differences of all the rest."[7] It is by means of this

conception of the ethical manifold that Adler saved both the individual and co-operatively democratic society in an ethical context.
The first principle of ethics which Adler derived from the ethical
manifold is that the individual should act so as to achieve uniqueness.
But we have also seen that to achieve one's own uniqueness is to
seek to bring out the diverse uniqueness in others. We may, therefore, give to this ethical principle yet another formulation: "Act
so as to elicit in another the distinctive, unique quality characteristic
of him as a fellow-member of the infinite whole."[8] Paradoxical as
this may sound, Adler found in the most completely individual of
acts, in the achieving of uniqueness, the ground and basis for the
achieving of sociality, and in the postulation of the ideal of a spiritual universe the only route to its realization.

There was still another version of the idealist perspective which
developed in the late nineteenth century partly under the inspiration
of Adolf Trendelenburg, who reinterpreted thinking in active and
dynamic terms, and partly under the influence of the Darwinian
theory of evolution. George Sylvester Morris, who taught at the
Johns Hopkins University and at the University of Michigan, was
primarily influenced by Trendelenburg in the development of the
view that the powers of mind are natural energies, moving forces,
directed toward purposes by will. To the extent that the powers of
mind are natural energies a study of their activities can become an
independent, experimental science of experience. John Dewey as
a student of Morris and later as his junior colleague at Michigan
developed Morris' position in a fashion more consonant with Hegelianism. Dewey's early text, *Psychology*, asserts that the unity of
man's psychical life is to be explained by the fact that man is a self.
The essence of selfhood is conceived to be will, which is a self-determining and self-objectifying activity. The objectifying activity of
the will is mind and its product is knowledge. The objectified will
is science, because the will universalizes itself in the process of objectifying itself. Mind as an agent in the world, and its resultant effects
can be studied in the same way that other objective facts can be
studied. The activity of the will is the basis on which mind is conceived as dynamic.

Alfred Henry Lloyd, who came to Michigan while Dewey was
still there but after the death of Morris, formulated his version of
dynamic idealism — the term is one of his contributions — with a

more explicitly evolutionary foundation. He asked, "What is thought in its simplest nature but the use of consciousness for some act of adjustment?"[9] Thought is a relation between consciousness and its environment; in traditional terms this might be called a relation between the self and the non-self. This relationship is neither formal nor mechanical. Since the relationship is an act of adjustment, it is dynamic. Consciousness as such, pure consciousness conceived as a separate entity, does not exist. Consciousness is transitive; it is consciousness of something. It must have an object. In general, the object of consciousness is the environment of the conscious self. But, Lloyd affirmed, "the object is only the self or subject over again."[10] What the subject regards as qualities of the object are, rather, his own states. Self and not-self are not, then, completely distinct. As soon as we begin to think about their distinction, we discover their identity. The not-self is a larger whole of which the self is a part. Since this is so, the larger whole, or not-self, has a social nature; it is made up of "other aspects of the same reality of which the self is but one."[11] Then the self, in relating itself to the not-self, is assuming a social responsibility. Matter, too, is regarded by Lloyd as a social institution rather than a substance.

Lloyd's universe is entirely constituted by relationships, and relationships are ever-changing. For this reason no final statement at any level either of universality or of particularity can ever be made about it. Thus when he talked about parts and whole, his definitions indicated that a part is one aspect of a relational system, and a whole is a relational system. This seems tangible enough, but Lloyd went on to say that anything is both a part and a whole; as one relational system, it is a whole, and it is also a relational part of another system or of many other systems. The multiplicity of dynamic relationships thus accounted for constitutes the meaning of a thing and its reality. Existence and relational activity are not two separate facts about a thing, but the existence of things is relationship. This leads to an intrinsically intelligible universe, because "intelligence is but the natural self-activity of a system of actual relations."[12] Things, then, insofar as they are real, are a relating activity to which Lloyd assigns the name of "mind." In this world of actual relations, change is not merely possible, but necessary and inevitable. A relational whole must create relations. It must be animate, or alive. An animate system of relationships is an organism. We can now say that the world of things is a spontaneously changing, self-active, living, intelligent organism. In this dynamic world, ideas are forces or plans and consciousness is always a planning. Planning is a process in which a number of things, of which the planner himself is one, assume an expression of their relationship which will set their activity free. Lloyd's idealism is so thoroughly dynamic that it has no fixed point from which a discussion of it can be started or at which a discussion of it can end.

When we come to talk of more recent American idealism, we find no single outstanding philosopher whose lead is followed by his fellow-idealists. There are, rather, a multiplicity of different idealisms. There is no single doctrine associated with earlier idealisms to which all of today's idealists would give assent. Idealism is to be sought in the temper of a philosopher's writing, in a preference for an emphasis on mind and its operations, more than in any specific doctrines. Idealists and non-idealists alike recognize that they are not engaged in two different spheres of philosophic activity. There is a community of concern. Both groups are aware that they are talking about the same universe. While there are differences in what is said and in the way it is said, there is merit in the point made by W. H. Sheldon of Yale that the differences between idealism and naturalism are less in life than they seem to be in theory. In part, this is the result of the relative absence from contemporary American philosophy of the extreme positions of subjective idealism and materialism. So, for example, Edgar A. Singer, of the University of Pennsylvania, refers to Nature as "ideal reality" and maintains that this ideal reality is the limiting conception that makes scientific progress possible. The function of the scientist is the reduction of his "probable error," the closer and closer approximation to this limiting conception or ideal, which is the culmination of both idealism and naturalism. Singer is careful to point out that the two types of philosophy asked for utterly different standards of evidence. Nevertheless, since the limiting ideal in both cases is the same, idealist and naturalist "are trying to think out an answer to the same ultimate question."[13]

Much recent idealism has moved away from eighteenth- and nineteenth-century mentalism and subjectivism and has resumed the ancient search for objective logical structure in the universe — objective mind. Typically, Clarence I. Lewis of Harvard, a student of logical theory in the tradition of Peirce, calls his theory of mind in the world order a "conceptualistic pragmatism," and maintains that pure rationalism and pure empiricism both attempt to separate "mind" from "experience." Both treat knowledge as a relation of one mind to an external world, so that in both the fact that other minds exist is not thought to have anything to do with the knowledge situation. Neither, he asserted, is sufficiently aware of "the sense in which our truth is social."[14] Lewis continued by pointing out that what we know as the world is constructed by our thought from sense data. This "reality which everybody knows" tells us as much about the structure of human intelligence as it does about the external source of our sensations. Experience can not be the fruit of a mind which is beyond experience working upon a matter which is beyond experience. Both mind and matter can be discovered only by an analysis of experience. "It is only because mind has entered into the structure of the real world which we know and the experience of everyday that analysis, or any attempted knowledge, may discover it."[15] Lewis, even more than the objective idealists of the Sage School at Cornell, somehow seems to stand between idealism and naturalism, as well as between rationalism and empiricism, and to be attempting to balance and mediate between their conflicting claims in his philosophy.

Similarly Frederick J. E. Woodbridge of Columbia stood between the two schools, bridging them by his concern for mind not as "an individual agent or being which thinks, but the realm of being in which thinking occurs."[16] This "realm of mind" has a logical structure; we can trace within it the interconnections of one fact or event with other facts or events. Men live in the realm of mind and are therefore able to gain unified and coherent knowledge. The realm of mind is not distinct from the realm of being; it is "the realm of being as known."[17] Woodbridge tried to avoid the materialist extreme of placing thinking outside of nature and the subjectivist extreme of making nature the product of thought. He emerged with the view that mind as a logical structure of existence is antecedent to thinking, and that our thinking as individuals is "a bodily activity congruent with that structure."[18]

Many of the trends of contemporary American idealism are in evidence in the writings of William E. Hocking of Harvard who believes that the universe has an objective meaning which is humanly discoverable, but is there independent of its discovery by men. We are not limited to the finding of "the bare facts of the natural order."[19] Since there is a meaning objectively present in the universe, we are justified in asserting that there is some kind of mental life at the core of reality. Philosophy, the attempt to penetrate to the core of reality, must be concerned with this mental life. This, to Hocking, means that philosophy must be idealistic. Furthermore, the pursuit of meaning which is the enterprise of philosophy is the search for values. The reality of things to which we reach out in our pursuit of meaning and value is a realm of the eternal emergence of ulterior values. "Values keep emerging as we enlarge our capacity and learn the adjustment of our instruments of vision."[20] For Hocking, just as for Woodbridge, the mental life has unity as well as objectivity. Unlike Woodbridge, however, Hocking was influenced by both personal idealism and the absolute idealism of Royce. He, therefore, conceives of this unity as a self infinite in depth and mystery. By this he means that all the meanings of things in the universe cohere in a single will. The finite human self is an imperfect image of the universe. It is a natural thing to be studied like other things; but it is also more than a natural thing because it is conscious of both facts and values. As a thing of nature, the self is completely determined. As more than a thing, the self is free because, out of a variety of possibilities, the self can and does determine what is to be the fact of the next moment. There is, then, an opposition in man between his subjection to the laws of nature and his transcendence of these laws. Hocking believes that this opposition is resolved by man's flinging a gesture of defiance at the laws of nature by means of the ceremonies of religion.

Body is explained by Hocking as a necessity for the actualizing of self. The self needs its body in order to be an actual, active, social, historical self. Nature is not involved in any particular self; it belongs to a community of selves. That is to say, nature serves the whole community of selves as the body serves and is the organ of the individual self. In either case, we talk about body belonging to self, not self to body; nature belonging to the community of selves, not the community of selves belonging to nature, because it is self which is the organizing and owning principle. The justification for Hocking's referring to a community of selves, for his assuming the interconnectedness of selves, is that there is an identical element in the wills of all human selves. This identical element Hocking expressed thus: "Human wills to live are always wills to live *with others*."[21] Mind, to Hocking, is that which holds together past, present, and future, fact and value, the actual and the possible. A natural object is an actual present fact. The mind can not be considered as a natural object, because in addition to actual present fact it is a hold on possible future value. Mind is the only organ which has this capacity. Mind is, therefore, the only organ for actualizing the future possibilities of value.

In Hocking's thought we find deposits from various types of idealism brought together into a system. Three of the earlier versions of American idealism which lie behind and contribute to this system merit consideration in greater detail — the personal idealism of Borden Parker Bowne, the absolute idealism of Josiah Royce, and the speculative, objective idealism of James Edwin Creighton.

II. PERSONAL IDEALISM: BORDEN PARKER BOWNE

George Holmes Howison did not succeed in writing an influential statement of the personal idealism which he taught at the University of California. Borden Parker Bowne, who taught at Boston University, was more successful in promoting personal idealism — or as he came to call it, "personalism" — in his books, because he was not only a system-maker but also the founder of a tradition and a school. His disciples have given continuity to his thought, which is influential in some religious circles in the United States and is widely studied in Latin America, where it is regarded as the culmination of North American philosophy. Although Bowne had read and studied the work of many philosophers, and although there is some reason to believe that the personal idealism of Herman Lotze (1817-1881) was a major inspiration to him, he seems to have wrestled with the problems of philosophy to a great extent as if they had never been studied before.

Bowne's philosophic career began and ended with criticism of the theory of knowledge of Herbert Spencer. In Bowne's day, Spencer was the outstanding representative of the Lockean tradition in British thought, and it was this tradition in its entirety which Bowne attacked for its insistence that knowledge begins in "atomic," discrete sensations impressed upon a passive mind. This sensationalism seemed to Bowne destructive of the idea of the self as a substance, the "substantial self," to the preservation of which his life in philosophy was devoted. When William James produced his conception of the "stream of consciousness," Bowne attacked this view, also, for similar reasons. He accused James of "smuggling" the characteristic activities of a self into the flowing stream, and failing to allow for a "unitary and abiding agent" whose activities they were. Bowne's criticisms of Kant, which we shall consider in more detail later, followed the same pattern. Kant and his followers, Bowne said, had paid so much attention to the forms by which the mind organizes experience that they had all but forgotten the self whose characteristic activity is to know by means of the organization of experience. Bowne, then, we may say, was the committed defender of the self, and he resented and rejected any philosophy which seemed to him to pay too little attention to the self. He was completely "self"-conscious.

There is a thread of common sense realism underlying Bowne's thought, as there is in many objective idealists. The substantial self in which he so firmly believed was not spinning an outer world from its own inner consciousness. Man's faculties, Bowne thought, give generally trustworthy reports. When, therefore, they report that there is an objectively existing world outside of ourselves, we must trust that report and accept their outward pointing as reliable. He believed that in the pointing of our faculties to other persons and to the external world we confront an objective order which we do not make, but discover. The outward pointing of our minds points to something real. Furthermore, Bowne insisted, this outer objective order plays fair with us; it meets our minds at least half-way. In the last analysis Bowne conceded that we know only our own states of mind — but our states of mind carry this outer reference which is not to be overlooked. We may say, if we like, that the process of arriving at a conviction that the world outside ourselves really does exist is an inference from our mental states; this is certainly true as soon as we begin to reflect upon the outer world. The fundamental act, however, is not one of inference, but one of faith that our minds in leading us to believe in an external world are not leading us astray. Granting his basic realistic faith in the objective existence of the external world, Bowne was, nevertheless, an idealist in the interpretation which he gave to this order in whose real existence he believed. Briefly stated, he considered the forces in the objective universe to be the expression of ideas. The material world is realized idea — idea which has somehow had force put into it.

The most characteristic of Bowne's ideas, that because of which he is called a personalist, is his view of the self. We can best come to understand Bowne's conception of the self by a consideration of the "mistakes" which he found in Kantian thought. Bowne pointed out that after emphasizing the power of the self in knowing, Kant then spoke of an underlying "thing-in-itself" which we can not know. In Bowne's view, the introduction of this unknowable "noumenon" weakened the correct account, that knowing is the constitutive activity of the self. Kant, he held, was led to this error by attempting to abstract thinking, a "will-element," from its meaning for thought. In the second place, Kant, and even more the followers of Kant, devoted so much attention to the study of the categories, or forms of the mind's activities, that they lost sight of the self. By concentrating on the mechanism of the knowing process, they minimized the importance of the knower. Bowne insisted that when we are dealing with the self, we must remember that it is the self which is basic in our study. We tell what the self is by watching what it does. The categories are only devices for classifying the activities of the self, and not in any sense necessary principles of the universe. It was at this point that Bowne passed beyond his teacher and friend, Lotze, to whom he dedicated his *Metaphysics*. For, although Lotze did emphasize the self even as Bowne did, the German thinker was still much concerned with the systematic study of the categories, whereas Bowne, especially in his later writings, tended to dismiss this study as secondary and of little importance, and to make the self central to philosophic analysis.

Bowne called his doctrine of the self a "transcendental empiricism." Basic to this doctrine is the belief that there is no reality except conscious experience. Everything real must be either a self or an idea belonging to a self. Any active being which is invariant — that is, which has self-identity, or remains constant in its own being in the midst of change — is a self. "We think of a thing as active, but still more as abiding. It has different states, but is always equal to, and identical with, itself."[22] The only type of thing which fulfills these demands for activity and self-identity is a self. When to these attributes we add self-consciousness and memory, binding the past and present together "in the unity of one consciousness," we have reached a conception of personality. In self-consciousness, the active being himself ties his past and his present together; thus his self-identity is the product of his own activity. "We become the same by making ourselves such."[23] The only true substance we know is the self, for it is only the self we know as a permanent thing with changing states. It is by analogy with our conception of the self as identical throughout changes that we form, misguidedly, a conception of non-personal things as changeless with changing states. Such a conception is misguided because "change penetrates to the centre of the thing, and the only thing which is permanent is the law of change."[24] Real being can only be personal being, for the idea of being must include permanence as well as change, identity as well as diversity.

Bowne wrote to A. C. Knudson, one of his disciples, "The question about my transcendental empiricism has no deep mystery in it. I simply aimed to call attention to the fact that intelligence cannot be understood through the categories, but the categories must be understood through intelligence, in that intelligence is simply a bottom fact which explains everything else, but accepts itself."[25] This is as true for the categories of being as it is for those of knowing. The categories of being are abstractions, "nothing but shadows," of the experience of persons. When we define "being" in terms of the categories of "action," "unity," and "identity in change," we must remember that the only way in which these categories acquire any concrete meaning is by their realization in experience. It is our own activity as persons which gives meaning to the category of action, our own unity of consciousness to the category of unity, our own consciousness of our permanence despite changes to the category of identity in change. Here personality is the "bottom fact" which explains the categories of being. These categories and those of knowledge — time, number, space, motion, quantity, being, quality, identity, causality, necessity, possibility, and purpose — are class terms, universals, having no real and independent existence. "The absolute person . . . is the basal fact of existence."[26] Men are, however, prone to the Fallacy of the Universal; they permit the general term to pass itself off as substantial reality. Thus, Bowne argued, the self is the only true cause that we know. To him this meant that whatever content the term "cause" had was derived from our consciousness of the actions of a self. The category of causality has to be understood in terms of a self. By the Fallacy of the Universal, however, we are tempted to make cause rather than the self central. We can not explain the self (as the materialists might), by any mechanical machinery, nor can we explain the self (as non-personalists might), by any metaphysical machinery. Bowne called any attempt to do so "inverted."

If we grant, with Bowne and other personalists, that ultimate reality is personal, and if we insist, as Bowne does, that other persons besides ourselves exist, then we have a basis for a personal pluralism, in which each person is a law unto himself. In order to convert this anarchy of finite individuals into a universe, some factor must be added to provide fixed laws by which the individual selves work. On any other theory transcendent action, or interaction, is contradictory. For action divides into two types: There is immanent action, such as thinking, in which the individual acts upon himself, and there is transcendent action, like attraction, in which the individual acts upon another individual. If each individual is self-determinative, then interaction — determination by another individual — is contradictory and community is impossible. This is not the old problem of action at a distance; the problem is "not to act across empty space, but to act across individuality." [27] Historically there have been many attempts to evade this problem, all of which have failed. Bowne's solution is to retain interaction at the expense of giving up the independence of the individuals. There is, he said, a constant dependence upon "one all embracing being, which is the unity of the many, and in whose unity an interacting plurality first becomes possible." [28] Interaction and independence are incompatible; the demands of system require interaction; therefore we must give up independence. What appears in finite terms as the transcendent actions of a plurality of individual selves is transformed into the immanent action of one fundamental, infinite, absolute, and independent being, of which all finite beings are created manifestations. These manifestations are able to interact, to determine each other mutually, because the same infinite being is present in them all, as their common ground.

This infinite being is a person. This, for Bowne, did not imply any limitation on the infinite being, for to be a person as he defined it was simply to be self-conscious — that is, to have knowledge of oneself and one's activities, and to determine oneself in accordance with this self-knowledge. Bowne maintained that the decisive argument for his personal theism is the intelligibility of the universe. The fact that our minds can comprehend the universe by thought is an indication that the universe was founded in thought. Were it not so founded, there could be no connection between our minds and things. There are various other arguments which Bowne used to demonstrate, from his standpoint, that the infinite being is an intelligent person. One is that we can know the nature of an active power by observing its acts, a rule which is generally true, but has special force when we are talking about mind. We do not directly observe the minds of our fellow men, but assert that they do have minds because their actions show order and purpose. Ordered and purposive acts are, then, the signs of mind. There are, he asserted, more evidences of order and purpose in the universal system of things than in human action. If we affirm mind in man, we have all the more reason for affirming it for the power whose works are revealed in nature. Furthermore, if we deny that there is a mind behind the system of things we must deny a mind to the finite persons, who, as we have already seen, must be manifestations of the infinite if there is to be any interaction among them. Moreover, a theory which denies a controlling mind in the universe shakes the finite mind's trust in itself, and is therefore untenable, because in establishing the theory we trust our minds to establish the untrustworthiness of our minds. "As philosophy can never be allowed to commit suicide, it is bound to take those views which are consistent with its own existence. Hence philosophy, when it understands its own conditions, must always be theistic." [29]

These arguments are all founded on the generally idealist position which Bowne advanced. He insisted that no matter what approach we take to the determination of the nature of reality, our thought issues in "contradiction and collapse" unless reality is conceived of as mental in its entirety. The only world we can know is a "thought world" of which "intelligence is at once the origin and the abiding seat." Unless we consider the idea of nature that conception which holds together its successive momentary phases and makes of them one system, we can not regard nature as being, for it is always a becoming. Thought can not deal with things, but it can deal with the rational ideas of systems of relationship in "what we call things."

These rational systems are what idealists in general concern themselves with; Bowne's personalistic emphasis was revealed by his refusal to consider the system apart from persons. "They are nothing," he wrote, "in abstraction from a mind which constitutes and maintains them." [30] Things are intelligible as ideas in a system, and system points to mind.

The fact that the universe is intelligible to our minds in any of its parts leads us to believe that it is intelligible to mind — though not necessarily to our finite human minds — in all its parts. The meaning of the universe in its fullness, the over-all system of its intelligible meanings, may take an eternity to decipher. Some of its meaning may lie forever outside the scope of finite mind, beyond human grasp; but the partial meaning which we can grasp makes us sure that there is an over-all pattern of meaning. We come back, at every turn, to Bowne's belief that we must trust our minds; our minds point to something. Again, in its outward reference, our minds point to things. If we take these things one by one, as isolated units, without relations, for Bowne insisted that there was no justification for considering relations as objective, these discrete units constitute the world of appearance, the phenomenal world. If, however, we take these things as co-implicated in a network of mutual relations, that network must be a system of ideas in some mind. But the co-implication of things suggests a unity of meaning which a finite mind can never complete in its limited experience. On these grounds, Bowne postulated an Infinite Mind.

He recognized, however, that this argument could not be used to prove as much as he wanted to prove. It must be remembered that Bowne's dominant interest in philosophizing was to find a rational justification for the religious beliefs to which he was antecedently committed. Intelligibility alone can not be used to prove that the Infinite Mind has a moral nature. The argument from intelligibility does not convert Infinite Mind into theistic God. Bowne realized, he said, that our full belief in theism can not be established solely on intellectual grounds. There are many other factors which enter into this belief. He thought, however, that one could find an intellectual starting-point which would most productively lead towards full belief. The individual self is constituted by the activity of knowing. This constitutive activity of the self always bears witness to something beyond itself. The power of the self may be indispensable, but it is a limited power. This individual self discovers other beings acting like itself and is convinced that there are other selves. The fact that selves act alike suggests that there is a "common-to-all," and this can be thought of best as the act of the World-soul. The World-soul has set finite selves over against itself; these finite selves share to a degree in the nature of the World-soul. On the basis of this common sharing in the nature of the World-soul, finite selves are able to enter into communication and interaction with each other.

The individual finite mind feels that it can know and that other minds can know. It is thus led to the assumption that it has been placed in a knowable universe. The mind, therefore, puts reason at the center of things. Things can not themselves have reason; we must assume that there is a God of Reason, or Infinite Mind. Because we have a regard for truth we assume that Truth has a cosmic embodiment in a God of Truth. A parallel argument holds with respect to righteousness and beauty. We find our minds and those of our fellows moving toward a regard for righteousness and beauty, and we assume, governing our actions by the assumption, that righteousness and beauty also have cosmic embodiments — that the God of Truth is also God of Righteousness and God of Beauty. It is in this way that we complete the God-idea; the merely intellectual conception of an Infinite Mind is filled out and becomes a theistic God. We must remember, too, if we would do justice to Bowne's thought, that this argument meant more to him than merely the view that God is a name for the sum of human ideals. He believed, although he knew that it could not be proved, that our ideals of truth, goodness, and beauty had an existence outside of our minds. He expressed this assumption in the statement that God is a Person living for a Truth, Goodness, and Beauty of which our best human understanding is only a feeble shadow. Any self which is capable of realizing values is a person; that Self which is the fulfilled realization of all values is the Supreme Person, or God.

III. ABSOLUTE IDEALISM:
JOSIAH ROYCE

The thought of Josiah Royce, professor of philosophy in Harvard University, is particularly interesting because of the way in which it brings together under one general system various types of idealist philosophy which were current in Royce's day. His central problem, one familiar to all idealists, was to avoid an extreme subjectivism in which the only existent which can be affirmed with certainty is the mind of the thinker, all other existents being assertable only as dependent upon this one certain mind, oneself. Once we accept the theory that what is called "matter" is only an appearance, a phenomenon, and that the only reality is mental, we find that we have opened the gate to difficulties in proving the real existence of an external world, and that we have also created a problem of proving the existence of other minds. We stand on the brink of "solipsism," the assertion that only the thinker himself exists. Royce's way of avoiding subjectivism was by means of his concept of the "Absolute Person" — a philosopher's way of saying God without involving himself in theological controversies — in whose mind the whole universe is a system of ideas in which finite minds share. At different stages in his philosophic development, as he fell under different influences, Royce reached this conclusion in different ways and expressed it in different terms, but the conclusion itself is constant.

Immanuel Kant had distinguished four fundamental philosophic problems: What do I know? What ought I to do? What may I hope? and, What is man? [31] Royce attempted to deal with the first two of these problems in his first philosophic book, *The Religious Aspect of Philosophy*, treating them in the context of theory of knowledge as they have been treated in the work of most modern philosophers. In the introduction to this work, Royce made a distinction between religion as a theory of morals (answering the question, What ought I to do?), and religion as a theory of faith (answering the question, What do I know?). That is, Royce separated, for purposes of his discussion, the ethical and the theological aspects of religion. He proposed to examine religion philosophically from these two approaches. He recommended the method of systematic doubt, scepticism, as proper for these studies. This sceptical criticism should be carried out by the philosopher in the area of religion as thoroughly and as fearlessly as in any other area. He must remember that he is not criticizing the truth, "if so be that there is any truth," but only human ideas, human notions, human approximations to the truth, in the hope that by his criticism he can lead these human ideas to a closer conformity with the truth. Sceptical doubt in matters of religion is "for a truth-seeker not only a privilege but a duty." [32]

As far as the philosopher is concerned, this duty to doubt is especially binding, because of the important role played by doubt in philosophy. Here we suggest one of the favorite themes of Royce's earlier work, that certainty first comes to the mind of the philosopher in the analysis of the process of doubting. He believed, and we shall soon present the argument by which he justified this belief, that the experience typical of the philosophic enterprise is "First, . . . the despair of a thorough-going doubt, and then the discovery that this doubt contains in its bosom the truth that we are sworn to discover." [33]

Let us now move with Royce to the conclusion of his early search for an ethical position. We find that he emerged into an ethical idealism whose highest ideal was the truly democratic one of resolving the confusions of conflicting wills. This ideal of a morality of harmony remains the goal of the moral life for Royce through all the different forms which his ethics took. In *The Religious Aspect of Philosophy*, Royce attempted to find a universal principle to serve as a guide for action in the morality of harmony. The principle might be called, in terms borrowed from Kant, a "categorical imperative." On the other hand, at least in its simplest form, it seems to be no more than an exposition of what the Biblical precept, "Thou shalt love thy neighbor as thyself" meant to Royce. For in its simplest form. Royce's imperative is "Insofar as in thee lies, act as if thou wert at once thy neighbor and thyself. Treat these two lives as one life." [34] There is an effort on Royce's part to reach a view broader than that of the individual without swallowing the individual up in the broader perspective. The task of ethics is to reach generality of perspective. This is so not only with respect to the intentions of the ethical act (as in Kant), but also with respect to the consequences of the ethical act (as in the Utilitarian position). In its definitive form, the Roycean imperative harmonizes the intention and the consequences of an ethical act, without losing sight of the attainment of a generalized standpoint: "Act as a being would act who included thy will and thy neighbor's will in the unity of one life, and who had therefore to suffer the consequences for the aims of both that will follow from the act of either." [35]

If we are to be able to speak at all of the resolution of conflicting wills, there must be some inner unity which makes this resolution possible. No person can be said to have an insight into the needs of the moral life until he has begun to realize the inner unity of nature among some of the actually existing conflicting wills which are to be found in the world around us. To know only the general rule, the imperative, is in no sense to have made a significant start on the living of a moral life. That start does not come without moral insight into the "true inner nature" of the wills whose conflicts the precept would have us resolve. The upper limit of moral insight, a limit which we are able to conceive by extension from the degree of moral insight that we have, would be an absolute moral insight which would be able to realize, at one and the same time, the inner nature of all the conflicting wills in the world. In addition to the realization that there is an inner unity despite the apparent conflict of wills, the nature of the moral insight leads those who have it to will to harmonize the conflicting wills in the world as far as this harmonization is possible. To harmonize these wills would mean to unify the lives of those whose wills and aims conflict, "to bring them into the unity of one life." Where only two wills are involved, mine and my neighbor's, then the demand of the moral insight on me is that I will to act as if he and I were "one being" whose aims included both my neighbor's aims and my aims. That is to say, I would try to think of my neighbor and myself as different aspects of a larger being, and act as this larger being would act in order to achieve as much as possible of the goals and purposes of its being.

When we talk of conflicting particular and personal aims the task of harmonization seems to amount to the seeking out of the most fruitful compromise possible. There are also more general aims, broad enough to serve as the goals of whole codes of morality, each accepted by large groups of people. Moral insight would require one's will to act as if the aims of all the people making up all these different groups were somehow to be included in one's own being. Inasmuch as the conflict among these general aims is apt to be on far more fundamental issues, it would be inadequate to do nothing more than compromise. To act "as if one included in one's own being the life of all those whose conflicting aims one realizes" [36] would necessitate making some kind of inclusive synthesis of the multiplicity of conflicting aims. Thus there is an Hegelian cast to Royce's early thinking as we move closer to the conception of an Absolute moral person. Moreover, as we have seen, there appears in Royce's thought a utilitarian concern for the consequences of the acts one wills. The moral insight on the individual level, where two wills are in conflict, involves my thinking of the consequences of my act in my neighbor's life and in relation to his aims. As a finite person, however, I could think of but a partial and limited set of consequences of any one act. An Absolute moral person with Absolute moral insight would stand committed in all his acts to a consideration of all the consequences of that act for all time as well as all the multiplicity of aims which will be touched by the act.

The moral insight, then, as it has been described above, is the foundation stone of Royce's ethical system. Moral insight is, in a sense, mediatory between the alternative positions of ethical dogmatism and ethical scepticism.

Ethical scepticism recognizes the actuality of many conflicting wills and many diverse aims, and sees in this plurality the ground for denying the possibility of a moral universal principle. It is in the intense study of the diversity proclaimed by scepticism that Royce found the certainty of an inner unity — the moral insight. Thus his ethical theory illustrates his belief that the discovery of certainty in doubt is a central stage in philosophic development.

Ethical dogmatism, on the other hand, is the assertion that there is one and only one proper end and aim for the moral life; over against this view, the moral insight insists upon diversity. Moreover, Royce believed that ethical dogmatism itself realizes the truth of a diversity of moral aims, "imperfectly and blindly." Because dogmatism does imperfectly realize the actuality of diversity, it tends to overstate its position and to hate and condemn all other aims. Ethical dogmatism, Royce maintained, is unthinking, irrational, capricious. An ethical dogmatist who seeks to ground his faith on reason can find no satisfactory rational position short of the acceptance of the moral insight. Moral scepticism, by continuing its reflection, and moral dogmatism, by making a beginning of reflection, both pass over into moral insight. "To get the moral insight, you must indeed have the will to get the truth as between the conflicting claims of two or more doctrines. This will being given, the moral insight is the necessary outcome even of skepticism itself." [37]

Even in this early period of his ethical thought, Royce had begun to recognize the importance of the organization of the moral life. His ethics was more social than individual. The individual, as such, has no rights; it is only as a fragment of "Life Universal" that my neighbor has any claims upon me, I upon him. My service to him is service to that larger whole, the "vast ocean of life," in which we are but drops, and to which we must be willing to sacrifice ourselves and our interests. Service to one's neighbor does not consist of increasing his individual happiness, hoping thereby to add to the "aggregate happiness of mankind." The aim of the moral life is unification, harmonization. Service to one another consists in furthering the cause of any work which serves to increase the unity and harmony of mankind. Almost as an afterthought Royce added that this must be done "without cramping the talent of any one of us." The task of the moral insight is to promote interconnectedness, relationship, union among men by means of its service to art, science, truth, and the state. Personal independence is but a temporary stage whose ultimate aim is the realization of the universal will. "The One Will must conquer." This One Will is not intolerant of diversity; it is an inclusive will. It is not "a one-sided will." It is the higher unity in diversity of all particular aims and all particular wills, save those which steadfastly deny unity. The One Will desires to include all purposes and all passions within itself to the end that all possible life may be realized. "Its warfare is never intolerance, its demand for submission is never tyranny, its sense of the excellence of its own unity is never arrogance." [38] It is thus that the Absolute Will stands at the apex of Royce's early ethics.

When Royce left the question, What ought I to do? and plunged into the attempt to answer the question, What do I know? — when he entered upon the search for religious truth, the discovery of certainty in doubt, and truth in error, which was of comparatively little importance to his ethics, became central. Royce pointed out that the attempt to live intellectually in a world of scepticism and doubt leads us for practical purposes into a world of postulations. Although we deny that any principles have absolute certainty and necessity, we recognize the demand for the making of assumptions in order that our practical life in many areas may continue. At the heart of the realm of postulates lie the postulate of science and the postulate of religion, which together present the basic conditions under which men are resolved to do their work. Men demand simplicity and rationality as the conditions of scientific activity. The postulate which makes religious activity possible is that that description of the world is true which arouses men's highest moral interests and satisfies their highest moral needs. On these two postulates a theoretical system of idealism is formulated, leading at its apex to an Infinite Knowing One, or Absolute Mind. This structure is entirely an intellectual one to this point. It is based upon postulates which express the requirements of human thought but say nothing about the objective truth of conclusions elaborated upon them. The one course by which Royce thought that his postulated system could be proved objectively true was by demonstrating, out of the nature of scepticism itself, that there are absolute and necessary truths.

Royce's method of demonstrating this was to show that the very admission of the possibility of error proves the necessity of truth. There is an indubitable principle left at the lowest depths of the most thoroughgoing scepticism, namely that "the conditions that determine the logical possibility of error must themselves be absolute truth." [39] It is a very simple matter that started Royce on the path to this discovery; to doubt our beliefs about the external world implies that we may be in error in our judgments. The fact of doubting means that "there is a difference between true and false statements about nature." [40] To affirm our belief also involves affirming that this difference is a real one. To deny our belief — or someone else's — also involves the same affirmation. Here then is a necessary truth — one which is indubitably true because it is involved alike in the affirmation and the negation of the same statement. It is certainly true that there is a difference between true and false statements about the world. Furthermore, Royce believed that his position provides an argument against the theory that all truth is relative because "different judgments in different minds or made at different times" [41] have no real object in common. For, he pointed out, if there is no real difference between true and erroneous statements, then the statement that there is such a difference is not truly false; and in the adverb "truly" the distinction which has just been denied is reintroduced. "If it is wrong to say that there is Absolute Truth, then the statement that there is absolute truth is itself false." [42] Is it false absolutely? If it is, then there is absolute truth and falsity. If it is false only relatively, then the question of absolute or relative truth and falsity must go on being asked until finally some statement is found on which the entire series is based. At the very least, Royce pointed out, if we would make sense, we must say "No absolute truth exists *save this truth itself, that no absolute truth exists.*" [43] Where the rational argument for absolute truth had become as sophistical as this, it is no wonder that the pragmatic and experimental theory of truth (see Chapter 7) was so welcome. On the basis of these proofs of absolute and necessary truth from the possibility of error, Royce proceeded to a rational establishment of the objective truth of the absolute idealism which he had stated earlier as a system produced on a postulational foundation.

In Royce's later works the themes which have been suggested are presented in changed dress, but with the same insights at their heart. In *The Spirit of Modern Philosophy*, after a careful and perceptive account of the thought of major German philosophers of the nineteenth century, Royce presented his own ideas in a series of "positive" chapters. Using precisely the same dialectical device by which we have seen him establish the necessity of truth, he now argued the necessity of objectivity on the ground of the possibility of meaning. Royce recognized that it was the same argument, and made reference in his later book to his earlier statement of the argument. It is here that Royce shows his concern with the problem of avoiding solipsism. "How," he asked, "does one ever escape from the prison of the inner life? Am I not in all this merely wandering amidst the realm of my own ideas?"[44] If we insist, with the idealist, that the world is not only real, but also rationally structured and knowable because of its rational structure, we are describing the real world as essentially a mind or a world of minds. In one sense, Royce admitted, this description of the world makes it impossible "to get to any truth beyond myself." This is all right, because there is an essential unity of all minds, so that "those other minds that constitute your outer and real world are in essence one with your own self." [45] Each of us is an inner self; but "the inner self is through and through an appeal to a larger self." [46] It is this larger self that knows all; when the inner and partial self inquires about any meaning, it is inquiring for something which, as a part of the larger self, it already in some sense possesses. Whenever my thought *means* a particular object, whether it means the object in doubt, in error or in knowledge, my thought and its object are both parts of one larger thought. "The self that means the object is identical with the larger self that possesses the object." A careful examination of our most trivial thought from this perspective would lead to a proof of an Absolute Self, all-knowing in whose mind the world is a system of ideas which, in all our in-tellectual activity, we mean. Unless this is so, Royce asserted, "I can't even be meaning that object yonder, can't even be in error about it, can't even doubt its existence." [47]

Again, in *The Conception of God*, Royce argued that our partial and fragmentary experience requires an all-inclusive, Absolute Experience for its interpretation. This Absolute Experience is Omniscient Being or God. Absolute truth, whose necessity we have already seen, can not exist for finite being, nor can finite experience recognize its own fragmentary character. In asserting the fragmentariness of finite experience we are implicitly asserting the necessity of an absolute Experience which, in its knowledge of the whole, can recognize the partiality and finiteness of human experi-ence. "The very effort to deny our absolute experience" implies its assertion.[48] In his Gifford Lectures on *The World and the Individual*, we find, more extensively stated, a similar argument leading to the conclusion that there is an Absolute Idea, or Self-Conscious Knower who is the ultimate fulfillment of all partial idea and is, therefore, all truth and reality. This is the full development of the "internal mean-ing" of the idea, that is, its "embodiment of a single conscious pur-pose." The idea also has an "external meaning" in its correspondence to facts which are themselves not part of the idea. Truth is defined as the correspondence of the internal and external meanings of an idea. It is the internal meaning, however, which is in the last analysis the dominant one for Royce. The completion and fulfilment of an idea means, then, that its external meaning (the "facts" or "exis-tence"), corresponds to its complete internal meaning (the "inten-tion" or "purpose"). "What is, or what is real, is as such the com-plete embodiment, in individual form and in final fulfilment, of the internal meaning of finite ideas." [49]

This emphasis on the importance of intention or purpose makes willing the key to all knowledge. In finite knowing processes, the complete internal meaning of any particular idea can never be known, for this complete meaning would be the entire system of all possible finite ideas. In order that there may be a complete internal meaning, the entire system, everything that is, must be known to "one final knower" in "one inclusive act." There is no fact except a "fact present to some consciousness." The whole world as a single fact can only exist as present to the consciousness of this one final knower. Ultimate purpose must be the purpose of this being, and all finite purposes, our purposes, must be justified as possession of a unique part of this unitary purpose. The uniqueness of each of our purposes is the safeguard of individuality; the inclusiveness of the ultimate purpose is the guarantee of rationality. The very fact that our finite purposes are distinguished from each other implies for Royce the existence of an Absolute Being whose purpose it is that our purposes should be distinct. "What is, is present to the insight of a single self-conscious Knower, whose life includes all that he knows, whose meaning is wholly fulfilled in his facts, and whose self-consciousness is complete." [50]

If we recall the discussion of Royce's early ethical theory, we shall remember that he sought to formulate a morality of harmony, to resolve the conflict of wills by bringing these conflicting wills into the unity of one life. In the early statement, there was a distinction between this ethical enterprise and the enterprise of knowing. Gradually, ending in the central emphasis given to will or purpose in *The World and the Individual*, Royce moved toward a view in which doing takes precedence over knowing. In Royce's last works the demands of the moral life are considered as primary, while the cognitive aspects of life run far behind. Furthermore, in the conception of the Absolute Person as it has emerged in the various works which we have discussed we have seen the forming of the outlines of that larger life in which conflicting wills can be comprehended as different aspects of One Will.

Because the moral and practical emphasis of Royce's thought became increasingly important through his career, his later reformulations of ethical theory are particularly interesting. In these works, in part under the stimulus of studies to which Charles Sanders Peirce (see Chapter 7, section II) goaded him, Royce developed his early theme of bringing many lives into the unity of a single life into a theory of community. In this newer approach, the Absolute, whose earlier form had been similar to the God of conventional theistic religion, was transformed into the Spirit of Community; the process of knowledge, which had been conceived in the traditional pattern of nineteenth-century German philosophy, was socialized into the process of interpretation; the world, which had been defined in idealist fashion as a realm of ideas, now was treated primarily under the aspect of a community of minds.

There is a transitional statement in his *Philosophy of Loyalty* (1908). In this book Royce defended the thesis that, for the loyal individual, loyalty itself, regardless of the cause to which it is devoted, is a supreme good. From the point of view of the world, however, it is necessary to decide what are the causes worthy of loyalty. Such causes must be those which join many persons into the unity of a single life. A cause worthy of loyalty would be one which had a concern for the individual in his uniqueness, and, at the same time, was super-personal. The only cause which emerges in Royce's discussion is the cause of loyalty itself. Loyalty to loyalty becomes, then, from the point of view of the world, the supreme good. The highest moral command is "Be loyal to loyalty." [51] At this point in his career, Royce was seeking for a more specific description of the unity into which he hoped to harmonize many lives. With the materials he then had available, the best he could do was to suggest that while loyalty is a good, loyalties may come into conflict. Yet even in the very conflict of these loyalties there is implicit an ulterior loyalty — to loyalty itself — on which all loyal individuals can unite. Like so many of Royce's other arguments, this is irrefutable and trivial. Something new had to be found before Royce could satisfy himself that he was saying something significant about social ethics.

When he studied mathematical logic at Peirce's suggestion, Royce found a hint which he elaborated into the latest form of his ethico-social thought. Here was the point: The relation between two things — objects, persons, minds — can never be an harmonious one; any pair is "dangerous" because of the possibility of misunderstanding, conflicts of interest, or mutual wrongs. The basic harmonious relation is not the pair, but the triad — the threesome — in which, whenever conflict develops between the interests of any two of the three, the third is present as a disinterested party to interpret his fellows to each other. The triad, is, then, the first community, and, inasmuch as its basic function is interpretation, Royce called it "the community of interpretation." This triadic community takes many forms; there are various communities of interpretation in society. What is common to all is that one member of the triad, C, mediates between two others, A and B, by interpreting A to B and B to A, thus minimizing or eliminating their conflicts. Royce hoped, especially as World War I began, that out of this conflict there might somehow develop an international community of interpretation of broader reach than the Hague World Court, which was one example of a community of interpretation. He regarded every judicial situation as a community in which the court was attempting to resolve conflict between plaintiff and defendant by a process of mediation or interpretation.

Royce considered insurance as one of the most satisfactory illustrations of the community of interpretation. He went so far as to propose a plan for world peace based upon international insurance. Without entering into the details of the peace plan, it is nevertheless important to see how the insurance company transforms a situation of conflict into a community of interpretation. "A" in this case is the Adventurer; he lives by taking risks. Some of these risks are financial, some involve his very life. "B" is his Beneficiary; if the Adventurer is successful in his risks and speculations, his Beneficiary profits. If the Adventurer is unsuccessful, his Beneficiary loses. The Beneficiary, naturally, wishes to restrict in one way or another the risk-taking of the Adventurer; the Adventurer resists any curtailment of his activities. Their conflicting interests constitute Adventurer and Beneficiary a "dangerous pair." Into this situation steps "C," the (insurance) Company, which reconciles the pair because it is the business of the Company to guarantee the Beneficiary against any loss into which the Adventurer may fall, and, at the same time, to add one more speculation, the insurance itself, to the risks which the Adventurer loves to take. The Company interprets the Beneficiary's need for security to the Adventurer, and the Adventurer's need for risk-taking to the Beneficiary. A and B learn to cooperate through the agency of C in at least this one respect. They are brought by C "into some kind of social unity, such as will make them act as if they were, in a certain respect, one man." [52] With this we find that we have made a full circle. In the last years of his life Royce found in the community of interpretation a satisfactory way of specifying what had to be done to bring many people into the unity of one life. Furthermore, inasmuch as the interpreter, C, is devoted to the cause of a union of wills of A and B, he is, in terms of Royce's transitional ethics, a "loyal" person. Thus the idea of a community of interpretation unified and completed the structure of Royce's philosophy.

IV. SPECULATIVE IDEALISM:
JAMES EDWIN CREIGHTON

About the beginning of the twentieth century many changes took place on the American philosophic scene. Partly as a result of the decisive defeats that theology had suffered in the controversies over evolution, partly as a result of the increasing influence of the German academic tradition on the American college, and partly as a result of the shifting interests of a generation of teachers of philosophy, the intimate relation between philosophy and theology in our colleges began to break down. Philosophy came into its own as an independent discipline with its own methods and its own subject matter, at least in the major colleges and universities in the United States. The process of emancipation from theology is still incomplete in some sections of the country, but by and large it was well advanced at the turn of the century, thus making possible a freedom of speculative thought which had previously been impossible.

As a result of this separation it became increasingly necessary to start non-theological journals and reviews in which the secular philosophers of America could publish their ideas for the information of their fellow-philosophers. The St. Louis *Journal of Speculative Philosophy* made a start in this direction at a non-academic level. It was not until the 1890's, however, that the first professional journals, *The International Journal of Ethics* (now called simply *Ethics*), and *The Philosophical Review* were established. Among the non-academic journals of the period which published articles of philosophic interest were Francis Ellingwood Abbot's *The Index,* which was later taken over by Paul Carus and retitled *The Open Court,* and Carus' *The Monist,* a publication of considerable philosophic distinction. In the early years of the twentieth century, *The Journal of Philosophy* was added to the list. These publications and other later additions provided an open forum for the discussion of philosophical issues. They have contributed importantly to the development of American philosophy in the twentieth century.

It was also at the beginning of the twentieth century that the American Philosophical Association, the professional society of the philosophic fraternity in the United States, came into being. Before this time various scientific societies had been formed, but philosophers had not seen any reason for organization. Despite the opposition of some of America's most distinguished philosophers, including William James, the Association was formed and has continued to flourish, to provide both a social and an intellectual stimulus for philosophers and teachers of philosophy. James Edwin Creighton, professor of philosophy in the Sage School at Cornell University, was the first president of the American Philosophical Association. In his presidential address (March, 1902), the forerunner of a long series of such addresses, Creighton spoke of the values of this new organization and of its tasks and purposes. Among other, more philosophical, comments which will be discussed later, Creighton discussed the need for face-to-face meetings with men of differing philosophic views. The personal acquaintance of workers in any field, he averred, is perhaps the best means of demonstrating to men their unity and agreement in purpose and the way in which their results are complementary. Personal relations among philosophers will breed a greater sympathy and understanding. "One may ignore or almost totally misunderstand the published views of another man; but when these are reinforced by the living personality they cannot so readily be either ignored or misunderstood." [53] Indeed, Creighton suggested (one hopes jocularly), that it is essential to the sanity and balance of philosophers that, at reasonable intervals, they should be "penned up and forced to listen to the views of their fellows." [54] Although the compulsory aspect of Creighton's suggestion has never been enforced, it is none the less true that as a general rule America's philosophers have learned in the give and take of philosophic congresses, many under the sponsorship of the American Philosophical Association, to be less fiercely partisan in their own views and to make an attempt at the sympathetic understanding of alternative views.

In addition to serving the philosophic community as the first president of its association, Creighton was for many years editor or co-editor of *The Philosophical Review*. From its foundation, this journal has been associated with the Sage School at Cornell, which has been a major influence in American philosophy for six decades. The first head of the Sage School was Jacob Gould Schurman, an enthusiastic student of the philosophy of Kant. Schurman gave the school at Cornell a characteristic temper which it has maintained throughout its history. In Schurman's version, this was a critical idealism, mediating between the exclusive claims of rationalism and empiricism.

He welcomed enthusiastically the independence of philosophy and made his own contribution by inaugurating the publication of *The Philosophical Review*, in order to supplement the specialized researches of philosophers by providing them with a common outlet. "It is fortunate," he wrote, "that the spirit of specialization has taken possession of Philosophy, and we may congratulate ourselves on the special investigations and special publications conducted by Americans. But division of labor is profitless without co-operation." [55] Schurman himself did little writing; in what he did we can see the effort to assert the independence of the discipline of philosophy by the assertion that Darwinism had no direct relevance to philosophic investigation and, in particular, to the field of ethics.

The era of the minister-presidents of colleges (see Chapter 3) had passed, and that of the philosopher-presidents had now arrived. In 1892, Schurman was elevated to the presidency of Cornell, and his place as head of the Sage School was taken by one of his students, James Edwin Creighton. Under Creighton's leadership the real distinction of the Sage School began. For more than thirty years, until his death in 1924, Creighton and his fine staff trained many excellent teachers who carried the moderating influence of their school throughout the length and breadth of the country. His administrative work as head of the Sage School, his editorship of *The Philosophical Review*, and his serious personal concern with his teaching and with the development of his students — a devotion repaid by their loyalty — combined to prevent Creighton from writing extensively. Much of what he did write was in the form of criticism of other philosophic positions current in his time. Only the main outlines of Creighton's philosophy can be presented, because he never developed its details. Yet there is enough to make it clear that his practical activities as educator, as editor, and as administrator were the active expressions of his theoretical views about the nature of mind, thought, and purpose. His philosophy and his life were not at war with each other, but were different aspects of one enterprise, the socializing of thought.

Creighton preferred the term "speculative philosophy" to describe his method. He intended, by the use of this descriptive term, to distinguish his thought from what he called "atomic realism," or the empirical tradition. For atomic realism the existences whose aggregation constitutes the objective world are in themselves without meaning. Atomic realism concerns itself, therefore, with the attempt to show how the "concrete" world is constructed out of "certain hypothetical elements." The relations between these elements are not internal; they are supplied by the mind from outside to explain what holds the elements together and builds a universe. So, too, "all significance and meaning are secondary and derivative, imposed upon the universe by the subjective mind." [56] Speculative idealism, on the other hand, insists, and has insisted throughout its long history, that existence and meaning are inseparable. Anything that exists is part of a system of relations and values. Merely to be, without being in such a system, to be as an entity in isolation, is an abstraction which can not be experienced. Historically, speculative idealism has taken its stand upon "reality in its concrete significance," and has attempted to understand things and their relations together. All our direct experience is experience of a "significant world," and speculative idealism "holds fast to the unity of existence and significance." [57] Essentially, what this involves is placing greater stress on value or significance than on existence, because existence is included within significance; part of the value of anything is its existence. If we start at the other end, with existent entities, we can not in any way build up to value; "there is no road to significance if one begins with bare existences." [58]

Although the philosophy of Berkeley has been called "idealism" it is actually in Creighton's opinion a "mentalistic" form of atomic realism. It is an attempt to show how the universe is made out of mental elements, not an attempt to understand the objective world. Berkeleianism says that everything that is is mental in character, either mental substance or the content of mental substance. Berkeley's philosophy is not a genuine idealism, because instead of striving to enter more deeply by reflection into the inner meaning of the outer reality which we know by intuition, instead of trying to penetrate to the meaning of human experience of the world, it "proceeds dogmatically to transform experience into an order of existing ideas, to elaborate a theory of active substances and passive ideas as the machinery through which it is to be understood." [59] Existence is no longer conceived to be located in an external order of things; its residence is thought to be the internal order of ideas. Existence is shifted from a physical to a psychological realm. But the relation between the mind and its objects is still conceived as an external and mechanical one. Simply to call things inner instead of outer, simply to convert existence from a physical to a psychological fact, does not convert existence into meaning. Creighton insisted that Berkeley thought of "experience as a collection of ideas, and each idea as a particular mode of existence, being nothing else than that which at the moment it is perceived to be," whereas for speculative idealism experience was to be regarded "as a system of developing meanings." [60]

Although there is some ambiguity in the philosophic position taken by Kant, so that from one point of view he seems to be involved in a speculative undertaking, Creighton found that in general Kant's philosophy was concerned with the attempt to build up objective reality out of "the disconnected particulars of inner representations," [61] so that Kant's work reinforced the Berkeleian type of realism rather than idealism. From his own speculative standpoint, Creighton regretted Kant's tendency toward a subjective placement of the center of the philosophic universe in the knower rather than in the known. Creighton's speculative idealism was an objective idealism; he thought that philosophy must begin, not with isolated mental states, but with an attitude of a subject to an object, that is, with a subject-object relationship. Subject and object, mind and nature, are not distinct types of being, but, on the other hand, the distinction between subject and object is not only a difference in their functions within experience. There is, rather, a primary duality within experience between the subject of experience and the object of experience, where the subject is not merely a passive "capacity for sensations or feelings" but is an active "process of objectification." [62] This is the core of Creighton's reply to Ralph Barton Perry's argument that to define experience in terms of the attitude of a self or subject to reality can yield only an individual and subjective experience — the argument of Perry's paper on "the egocentric predicament." Speculative idealism has never considered the mind as a thing apart from the external order of nature. Since it recognizes no "ego 'alone with its states,'" it has no egocentric predicament. Problems of how the mind as such can know reality as such speculative idealism dismisses as meaningless abstraction. "Without any epistemological grace before meat it falls to work to philosophize, assuming, naïvely, if you please, that the mind by its very nature is already in touch with reality." [63] The relations between what is called mind and what is called nature are internal relations. To be a mind at all is to be in relation with nature. The reciprocal relationship, that to be nature at all is to be in relation with mind, Creighton did not insist upon, but he did assert that "the external order that we call nature is something that is at least knowable by mind . . . that 'knowability' is a genuine characteristic of things, not an accident external to them." [64]

For Creighton, then, subject and object are correlative terms. Any defect in our conception of either involves a corresponding deficiency in our conception of the other. "Without a genuine subject, no objects, and without real objects, no possibility of a true subject." [65] It is important, if we would fully understand what Creighton meant by this, to recall that the term "subject" is used by Creighton in the sense of "a process of interpretation in terms of ideas and universal relations." [66] Experience is the expression of a self-conscious subject. As such, experience is guided and determined by the values and purposes which the subject accepts; experience is directed toward ends. It is teleological. These values, purposes, ends, and ideals, which the subject accepts and which determine experience are not, however, merely personal attitudes, hopes, desires, or wishes, operating in some haphazard fashion. They are, rather, universal demands which are binding on all subjects and which are systematically interrelated and interconnected, that is, in a word, rational. An account of experience which describes it as the attempt to realize a rational life is the only sort of account which is true to the nature of experience. Experience is, then, both life and something more than life; it is "a life consciously lived in relation to an environment." [67] The subject-object relation is a constituent of rationality, for rationality implies that there is "an objective order to be known." [68] This objective order is the tool which must be used by the subject in all his practical activity; its nature and limitations as a tool define the limits of his practical activity.

Our experience is constituted just as importantly by our relation to other subjects as it is by the subject-object relation. The difference between the two types of relation is that these other subjects can never be tools or means to us. They are co-sharers with us in a common experience and they cooperate with us in the effort to realize common goals. A rational life can not be lived without such relations with other subjects. "The demand for a rational life there-

fore carries with it a demand for a social life." [69] It is in this way
that experience, although it remains personal, nevertheless is objective; its validity is not limited to the passing moment, nor is it completely bound in by one's mental states. Experience is a rational order
which is shared by many individuals. Thus there are three "moments"
whose interrelations experience defines. "Experience is at once an
explication or revelation of reality, a comprehension of the mind of
one's fellows, and a coming to consciousness on the part of the mind
of the nature of its own intelligence." [70] Of these three processes,
it is the second, the development of the social nature of intellectual
life, which is the most characteristic theme in Creighton's thought.
He believed, and lived by his belief, that the intellectual life can not
be led in complete isolation. It can be realized only "through membership in a social community." [71] Individual minds are bound to
each other by mutual participation in a realm of ideas or meanings.
At no point in its career is thinking an individual project; it is always
a social venture. Thinking requires a very close and understanding
partnership with other minds. There is always a discussion involved in
any act of thought. Certainly the verification of the truth of any idea
requires "the coöperation and interplay of a plurality of minds." [72]

A view of this sort demands the reconsideration of our notion of
the philosophic individual, even as we have reconstructed our idea of
the moral or political individual. We must recognize that one of the
essential elements of individuality is internal relations with his fellow
men. "We have been forced to abandon the notion of *exclusive* individuality, and to recognize that individuals have reality and significance . . . just in so far as they embody and express the life and
purpose of a larger social whole of which they are members." [73]
Without society, there can be no individual. To this conception
Creighton assigned the term concrete individuality, that is, individuality as the particularizing of some social universal. The idea
of an exclusive individual is abstract; that of a social individual is concrete. The older conception of exclusive individuality provides no
basis for a theory of coöperation. The newer conception of concrete individuality does furnish the ground for such a theory, because
it conceives of what each individual brings to the coöperative effort
as itself the product of a collaboration of minds. It builds coöperation on a foundation of coöperation, rather than attempting to
ground a social phenomenon on a self-centered base.

Creighton divided an act of thought into three parts — "the formulation of the problem, the ideational construction, and the process of verification." [74] He made the claim that, if we consider actual cases, each of these three stages of the act of thought is social. In each stage the thinker uses the mind of his fellow men. Our problems grow out of the requirements and the interests of our society; this may mean that we are roused to opposition by some condition existing in the society or that the problem is brought to consciousness in us by the leading of other minds. When we attempt to solve the problem, other attempted solutions of this and similar problems by other minds are our constant resources and point of reference. Discussion, oral and internal, is the characteristic form taken by attempts at problem solving. Finally, verification, as we have already suggested, is a social process; "our thoughts gain their certificate of truth only after being sifted, tried, and tested by a larger and more complete experience than that of any individual." [75] To think at all is to enter into a working partnership with our fellow men. This is what Creighton meant by "the doctrine of the social nature of thinking."

A specific opportunity to express this ideal came to Creighton as first president of the American Philosophical Association. He told his colleagues that he conceived of this association as the model of a rational society where, if anywhere on earth, there would be found those who might "preserve the vitality of thought" by "a genuine give and take process." [76] He spoke to his peers of the task of thinking together, urging them to remember that by such conscious intellectual coöperation the sciences had made their notable advances. In philosophic work, there is a double form which this coöperative effort must take. In the first place, philosophers are especially bound to build on the work of their predecessors; philosophy is not the history of philosophy, but the study of the great historical systems of the past can help us to understand contemporary questions and to formulate them intelligibly. He did not call for an uncritical acceptance of the past, but for a recognition that "there is a dead as well as a living past," [77] and that our obligation is to the study of the living past. Only in terms of present problems is it possible to distinguish what is living in the past — so that "the history of philosophy is only intelligible when read in the light of present-day problems." [78] In the second place, philosophers are especially bound to make use of the coöperative method of discussion among the members of a generation. All the philosophers of a generation are not at work on the same problems, but they are working on closely related ones, because "there is in every generation a main drift of problems." [79] Unless we work within this main drift, our work is unfruitful. The more philosophy abandons the attempt to work out a system of the universe by deduction from fundamental principles, and bases itself upon inductive procedures starting from the facts of experience, the more vital it becomes for philosophers to work together. It is far easier "to lose oneself in subjective fancies in this field" than in others; coöperative effort is a way to keep our fancies under control. Generally, "the task which seems too hard for the individual appears in a different light when he regards himself as a member of a body of organized workers." [80] It was as such a body exemplifying intellectual society that Creighton envisaged the American Philosophical Association.

Creighton was criticized on the ground that his concern for social mind and for experience as objective and sharable did not take adequate account of the quality of experience as the inner life of a subject. He replied that to view experience as the conscious life of a subject is the important difference between philosophy and science. He held, however, that the inner life of a subject is not subjectivity, singularity, and uniqueness, but is, rather, the attitude of the subject toward objects and other subjects. "The true inner experience is the rational life of a subject" [81] including objective relations to things and other persons. The mental states, affections, and volitions which are referred to by some philosophers as constituting the inner life of a subject are abstractions from the inner "concrete" experience to which Creighton had reference. Creighton's thought is consistently free from the psychological theory of knowledge which bases itself on separate and isolated mental states inhering in a mind or mental substance.

The attitude of a human subject to the world has been described in Creighton's terms as a demand for a rational life, and experience has been characterized as the process in which that demand is progressively realized. The life of knowledge, which is "a process of mediation and interpretation," [82] was ranked by Creighton as more important than the life of the emotions or that of the will, for, to him, the meaning of these is to be sought in the more universal and inclusive life of knowledge. The activity through which the subject realizes its demand for a rational life is judgment. Judgment and consciousness are identical conceptions; the conscious life is an activity of judging. "To be conscious is to judge; to be in consciousness, is, to some degree, to be already interpreted and universalized. . . . At any given point, then, we may describe the conscious life as a continuous judgment, which not only embraces and gives meaning to all the states of the moment, but includes and supports the whole system of our knowledge up to date." [83] Such a judgment is never completely harmonious and coherent, and, therefore, each judgment leads on to further processes of analysis and interpretation. The conscious life is always in process of becoming; the judgments we make are not separate and detached functions, but are the means by which at any given moment experience is progressing toward its ultimate goal of rational life. It is in these terms that Creighton reintroduced purpose into his philosophic perspective. The complete continuity of experience involves the subordination of all the various ends of life to the one all-inclusive purpose of the attainment of rationality.

It is clear that Creighton shares with Royce, and in general with recent idealism, a concern for the theory of community; it is also clear that he differs from Bowne and all who stress personal identity as a basis of reality. The additional point that in Creighton idealism has reached a standpoint that is very close to that of the new naturalism will be clarified by discussion in Chapter 9. There are differences, especially in the privileged status which Creighton's philosophy assigns to mind and in his association of existence and value. This is partly a result of the Sage School conception of the office of philosophy as mediatorial and partly a result of the generally secular tone of his philosophy. Whatever the reason, Creighton gives evidence that twentieth-century American idealism has taken a new departure which may, in time, lead to a vigorous development of speculative philosophy in America.

7

PRAGMATIC PERSPECTIVES

I. TECHNIQUE OR TEMPERAMENT

Of all the philosophies we discuss here, pragmatism has seemed to many to be the most distinctively American in its outlook. This comment has seldom been meant as praise of pragmatism or of the pragmatic outlook. It is, rather, intended as a derogatory dismissal of pragmatism because of its sharp break with the traditional canons of philosophic respectability, its impatience (at least in its popular form), with precise analysis, its opposition to granting any privileged status in the universe to the human mind, its bold sweeping away of distinctions which had stood for centuries, and its post-Darwinian biological emphasis on change, growth, and process as the object of philosophic understanding.

Arthur O. Lovejoy, long professor of philosophy at the Johns Hopkins University and adherent to the school of critical realists (see Chapter 8, section I), wrote one of the most penetrating criticisms of pragmatism. He pointed out that the very term "pragmatism" itself was so uncritically used that it had thirteen different meanings in the literature of the then (1908) still young movement. It is true, of course, that some of the differences which Lovejoy found were so slight and trivial as to be of no account save to a determined opponent. It is also true that the pragmatists themselves had pointed to the most important of Lovejoy's distinctions. Nevertheless the fact that such a criticism could be made indicates a fair degree of technical carelessness in the pragmatic writers.

There is a sense in which we can refer to pragmatism as distinctively American without indicating either praise or blame, eulogy or derogation. To suggest this in any detail would require a lengthy discussion of the distinctive elements in American culture and a demonstration that pragmatism is the expression in terms of a philosophic movement of these culture patterns. To do this exhaustively would be beyond the scope of this work, but the direction of this sort of discussion can be shown in one illustration. American society has not been marked by fixed lines of demarcation between classes. It has not been a society in which the social position of any individual is irrevocably fixed by that of his ancestors. The criterion of social position has been the achievements of his life, not his ancestry. In line with this social mobility, there has never been a sharp line drawn between intellectual activity and manual activity. To some extent at least, every individual has been educated for both head work and hand work. Politically, the extended franchise has been the expression of the view that every man is intellectually capable of making decisions in matters which affect his welfare and that of his society. There have been some distortions of this tradition in the spoils system, based upon the view that every man is equally competent for any governmental position. By and large, however, the effect has been to keep intellectual life and practical life in close touch with one another.

Thus, the American philosopher, however academic his philosophy, has been no academic recluse. He has a familiarity with the farm, the factory, and the marketplace which is bred of the associations of his life, and not gained solely from the reading of books about agriculture, industry, and commerce. When pragmatic philosophers keep their ideas close to the practical concerns of life, utilizing metaphors drawn from the fields or the workshops, they are not so much giving expression to "American practicality" and "Yankee materialism" as reflecting in their philosophies the continuity of the practical and the intellectual life by celebrating the interpenetration of practice and theory.

What we learn from an investigation of this sort, is the nature of pragmatism as a temperament among American philosophers that was produced in some measure by the culture in which they were nurtured. H. Heath Bawden, one of the lesser pragmatists, wrote "The spirit of democracy has at last reached the metaphysicians. . . . The new philosophy called pragmatism [is] . . . a sign that the democratic ideal is destined to transform our thinking as well as our conduct."[1] We discover pragmatic statements made by philosophers who would have resented strongly any suggestion that they were pragmatists, like Joseph Le Conte of the University of California, teacher of Josiah Royce, who said "Whatever doctrine or belief, in the long run and throughout the history of human advancement, has tended to the betterment of our race, must have in it an element of truth by virtue of which it has been useful." [2] We find intimations of a pragmatic attitude in Jonathan Edwards' criteria for the graciousness of affections (see Chapter 1, section II), in Benjamin Franklin's schemes for the improvement of himself and his community (see Chapter 2, section I), and in Ralph Waldo Emerson's argument for an ideal philosophy (see Chapter 4, section II), as well as in many other American thinkers. We might even make sociologically intelligible the fact that pragmatism was first formulated in America and that it has gained comparatively little support outside of America. But we would not learn anything about the nature of pragmatism as a technical philosophy centering in a theory of knowledge which arose historically in the criticism of the thought of Immanuel Kant, and which had ramifications in legal, social, religious, and political philosophy, and some important consequences for philosophy of science. Nor would we learn in what sense pragmatism is to be regarded as one development among many in the long history of British empiricism. So, although the study of pragmatism as a temperamental phenomenon is interesting, it will be subordinated in the balance of our treatment to the more technical aspects of the pragmatic movement.

John Dewey, in a sketch of the development of pragmatism in America, suggested that when William James referred to pragmatism as "a new name for an old way of thinking,"[3] the historic ancestry implied was to the work of Francis Bacon (1561-1626), who made important contributions to the development of empiricism in the British tradition. Whether the specific reference was to Bacon, we do not know. Dewey was correct, however, in emphasizing the importance of British empiricism to American pragmatism. Whereas the empirical philosophy which has been dominant in Britain for so long is concerned to analyze the process by which generalizations are built up out of experience, pragmatism has been far less interested in how we reach generalizations in our thinking and far more concerned with the consequences of our belief in these generalizations. British empiricism is based upon a backward look, searching for the elementary components of the mental life. Having found that these elements can be nothing but states of mind, the

British empiricists have been faced with the problem of determining the relation between these elementary "ideas" or mental states, and an objective external reality existing prior to our knowledge or our perception of it. Somehow our ideas copy this reality, an i somehow the mental operations which we perform on these ideas enable us to control the external world. "Knowledge," as Francis Bacon said, "is power." But *how* the relation between knowledge and power arises and *how* the equation between our ideas and the antecedent reality they copy is established has been a perennial problem. If the agreement of our ideas with reality is what we mean by truth, and if we can know only our ideas of the reality and not the reality itself, how can we ever know whether our ideas are true? If the conclusions that we reach by building up a generalization on the basis of a limited number of particulars can be regarded merely as probabilities, where are our certainties, our absolute truths, to be found? Problems of this sort loom large in the literature of British empirical philosophy.

There are some areas of thought, however, in which, whatever our doubts about the foundations of our knowledge, we can not permit these doubts to paralyze our actions. Ethics is a field of this sort; whatever insecurity we may have about our ethical knowledge, we must act, we must make ethical choices. "A belief," said Alexander Bain (1818-1903), "is that upon which we are prepared to act." Side by side with their highly tentative, sceptical theory of knowledge, British philosophers developed the ethical position of utilitarianism which replaces analysis of the grounds of any ethical belief by estimation of its consequences. Similarily, British scientists had by-passed the question of the legitimacy and certainty of the intellectual operations on which their hypotheses were founded and had tested these hypotheses by an experimental verification of their predicted consequences. What America's pragmatic empiricists did was to accept the procedure of the utilitarian ethical philosophers and the experimental scientists as a method of breaking through the roadblock in theory of knowledge, theory of meaning, and theory of truth. The pragmatists disclaimed the search for an absolute truth and the analysis of the grounds of knowledge. They abandoned the retrospective pattern of British empiricism and centered their attention upon ideas as instruments of control and the forward look into the consequences of belief. Addison W. Moore, one of the students of John Dewey at the University of Chicago, pointed out that while pragmatism is, in truth, a new name for an old way of thinking, it is an old way of thinking in science and in practical life, not in philosophy. In scientific and practical thought, regard for consequences is both an old and a universal method; "as a *conscious and acknowledged method in philosophy* it is neither so 'old' nor so 'universal'."[4]

There are four major figures in the history of pragmatism in America: Charles Sanders Peirce, William James, George Herbert Mead, and John Dewey. In his long and fruitful life Dewey incorporated his pragmatic method or instrumentalism into the larger view of "experimental naturalism." We shall, therefore, reserve extended discussion of his work until later (see Chapter 9, section IV) and comment on his contributions to the pragmatic movement only incidentally here. Peirce, James, and Mead will be presented in later sections of this chapter. James, who is responsible for the popularization of the name "pragmatism," although he preferred to call his own system "radical empiricism," declared that Peirce came to the guiding conception of pragmatism first. Peirce himself allows that Chauncey Wright (see Chapter 5, section III) had something to do with it. Peirce also mentioned the influence of Bain's definition of belief which was quoted by Nicholas St. John Green, himself a lawyer and member of the faculty at Boston University Law School.

At all events, pragmatism was born out of the discussions that took place in a group which met frequently but informally in Boston and Cambridge about 1870. Peirce called this group "the metaphysical club," though more recent historians have cast doubts upon whether the "club" was as organized as this name suggests. In his memories of this group, Peirce wrote "Wright was the strongest member and probably I was next — then there were Frank Abbot, William James and others."[5] Frank Abbott is a nickname hiding the scientific realist Francis Ellingwood Abbot (see Chapter 5, section IV). Among the "others" were Nicholas St. John Green, John Fiske, America's cosmic Spencerian (see Chapter 5, section II), and Oliver Wendell Holmes, Jr., then just returned from his experiences in the Civil War, who was later to become Chief Justice of the Massachusetts Supreme Court, and Associate Justice of the Supreme Court of the United States. Though the brilliancy of their later careers was still unrealized, this must have been a remarkably able group of young men. "It was there," Peirce added, "that the name and doctrine of pragmatism saw the light."[6]

Pragmatism is, then, an attempt to explain in empirical terms the place of thinking and of knowledge in the world without falling into the difficulties which beset other empiricisms. In addition to utilitarian ethics and the general practice of scientists, both of which anticipate the pragmatic method, the work of Charles Darwin in proposing the theory of evolution should be singled out as an especially important stimulant to the pragmatists. As we have pointed out (Chapter 5, section I), one of the philosophic results of Darwinism was to concentrate attention on process instead of on structure, on becoming instead of on being. In terms of the Darwinian theory, the origin of thinking could be readily explained as the development by the human animal of a special instrument of adaptation to his environment, as one aspect of the process of becoming a dominant species within nature. Thinking became for the evolutionary naturalist a form of conduct directed toward the end of survival. This was an extremely important contribution to philosophy in that it considered thinking as a natural process developed in a natural context and thus helped to break down some of the difficulties which earlier philosophies had faced in explaining the nature of knowledge.

There was, however, one decided deficiency in the evolutionary view of thinking; if the purpose of thinking was always natural survival, and thinking among human animals was like flight among birds and other instruments of natural survival, then the purpose involved was always nature's purpose working through unconscious mankind. Men are not in control of their thinking; they are pawns in nature's game. Darwin's assertion of the variation in species was welcomed as liberating men from the uncontrollably fixed species of earlier tradition, both philosophic and scientific; but if men were not in control of their own purposes, then the variety and change which Darwin proposed was just as uncontrollable.

The pragmatists ingeniously suggested a way in which the general outline of the Darwinian position might be held without denying existence to self-conscious purposive thinking by men, to human self-control. Why, asked Addison Moore, should it not be possible, within the terms of the evolutionary hypothesis, that thinking itself, which was naturally selected as an advantageous variation, should develop natural varieties of which reflective, deliberate thinking is one? "Must not variation in species admit variation in species of variation as well?"[7] At the very least it must be allowed that there is a possibility that one of the effective and, therefore, naturally preserved variations will be conscious and purposive thought, which will be one method of producing novelty in the world. If deliberate and reflective thought is thus allowed as a development of the evolutionary process, this thought must be creative, not merely representative. It must have a function in ongoing biological situations. This must not be taken to mean that ideas somehow produce reality out of nothing. The creative function of ideas is manifested in the reconstruction of the existing elements in any situation into a new combination which better satisfies human needs. When the elements of a situation are confused and problematic, nonreflective behavior is unable to complete itself save by the happy accident of trial and error. Reflective behavior or thought symbolizes the actual situation and its elements in some ideal form; then it works over these ideas until it has, in thought, discovered a likely possibility for transforming the confused actual situation into a less confused situation. This likely possibility or hypothesis is then tried. If it succeeds in resolving the actual situation, if it does what it was intended to do, then we can pronounce it true in that situation. It has proved itself by its effects, pragmatically. From materials already present in an experienced situation, thinking constructs a new situation, leads to a revised experience. Reflective thinking is always a stage in activity, according to the pragmatists, and it is fair to call it the problem-solving stage or "inquiry."

One point on which the pragmatists were insistent was that thought is active. Our ideas do not simply copy or represent, in some passive sense, the objects of our knowledge. For pragmatists, the "facts" are not before us; they become facts in the process of being known. A fact is the name for a particular interaction between the knower and his external environment. Again, this does not mean that facts are created out of nothing by the mind; the pragmatists avoided extreme subjectivism. What is meant is that in some sense the facts are changed by becoming known. Here is the point at which there developed the controversy between the pragmatists and the "new realists" (see Chapter 8). The new realists argued that the only difference that ideas make to the facts is that thought is added to the situation. Thinking, they maintained, does not make any essential difference to the things that are thought about. The reply of the pragmatist was to say, with Bawden, "If by knowing [the facts] we mean anything more than mere familiarity with them and practical use of them, then cognition is more than a merely revelatory process, — it is constitutive and determinative of their nature as facts." [8] Thought is part of a process of reconstituting facts in the direction of some standard, some criterion of values. All theory is practice in the process of undergoing transformation.

The realist argues that reality exists in independence of human knowledge of it. The idealist counters that there is no reality apart from some form of knowledge of it; perhaps the self's knowledge of it, in which case he is a subjective idealist; perhaps the knowledge of it in the mind of some Absolute, in which case he is an absolute idealist; perhaps the knowledge is in some sense social, that of a community of minds, in which case he is an objective idealist. The pragmatist reply to both positions is that each is a half-truth; that reality exists completely neither in a physical fact nor in a mental fact, but in a situation which includes both. Reality (the word more frequently used by pragmatists is "experience") *is* change, *is* becoming, *is* movement, *is* process. Both physical fact and mental fact, both object and knowledge, are within this process. Reality is the bringing of the object to consciousness in knowledge. Since thought, the having of ideas, is connected in pragmatist theory with the arising of a problem or obstacle to the functioning of habit, the pragmatist restores to the word "object" an etymological meaning of "that which objects, or obstructs." What we call "objective" or external to ourselves is that which seems for the moment, to lie beyond our control. Henry Waldgrave Stuart, another of the lesser pragmatists, remarked that our feeling that there is something unsatisfactory in our experience "suggests the differentiation of subject and object and the postulation of the latter as an alien 'other,' causing the unsatisfactoriness." [9] In a certain sense, John Dewey said, bringing an object to consciousness, knowing it, must involve its being innocently "subjectified." "Knowledge," he went on to say, "is always a matter of the use that is made of experienced natural events." [10] Knowledge, then, is always an instrument or tool in the change from an unsatisfactory reality to a more satisfactory reality.

Inasmuch as pragmatism made the claim to be "a recovery of philosophy," which (again in Dewey's words), "ceases to be a device for dealing with the problem of philosophers and becomes a method, cultivated by philosophers, for dealing with the problems of men,"[11] and inasmuch as the test of truth of a theory, for pragmatism, is to be found by an examination of its consequences, it is only fair that we should consider briefly some of the consequences of pragmatism applied to the problems of men. We must judge the success of pragmatism by the only test a pragmatist would be willing to apply, its contribution to the solution of some of the besetting confusions in various areas of twentieth-century life. We shall not, of course, be able here to deal with this question exhaustively. What follows, then, is a few suggestions, not a catalogue, of the applications of pragmatism in various areas of contemporary American life.

Education is probably the first such problem area of which we would think, partly because of Dewey's contributions to the study of this field, and partly because the application of pragmatism to education has been most widely publicized. Here we should say that not all "progressive" education is to be regarded as "Deweyan" or pragmatic. The general principle to be looked for is that to the pragmatic educator, education is neither the imposition upon the child of a pattern nor the completely free and uninhibited activity of the child. The first, or traditional, theory is prominently called "subject-centered;" it includes a rigid concept of control from above, and makes of the school an organization most unlike the less highly regimented society in which we live. The second progressive theory is frequently called "child-centered;" it is based upon the expression of the child's individuality; in the complete absence of control, it makes of the school an organization most unlike the society in which we live. Between these extremes, though somewhat closer to the second type, there lies the pragmatic type of progressive education, in which an attempt is made to discover the function of subject-matter and of organization within the experience of the child. "When external control is rejected, the problem becomes that of finding the factors of control that are inherent within experience.[12] The cultivation of the child's individuality in terms of his unique relation with the world, and the expression of this individuality in forms appropriate to the age and the maturity of the child are considered more suitable than the application of adult standards to the child; but this is not taken to mean that there is to be *no* standard whatsoever. Free activity is preferred to an imposed pattern of discipline, but "free" is not taken to mean "anarchic;" what is being sought is self-motivated activity, under the guidance and stimulation, instead of the direction, of a teacher.

Learning is declared to be achieved through "experience," as opposed to memorizing of texts or listening to expositions. This does not mean, however, that any and all experience is equally educative. Some experiences seem to stimulate and some to retard the possibility of further experience; only those experiences which are properly stimulative can be considered educative. "It is not enough to insist upon the necessity of experience, nor even of activity in experience. Everything depends upon the *quality* of the experience which is had."[13] This quality, of which Dewey speaks in the passage just quoted, has two sides. It is immediately pleasant or unpleasant; this the child can determine. It has remoter effects on the stimulation or retardation of further experiences; this the educator must judge. The educator's problem becomes, then, the selection out of a wide variety of possible experiences (including those of contact with the ideas of the past), those which in his mature judgment are likely to have beneficial results in the future experience of the child and which he can arrange as experiences which the child meets without being repelled by them. The child should not meet random experiences in the school; the experiences of the schoolroom must be planned very carefully, in the light of the particular individuals in that schoolroom, and not improvised on the spur of the moment. Furthermore, what the child learns through educational experience is not an isolated fact to be stored away until needed but a pattern for dealing with an immediate situation in his present environment. Education is life for the child at the same time as it is preparation for his adult life.

Another area in which pragmatism has had important consequences and applications is in legal theory. These two have been closely connected since the very earliest days of pragmatism, for, as we have pointed out, there were lawyers and teachers of law among the associates of Peirce, Wright, and James in the "metaphysical club," in which pragmatism was first explored. One of these lawyers among the philosophers and philosophers among the lawyers was Oliver Wendell Holmes, Jr. Holmes was a hard-headed believer in the influence of economic and political realities who thought James' form of pragmatism "an amusing humbug."[14] He tried in discussions over a number of years to make James more aware of the power of social forces. In general, despite his sentimentalized version of some of Darwin's ideas — he thought of the "struggle for survival" as a glorious adventure — Holmes was a consistent empiricist who insisted that "The life of the law has not been logic: *it has been experience*."[15] Again, he declared that, "*experience is the test* by which it is decided whether the degree of danger attending given conduct under certain known circumstances is sufficient to throw the risk upon the party pursuing it."[16] On the basis of this theory of law, Holmes or any other judge who accepted his theory could determine the meaning of a law in terms of its social consequences rather than by deductions from its language.

Holmes' sociological view of the law led him to define it pragmatically as "the prediction of the incidence of the public force through the instrumentality of the courts."[17] Dean Roscoe Pound of Harvard Law School made theoretical contributions to the amplification of this view, insisting that the judges made the "actual" law "by a process of trying the principles and rules and standards in concrete cases, observing their practical operation and gradually discovering by experience of many causes how to apply them so as to administer justice by means of them."[18] Many judges in both state and federal courts have given expression to this legal pragmatism in their judicial decisions.

There is a somewhat more extreme form of pragmatism which, under various names — of which legal realism is the most usual — has gained some strength in American law schools and law courts. In this group the sociological emphasis of Holmes and Pound and their followers has been absorbed into a broad theory as one point among many. Although there is a great diversity among legal realists, Professor Karl Llewellyn of the Columbia Law School has summarized nine points of agreement. Law is conceived as changing, not static. Society is also regarded as changing. Law is thought of as a means to social ends. For purposes of study it is important to distinguish description from evaluation, what is from what ought to be. Traditionally held legal rules and concepts are distrusted. There is a special doubt of the importance of prescriptive rules in reaching judicial decisions. The realists believe that there is value in reconsidering the categories under which cases are grouped and trying to narrow these categories. They insist upon evaluations in terms of effects. Finally, they regard as desirable a sustained attempt to put their views over as a program. Thus far the activities of this group have been more largely devoted to criticism of earlier theories of law and to a study of the practical techniques and the ways of thinking of lawyers than to the use of their method to refine and redefine the pragmatic meaning of legal ideas.

Pragmatism as applied to politics and political science has taken many forms both theoretical and practical. One of the more interesting is the study of politics as the interplay of pressure groups, which has been carried forward notably by Arthur F. Bentley. The only foreword to Bentley's book, *The Process of Government*, is a single sentence indicating his instrumentalism: "This book is an attempt to fashion a tool."[19] For Bentley, we block interpretation when we attempt to interpret what goes on in a society in terms of the ideas and emotions of the men who make up that society. He calls interpretations of this sort "animistic," by analogy with primitive animistic accounts of nature; just as natural science could not develop until "the animism of the forest" had been cleared away, political science can not develop until the animism of society has been discarded. All our theories have been built up animistically; they must be tested in social life and activity to discover whether they have any scientific value, whether they have any use, whether they can be made to work. Bentley's critical point is that the feelings, ideas, and ideals resorted to as principles of social and political explanation are not definite things in and behind society which work upon society as causes, but rather that when terms like these are used we are restating our problem, not solving it. Terms like "anger" or "liberty" never lose their social reference; they may be used as convenient shorthand expressions for indicating some causal connections which have been worked out. But we must never confuse the issue by considering anger and liberty as solid facts on which to base a social explanation. The "angry" man is never angry except in certain situations. Anger has no meaning apart from these situations. We can not "give values to the man's present attitude" unless "we state the full situation in terms of all the activities entering into it."[20]

If these "occult causes" are disposed of, we can go on to study the process of government by analyzing the pressures on government. Our raw materials are activities, "first, last and always" — the activities of government itself and of related groups. It is changing men's conduct, or resisting such changes; it is grouping forces or breaking down groupings of forces. Writing and talking are, of course, to be considered as activities. When we view the activities of government in this way as the competing activities of groups of men, we see that all the phenomena of government are those of force or pressure. These group pressures acting upon and against each other, now in balance and now out of balance, make up the existing state of society. Government is an organized network of activities and agencies designed to bring about the adjustment of the interest groups. Law is not the result of government, but another name for the process of government. Law is the statement of the ideal adjustment or balance which is never achieved. This statement must be constantly changing as the state of society is ever in flux; law is an activity struggling for the systematic adaptation of group interests. Thus the political theory of a pragmatist like Bentley comes to a view of the nature of law which is similar to that of the legal pragmatists.

These three illustrations will have to serve us here as evidence that in many areas of human questioning the pragmatic approach has been rewarding. It has led to the dismissal of older views which have hampered understanding, and has cleared the ground for new views even where it has not been able to formulate novel interpretations. Since pragmatism made its chief claim that of being a method for reconstructing our thinking and thereby recovering philosophy, what has been done beyond the first critical steps has differed from pragmatist to pragmatist. The remainder of this chapter will follow the original pragmatism of Charles Sanders Peirce, William James, and George Herbert Mead into the wider speculative reaches of their differing philosophies.

II. PRAGMATIC MEANING: CHARLES SANDERS PEIRCE

Pragmatism has a double aspect. It is of interest as a temperamental proclivity among philosophers; this is particularly apparent in the philosophy of William James. It is also interesting as a body of technical answers to a set of technical questions within the general area of theory of knowledge. The central question to which pragmatic empiricism attempted to provide an answer was, "What is an idea?" We have already seen that the pragmatists rejected the realists' answer that an idea is a presentation of reality and the idealists' answer that an idea is a representation or copy of reality. Both the pragmatists and the idealists considered the universality of an idea as a generalization, not as an abstraction. The pragmatists, however, asked a further question with which idealists did not concern themselves. The pragmatists wanted to know why we generalize. To this query they supplied an answer in terms of the way in which an idea, or universal, functions within experience. Their ultimate answer to the question about the nature of an idea was given in terms of what an idea *does* rather than what it *is*. To the pragmatists an idea functions within life as a plan of action. The value of an idea is its success as a plan for getting where, in a particular situation, we want to get.

Among those for whom pragmatism was a technical discipline, a method of carrying on a part of the philosophic enterprise, Charles Sanders Peirce is outstanding. Although his was one of the great "seminal minds" in American thought, he did not have the easy fertility of speculation which one might think of as the progenitor of novelty. When he wrote to James in 1897 explaining why it was so difficult for him to change his intentions with respect to a course of lectures which he was to give, he declared that his philosophy was not "an 'idea' with which I 'brim over'; it is a serious research to which there is no royal road."[21] Another of Peirce's difficulties was that his typical method of approach to any question was half earnest and serious, half ironic and playful. Many times he would start a discussion of some subject in serious vein, and then his humorous vein would prevail and complete the discussion. This variety made him difficult to understand from the lecture platform, and it still contributes to the difficulty of reading his works.

Furthermore, for reasons both serious and playful he was a chronic and incurable inventor of new and often barbaric terms. His serious reason for advocating and practicing the creation of vocabularies was that words used by the loose thinkers of everyday life carry with them into technical usage all the loose ends of association of their misuse and thus lose their technical usefulness. He demanded of any science that it should have "a suitable technical nomenclature

. . . whose vocables have no such sweetness or charms as might tempt loose writers to abuse them,"[22] as well as an approved method for coining new terms and assuring their acceptance among scientists. The term "pragmatism" was one of his own creations; when he felt that it had been too loosely used to be thoroughly reputable, he invented the term "pragmaticism" to replace it, hoping that the new coinage would be ugly enough to discourage its appropriation for use in everyday speech. Finally, in an age when, in America, the study of logic beyond its simplest elements was most uncommon, it was one of Peirce's distinctions to be a superior and creative logician, pressing forward to new frontiers in symbolic logic. For all these reasons, Peirce received neither the recognition that his work deserved nor the audience that his thought merited.

As an evolutionary thinker, first in the vein of the romantic philosophy of nature of Schelling — one of the early and persistent influences on Peirce's thought, and later with a Darwinian bent, Peirce became interested in the law of habit-formation. Baldly stated, his belief was that the universe forms habits, generalizes, and becomes more and more orderly. Life, as distinct from merely mechanical behavior, is the falling into patterns of order; physical laws are habits of lesser inclusiveness than the laws of vital organization. Insofar as human beings tend to develop habits they exhibit in their life the generalizing pattern which is characteristic of all life. In mental activity there is one basic and primary law, which is that thinking is a tendency to generalization. Ideas "reproduce themselves," take in more and more territory, become increasingly inclusive. Feelings of comfort or discomfort in any part of the body tend to spread until we feel comfort or discomfort throughout the body. Relations among feelings and associations among ideas tend to produce new feelings and novel ideas. In all these ways mind grows by generalizing. When there is any disturbance, creating new patterns of relationship and ultimately new feelings and ideas, we are conscious that we have gained something, and when another disturbance comes along, we tend to assimilate it to the earlier one, and thus to begin the formation of a new habit. "Feelings, by being excited, become more easily excited, especially in the ways in which they have previously been excited."[23] We develop a habit of response. Our consciousness of such a habit of response constitutes a "general conception," idea, or universal.

The generalizing process which has been described does not take place in a "mind" somehow separated and distinct from nerves and muscles, and, in general, the body. When there is any stimulation (external or internal), to a particular group of nerve cells, the ganglion, or tissue in which the nerve cells are located, connected most closely with that group of nerve cells is irritated into activity. This activity occasions movements of parts of the body which are controlled by that ganglion. If the stimulation of the nerve cells is continued, as in prolonged tickling, the irritation is not confined to the single ganglion, but spreads from one center to another throughout the body, usually increasing in intensity as it spreads. Movements of other bodily parts are induced by the spreading irritation. The response has been generalized in the nerves and muscles. Perhaps, too, fatigue weakens or halts the activity of the parts first stimulated; if the stimulus continues, the response of parts which have not become tired will continue long after activity stops in the parts directly stimulated. Finally, when for any reason the stimulation stops completely, the activity stops almost immediately. From this physiological and neural account of the response of the organism to stimulation, Peirce concluded that, whenever a nerve is stimulated, the reflex action which is called forth, if in its first form of activity it does not succeed in halting the irritation, will change its bodily manifestations again and again until it is finally successful in halting the irritation.

We have seen that "all vital processes tend to become easier on repetition."[24] If there has been a "discharge" of nervous energy along a particular path, the likelihood of another discharge along that path is increased. If, then, the same irritation of the nerves — again, let us think of tickling — recurs, all the connections and all the actions which have taken place in consequence of the earlier stimulus are more likely to take place on the second occasion. Assume a repeated recurrence of the stimulation. Of the many possible actions that may be called forth, only the one that ends the irritation is sure to occur every time. The other actions may or may not have taken place, but since action is continued in changing forms until the irritation is stopped, that final action must have been performed every time. With each repetition it is increasingly likely that this action will be performed soon, because "a strong habit of responding to the given irritation in this particular way"[25] will have been established. When a habit of this sort has been developed it is possible to say that our reaction to that stimulus has become generalized, or, to put it another way, we do not react to the particular event but to its probable consequences. The "idea" of the stimulus, or its "meaning," is its consequence in our behavior. These ideas, these meanings, are universals which are not merely names for a common quality abstracted from things, nor entities existing in some non-natural realm. They do exist, objectively, "among things." They are habits in nature. Nature can and does form habits, but not as freely as organic being. "What we call matter," said Peirce, "is not completely dead, but is merely mind hidebound with habits." [26] Peirce's theory of universals looks back to the medieval realism of Duns Scotus (1266-1308), though it is likely that Peirce's acquaintance with the works of Scotus was quite perfunctory.

Whenever an event or a stimulus has a belief as its consequence, it has an idea or meaning. The stimulus or event is, then, the sign of the meaning. In action, ideas are beliefs; beliefs are plans of action. Peirce's theory of knowledge does not begin, like that of Descartes and his followers, with doubt; nor does it begin with sensation, in the Lockean tradition. It begins with belief, and belief is closely related to conduct. When we come to the discussion of belief and meaning, we have reached the heart of Peirce's pragmatism, because for him pragmatism was a method leading to the solution of the problem of meaning. For Peirce the meaning of a concept must be interpreted in terms of conduct, not of sensation. If we wish to discover the meaning of our conception of any object, Peirce said, we must "consider what effects, which might conceivably have practical bearings, we conceive the object of our conception to have. Then our conception of these effects is the whole of our conception of the object."[27] The effects of which Peirce was speaking were not, however, the "particular sensible consequences" to which (as we shall see in the next section), James referred in his California address of 1898. They are general and active consequences, for as Peirce went on to say, "The entire intellectual purport of any symbol consists in the total of all general modes of rational conduct which, conditionally upon all the possible different circumstances and desires, would ensue upon the acceptance of the symbol."[28]

Peirce was struck by the historical fact that some intellectual problems are ultimately solved, when the advance of human knowledge provides the material for a solution, whereas other problems remain permanently unsolved. The permanently unsolved speculative posers include such questions as "Are mind and matter essentially different from each other?" and, "Is there an immortal soul?" and others of the same sort. Peirce asked whether problems of this order were merely unsolved, that is, whether the fault lay in the deficiency of our techniques of problem solving; or whether they were insoluble, that is, whether the problems themselves were at fault. Having decided that such problems are insoluble, he went on to ask in what sense, if they are insoluble, they can be considered as problems at all. A genuine problem should be capable of solution although at the present moment it is unsolved. If it is not soluble, a question is no problem because it is not significant, not meaningful. An insoluble question is a non-meaningful question expressed in the literary form of a problem. Peirce called it a "pseudo-problem." The so-called "problem" precludes the possibility of its solution because its subject is absolutely "unknowable," in human experience, at least. To exclude pseudo-problems from consideration in his philosophy Peirce developed a rule specifying the conditions under which the language men use is meaningful. The meaning he is concerned with is, of course, the objective, public meaning, the "general modes of rational conduct" which are the consequences of the terms of the language. The psychological, individual content and effect of terms, which was of concern to William James, would lead to a private solution of problems under consideration, and to Peirce a private solution is no solution at all.

As far as the elements of language are concerned, Peirce's pragmatic standard of meaning required that any term or word designating an object must be definable in such a way that the object signified by the term is identifiable in experience. In the repetition of the suffix "able" we have the consistent reference to the future of all pragmatists. To define a word meaningfully, we must describe the experimental conditions which would enable anyone to discover in his experience the object to which the term refers. If we do this, we establish a standard of agreement and of universal intelligibility. The value of a standard of this sort is evident when we consider how beneficial a public and universal definition of such terms as "freedom," "aggression," and "democracy" would be in our age. It is not to be wondered at that in our age the important intellectual enterprise called "semantics" has attempted to develop a more critical theory of language use along Peirce's lines. For sentences and propositions to be meaningful Peirce required that the terms of which they were composed should themselves be meaningful, and that the truth or falsity of the statements should be capable of investigation by the use of scientific methods. The meaning of a statement, then, consists in the sum of its verifiable consequences, where by verifiable we understand the possibility of investigation in a manner comparable to that of a scientific laboratory. Now we can return to our starting-point, the question, "When is a problem significant?" For Peirce, a problem is genuine, significant, and meaningful if the possible answers to it are experimentally verifiable statements.

Peirce's pragmatism involves a theory of meaning which is operational; his definitions are, as he put it, precepts. The definition of a word leads the investigator to the object denoted by the word. "The rational purport of a word or other expression lies exclusively in its conceivable bearing upon the conduct of life." [29] Similarly, the association of the meaningfulness of a statement with the possibility of proving it true or false experimentally is equivalent to saying that a statement means that "if a given prescription for an experiment ever can be and ever is carried out in an act, an experience of a given description will result." The meaning thus given will always be a general statement, conditional in its form; it is "the general description of all the experimental phenomena which the assertion of the proposition virtually predicts."[30]

The simplest statement makes a limitless prediction of experimental results. As Peirce pointed out, merely to say of a particular stone that it is hard is to predict that *whenever*, and *no matter how often* a certain testing experiment, say, scratching, is performed on that stone, the test will fail to mark the stone. Because there is an unlimited series of testing operations involved in any statement, "the rational meaning of every proposition lies in the future."[31] Rationally, then, and with our eyes on the future, two statements which are verbally different but which have the same verifiable consequences have the same meaning and are, therefore, logically identical; two statements which are verbally alike but which have different verifiable consequences have different meanings and are, therefore, logically distinct. Peirce formulated the central insight of his pragmatic theory of meaning in various ways. In none of these expressions is there any modification of the forward-looking aspect of his theory. At some times he seems less precise than at others in specifying that the behavior which identifies a meaning must be laboratory behavior. He seemed almost Jamesian when he said, "Our idea of anything *is* our idea of its sensible effects."[32] More often, however, his statements are carefully phrased to fit the interpretation which we have given. He insisted that "The whole function of thought is to produce habits of action. . . . What a thing means is simply what habits it involves."[33] His theory of meaning is closely associated in his philosophy with the evolutionary discussion of the nature of habit to which we have already referred.

Peirce was careful to point out that his pragmatism led to a theory of meaning, to a concern for the meaning of ideas and not necessarily their truth. "The battery in my car is dead" is a meaningful statement because it can be translated into a general conditional statement prescribing a series of experimental tests to be performed. It is not necessarily a true statement because the performing of these experimental tests may show that my battery is capable of starting my car. We must be careful to make the distinction between meaning and truth in this context especially, because, for William James, pragmatism does lead to a theory of truth. This is not to be regarded as a major difference between Peirce and James; the title of the book in which James expounds his theory of truth is *The Meaning of Truth*. James is making a particular application of Peirce's theory of meaning (as he understood it), to the term "truth" and to statements which assert the truth of anything. The difference between Peirce and James results, rather, from the concern of Peirce for the general, operational consequences of any statement and the concern of James for the particular, sensible consequences.

Peirce did, of course, have a theory of truth which is clearly indicated in his discussion of how we fix our beliefs. We engage in processes of reasoning, he pointed out, in order to extend our knowledge from something we do know to something else which we do not know. Reasoning is good if it carries us from true premises to a true conclusion. But man is not a logical animal and, therefore, although on some occasions he may reason correctly and reach conclusions which are true as well as satisfying, for the most part, it is not the truth or falsity of the particular conclusions which leads him to regard a certain piece of reasoning as good. There is a "habit of mind, whether it be constitutional or acquired"[34] which leads us to draw one set of inferences rather than another from a set of premises. It is this habit which we designate good or bad, according to whether in general it will yield true conclusions. If the habit of mind is such as will generally lead to the inference of true conclusions from true premises, we call a particular inference valid without regard to its truth, as long as it was made in accordance with a "guiding principle," or formula, expressing the nature of the determining habit. We notice in this statement the effect of Peirce's concern for the habit or general pattern over against the particular instance. To know these guiding principles is to have solid grounds for our affirmations of belief.

Yet there is an assumption which precedes any application of these habits of inference, namely, "that there are such states of mind as doubt and belief — that a passage from one to the other is possible, the object of thought remaining the same." [35] There is a practical difference between doubt and belief, as well as a difference between the feeling we have when doubting and that which we have when believing. Belief, as we have pointed out earlier, is associated with action, while doubt has no such effect. "The feeling of believing is a more or less sure indication of there being established in our nature some habit which will determine our actions." [36] Another difference between doubt and belief is suggested by our account of an irritant stimulus. Doubt serves as an irritant which is not allayed until a state of belief is reached. Belief is "a calm and satisfactory state" which we do not wish to change. "We cling tenaciously, not merely to believing, but to believing just what we do believe." [37] Peirce uses the word "inquiry" to mean the struggle to change from a state of doubt to a state of belief. For the most part, whatever our pretensions, Peirce insists that we are not concerned in the truth of what we finally believe but only in the fact that we finally do believe. At best, "we seek for a belief that we shall *think* to be true." [38] Where there is no real doubt there is no inquiry; where there is belief it is useless to attempt to pursue inquiry any farther. Inquiry serves the purpose of fixing belief.

The first method of the fixation of belief Peirce called "the method of tenacity." It involves the reiteration of a particular answer to our questioning, until a habit of answering that question in this way has been firmly established. Concomitantly, there is a deliberate refusal to face or to listen to any other answer. This is a method in very common use, Peirce avers, and it has the advantage of yielding "great peace of mind," especially since a believer will steadfastly refuse to admit the inconveniences of his belief. This is, of course, not a rational method of fixing belief, but inasmuch as a state of believing and not rationality is what users of the method aspire to, it may be for some and for a limited time successful. As a general rule the social impulse works against the permanent success of the method of tenacity. Men in normal social life influence one another's opinions. Any individual who was not a hermit would have to be most bull-headed to maintain his private belief against that of everyone else with whom he comes in contact.

Because there is an interaction of beliefs and opinions, the need is for a method of fixing belief for the community rather than for the individual. The method of authority is developed to meet this need. It is superior to the method of individual tenacity and has had a far greater success. In practice it amounts to tenacity maintained by the state or other organized group rather than by the individual. This Peirce allows as possibly the best of methods for the mass of mankind, yet his description of the operation of this method is repulsive in the extreme. He describes a process of totalitarian "thought-control" instituted by the state or other power, using terror and inquisition, cruel atrocities and the massacre of dissidents as its weapons when it has the power. This method, he added, "has, from the earliest times been one of the chief means of upholding correct theological and political doctrines." [39] No such institution can, however, fix belief upon every subject and every aspect of each. Only the central and most vitally important beliefs can be taken care of, and, for the rest, men must be left to their own devices. For the mass of unquestioning mankind, there is no need for a method beyond that of authority.

There will be found some in every society who seek a more suitable method of fixing their beliefs. They have sufficient knowledge to see beyond the strictly local and temporal, and sufficient intellectual integrity to be able to admit that other societies may produce opinions of value at least as high as those produced in their own society. They are unable to accept either the capriciousness of the method of tenacity or the arbitrariness of the method of authority. In seeking for a way to resolve their doubts, they develop the method of discussion, whereby men, consulting and conversing together, create in each other an impulse to believe and also determine what they are to believe. Beliefs reached by this method have characteristically been unrelated to experience, but "agreeable to reason." This has been the traditional method of "metaphysical philosophy." Despite its long history and its intellectual respectability, the failures of this method have been most clearly marked, because it makes inquiry a matter of developing taste. Beliefs are still determined by human preferences, not by "some external permanency — by something on which our thinking has no effect." [40]

The search for an adequate method of fixing belief led finally to the method of science, in which the "external permanency" consists of the fact that the source of our belief is public, not restricted to a particular individual or group, but open to every man. The effect may differ from individual to individual, yet the method should lead all to the same conclusion. This is the only method which Peirce considered worthy of pursuit. Only in terms of scientific method is belief more than private. An idea becomes clear insofar as its consequences can be told to some other mind, with whom we share plans of action, at least to the extent that we use the same terms to define beliefs which have the same consequences. The minds communicating in this fashion constitute a community; the best exemplification of such a community is to be found in the scientific laboratory. Granting that there is a laboratory community, we have an implicit definition of Truth: Those beliefs are true which would be agreed upon by an infinite community of laboratory scientists who carried inquiry sufficiently far. The need for an infinite community and for an indefinite continuation of inquiry will be clear if it is remembered that the simplest of statements implies an unlimited number of experimental predictions. To this view of the ideal nature of truth Peirce gave the name of "critical common-sensism." For any partial and finite human needs to fix our beliefs, it would not be necessary to know whether, in this remote sense, the belief is true; all we have to know is whether it is useful to submit our ideas to the laboratory community for investigation. Ultimately this depends upon the processes we have used in our inquiry and our drawing of inferences. "As all knowledge

comes from synthetic inference, we must also infer that all human
certainty consists merely in our knowing that the processes by which
our knowledge has been derived are such as must generally have led
to true conclusions." [41]

Peirce was especially interested in what may be called the second
degree of habit formation. We have seen that any generalization is
a habit. Peirce wanted to understand the habit of generalization,
the habit of forming general ideas. The traditional logical processes of induction and deduction, which he considered carefully,
seemed to him not to lead to new ideas. But he distinguished and
named a third logical process, which he called "abduction." He
insisted that "the abductive suggestion comes to us like a flash. It is
an act of *insight*." [42] An abduction is an hypothesis which joins
together our otherwise unrelated observations. Abduction has neither
the logical necessity of deductive reasoning nor the factual accuracy
of induction. It is merely suggestive of a possibility. Induction can
be said to lead to laws of nature; abduction leads only to hypotheses.
There is a continuity in induction; the conclusion is an inference that
in cases like those which have been observed similar phenomena will
be observable. In abduction there is discontinuity; the conclusion
suggests an explanation in terms of "something of a different kind
from what we have directly observed, and frequently something
which it would be impossible for us to observe directly." [43] We can
have no assurance of certainty about an abduced hypothesis. We
can not be sure that it will prove successful in explaining what it
is suggested to explain. Like William James' "will to believe," of
which we will talk in the next section, abduction is entered upon
in pragmatic desperation, "its justification being that it is the only
possible hope of regulating our future conduct rationally." [44]

In concentrating our discussion on one aspect of Peirce's philosophy, his pragmatism, we have, perhaps, been unfair to other,
more speculative sides of his philosophy and his character. What
we have done here is to sketch the foundations of one of the most
suggestive philosophic systems to have been attempted by an American writer. There is more justification for the incompleteness of
this account in that Peirce himself did not complete the work he
planned. Most philosophers are of little importance even a half-
century after their work has been done. It is only the greatest
whose ideas live on and even increase in significance centuries after

their authors have died, and in places remote from where they
lived and worked. That today far more is known and studied of
Peirce in both America and Europe than during his lifetime is, perhaps, an indication that when the ballots of posterity — the future
which Peirce was so ready to trust — are finally cast, he will rank
with the few who achieve true immortality in their ideas.

III. PRAGMATIC TRUTH: WILLIAM JAMES

In his youth, William James could not decide whether he wanted
to be a scientist or an artist. The indulgence of his father (see
Chapter 4, section IV) made it possible for him to study both, in
Europe as well as in America. This early experience of two distinct
disciplines and two different worlds may account in part for the
breadth of James' interests and for his openness and tolerance of
diversity. By the time he was thirty, William James seemed settled
in a scientific career when he was appointed to teach physiology at
Harvard. Again, however, his interests broadened. First, he became
concerned with physiological psychology, and, under the influence
of this interest, established (in 1876), one of the first psychological
laboratories in America. Next, his interest in psychology became
more general. He devoted himself to studying psychology until, in
1890, he came forth with his extremely influential two-volume
Principles of Psychology. This work marked a radical shift in
psychological perspective and furnished the basis for an equally
radical change in philosophic emphasis. The shift was from a psychology which stressed the mechanical association of similar ideas
to one in which mind was a dynamic and functional instrument of
adaptation to the environment; mind, for James, was a name for a
certain type of behavior.

James' psychology broke down the separation between mind and
body by considering what had traditionally been called "mind" as
man's conscious, intellectual behavior and what had traditionally
been called "body" as the biological context in which this behavior
takes place. Thus his work provided a psychological basis for the
overthrow of the dualism of mind and matter which had been the
starting-point of most "modern" philosophy. At the same time, by
insisting that mind is not a substance, but an activity, he was cutting

out the underpinnings of the psychology of "mental states" which lies at the heart of the British empirical tradition since John Locke. We must, James thought, renounce the conception of mind as an independent "stuff." He loved to translate the German "Stoff" by this less formal word, rather than by its more formal synonym, "substance." Mind is no stuff which can be cut up into fragments labeled "sensations" or "ideas" or "mental states." It is activity. It is the dynamic and continuous process by means of which the organism and its environment are integrated. Although in man, at least, the process of adjustment is intelligent and conscious, consciousness is internal to the process, not added to it from without.

James sincerely tried to exclude philosophic considerations from all except the final chapter of his *Principles of Psychology*. His philosophic views, however, and the implications of his psychological position for philosophy kept coming to the surface of his mind. He had always been interested in the problems of philosophy. In his youth he had become accustomed to discussions of philosophic issues which his father started as the family sat at dinner. Prior to his appointment in physiology at Harvard he had been one of the regular participants in that informal group which Peirce called the "metaphysical club." He had written a few articles in which there were foreshadowings of his later philosophic themes and positions. Now he was driven to philosophic speculation by his own psychology. In 1897 he began an almost exclusive devotion to philosophy to which he gave the remaining thirteen years of his life. For various reasons, of which persistent ill-health was most important, he was never able to complete a systematic presentation of his philosophic position. In what he did write, however, enough of his ideas emerged for us to be able to gain an understanding of his thought.

The complete structure of James' philosophy he preferred to call "radical empiricism," reserving the term "pragmatism" for the method of his philosophic study. There is a very brief statement of James' radical empiricism in his "Preface" to *The Meaning of Truth*. Here he asserts that "Radical empiricism consists first of a postulate, next of a statement of fact, and finally of a generalized conclusion." [45] The postulate of radical empiricism is expressed in a way which Peirce would have found acceptable. It insists upon a limitation of materials for philosophic debate to things which can be defined in terms drawn from human experience. James did not deny that the

universe might conceivably be full of suprasensible things. His insistence was only that, whether or not things which are unexperience-
able exist, one can not hold a meaningful philosophic discussion about
them. He did not go so far as to identify the existence of any thing
with the possibility of its being experienced in some fashion by men;
he did not say "To be is to be experienced." But he did hold that
to be with any human significance is to be experienced. Had James
not added his "statement of fact," his empiricism would have differed
scarcely at all from that of the British school. In this statement,
however, he departs radically from traditional empiricism by asserting that the relations between things "are just as much matters of
direct particular experience, neither more so nor less so, than the
things themselves." [46] Relations are neither transcendent aspects of
the structure of the universe nor arbitrary principles by which the
mind orders and organizes experience. No more are they inferences
from experience. They are parts of experience. The view (James
called it a "fact") that relations are directly experienced led him to
the generalized conclusion that we do not have to assume an "extrane-
ous trans-empirical connective support" for the universe as we apprehend it. Experienceable things are connected by experienceable
relations. The world "possesses in its own right a concatenated or
continuous structure." [47]

James considered the establishment of a pragmatic theory of truth
to be a primary step in gaining acceptance for this empiricism. This
theory of truth is the philosophic position most usually associated
with his name, and also the point at which his differences with Peirce
appear most clearly. When James lectured at the University of
California in 1898 on "Philosophic Conceptions and Practical Results," he twisted Peirce's argument for pragmatism by asserting that
the meaning of a "philosophic proposition can always be brought
down to some particular consequence in our future practical experience." [48] The experience, he said, might be either active or passive;
this made no difference to its being meaningful. The experience must,
however, be particular, not general. Peirce's concern for generalized
consequences does not appear in James, nor does James' concern for
the particular sensible consequence appear in Peirce. As we have
seen, Peirce talks of meaning in terms of a habit, a general attitude of
response which is set up as a consequence of our experiences with a
thing. James, on the other hand, discusses meaning in terms of its

particular uses. Because of this difference, Peirce and James diverge widely in their theories of truth. For Peirce, truth depends upon public verifiability, thought of as a sort of scientific method, whereas for James truth is "a class name for all sorts of definite working-values in experience." [49] These working-values, or uses, are in future experience. Truth *becomes* true for James.

James' theory of truth is founded in a pragmatic orientation, "the attitude of looking away from first things, principles, categories, supposed necessities; and of looking towards last things, fruits, consequences, facts." [50] It was out of such an attitude that James produced his chief theses about truth. Ideas are true if they can be assimilated, validated, corroborated, and verified by men. There is no "stagnant property" of truth in an idea. "Truth *happens* to an idea. It *becomes* true, is made true by events." [51] The truth of an idea is an event in the process of its verification, as the validity of an idea is an event in the process of its validation. We must, however, be sure that we give terms like verification and validation a pragmatic interpretation; if we do not, we have but shifted from one static position to another. Validation and verification mean pragmatically "certain practical consequences of the verified and validated idea." [52] James conceived these practical consequences as "agreeable leadings."

Truth, then, is for James synonymous with a certain way of regarding usefulness. James' pragmatism is practicalism. Of any particular idea, said James, we may say, "It is useful because it is true," or, "It is true because it is useful." Pragmatically these two phrases mean exactly the same thing, that the idea can be fulfilled in practice and can be verified. "True is the name for whatever idea starts the verification process, useful is the name for its completed function in experience." [53] To verify an idea we must ask what concrete and particular experiences in anyone's life will be affected or altered by the fact that the idea is true rather than false. Metaphorically, James referred to this as "the truth's cash-value in experiential terms." [54] Vivid and happy as the literary quality of this metaphor may be, it was an unfortunate choice. It provided an opening that opponents of pragmatism were not slow to recognize. They could now argue that pragmatism was a crass and materialistic philosophy whose only use for ideas was their "cash-value."

Whatever opponents thought of his metaphor, James liked it, continued to use it, and even extended its use. The extension given to the metaphor by James brings us back to Peirce's criterion of meaning, verifiability — and not necessarily previous verification. James maintained that there are various forms of the truth-process in experience, but that all of these lead back to one primary type, "simply and fully verified leadings" with respect to common sense things or relations. These everyday truths are the prototypes of all truths. Yet in many and perhaps most of the "truths we live by," we do not bother to verify; we let our notion pass for true. The reason for this is that we are confident that verification is possible, and that the notion is verifiable — as long as everything goes on all right. And then James stretched his metaphor of "cash-value" to cover this idea. "Truth lives, in fact, for the most part on a credit system. Our thoughts and beliefs 'pass,' so long as nothing challenges them, just as banknotes pass so long as nobody refuses them." [55] A notion which is potentially verifiable may be accepted with as much confidence in its truth as one has in a notion which has been fully verified. Verifiability is as good as verification.

Truth in James' thought, as in that of the other pragmatists, had social reference. True ideas lead one into fruitful relations with one's society, "away from excentricity and isolation, from foiled and barren thinking." [56] But whereas, in Peirce, the social dimension of thought led to a restriction of truth only to those ideas which would be agreed upon by an infinite community of laboratory scientists, James' "large, loose way" of interpreting agreement (as agreeableness), made for an almost unlimited possibility of attributing truth-value to an idea. As long as an idea has agreeable consequences in the particular experience of some individual, somewhere, the idea has truth-value.

It is his concern for the particular consequence that leads James to reach this conclusion so unlike that of the other major pragmatists. It would be extremely difficult to find a statement which would be agreeable to no one anywhere in the world. In fact, on James' view, it would be quite possible for the same form of words to have different consequences in the experience of twins, agreeable and therefore true for one, not agreeable and therefore false for the other. James' way of regarding the truth of an idea made it depend upon its usefulness or expediency for an individual thinker. Indeed, he said, summing up his theory of truth, " 'The true,' to put it very briefly, is only the expedient in the way of our thinking, just as 'the right' is only the expedient in the way of our behaving." [57] He qualified this somewhat by insisting that our consideration had to be given to the long-range expediency of an idea; one which satisfies expediency for "all the experience in sight" will not necessarily be as successful in dealing with future experience. But this qualification was not sufficient to allay the force of Josiah Royce's shrewd comment that James would put a witness on the stand and ask him to swear "to tell the expedient, the whole expedient, and nothing but the expedient, so help him future experience." [58]

James could reply to Royce and other critics that differing philosophic positions are basically expressions of differing temperaments. Whenever a philosopher is engaging in his professional activities, he urges impersonal and objective reasons for conclusions to which he is temperamentally led. "His temperament really gives him a stronger bias than any of his more strictly objective premises." [59] Royce, he would have said, is essentially of the "tender-minded" temperamental type, and reveals this temperament in his philosophy. Tender-minded philosophies are rationalistic, intellectualistic, idealistic, optimistic, religious, free-willist, monistic, and dogmatic; a philosopher of the tender-minded type can be satisfied only by a closed system, a block universe. James regarded himself, on the other hand, as closer to a tough-minded type. Tough-minded philosophies are empiricistic, sensationalistic, materialistic, pessimistic, irreligious, fatalistic, pluralistic, and sceptical. A tough-minded philosopher demands a system which leaves the universe in thought as open as it is in actuality. Wherever James may have derived this theory of temperaments (and this is a moot point), it is certainly an excellent argument-stopper. One picks his philosophy by temperament; there is room for exposition and development, but not for basic controversy.

In one respect, at least, James' pragmatism was not tough-minded. One manifestation of his use of the large, loose way of interpreting agreement was his doctrine of the "will to believe." There are certain ideas that agree with the evidence; these are verified, true. Other ideas run counter to the evidence; these are disverified, false. There are still other ideas for which there is either no evidence, or not enough evidence to justify declaring them true or false. In the case of these latter ideas, in areas in which exact scientific knowledge is impossible, we have a right to accept, at our own risk, such beliefs as seem likely to prove fruitful in our lives. Furthermore, James argued, our belief in a proposition may be a condition of happenings which confirm its truth. One's faith in the honesty of some other person may be the ingredient which inspires that person to be honest. A woman becomes more beautiful by being told convincingly that she is beautiful. In terms of this doctrine, James justifies religious faith, because its augmentation of hope and courage may be the cause of beneficent consequences in the life of the believing individual, and may thus justify or confirm his faith.

In some ways this argument for the will to believe parallels the argument James used to justify the theory of the emotions which he published in 1886, and C. Lange came to independently a year later, and which is, therefore, called "the James-Lange theory of the emotions." It is worth our while, in the light of some of the misunderstandings of James' essay, to remind ourselves that he was not arguing for unlimited credulity and an absence of critical standards with respect to matters proposed for our belief. He was, rather, developing a corollary of his notion that the proper function of thought is to lead to considered action. Where there is a clear verification or disverification, the action which is called for is easily determined. If we are too careful in the intermediate, twilight zone then we shall fail to act at all in many areas of life, and this default, he felt, is worse than acting in partial or total ignorance, taking a chance, in the two types of case which he specifies: The first type of case is where, unless we do accept some belief, we lose all chance of ever attaining truth, that is, where, in the nature of the case, no confirmatory evidence is possible; and the second is where there is a likelihood that the effect of our belief will be to breed verifying facts, where "the thought becomes literally father to the fact, as the wish was father to the thought." [60] He urged in these cases the claims of belief against the sceptical doubts of the positivists of his time.

James' tough-minded pluralism arose, as his biographer Ralph Barton Perry demonstrated, out of two distinct motives. One, to which James never wholly surrendered, was the belief in a plurality of personal wills. This gives to each a freedom from involvement in others. We can not, in such a world of plural souls, either approve or condemn the world as a unit, but must judge it piecemeal, each individual being distinguished by a "personal sacredness" or privacy, though all together "sit at the common table of space and time." [61]

The will of such irreducible personal units he conceived as free; and, in the context of his essay on "The Will to Believe," this would mean free to believe or to disbelieve where the available evidence did not necessitate a conclusion. Moreover, since we have seen that in some cases James thought the affirmation of a belief might be a pre-condition of the occurrence of verifying facts, the free personal will would be creative of truth. Because there is this diversity, James argued in an essay, "On a Certain Blindness in Human Beings," it is desirable for men to discipline themselves to enter vicariously into the experience, the emotions, and the thoughts of others of a radically different position in life; the idea here, though the language is totally different, is closely similar to the view of George Herbert Mead (which we shall meet in the next section), that mind arises in society when a biological individual develops the ability consciously to look at his own behavior from the perspective of the other.

James, however, did not remain satisfied with this ethical idealism. He later developed a less sentimental version of pluralism inspired by the view that the world is composed of an infinite diversity of qualitatively different stuffs. He once described the world, in a letter to Josiah Royce, as "the whole paradoxical physico-moral-spiritual Fatness, of which most people single out some skinny frag-ment." [62] For himself, James wanted no such slenderizing abstraction. He wanted to comprehend the world's multiplicity in his vision, perhaps not to account for it, but at least to take it into his account. The later pluralism of James' *A Pluralistic Universe* maintained that in accepting pluralism we describe the constitution of reality to be in the large what we find it to be in our small experience. We find in the least segment of our experience not simplicity, but multiplicity, "plurally related." These relations are not in any way mutually im-plicated in each other. "Each relation is one aspect, character, or function [of experience], way of its being taken, or way of its taking something else." [63] There is no suggestion that all of these relations are simultaneous, nor is there any limitation of the possibility that in some situation all might be simultaneous. There is an interpenetra-tion of relations, but not an interdependence. The relations, which as we have seen, are integrally parts of the flux of sensory experience just as much as things are, are of all sorts, not merely relations of dis-junction, but also relations of conjunction. In one listing James specified relations "of time, space, difference, likeness, change, rate, cause or what not." [64] The sensory flux is composed of transitory, impermanent and particular things; James argued, therefore, that relations as given in experience are not permanent, eternal, and universal, but also transitory, impermanent, and particular. A thing, then, may enter into relations with another thing, or drop its relations. There is a wide variety of possible combinations of things and relations; this is the warranty of the openness on which James insisted as a character of the universe.

The monism which James combatted, the monism of the block universe, is a system of complete interdependence. No matter where or with what we start, the whole system, the universe in all its ramifications, is implied. Relations are part of the permanent structure of the universe; if anything were out of relation with another thing at one time, it could not come into relation at any time. This, James pointed out, makes a definite pragmatic difference between a pluralism and a monism. "If *a* is once out of sight of *b* or out of touch with it, or, more briefly, 'out' of it at all, then, according to monism, it must always remain so, they can never get together; whereas pluralism admits that on another occasion they may work together, or in some way be connected again. Monism allows for no such thing as 'other occasions' in reality." [65] Actually, the monism which James describes is an exaggeration — we might almost call it a straw man. His exaggeration, however, is designed to aid in distinguishing two ways of thinking about reality, which he calls the "each-form" and the "all-form." Any absolutistic philosophy, like that of Royce, for example, considers reality under its collective form. It regards the form of totality as the only rational way of thinking about reality. In this monistic, collective view of reality, there is an eternal pattern of "universal co-implication."

The "each-form" or "distributive theory of reality," which James espoused and which he equated with pluralism and with radical empiricism, is prepared to concede the possibility that some reality may not be included in any collective account, however large the collection may be. It sees no logical objection to allowing a "strung-along type" of connection as alternative to the collective "through-and-through unity of all things at once." [66] James, at least, goes farther than this, asserting that he considers the distributive theory to be empirically as probable as the collective theory. In the "each-form" there are many possible relations which are not actual at any moment, and which may or may not be actualized at some other moment. "The word 'or' names a genuine reality." [67] There are alternatives in every situation, not complete determinations. The parts of reality may not be in the same sort of direct connection with each other which is suggested by the word "co-implication." Yet we need not deny that reality distributively described is coherent; James suggested that "a thing may be connected by intermediary things with a thing with which it has no immediate or essential connexion." [68] Each part of reality is in actual connection with some other parts, in possible connections with many other parts. This multiplicity of actual and potential relations leads ultimately to a mediated connection, however remote, between every part. Pluralism does not destroy the possibility of a *uni*verse; it does, however, reject the type of rational universe accepted by the absolutists. Reality has the continuity of a chain, in which each link is directly connected with but two other links, one on either side, and yet, through inter-mediation, each link is in some remote fashion connected with every other. The distributive theory, then, assumes that there is no sharp and unbridgeable distinction between reality, conceived in this fashion, and appearance, which also is manifested in an "each-form." Reality is what it is experienced as being.

With this assertion that reality is to be regarded under the same form as our experience, we can begin to appreciate the importance to James' philosophy of the position he took in *The Principles of Psychology*. For it was in his psychological masterwork that James proclaimed the theory of the "stream of consciousness." This psychological theory, which has had striking literary development as a fictional technique, insists that experience is not composed of separate units of perception somehow imbedded in "consciousness" (a hypothetical substance whose real existence and necessity James doubted). James, both as psychologist and as philosopher, preferred to consider "consciousness" as a name for the flux of experience, "the confluences of every passing moment of concretely felt experience with its immediately next neighbors." [69] The flux of experience is the stream of consciousness. Both experience and consciousness evince a "strung-along" sort of order; now James adds that the order of reality is no more rational than that of experience or that of consciousness.

In James' pragmatic philosophy his temperamental antipathy to the rational conception of a universe completely systematic, orderly, precise, and predictable was given full scope. All his sympathy for the irrational and the extraordinary, all that drew his attention and interest to psychic research, "new thought," and similarly out-of-the-way manifestations of the human spirit, all that led him to the investigations which lie behind his lectures on the *Varieties of the Religious Experience*, are at home in his open universe as they could never be in any closed system. Even his concern for the particular, which his friend Peirce could never understand, becomes readily understandable if we realize that it is only in terms of a universe of particulars that one can give a proper place to the singular.

IV. SOCIAL BEHAVIORISM: GEORGE HERBERT MEAD

Of the major pragmatists, George Herbert Mead of the University of Chicago is the least known, but by no means the least interesting. This can be explained in part by the fact that Mead himself made no full-dress statement of his position. Even his Carus lectures were never completed by Mead; in their published form, under the title *Philosophy of the Present*, they were edited by Arthur E. Murphy. An editorial committee headed by Charles W. Morris has compiled three other books out of student notes, stenographic records of some courses given by Mead, and fragments of manuscript or short published articles. Thus we have no real indication of what Mead's own final statement of his philosophic position might have been. Like William James and John Dewey, and largely under the influence of Dewey, Mead worked in psychology as well as in philosophy. His psychology of social behaviorism gave him the leverage to free both his theory of knowledge and his theory of value from the dualism of earlier thinkers. He attempted with but moderate success to develop a metaphysical position consistent with modern physical theory.

Mead's interest in social psychology was an outgrowth of his philosophical concern with evolutionary biology. In any age, he thought, philosophy is the attempt to interpret the knowledge which seems then to be most securely grounded. In the 1890's, when the foundations of Mead's later work were begun, evolutionary biology seemed to be a very secure part of human knowledge. To Mead, as to many other philosophers of the period, the acceptance of evolution seemed to demand that not only the life of the organism, but also the life of the mind, was to be given an evolutionary interpretation. Mind was conceived to have arisen, like other evolutionary developments, in an interaction between the organism and its environment. As we have seen in our discussion of the ideas of John Fiske (Chapter 5, section II), even societies were viewed as complete biological organisms, and their origin and development fitted into the pattern of evolutionary thought. Mead's work in social psychology contributed to the interpretation of evolution a theory of mind and of the self which was designed to set thinking man wholly within nature rather than beyond nature. Mead's view of man denied the transcendence of any aspect; he did not accept the Greek idea of a reason beyond nature, or the concept of a soul beyond nature of Christian doctrine and medieval philosophy, or the modern philosophers' dualism of mind and body which set mind beyond nature.

In developing this position, Mead came to the realization that psychology had been at fault in its exclusive concern with the study of the individual self or mind. He rejected this traditional individualism and replaced it with the view that mind emerges as an incident in man's social activity; "the social environment is endowed with meanings in terms of the process of social activity." [70] The suggestion which led Mead to this result seems to have come to him from his study of the work on gesture by the German psychologist, Wilhelm Wundt (1832-1920). Wundt saw the gesture in a social context where Darwin, in his book on *The Expression of the Emotions in Man and Animals*, had treated gesture in a purely individualistic context. For Wundt a gesture intended communication of meaning; for Darwin it was merely self-expression. Mead, however, went farther than Wundt in thinking of the gesture in social terms. He traced the whole development of genuine communication in language from gestures. He made two basic criticisms of the work of all his predecessors, including Wundt. The first was that, in some way or other, each of them assumed that minds or selves were in existence prior to society, and used these antecedent existences to explain the start of the social process. In the second place, even when they did try to account for some aspects of mind on a social basis, they did not succeed in specifying the mechanism involved in the social emergence of mind. Mead himself tried to overcome the first of these by showing that mind and self are entirely and without residue developed in the social process, so that no aspect or phase of mind or self has to be accounted for in any way except socially. In his own theory he met his second criticism of other theories by presenting the view that language, considered as vocal gesture, is the mechanism by whose operation mind and self emerge out of the social context.

This theory represents a fusion of biological and social approaches. In it Mead asserts that there is an ongoing social process of interactive biological organisms, communicating by means of gestures. Minds and selves arise when the "conversation of gestures" is internalized. The individual act is revealed within the social act; it is the social act which is primary. This is the ground for describing Mead's psychology as social behaviorism. It must not be confused with the more widely publicized individualistic and mechanistic behaviorism of John B. Watson. For Mead, language is an objectively observable factor, one of the forms of interaction within a social group. Even after it has been internalized and has thus become the factor which constitutes what we call the human mind, language remains basically social. Mead did not use the term "behaviorism" to indicate any dismissal of consciousness or neglect of the private. He used the term to describe his approach to all experience in terms of behavior; mind (mental behavior) is not reduced to non-mental activities, but it is understood as a special type of behavior which emerges out of non-mental types of behavior under certain conditions. First the non-mental, and then the mental, types of behavior are relating activities, part of a network of objective relations of which social environment is the organization.

By means of language, then, the biological organism within the social process is transformed into the "minded" individual, the self. For language to develop, a society of a certain type must exist as well as certain physiological capacities in the individual organisms. The very minimum society which is conceivable is composed of more than one biological individual, jointly carrying on some social act. At the very least, carrying on a social act means that the individuals are using each other's acts as gestures, as guides to the completion of the act. There is, for example, a minimal social act involved in a dog fight, for the beginning of each act of one dog guides the other dog in determining what his behavior is to be. Thus the gestures of the first dog have a meaning for the second, in the same sense that the clenched fist under certain circumstances means the blow. These meanings are not in any private, subjective consciousness; they are present objectively in the social situation. Of course, a dog fight is an example of the lowest common denominator of social communication. It might almost be called subsocial communication, and the gestures, in this case, are not language, because the dog enacting these gestures does not intend to communicate by means of them. In a dog fight, the participating biological individuals have not yet become consciously communicating selves. They communicate only because they can not help doing so.

When the gestures are transformed into what Mead calls *significant* gestures, we can begin to talk about a minded individual. In order that a gesture may be considered significant, the individual must be able to interpret the meaning of his own gesture. He must be able to call forth in himself the response which his gesture will produce in another individual and be able to use his foreknowledge of the response that the other will make to control his own conduct. At this point the individual is communicating what he wants to communicate, rather than what he can not help communicating. This is the stage of true language; the biological individual has acquired a mind and is on the way to becoming a self. Like Dewey, Mead considers thinking a planning or mental rehearsal of what is to be done. "We are conscious when what we are going to do is controlling what we are doing." [71] Instead of assuming the existence of mind to start with and working out from mind to society, Mead starts with objective social process and works inward to the mind, importing the social process of communication into the individual by means of significant gesture. Mind, developed in this way in a social context, remains social. Thought continues in the same way in which it started, by our taking the part of others and controlling our overt behavior in terms of this inner realization of the way in which others will respond to our actions.

Now we have arrived at the characteristic trait which distinguishes a self. When a minded individual becomes the object of its own thinking, it is a self. Not by a vague consciousness of one's difference from one's environment, but through an awareness of oneself as seen from the perspective of the other does selfhood arise. Incidentally, this "other" whose response to one's behavior must be anticipated as an inner response is not a specific person different from oneself. We do not take the role of father or teacher or minister or employer; it is what Mead calls the "generalized other," any other participant in a common activity. The generalized other is *any* fellow-member of a social group. It is, however, important to remember that, although this conception seems to impose a rather rigid control of the individual by social pressures, and although, as we have seen, both mind and self are social emergents, Mead does not lose sight of the individual, or dismiss the individual as of no account, or completely submerge the individual within society. The inter-action of society and individual is a two-way process in the course of which society both acts upon and reacts to the individual, the in-dividual both acts upon and reacts to society. Every action of every individual changes the social structure to some slight degree. This is true of thought as well as of overt physical action. Mead (like Dewey) conceives of thought as one sort of reconstructive behavior. "In our reflective conduct we are always reconstructing the im-mediate society to which we belong." [72] In the emergence of the self, society is transformed. It develops a distinctively human or-ganization. It becomes a community of selves, rather than a collec-tion of biological units. As mind emerges from society, the idea of society (in the form of the conception of the generalized other), enters into each of its component individuals. Thus society regulates the behavior of the individual in terms of his consciousness of the effects on others of the actions which he is considering.

We may justly assert that this entire theory of the social emergence of mind and self and the corresponding transformation of society from an aggregative to a moral grouping depends upon the view that the basic act is a social act. In recognizing this we are led to want to know more about what Mead thought about the act itself. What was Mead's theory of the act, his pragmatism? Here Mead dis-tinguished any act into a process of four stages — impulse, percep-tion, manipulation and consummation. Except where there is a blockage, preventing the completion of the act, this is the pattern of the act at any level of organic behavior. If, however, there should be any block, any barrier to the completion of the act, only man among all the animals has developed a technique for dealing effec-tively with the problem created by the blocking. Thought in man is the problem-solving activity. This is Mead's version of Dewey's in-strumentalism (see Chapter 9, section IV); all thinking is instrumental to the completion of an act by leading to the consummation of an impulse or interest. The blocked impulse is freed when the individual indicates to himself the possible causes of the difficulty, sets up possible hypotheses to guide his action to the elimination of these possible causes, and, therefore, to the removal of the barrier to consummation, and, finally, tests these hypotheses by overt behavior. The physical world as it is understood by science is not the world in which the act takes place (or is blocked). The scientists' world is, rather, an abstraction from the manipulative stage of the act. This abstraction is not random but purposive and instrumental. In overt behavior the manipulative stage of the act involves physical manipulation; in thinking it is hypotheses or ideas which are manipulated. In science we draw this stage temporarily out of its context, but we do so in terms of communication or language, which is the social dimension of thought. Other animals, without the power of linguistic communication, live in a world of events. Man, who has developed linguistic communication, is thereby enabled to live in a world of shared meanings.

Pragmatism's double ancestry, its background in British empiricism and in evolutionary biology, seemed to Mead to create for the pragmatist a problem in reconciliation. As an empiricism, it accepts scientific methods as those of philosophy. To emphasize this would involve regarding the organism as one more object in a world of objects, without any special status. Organisms are given in a world along with other things. As a biologism, however, it must be concerned with action, and particularly with the interactions of organism and environment; in this view organisms are not simply one unprivileged class of objects among many others, but have a special place. The biological emphasis leads to the consideration of other objects as appearing only at certain stages in the activity of the organism. The world which appears for our observation is a function of impulses in the organism seeking an expressive outlet. Both empiricism and biologism locate truth in the verification of ideas; but where empiricism requires that the description of a meaning should be verifiable by the appearance of what was meant (as we have seen in Peirce's theory of meaning), biologism finds truth in an idea when it leads to the unblocking and eventual consummation of the act. Mead tried to combine the two emphases, though his own thought was primarily biologistic, by asserting that the verification which scientific method demands of an idea is that it shall be instrumental in unblocking blocked conduct. "The testing in its working-out means the setting-free of inhibited acts and processes." [73]

Mead's subtle discussion of the status and nature of universals is related closely to his theory of the "generalized other" and to his view that relations are objective. As we have seen, Peirce had recognized that universals are connected with habits. Mead's thought was, in the context of his total philosophy, similar. An act, he said, is universal inasmuch as the impulse to the act can be stimulated by a wide variety of objects, and it can be brought to consummation by the manipulation of a wide variety of objects. Many possible stimuli may induce the impulse to an act of sitting; many possible objects may be manipulated in such a way as to satisfy the impulse by consummating the act of sitting. Any object that one can sit on, and thus consummate the act, is a "seat." Similarly, any object that can dig a hole is a spade. The terms "seat" and "spade" are not particular concepts; they are universal ideas, located neither in an independent realm of universals, nor directly in things, nor in the mind, but in the attitudes of an agent to an object in the context of a total act. The concept or idea denotes whatever objects can be used in the course of an act. Universals, then, are not entities; they are relations. When we talk of universal terms the relationship is one of symbolization; a universal term is the symbol for any object which can complete a particular phase of an act. In the same way as colors are objective in the relationship between a sighted organism and an object, universality is objective in the relationship between an acting organism and an object. The universality of objects is in relation to an act which may be carried on by means of any of the objects. The universality of an act lies in the fact that it can be carried on by means of any of a wide range of objects. The universality of a term lies in its symbolizing any objects which fulfill the requirements of the act.

The meaning of the universal does not reside in the term itself. "Meanings have emerged in social experience, just as colors emerged in the experience of organisms with the apparatus of vision." [74] Meaning develops in experience because the individual stimulates himself to take the attitude of the other in responding to an object. Meaning is public and objective as long as it "can be indicated to others while it is by the same process indicated to the indicating individual." [75] Meaning is, therefore, that which is identical in different perspectives — in one's own perspective, as indicated to oneself, and in the perspective of the other, as indicated to him. Meaning is, then, universal in that it unites different perspectives into a single perspective. "The significant gesture or symbol always presupposes for its significance the social process of experience and behavior in which it arises, or . . . a universe of discourse." [76] By a universe of discourse Mead means nothing more than a system of shared meanings. Universality has a social dimension insofar as what an individual says or what he does is understandable and acceptable, within a system of shared meanings, to any other participant with him in a common activity. Universals have no meaning apart from the social acts in which they arise and from which they draw their significance. In the last analysis universals are ways of behaving — "alternative ways of acting under an indefinite number of different particular conditions or in an indefinite number of different particular situations — ways which are more or less identical for an indefinite number of normal individuals." [77] In defining the meaning of universals in terms of ways of acting, Mead was providing a capstone for the technical structure of pragmatism, while his insistence on the social emergence of meaning furnished a link between his social psychology and his pragmatism.

The latest stage of Mead's thought was a concern for the development of a metaphysics continuous with these other aspects of his philosophy. In his lectures on *The Philosophy of the Present*, Mead suggested a theory of time, a theory about the social implications of relativity, and a final synthesis in which sociality appears as a trait of emergent evolution. This aspect of Mead's philosophy was not fully worked out, and it is extremely obscure and difficult. In particular, the interpretation of relativity which he presents has been very sharply criticized. Nevertheless, it is worth our while to try to explain Mead's metaphysics in as simple a fashion as we can, bearing in mind that any simplification is apt to be a distortion.

Mead's theory of time depends on the view that anything real must be so in a present (not "the" present), or in relation to a present; the present is the locus of reality. In relation to any present there may be raised the question "What is the status of its past?" A past is clearly not just an antecedent present. "A string of presents conceivably existing as presents would not constitute a past." [78] A past is, rather, the causal determinant which makes possible the occurrence of a present, and which conditions this present by prescribing to it the relations which must be carried on. However, the continuity with its past which is indicated by this statement is never the whole of any present; each present is in some respect discontinuous with its past. In it there is an "emergence" of something novel, of something not completely determined by its past.

The problem which this creates for us is to reconcile determination with emergence. Mead suggests that before the novelty has emerged and at the moment of its occurrence, it does not follow from the past; it is discontinuous. After the novelty has occurred, however, we try to reconstruct experience in terms of the novelty. We try to conceive of a past from which the novel element does follow, and thus we seek to eliminate its apparent discontinuity. We strive to attain a new standpoint ("perspective" is Mead's word), from which we can understand completely the conditions which determined the present. Each new present requires the construction of a different past; its novelty is rationalized after the fact. New pasts "arise behind us" as each new present "marks out and in a sense selects what has made its own peculiarity possible." [79] A present is, then, the center of a "temporal perspective;" around this center a set of relations to past events is organized. The transition from one present to another involves a shift from one temporal perspective to another in the process of which the past is reconstructed. Mead's theory of time leaves us with a special kind of relativity, a relativity of temporal perspectives.

We have now come with Mead to his special theory of relativity; we must see what he makes of a more general theory of relativity. For Mead, relativity has made the world of material objects secondary and derivative in scientific investigation. Relativity theory has broken down the distinction between space and time; this seems to Mead to have made it impossible for us to isolate our conception of a physical object from the changes that are taking place in it. The physical object is no longer to be regarded as permanent. This newer conception of the physical object has to be defined in terms of values which are essentially relative; "energy, like space-time, is a transformation value." [80] Energy is a variable; space-time is a variable. Yet energy and space-time are the properties by which we identify an object. This poses a metaphysical question which one will find profound or idle according to his temperament: "Can a thing with changing spatio-temporal and energy dimensions be the same thing with different dimensions, when we have seemingly only these dimensions by which to define the thing?"[81] A similar question arises with respect to distance; in the light of relativity theory, we can no longer interpret distance values in terms of possible contact experience. We have no longer any right to assume that the properties which a thing has where it is would remain constant if the thing were in a different place. The space and time values which an object has from a distance under conditions of relative motion will not be identical with a measurement of it in its own space and time units. These are typical difficulties which seemed to Mead to arise in philosophy because of the advance of relativity theory.

He attempted a resolution of these difficulties which depends upon his account of social interaction. Mead asserted that, whether we are dealing with the physical field as it was understood by pre-relativity science or with that which the theory of relativity requires, social interaction is the model we follow. The correction and organization of our relative experiences in terms of the "real" objects to which they refer does not involve a non-empirical reality to which, somehow, our experiences must correspond. This scientific correction involves, rather, a way of acting which relates past and future to the present from the perspective of its widest social meaning. Mead considered the scientific view a special type of "taking the role of the other." In relativity theory, the range of our generalization takes us far beyond the physical object to a realm of the "generalized other." Here we have an attitude which makes it possible for us to pass from any physical perspective to any other, identifying in each perspective only that which is in fact identical, namely, the formula which justifies our making the transition from perspective to perspective. The concept of space-time does not give us a new and altogether unattainable sort of object. It is, rather, a wider generalization of social objectivity. It extends our capacity for taking the role of the other from our merely terrestrial neighbors to our stellar neighbors. The theory of relativity is one phase of the process by which man achieves social objectivity; in all its phases this process is one of organizing relative perspectives.

When scientific thought in its broadest reach has thus been lined up with the rest of Mead's thought, we are ready for the last, incomplete, and only fragmentary suggestion in his philosophy. This comes in his attempt to generalize sociality into a characterization of the whole course of natural development. "I have wished," said Mead toward the end of his life, "to present mind as an evolution in nature, in which culminates that sociality which is the principle and the form of emergence." [82] There is a plurality of relational systems; an object belonging to two such systems at once brings into each a character which it has gained by its presence in the other. The process of readjustment in which the object maintains itself in each system by being also in the other is sociality. Thus sociality emerges into higher and more complex objective forms of expression, as mind evolves out of animal behavior. An animal is involved in two relational systems simply by being both material and alive. The animal is, however, not conscious of being in two systems because it is unable to take the role of the other. Sociality among animals is, thus, of a low order; out of it, however, emerges a higher level of sociality, conscious experience, in which an individual can grasp meanings in their widest generality. Once this level has been reached, the self commands so wide a variety of perspectives toward his world as to be able to identify that which is common to all perspectives, and which would therefore be valid for any rational animal. To be able to isolate the identity in all perspectives is to take the role of the generalized other, and this is what the scientist does. The meanings which the sciences find in the world are those which would be revealed in this most impersonal of perspectives. There is a fillip of paradox in Mead's view. To be a real member of the community of rational beings is what it means to be a person; yet one becomes a member of this rational community precisely by taking the most impersonal of standpoints. It is by achieving the greatest impersonality of perspective that an individual becomes a person.

For Mead this culminating vision of his philosophy led to freedom from both past and future. The present is where our values lie. The past and the future provide us with the means and strategy for working for their realization. "The present is the scene of that emergence which gives always new heavens and a new earth, and its sociality is the very structure of our minds. Since society has endowed us with self-consciousness, we can enter personally into the largest undertakings which the intercourse of rational selves extends before us. And because we can live with ourselves as well as with others, we can criticize ourselves, and make our own the values in which we are involved through those undertakings in which the community of all rational beings is engaged." [83]

Surely the objective idealism of Peirce, the radical empiricism of James, and the metaphysics of sociality of Mead are totally dissimilar outcomes. Yet all are alike founded on a pragmatic base, and in all there is the attempt to understand the realm of thought as the community of scientists might understand it, as an instrument in the adaptation of man to his environment and of the environment to man. In all there is an attempt to see ideas arising within a natural setting and functioning therein as plans or instruments. To Peirce, James, and Mead, alike, the world is still in the making, and man is one of the makers. This is the unity among these diverse pragmatic philosophies.

8

CROSS CURRENTS OF REALISM

I. THE SEARCH FOR A PLATFORM

The successors of Kant in Germany, England, and America accepted his elaborate and careful criticism of man's knowledge of nature with far less critical limitation than he would himself have approved. He wished to establish the limits within which scientific knowledge could be considered valid, and to restrict somewhat the claims made by the thinkers of the eighteenth-century Enlightenment for the range and certainty of human reason. His followers among the idealists considered his attempts to fix the limits of validity for natural science as an invalidation of natural science. They developed, to replace science, a superscientific view of the universe based upon the belief in a super-Reason able to comprehend the Reality behind the fragmentary world of appearance, and of phenomena, to which science was restricted. The empirical method of the scientist, they asserted, could result in but a relative, particular, and partial knowledge of true being. Even the particular facts which scientific inquiry could reach were, by this interpretation of Kant's thought, infected with a subjectivity arising out of the inability of the human understanding to grasp things as they are in themselves — the necessity of regarding things in internal relationships which are supplied by the mind. Only by means of philosophic speculation which leaves particular facts and human experience far behind, and which soars into realms completely transcending the physical, did they believe that men could gain a knowledge of absolute, universal, and unitary Being. This metaphysical Reality they considered to be the only source of human comprehension of the complete pattern of the universe. For some, this superior Reality was a Mind, for others, a Person; for still others, a Will. In all of these interpretations, the consequent philosophical system was described as an "idealism." And in all of these idealisms as well as in some of the earlier versions of pragmatism, the objects of human knowledge were somehow thought to be changed in the act of knowing them, so that men could never know what they were like independent of their being known.

At the beginning of the twentieth century, in Europe, England, and America, there were developed, almost simultaneously, philosophic systems designed to refute the idealist view and to insist that things are not significantly changed by our knowing them. These various movements, because of this central insistence on the independent reality of the objects of human knowledge, were known as "realisms." In France there was a revival and a refurbishing of the ancient philosophy of St. Thomas Aquinas, known as "neo-Thomism;" more recently the realistic philosophy of neo-Thomism has appeared as a minor but significant force in American philosophic thought. In the German countries, the realistic school developed as Phenomenology, which has also made for itself a place in American philosophy. In England, G. E. Moore, Bertrand Russell, Alfred North Whitehead, and their followers in the so-called "Cambridge school," were explicitly realistic in their philosophy. Whitehead came to America, and, in a distinguished career as a teacher of philosophy at Harvard University, led many students to a view which, though realistically grounded, developed an elaborate metaphysical superstructure whose kinship to realism is far from clear. Other, chiefly younger, American philosophers have gone directly to the fountainhead and have returned from their studies in England as confirmed realists. In America the cause of realism was fostered by William James, and its development carried on by many of his students. Among these students and others who were in basic sympathy with them the search for a realistic platform, which is the theme of this section, was carried on during the first two decades of the twentieth century.

Although the stirrings of realism in America were felt at the very beginning of the new century, and such critiques of idealism as Ralph Barton Perry's article on "The Egocentric Predicament" had been published earlier, realism as an organized and cooperative search for a platform can not be said to have begun until 1910. In the spring of that year a group of six young American philosophers met together to define the basis of their agreement and to formulate and expound a realistic philosophy which they regarded as novel. The members of the group were affiliated with different universities: Ralph Barton Perry and Edwin B. Holt were then teaching at Harvard; William Pepperell Montague and Walter B. Pitkin (later to become known in less philosophical circles as the author of *Life Begins at Forty*), taught at Columbia; Edward Gleason Spaulding was at Princeton; and Walter T. Marvin taught at Rutgers. The total world-views of these six men were by no means identical. Beyond their fundamental agreement on the realistic approach they made no attempt to enforce any unity. Their first cooperative statement, published in July, 1910, after several meetings, was called "A Program and First Platform of Six Realists." Two years later, the group published a volume of "coöperative studies in philosophy," entitled *The New Realism.* Their joint authorship of this volume earned them the group name of "the new realists."

The area of agreement among the new realists was small. They expressed complete agreement on two working procedures, and agreement with reservations on three principles of the theory of knowledge. Beyond this small area they broke up, devoting their energies as much to crusading each for his own interpretation as to the conduct of their joint enterprise. As far as the method of philosophic study is concerned, the six were as one in believing that philosophers, like scientists, should cooperate instead of working alone. *The New Realism* was to exemplify this pooling of philosophic concern not by seeking unanimity on each point discussed in each essay, but by a process of mutual criticism and adjustment aimed at making each article generally acceptable to all. In the second place, they agreed, again with the example of scientists in mind, that it is possible for philosophers to isolate each of their problems successively and to study and analyze them one by one. In effect, they abandoned here the traditional search of philosophers for an all-embracing system, and contented themselves with a step by step advance toward an understanding of the universe and man's relation to it. By agreeing on this procedure, they thought that they could study the knowledge relationship between a knower and a thing known without concerning themselves with the nature of either, or, for that matter, with the status of relationship itself. Thus, even in this agreement, seeds of later disagreement were sown that soon bore fruit.

The three positive principles concerning the knowledge relationship on which the new realists agreed with reservations represent the merging of three earlier types of realistic philosophy. The realism of common sense, everyday experience, opposed sharply to a Berkeleyan mentalism, is evident in the assertion that there are, in fact, some particular things which exist when no one is conscious of them. The existence of particular things is independent of human knowledge. The defense of this principle was based upon inferences from our experiences designed to show that although consciousness or knowledge is necessarily a factor in the situation when we are conscious of, or know, an object, this does not necessarily prove that the existence of the object depends upon consciousness. We must decide whether the object is dependent or independent by charting its behavior while it is under observation. The result of this investigation is to show no influence of consciousness on the behavior of objects. Quite the reverse, as Montague pointed out: "They come and go as they list, and while our experience and its changes depend largely upon them and upon their changes, the converse is not true." [1]

The second type of realism expressed in the principles of the new realists is that of the Platonic tradition in philosophy. There are, it was asserted, some universals or essences which subsist — that is, which may be logically identified though they can not be empirically observed — when we are not conscious of them. The argument which the new realists used in the attempt to demonstrate this principle parallels that which they used for their first principle, but does not carry as much conviction because it lacks a foundation in experience. They maintained that the relations of numbers and of such qualities as colors are independently subsisting universals, entirely indifferent to human consciousness of them. Again to quote Montague's historical account: "That $7 + 5 = 12$ is entirely explained by the natures of seven, of five, and of twelve, and not in the least by the nature of consciousness." [2] One might point out that the nature of "plus" and "equals" must also enter into the explanation, and that in all these cases the nature of the universal is merely its conventional definition. It would be more difficult to show that if yellowness is added to blueness the result is greenness even though every child knows as a rule of thumb that the combination of blue paint and yellow paint will enable him to make a green mark.

It was in their third principle, which asserted the realism of Thomas Reid's theory of perception against that of Descartes and

Locke, that the arguments of the new realists began to show their basic lack of agreement. The principle is that of "presentative realism," which states that some of the real things which exist independent of our knowledge of them are grasped intuitively and directly by the mind, rather than indirectly through mental copies or images as Locke had asserted. Thus there are not two "things" — the thing as it is in itself, and the thing as it is in our consciousness of it — whose identity may be assumed or denied, but only one "thing." It is true that before the human organism can perceive an object there must be some change in the organism; the new realists declared that Descartes, Locke, and all other philosophers who accepted their view wrongly drew from this fact the fallacious conclusion that what we perceive is not the object but the change, the effect it produces in us.

Thus far there was a large measure of agreement among the new realists, perhaps as much as philosophers can ever hope to reach. It was at this point, however, that the new realists began to expand and to expound their disagreements instead of following their original plan of concentrating on the amplification of those points on which they agreed. Instead of concentrating their fire on their common enemy, they fell into internecine strife. Their cooperative book itself contains an appendix in which Montague attacked two of the positions taken by Holt in his article. Holt's reply to Montague's comments is appended. In a further comment, Pitkin aligns himself with Holt on the issues which Montague raised; he indicates, however, that he understood Holt's position in a different sense than either Holt himself or Montague understood it. Perry also wrote in support of Holt. Here, among but four members of the group, there were already three varieties of new realism. By virtue of his differences from Holt and Perry on these two issues, Montague later asserted that he represented the "right wing" of the new realism.

The points he raised were these: First, Perry and Holt, undoubtedly under the influence of the functional and behavioristic schools of psychology which were then widely accepted, had maintained that what we mean by saying that an individual is conscious of an object is that his bodily organism manifests some "specific response" to the object. Montague held that a response of an organism must mean a motion of some or all of the material particles which compose the organism. A motion must take place spatially and in a definite direction. Such a spatial and directional motion, he thought, can not constitute "what we experience as 'the consciousness of' an object." [3] Whatever our awareness may be, Montague insisted, even if we wish to regard it as a definite part of the organism, we must surely avoid defining awareness as a motion of any sort. Our awareness enables us to be conscious of what is outside ourselves. By means of it we are able to come into relation with objects which "are either in other places and times or not in space and time at all," [4] and this last point precludes any possibility of regarding awareness as motion. Holt and Perry dismissed this argument by denying Montague's identification of "response" with some kind of material motion.

The second difference of opinion between the right and left wings of the new realism was both more complex and more fundamental. It involves the way in which Holt and Perry on the one side and Montague on the other interpreted the fact of our susceptibility to error. We have pointed out that for the realists some of the objects of our consciousness exist even when we are not conscious of them; the question which is now raised is whether, if our consciousness or experience is illusory or erroneous in any particular instance, the object of our consciousness in that instance can be said to have objective, independent existence. Holt's position, with which Perry agreed, was that contradiction, error and unreality exist objectively; they are not distortions introduced by consciousness. "It seems to me," Holt wrote, "that the extra-mental world is teeming with contradictions and unrealities, and that these can come to consciousness by virtue of a psychical process, which presents no elements of 'distortion.' " [5] Montague took exception to Holt's view that "objective contradictions constitute the content of an erroneous experience and cause its occurrence." [6] He was willing to grant subsistence out of the mind to an unreal object; he boggled, however, at allowing it any causal force, because, as he put it, "It is the nature of the unreal, or merely subsistent, to be sterile of consequences." [7] We can know an unreal object, but it can not be the cause of our knowing it. Montague later came to realize that his protest at this point was based upon his unwillingness to go along with Holt and some of the other new realists in admitting (with William James), that the relations between things are as objective and independent of our consciousness as are the things themselves.

There were, in addition to the two differences of opinion we have considered, many other differences among the new realists and their followers. The philosophical journals of the period were full of criticism, refutation, and counter-refutation. It became clear that there was actually only a very slight basis of agreement among the members of the school and that even this was almost entirely involved in their criticism of the metaphysics of the idealist successors of Kant and of the dualism of real object and mental object in the Lockean tradition. Certainly, although the acuteness of their analysis can not be denied, they left behind them no affirmative position to serve as a foundation for later philosophic activity. They helped to destroy the dominant system of philosophy in their time, but failed as a group to give any positive content to their realism.

Whether because of this failure of the group, or because of their failure to answer adequately criticisms of their view of the objectivity of relations, or because of some other reason, some deficiency on the part of the new realists led to the rise of another group who called themselves "critical realists." This group of seven American philosophers carried on its cooperative activity chiefly between 1916 and 1920. The members of the critical realist group were Durant Drake of Vassar College, Arthur O. Lovejoy of the Johns Hopkins University, James Bissett Pratt of Williams College, Arthur K. Rogers of Yale University, Roy Wood Sellars of the University of Michigan, George Santayana who had taught at Harvard but was no longer there, and C. A. Strong who had taught psychology at Columbia but who had, like Santayana, retired from active teaching. The book which these seven wrote conjointly, called *Essays in Critical Realism,* was given the subtitle "a cooperative study of the problem of knowledge." Here, as in the earlier collection of new realist essays, the limitations of philosophic cooperation are again revealed and frankly admitted. The seven sought for no agreement except in the specific area of their immediate concern, the problem of knowledge. They regarded their new realist predecessors as naive in the analysis of the act of knowing. They adopted the adjective "critical" to describe their own more elaborate analysis, which was essentially a careful combination of the insights of subjective and objective theories of knowledge.

They held that in certain contexts it is proper to draw a distinction between the object which is known and the state of consciousness which is the vehicle of that knowledge. Thus the critical realists accepted for some purposes the dualism against which their predecessors had revolted. In making and even emphasizing this distinction, however, the critical realists did not mean to say that what we know is a state of mind or consciousness. We do not know a mental state which is itself an existent and from which we must infer the existence and the character of an external object. The critical realists maintained, rather, that what we are in any way conscious of, whether we perceive it, conceive it, or remember it, is the external object itself, which is independent of the process of knowledge and beyond which there is, despite what Kant had said, no ulterior reality.

There is something in each case in which we can talk about knowledge which is the starting-point for knowledge. This something is not itself the product of any aspect of the act of knowing; it is "given" to the knower in the same sense as the conditions of a problem are given to anyone who attempts a solution. The "given" is that with which the knowledge process starts; the realists referred to it as the "datum." The heart of the critical realist view of the nature of knowledge is the distinction between the object and the mental state by means of which it comes into consciousness. Some of the critical realists believed that the mental state is internal to the knower, and hence distinguished the "datum" as objective. The "datum" is, however, clearly not the physical object itself; in knowledge we do not literally grasp the object of our knowledge, although we seem to an unsophisticated analysis to do so. On the other hand, some of the critical realists thought of the "datum" as a distinct being, separate from both the object and mind, and yet in some way representing the object to the mind. The "datum" is an essence, a character, by means of which the "whatness" of the object is known. When the seven cooperating critical realists came to specify more exactly the nature of the "datum" they broke into two groups. Lovejoy, Pratt, and Sellars held that whatever object is present to the mind at any moment is made up of particular sense-data. The other four thought of the "datum" as more complex, having been influenced by William James' account of the given. The limits of cooperation within such a group are again evident in this splitting of views.

Another aspect of the polemic of the critical realists is shown in Lovejoy's attempt to prove that a "true" pragmatism would have to be founded on a theory of knowledge like that of the critical realists.

All instrumental knowledge involves a representation, by "data" which *are* present to the mind, of existents which *are not* present to the mind. Knowledge thus necessarily requires the consideration of non-present existents, which Lovejoy insists are "transcendent" of the particular experiences of knowing in all cases, and, in some cases, "transcend the total experience of the knower." Furthermore, if we assume that there is a "real" physical world whose character is described by natural science, some of the content of experience, specifically those parts which enter into experience as recollection of things past or anticipation of things future, can not be considered as belonging to the real physical world. There are entities, then, which are experienced but not physical. These entities Lovejoy called "psychical," and he insisted that, inasmuch as knowledge is mediated through such psychical entities, it would be impossible without them.

James Bissett Pratt concentrated his fire against Kant's "reluctant witness for idealism." For the Kantian philosophy, he pointed out, there is an impassable gulf between the realm of the knowable, the world of phenomena, and the realm of the real, the world of things-in-themselves. Critical realism is an attempt to bridge this chasm by regarding knowledge as "that situation in which one is forced to distinguish between the object of one's thought and the thought itself." [8] Physical objects do not exist in a different realm from men, as do Kant's things-in-themselves. They are in the same world as the minds which know them; they affect men's lives and in some cases are affected by men's actions in ways which are not dependent upon the process of knowing them. This much our practical experience teaches us, so that we can define physical objects in such a way as to know what we mean by them as well as "to make that meaning perfectly plain to everyone but the perversely blind." [9] The laws according to which physical objects act, and their relations to each other as well as to men can be investigated by the methods of physical science. The results of scientific study give us "true knowledge of reality," because the relations which are studied are external, not mind-dependent. Both science and our everyday actions verify the hypothesis of critical realism that physical objects are both independent and knowable.

These brief summaries will serve as samples of the ideas and themes, the agreements and disagreements, of the critical realists, as our earlier summaries have suggested the enterprise of the new realists. There were other American philosophers of this period who were more or less akin to these realists in their theories of knowledge but who remained outside of the cooperative groups. But there is little more to add to the story of American realism as such. Its exclusive concern with agreement in theory of knowledge reduced it to barrenness as a system of thought, although its insights and emphases have merged into other philosophic positions and have strengthened them. It is not too much to say that, between them, realism and pragmatism destroyed the thin and bloodless academic idealism of the late nineteenth and early twentieth centuries, making it necessary for a more "tough-minded" type of objective idealism to develop in order that idealism as a way of thought might survive. It is certain that realism was, in part, responsible for the change of philosophy in the colleges from what has wittily been called "a combination of the paradoxical and the unimportant" [10] to a renewed association with the natural and social sciences. There is a realistic temper in contemporary American thought even though there is no vital school of realism. The new realists, the critical realists, and those who were realists without any epithet have taken their theories of knowledge with them into other movements in American thought. In the rest of this chapter we shall examine the philosophies of Ralph Barton Perry, a new realist, Roy Wood Sellars, a critical realist, and Wilbur Marshall Urban, whose standpoint is beyond realism and idealism.

II. THE NEW REALISM:
RALPH BARTON PERRY

Ralph Barton Perry's undergraduate years were spent at Princeton, where his chief teacher was a typical academic idealist, Alexander T. Ormond. When Perry in later years described his move to the Harvard of William James, Josiah Royce, George Santayana, Hugo Münsterberg, George Herbert Palmer, and Charles C. Everett, for graduate study, he called the shift "an abrupt transition from faith to criticism." [11] This transition was not only an important part of Perry's biography, but also a vital factor in the emergence of new and critical philosophies in the last years of the nineteenth century in America. It was the age of the counter-puncher in American philosophy. The chinks in the armor of absolute idealism were becoming visible. The newer biological insights of the evolutionists and the new functional psychology were at hand to furnish weapons for the assault. In the end, the old form of idealism was beaten to its knees, perhaps never to rise again. From his philosophic youth, Perry was one of the better counter-punchers and critics. We shall see here how he moved from criticism to the construction of a philosophic position on realistic lines.

Perry's article on "The Egocentric Predicament" was one of the sharpest weapons in the armory of the critics of idealism. The essential argument of this essay was that, necessarily, when any human observer or thinker perceives or thinks about the world, he thinks about it in relation to himself. This is true regardless of the philosophic school to which the thinker belongs; it is as true of the realist as it is of the idealist. The fact that there is a relation of this sort in all our thinking is one of the difficulties with which thought has to contend, but Perry said, the omnipresence of this factor in thought does not indicate that it is fundamental for reality. For the idealist who equates being with being perceived, the subjective idealist, the "him-ward aspect of things" [12] is considered as affording the deepest insight into reality. True as it must be that no philosopher can discuss anything which is not an idea, because in discussing it he converts it into an idea, all that this proves is that "every mentioned thing is an idea" not that "only ideas exist." [13] The egocentric predicament is characteristic of thought, not of being. Confronted with this truism, that nothing can be thought about without being thought about, the subjective idealist has thrown up his hands in despair and insisted that nothing can be without being thought about. "Idealists have used as an argument what is, in fact, only a difficulty." [14]

Perry's argument from the triviality and redundancy of the egocentric predicament destroyed the foundations of subjective idealism, and he believed that all idealism was infected with subjectivity. He saw no essential difference between the idealism which Berkeley gave to the world in the early eighteenth century and that of the German post-Kantian schools of the nineteenth century. This later idealism, however, did claim a difference from that of Berkeley, insisting that the difference made of their idealism an objective rather than a subjective variety. For objective idealism, the error of Berkeley was his failure to recognize that the "mind," to which reality was reduced was not the human mind, but some sort of universal mind, "a super-personal, or impersonal, logical consciousness." [15] The content of this cosmic consciousness is objective reality for the individual thinker. Perry's reply to this line of thought was that to the extent that objective idealism repeats the Berkeleyan argument, it is subject to the same criticism; to the extent that it does not, it is unproved. Perry's arguments against idealism all involve the discovery of either the fallacy of the egocentric predicament or of "definition by initial predication" [16] — that is, of regarding that aspect of things in which they are first presented to us as their definitive character.

Although Perry was not a pragmatist, his criticisms of pragmatism were never as sharp as his criticisms of idealism, or of what he calls "naturalism," which includes a wide variety of types of positivistic philosophies. It may be that his devotion to his master, William James, led him to a somewhat more tender treatment of the pragmatic position with which James' name was associated. It may also have been a feeling that, properly limited and applied, pragmatism might re-enforce the realism to which he was devoted. Perry considered the philosophy of James to be just such a desirable combination of pragmatism and realism. To reach such a satisfactory outcome, Perry thought, the pragmatist must carefully restrain his metaphysical tendency to suggest that "knowing *makes* reality." [17] If pragmatists should not hold the reins firmly on their own tendencies, they can develop a subjectivism as extreme as that of the idealists, with less theoretical justification. For a subjective pragmatism would end in a complete relativism. Not only would there be no fixed truth — this Perry could accept; but also there would be no fixed fact, no fixed being. If the objects of judgment are regarded as created by judgment, then the objects are inescapably linked in the conflict of judgments. A balanced pragmatism must insist on the distinction between truth and reality, lest reality become what truth is for the Jamesian pragmatist, "a specific and characteristic form of human success." [18]

These critical and negative comments served Perry as a spring-board from which he could leap into the discussion of his own realistic philosophy. Here, as in most modern philosophy, the starting point was theory of knowledge. Yet, in describing his theory of knowledge, Perry introduced a procedure unusual in his group. The problem of knowledge, he said, is the problem of defining the "relation between a mind and that which is related to a mind as its object." [19] The feature which is present in both terms of the relation is mind. Perry, therefore, started with the attempt to find out what sort of thing mind is. This investigation may be accounted as Perry's technique for eliminating the egocentric character as far as possible from his own thought. By a careful study of mind and its operations we can learn what to discount from our perceptions in order to find the mind-independent object. Now, there are two classic methods for the study of mind; one is to observe it as it appears in nature or society, the other is introspection. By each of these methods it is possible to work out a view of the action of mind and of the content of mind — both thinking and thought. It has long been realized that the pictures of mind which these alternative methods produce are so altogether different as to lead to the conclusion that what is accessible to observation is not mind at all, but some non-mental shell or exterior from which we can infer the existence but not the nature of the mind within. Perry's suggestion is, rather, that mind without and mind within are parts of the whole mind, related to each other and to the whole of which they are parts in the same fashion as the concave and convex aspects of a whole shield. When looking at the shield, we tend to regard it as concave or convex depending upon what aspect we are first aware of; yet it is possible to overcome this "initial bias" and know the whole shield in its full concavity-convexity. Similarly, Perry holds, either the mind within or the mind without may assume undue prominence because of our "cognitive starting-point." Yet here, too, an initial bias may be overcome and the whole mind known in its full internality-externality.[20]

Most of the technical material, chiefly physiological in nature, which Perry used in his argument, was based upon the work of E. B. Holt and does not call for elaboration here. We may briefly summarize Perry's conclusions: What is directly known, whether by observation or by introspection, is the real mind. In neither case, however, is the whole mind what is known. Rather, the results of observation and those of introspection must be fitted together to supplement one another. The method of observation tends to slight the contents of mind and to emphasize its actions; the method of introspection tends to slight the actions of mind and to emphasize its contents. When these factors are brought together they compose a whole mind, no part of which is shut away from any knower. Mental content can be inferred from mental action, and thought from behavior. The reason this is possible is that the elements of mental content are neither exclusively mental nor exclusively the property of any one mind; they are "neutral and interchangeable." [21] It is the grouping or relation of these elements which is peculiar to one mind, and the principle of this grouping is the interest or desire of the individual. Each mind contains not its whole environment, but an abstracted segment of its environment; we can infer what segment that is by observing toward what part of the individual's external environment he acts in an interested fashion. A mind is a complex organization which acts according to its interests. The basic interest of self-preservation has been supplemented in the course of evolutionary development by a variety of special interests, some peculiar to a species, some peculiar to an individual. The nervous system and other bodily instrumentalities further the interests of the mind by making possible its active relation to its environment. It is the interests and instrumentalities taken together which constitute the action of mind. The contents of mind are "parts of the environment, with which it deals through its instrumentalities and in behalf of its interests." [22] The human mind exceeds other minds both in variety and coordination of interests and in the discrimination and range of its contents. "It acts on abstractions and principles, on an innumerable variety of complex objects, and on remote regions of space and time; all of which lie outside the practical economy of animals comparatively deficient in sense, memory, imagination, and thought." [23]

A mind thus constituted is the knower with respect to which Perry worked out his theory of knowledge. This theory as Perry propounded it, is a combination of two theories, the theory of immanence and the theory of independence. Any realistic position must assert that in some sense things exist in independence of a mind which knows them. Having made this assertion, a realism must then explain how independent things become the contents of mind. The theory of immanence is Perry's way of explaining this. If we recall what was said above about the neutrality of the contents of mind, it will be easy to understand Perry's assertion that the same elements compose mind and body. Reality is not divided into a realm of mind and a realm of body, but is, rather, "a field of interpenetrating relationships." [24] When any thing is known, it enters into a relationship which constitutes it as the content of a mind. Things, in the relation of being known, are ideas. These things may simultaneously maintain a variety of other relationships. Things are immanent in the cognitive relation, but are not constituted by this relation because they transcend this relation by appearing in other relations at the same time. But the most important point here is "that the difference between knowledge and thing, like that between mind and body, is a relational and functional difference, and not a difference of content." [25] It is the thing in itself which enters into the knowledge relation.

The theory of independence by which Perry supplements this theory of immanence says that neither the existence nor the nature of what is known or otherwise experienced is determined by the fact of its being known or experienced. Since we have discussed the question of independence in the last section, we need add here only that Perry felt that the arguments which had been used by other philosophers, especially by the British realists Bertrand Russell and G. E. Moore, to establish independence are inadequate. The inadequacy he thought the result of their dialectical character, and their failure to base themselves on observation. His own theory of mind, which we have summarized above, seemed to Perry adequate for establishing the independence of things on an observational base. By combining his theory of immanence and his theory of independence into one broader theory, Perry contended he had established that "the cardinal principle of neo-realism is *the independence of the immanent*." [26] Knowledge always involves the facing of independent facts.

It is a temperamental preference for facing the facts as he understands them which lies at the heart of Perry's ethical and social philosophy as well as his theory of knowledge. Our belief must be brought into conformity with facts which are fixed, not absolutely, but relative to the belief. If the key of our belief does not fit the lock of what our belief is about, we need a better key. From his technical realism, Perry moved on into a practical realism. In his *General Theory of Value*, we have the meeting of the two strains, for here he presents an elaborate analytic argument for his temperamental tendency. Here value (whether ethical, social or esthetic), is found in particular relations of the object to mind. The value of an object is shown by its power to move minds. Value may be positive or negative; a positive value would be manifested by attracting minds, whereas a negative value would be manifested by repelling minds. The terms attractiveness and repulsiveness are inclusive terms; each has different modes in relation to different objects. Value, then, does not reside in the object alone. Value is not a quality in the object. But neither does value reside in the mind alone. It is not a subjective quality. Value is a relation. We can not abstract attractiveness from attracting; we can not talk of attractiveness as an element in an object "*by virtue* of which it evokes feeling or will." [27] Attractiveness is the evocation of the feeling or will. Furthermore, and in line with Perry's view of the nature of mind and his theory of knowledge, a particular individual need not himself be attracted or repelled in order to know that an object is attractive or repulsive, "any more than, in order to know that an object is destructive, it is necessary that he should be destroyed by it." [28] The knowledge of value involves no more than any other kind of knowledge. An individual can derive knowledge of value from his own consciousness of being attracted or repelled by an object; he can equally well derive knowledge of value from the consciousness that others are attracted or repelled by that object. Men are able to discover or to recognize a value which is antecedent to their discovery of it. A value may have an independence like that of a fact. Thus Perry's realistic theory of value makes interests in general, not the interest of a particular judge, the criterion of value.

Within this general perspective, Perry might be described as a conservative liberal in his moral and social thought. He has himself used the phrase "one who is revolutionary enough to remain loyal to the great revolutions of the past." [29] His ethical thought, as suggested in his book, *The Moral Economy*, reveals the closeness with which a realistic ethics can emerge as a non-doctrinaire humanism with a strong tinge of ideality. The method Perry used is broadly empirical; he derived his moral ideas and moral laws from a study of life, not from a study of other ethical systems. He found, with the naturalists and humanists, that nature itself is neutral, impassive, on questions of value. With the introduction of life, however, the terms of value begin to have a meaning. "The organism inherits the earth." [30] Neutral, mechanical nature becomes the environment to an organism, to be manipulated on behalf of its interests and satisfactions. For the non-human organism, goodness may be described as fulfillment of interest, or biological preservation. For the human organism, goodness consists of the satisfaction of desire. Goodness is a relation between organism and object; interest or desire is the particular mode in which attractiveness is manifested in this context. Mechanisms themselves neutral enter into relations with organic life. In these relations their neutrality is transformed into good when it is good for the organism.

Inevitably, however, this simple division of the natural environment into good and bad passes over into "the moral drama." When one interest conflicts with another, when what is good for one is bad for another, the moral situation has come into being. Every unit of life must come to a dual recognition of other units of life. They are parts of its environment; their interests are factors in a total situation which are good or bad for its interests. But they are also partners with it against mechanical nature. The principle of moral action, the moral idea, arises when interest allies itself with interest to gain force "against the common hereditary enemy, the heavy inertia and the incessant wear of the cosmos." [31] The plurality of interests becomes by alliance a community of interests, a moral economy. Morality, then, is cooperation against the cosmos instead of the warfare of conflicting interests. It is "the forced choice between suicide and abundant life." [32] Moral good (as distinguished from mere goodness), is the fulfillment of an organization of interests. To the value of fulfillment, of satisfaction, there is added in moral goodness the value of harmony and mutuality.

Since life means the manipulation of the environment on behalf of the fulfillment of vital interests, morality is organized life. The merely biological struggle for existence is replaced in the moral economy by the social drive for progress. The moral economy is, in ideal, universal. It includes all actual desires and all possible desires, and while it can not provide for the full satisfaction of all, its aim is to make the most liberal provision for each. The moral good is that which satisfies the greatest possible number of interests in a particular situation. Value and interest are connected by an objective relation; on this relation Perry rests the logic of his moral theory. A value which fulfills the greatest and most inclusive organization of interests is preferable to one which fulfills a lesser. In any particular set of circumstances, "that act is morally right which is *most right*." [33] To hold this view requires acceptance of the principle which Perry calls that of "the objective validity of interests." [34] The fact that at a given time a particular interest happens to be motivating me does not justify my disregard of other interests. It also requires the admission of a quantitative element in moral preference. The unit of value is one fulfilled interest. No simple interest can be ranked above another on grounds of quality, for to do so would require that value be considered as residing either in the object or in the subject, and not in a relation. If this be so, then the fulfillment of two interests is better than the fulfillment of one, because it is quantitatively larger. Thus Perry accounts for the priority of the maximum good over any limited good by the quantity factor. In this context, what we mean by duty is the obligation to control our actions in particular situations by the fullest possible realization of their consequences.

Morality, then, can be rational. "To be moral is . . . to be right-minded and open-minded in the unavoidable business of living." [35] But it is not easy to be right-minded and intelligent. Every particular situation in which we may be called upon to act appears on reflection to be extremely complex. To attempt to consider each situation afresh would be to paralyze action. For the most part, therefore, the individual guides his life by certain precepts of varying degrees of generality. These precepts or general rules of conduct are known as virtues. These virtues are, as it were, moral hypotheses whose verification is the cumulative experience of human beings in living together. The verification required of such hypotheses would be evidence that they lead to the satisfaction of as many desires as possible. Virtues can not be verified by any abstract, theoretical procedure; "Life is the only adequate experiment in living." [36] Nor, since morality has been defined in terms of the organization of life, can virtues be verified in the life of the individual. Verification of virtue takes place in the history of society. Virtues are verified by the institutions to whose development they lead and by whatever evidence we can find that civilization as a whole is progressing.

With such a view, it is clear that Perry's social philosophy must stress democratic harmony, peace, and international cooperation. It is less clear, except in the light of Perry's background and his early intention of entering the ministry, why he introduced Puritanism as well as Democracy into his social theory. His social philosophy is one of the rare attempts in recent times to provide an intellectual formulation for a conservative liberalism, distinct from both revolution and reaction, which is a "discriminating and forward-looking fidelity" to a past "perpetually rediscovered and renewed." [37] It is blind faith in neither old gods nor new sciences; it is a combination of reverence and scepticism toward both, with a clear sense of moral direction. Most of the time, when Perry talks of puritanism or of democracy, he is talking not of historic movements but of this moral attitude as expressed religiously or politically. Thus he is enabled to speak of men who were in no sense Puritans as puritans; men who were not Democrats as democrats. He is talking of "puritanism and democracy" and by using capital letters for these two attitudes, creating the impression that he is talking about the dominant strains in American thinking in the seventeenth and eighteenth centuries. To put it another way, he sees both puritanism and democracy as in his view they should have been rather than as they actually were. Perry's "puritanism" arises from man's feeling that there is a best to which he must aspire; whenever he falls short of his aspiration, he feels a sense of guilt. Democracy, too, is a moral movement, optimistic where puritanism is pessimistic, seeing not "man's present predicament" but "his hopes and possibilities." [38] It is the belief of the democrat that if human nature is permitted to develop in freedom man will cooperate intelligently with his fellow man to build a better world.

Naturally, the extremism of both of these "historic" movements of what Perry calls "moral liberalism" has produced exaggeration of defects. In the case of puritanism, the defect was of excessive pre-occupation with the letter rather than the spirit of morality, and consequently, a neglect of the human factor in morality. Democracy has suffered because of its over-optimistic view of human nature and its confusion of public good and self-interest. It has also exaggerated the influence of reason and goodness in the world and has therefore failed to build a moral armament against disillusion.

Now if we assume that there is an ideal of puritanism of which historic Puritanism was the shadowy expression, and an ideal of democracy to which historic Democracy (in America) is the approximation, it will be seen that these two moral movements were both complementary and mutually corrective. To these two movements Perry proposes to apply his critical conservatism, to "take puritanism and democracy as symbols of piety, reaffirming that which we find true, looking for their constituents of truth in order that we may reaffirm them, reaffirming them in order thereby to maintain our moral identity and the stream of the national life." [39] In short, Perry's conservatism is a demand for a reconstitution of American thinking on the basis of lasting elements in seventeenth-century religious pessimism and eighteenth-century political optimism welded together into a positive creed of inclusiveness and non-conflict.

In a later book called *One World in the Making*, Perry makes a specific and concrete application of his social position to the question of international organization. Perry's thesis in this work is that the world is already a technological unity, but has yet to become a moral and social, that is, an institutional unity. This moral unity is what we are today attempting to forge. Here Perry asserts that as the basis of any lasting peace, "that which has to be built is a system of institutions which shall not only embrace the whole surface of the earth but also represent every human interest." [40] Before this can be done, a world-wide conscience must be developed; this will underlie the political, legal, cultural, educational, and religious achievements "which in their sum will constitute that moral unity of man's world for which the unity of his dwelling place has paved the way." [41] Politically, Perry regards true world government as the ultimate development, but sees a gradual approach to this through cooperation by existing national governments in limited areas. The fuller development of political world unity is conditioned on the development and enforcement of an international law; the development of a world economy of abundance, freedom, and justice; the recognition of both cultural diversity and the growing areas of cultural universality, for example, in science; and the reorientation of education on global lines. Finally, world organization must be aided and augmented by a religion of humanity supplementing the various historic religions and sanctifying the ideal of a morally unified mankind. Thus world unity is the political expression of the moral economy.

III. CRITICAL REALISM: ROY WOOD SELLARS

The plain man, whose thought has not been touched by philosophic considerations, is a realist. The world is there, outside himself. It contains physical things in a definite order of both space and time. He sees, hears, or otherwise perceives these physical things; he approaches them or retreats from them, manipulates them, uses them in whatever fashion he can. By and large, except for an occasional moment of wonder about the relation to things of men who lack one or more of the senses, he is convinced that the way in which he experiences things is typical, and that it is the normal human experience. He believes that the physical things were there before he perceived them and that they remain there afterwards. Their existence does not depend upon him, nor have their properties any unique relation to his mind. When he calls something to the attention of another human being, that other perceives and handles the same thing. Things are both independent of men and common to men. Physical objects are considered as permanent and unchanging. Apparent variations in the object are explained as changes in the relation of the perceiver to the object, not changes in the object itself. Nor is there on this view anything special about the perceiver. He is a concrete individual, a particular kind of thing, as real as the things he perceives. Part of his nature as the kind of thing he is, is that he can perceive and be aware of other things as well as of himself. Knowledge is not a problem but a fact.

To this realism of the plain man, Roy Wood Sellars gave the name "natural realism." He added the caution that we must not regard natural realism as a theory of what actually occurs in knowledge but rather as a "statement of what *appears* to take place." [42] Although this uncritical and unreflective view stands in obvious need of revision as soon as philosophic doubts begin to emerge, Sellars insisted that its essentially realistic character must not be violated in revising it. The task of theory of knowledge is so to refine natural realism that it will be philosophically justifiable, not to introduce a totally unrelated hypothesis founded upon a different and unnatural standpoint. The task is to use our improved knowledge of psychology and logic to found a critical realism which corrects natural realism in detail, but does not destroy its insistence on the independence of the object. Critical realism is, then, to be a clarification of natural realism which studies the mechanism of knowing in order to overcome certain illusory views about the nature of knowing. For critical realism, as for natural realism, "it is the external object which is known, and *not* the idea of the object." [43] Critical realism elucidates natural realism; it does not replace natural realism. Underlying all the subtleties of Sellars' analysis of knowledge is a profound regard for the view of the plain man. The starting point for Sellars' revision is concern for the theory of perception, because an act of perceiving is the simplest unit of knowledge.

To the perceiver it seems that his act of perceiving is a knowing of independent objects directly. Sellars developed his criticism of this claim to show that perception is not an "event in which things directly reveal themselves," [44] but that it is rather a process in which various factors, both external and internal to the perceiver, mediate between the object and the perceiver. The view of natural realism that what is perceived is the object itself can not be maintained, except as an expression of the intention of the act of perceiving. No more can the position of Berkeleyan subjectivism that ideas are the objects of perception be affirmed. Instead of these views, Sellars proposed that perception is a twofold process, first of selecting, actively, certain external things, and then of characterizing or interpreting them. Thus, both external things and ideas are elements of the process of perception but neither is an exclusive constituent. Perceiving, then, is not a simple and direct affair, but "an interpretative operation in which sensa are taken up into a directed characterization of external things." [45] What we perceive is not physical things but percepts, which are "thing-experiences." Perception is neither under the exclusive control of the physical thing nor under the exclusive control of the perceiver, but under joint control. If this is so, whatever we may say about the independence of the physical thing, we can no longer talk about it as common to many perceivers. There may be a correspondence between the percepts of different individuals, but different individuals do not see the same thing. The object is a source of stimulation to the organism, and the stimulation is patterned. But this is only the occasion of perceiving. This patterned stimulus must be taken up into the activity of the organism for interpretation. The organism is not passive in perception. "When a satisfactory perceptual experience is delayed because of uncertainty, the percipient focuses on the object, trying to get clues for a satisfying *interpretation*." [46] Even at this elementary level of knowing the mind is operating in terms of categories of interpretation.

With this introduction we are ready to consider Sellars' theory of knowledge. An act of knowing (like an act of perceiving), is a complex process having definite structure. In knowing, we have a sense that what we know are external things. There may or may not be an actual object when we have this sense; for our knowledge to have objective reference it is essential only that there should be the sense that our knowledge refers to external things. The structure of real knowledge and the structure of illusion are alike. When things, which exist independently, are selected by an act of reference of a knower, the selected things become objects of knowledge. As objects they can be referred to, interpreted, and judged in the absence of the external thing. There is no literal connection between the mind and external things; rather, the knowing mind has a content which, it believes, discloses the thing taken as object. The consequence of this is that knowledge of a no-longer-existent past is neither paradoxical nor problematic. The past need not be actually existent in order to be referred to, to be taken as object.

There are various levels of knowing, some of which are unconscious and implicit, while others are conscious and explicit. The problem of knowledge arises only in connection with the latter, yet the former indicate "the organic setting" or matrix of knowledge-claims and thereby reveal the natural antecedents of cognition. Implicit knowing is an instrument of biological adjustment; as such it is structured and directed outward. Whether or not we agree to use the word "knowing" of this implicit knowing, "the rise and use of an actively reproduced pattern," [47] Sellars asserted that this is the foundation out of which explicit knowing grows in a natural fashion. Were there not such a background, the fact of knowing "would be as mysterious and non-natural as innate ideas and supernatural revelation." [48] Perception and perceptual knowledge is one of the lower degrees of knowledge. It can not be taken as absolutely accurate knowledge, though in its own higher levels of scientific observation it approximates accuracy more closely than "quick practical perception." [49] As perceptual knowledge passes over into scientific observation, we move from implicit knowledge to explicit knowledge.

Explicit, scientific knowledge builds upon the "organic technique" of perceptual knowledge to the point where the relativity of perceptual perspectives is replaced by measurement. There is conscious effort to achieve a more accurate approximation of the object. Knowing, in either form is a "descriptive interpretation" of objects; and in the interpretation of the object, there is a disclosure of the thing which the mind has made the object. Throughout his discussion of knowledge, Sellars moved toward the recognition that all knowledge is "approximative" rather than absolute. At different levels of knowing the types of predicates that we use are appropriate to the disclosure of characteristics of the object. "Red" and "green" are predicates which might be acceptably used about an apple at the perceptual level, whereas at the scientific level our predicates would be measured light frequencies reflected from the apple.

There are two factors in the knower, and a third which is external to the knower, which are involved in the question of truth. In the knower there is, first, an attitude of belief, and, second, the content of that belief. Outside the knower there is a state of affairs which the belief denotes. Truth is a term applied to the second internal factor when it gives accurate knowledge of the external factor. To give accurate knowledge of this factor, it must correspond with the object denoted. Truth is a correspondence of the content of our beliefs with the external state of affairs in such a manner that our beliefs do actually give knowledge of the object.

Thus far we have been concerned with Sellars' version of the critical realist theory of knowledge. We now turn to a summary of his metaphysical views to which we may assign such descriptive names as "physical realism," "naturalism," or "materialism." Sellars himself has at various times in his career used each of these names, and he considers that the views they suggest are closely similar. Physical realism has historically differed from naturalism only in maintaining the dualism of mind and body which modern philosophy inherited from Descartes. Inasmuch as Sellars had rejected any suggestion of special status for mind and had always considered mind as an intrinsic element in the organism, his version of physical realism was actually a naturalism. Naturalism, as he used the term, involved, in addition to the rejection of special status for mind, the assertion, contrary to supernaturalism and transcendentalism, that nature needs no non-natural support; the belief that space, time, and causality have basic significance for the world in which men live; and the denial that there is any "concentrated control" in the universe, which amounts to an assertion of pluralism. Finally, in regard to the use of the term materialism, Sellars felt that its traditional use was insufficiently flexible, and that the mechanical view of the world associated with that earlier use underemphasized the importance of mental activity and of values as human motives. He has suggested, however, that naturalism as he understands it is "a new materialism."[50]

The naturalism to which Sellars adheres is justly prefaced by the adjective "evolutionary." The qualification is intended to suggest that organic life and mind are novelties which have developed in nature under certain favorable conditions. There is an uneven diffusion of matter in the universe; just so, Sellars holds, there is an uneven distribution of "conditions making for complicated organic syntheses such as life and mind." [51] Sellars does not assert that the universe as a whole is evolving, but only that particular physical systems within the universe are. Life and mind, then, are particular developments within physical systems. They have been "physicalized" in Sellars' thought. Again, in being physicalized or naturalized, they are not denatured. Sellars' willingness to think in terms of levels and patterns, which we have already seen manifested in his theory of knowledge, is operative in his metaphysics as well. What have evolved are patterns on different levels of complexity of organization. "The new materialism acknowledges the immense variety and fertility of the physical and will reject none of its actual forms, from star-dust and the stripped atoms of incandescent suns to the primeval slime of the surface of this earth of ours and the intricate organization of human brains." [52] All of these are material, all are physical, all are real. The physical and the real are identical. All that exists is subject to spatial and temporal conditions and to physical causation; all existence is, therefore, either itself describable as a physical system or else inseparably bound up with a physical system.

For Sellars the actual world in which we live is the real world — the *only* real world. It is a substantial world. The category of substance has been an unfashionable one in recent philosophy, and it may be well, then, for us briefly to rehearse Sellars' defense of substance. By substance he means something different from the material substratum of Locke. The essential feature of substance for Sellars is continuance. A substance is a thing or being which persists through a measurable amount of time, and which is not destroyed by change of place. Substances can become objects in an act of knowing. They are self-existent, but not necessarily isolated. They may enter into relations with other substances. "The essential notes in the category of substance are endurance and being; but there is nothing in these notes which excludes relations." [53] To substitute the category of events for that of substance is, to Sellars' mind, inadequate, since we usually think of an event as part of a physical system in space which is more enduring than the event it includes. His critical realism enables him to reply to Berkeley's criticisms of substance; in particular he can insist that it is not the object itself which is given in the cognitive act, but the idea or character of the object, and that to think the character of external things is in no sense to assert that the things themselves are ideas or internal events. When we think about things it is their pattern and not their stuff that we think about; but this does not mean that the thing is nothing but a pattern. A substance can become the object of an act of knowing, but it is not constituted by being known. Much difficulty was created by Locke's reduction of substance to the substratum in which properties or characteristics inhere. Sellars points out that the thing, the substance, the material system is the entity; whereas Locke made entities out of the characteristics and left no role for substance but that of the supporting substratum. Extension, structure, mass, and causal efficacy are adjectival to that which is extended, structured, massive, and causally effective.

In Sellars' philosophy, then, it is matter organized as physical systems which is ultimate. There is nothing "mere" or "brute" about matter. There is an intrinsically dynamic character in nature; the principle of activity does not have to be introduced from outside. A physical system is a unit of activity. When, under appropriate and favorable conditions, new physical systems emerge, their new properties and new activities are expressions of their new organization. This is the theory which Sellars holds even when the new properties are those we call life or mind. "Life is not a non-natural force coming from outside, but a term for the new capacities of which nature has found itself capable." [54] Vital organization is a higher level of physical system; mental organization a still higher level. Both, however, are types of physical system. Sellars' materialism is certainly a far cry from the older materialisms which attempted to reduce everything to a mechanical uniformity of material particles in uniform motion. The difference arises from Sellars' stress on the importance of organization, leading him to emphasize the relations within a physical system which constitute the system as a unit. The endurance or substantiality of a physical system is secondary; primary endurance is being itself. Change is an alteration of the patterns of organization of complex and secondary systems. The elements of being never cease to be, but the combinations in which they occur are many and changing.

The universe taken as a whole is not a homogeneous system but a heterogeneous one. It is composed of many systems, each of which is controlled by its own organization. If it were otherwise, if the universe were homogeneous, then the pattern of the whole would be controlling for all the component systems, and, for any particular system, control would be predominantly external. The conditions of activity of the particular system would be set outside of itself. To the extent that we are able to regard the universe as heterogeneous there is a large measure of autonomy in its parts. Sellars even sees struggle between the parts within this universe. It is by virtue of this interpretation of the character of the universe that Sellars' perspective emphasizes freedom rather than necessity. The freedom of the part may increase; it "may achieve new ways of doing things which give it new degrees of freedom." [55] This freedom is what permits activity and creativity in nature, but it is not to be equated with the "free will" of older philosophies. Free will theories are dualistic. The free will is not an intrinsic characteristic of the physical system, but is a non-physical addition to it. The creative freedom of the physical system in Sellars' thought is intrinsic. It is "the expression of the system undergoing change." [56] Freedom is understood as the self-determination of a changing system.

We have moved with Sellars through a critical realist theory of knowledge and a materialistic metaphysics. We have now to see how he supplemented these views with a humanistic theory of values. Even to suggest that a theory of values consistent with his metaphysics can be constructed is to indicate how far Sellars' philosophic materialism has moved from the older materialism. For when materialism meant the reduction of everything that is to atomic particles in determinate motion it was foolish to talk of values. Even today there are many difficulties in defining the nature and status of those judgments which we are constantly making about the value of acts or of things. Sellars pointed out that the terms we use in making value judgments, terms like good, bad, beautiful, ugly, useful, and harmful, are not to be found in the vocabularies of the inorganic sciences. These terms apparently do not refer to natural attributes, and yet the statements in which we use them seem to us to be justified. There is a difference between valuational statements and other judgments; our intention in making the statements is different. In judgments of fact or existence, or what Sellars calls cognitional judgments, the intention is to call attention to a state of affairs which is itself independent of the judgment and its formulator. The intention of a value judgment seems to be to estimate an external object or situation *"with respect to* human living." [57] Sellars treats value as a kind of interpretation of an independent object, and to this extent his view may be called consistent with his critical realism, in which all knowledge is regarded as interpretative and judgmental. The particular type of interpretation which he considers it to be is less objective. It is, he says, "an interpretation of an object as having the *capacity* to enter human life with certain consequences of importance to the self or to a social group." [58] In a word, value-judgments are humanistic interpretations.

Sellars finds value experiences, or implicit valuations to be prior to value judgments, or explicit valuations. These experiences refer directly to a human being, who has a good time or a bad time. There is in value experience a reflection of the person whose experience is referred to. A misanthrope has a bad time at a family dinner. For the most part, the components of a value experience are feelings, which are psychical, and desires, which may include psychical and physical elements. Sellars holds, however, that even in value experience there is an intellectual component which adds depth and breadth to the experience. When we move to the level of value judgments, the feelings and desires which entered into value experience are still important, but there is an enlargement of the intellectual component. A value judgment expresses an interpretation of an object in terms so similar to those which are used in cognitive judgments that the problem is to decide in what way they differ from cognitive judgments. Sellars maintains that in practical life the distinction between cognitive judgments and value judgments does not appear. "Value predicates mingle with descriptive predicates." [59] The specialized disciplines of economics, morality, art, and politics retain the mixture characteristic of practical life. They differ from the sciences because in the sciences we are trying to find out the nature of the object itself whereas in these fields we are interested only in the bearing of the object on human life, on ourselves.

Valuing, then, is a human activity of a different sort from knowing. To the extent that there are creative possibilities in the external world, new objects are constantly appearing to human perception. In themselves, like other physical systems, these new systems are perceivable; that is, they can be referred to and characterized as objects. They are also evaluable; that is, they are open to value judgment and interpretation. Value judgment is the interpretation of the object by means of a value predicate. "When we assert that a person *is agreeable* we mean that he is rightly interpreted as the sort of person who would give us agreeable experience in intercourse with him." [60] This, Sellars asserts, is one way of thinking the person, and is not radically dissimilar to other ways of thinking. The value predicate "agreeable" is assigned to the object as a result of our actual experiences with the object or as a prediction of our possible future experiences. The object then, is some thing, person, or act which has already entered into our lives or which we conceive as possibly entering our lives at some time, with results which are expressed in our judgment. Inasmuch as this judgment is expressed with respect to the situation as it now exists, and this situation may change, values are not necessarily stable, fixed, and permanent. Objects enter into human life at different times with different results unless human life remains a constant. There is no intrinsic value. "Gold in a desert may have no value but be only a mockery." [61] This does not mean that values are subjective, merely expressions of a personal preference. It does mean that part of the objective ground of value is to be sought in environment and in personality. Some of the factors entering into evaluation are subject to individual variation. Sellars does not believe that this will lead to an anarchy of values; he thinks, rather, that there will be a few themes on which individual differences will play symphonic variations.

IV. IDEALISTIC REALISM:
WILBUR M. URBAN

Of all the movements we have thus far treated, the realist movement has been the most technical and the most analytic. Yet we can see in both Perry and Sellars that beyond their tight technical interests and their careful discriminations there is a speculative outreach and a concern for meaning and value which carries their thought into the broader questions of perennial philosophy which have puzzled men for thousands of years. Yet the philosophies of these two realists are in some ways more closely akin to pragmatism than to the older philosophical tradition. Despite their special characteristics and internal varieties, pragmatism and the realisms of Perry and Sellars have had a common thread, a common temperamental tendency which has two aspects. First, positively, all these philosophies have announced a regard amounting to blind faith for the laboratory method in philosophy; second, negatively, they all deny that mind has any special status in the universe, and therefore they distrust the sort of philosophic speculation which has traditionally been called metaphysical. This affirmation and this denial have had noteworthy consequences beyond their immediate application. For example, they have led to many difficulties and ambiguities in the discussion of the theoretical basis of human values and to the virtual elimination of theological principles as significant for philosophic explanation. Perhaps the most important characterization that can be given of the effects of these modern philosophies is that they have denied the over-all intelligibility of the universe. Knowledge and understanding are viewed as piecemeal interpretations of fragmentary phases of human experience. These modernisms have denied the possibility of a systematic understanding of the universe.

Needless to say, this new departure, this "reconstruction" in philosophy, has not been acceptable to all the Americans of our age who have practiced the ancient art and mystery of philosophizing. In various ways those who are unwilling to surrender to the modernist limitation and contraction of the scope and outreach of philosophy have striven to spur a return to the conception of philosophy in "the Great Tradition" — from Plato to Hegel.

Except in the central desire to restore the older and grander conception of the nature and function of philosophy, there has been no more unity among this group than among the "reconstructionists" whom they oppose. There are schools of philosophic thought among advocates of "the Great Tradition" revived. But there is one common assumption underlying their diversities which leads to our grouping them here together as manifestations of a distinctive spirit in recent philosophy. This is the assumption that all of reality is intelligible, intelligible as a totality. "From Plato to Hegel," Wilbur M. Urban of Dartmouth and Yale said, "this perennial philosophy has been characterized by the notion of an *intelligible* world, in some sense 'beyond' the sensible and the phenomenal."[62] It may be that later historians of American philosophy will consider neo-Thomism as the most important of these schools. This revival of the philosophic outlook of the medieval thinker, St. Thomas Aquinas, has spread beyond the religious sources in which it is rooted. Neo-Thomism in America, however, has developed no profound and original thinkers and it is chiefly for this reason that, despite its pervasiveness and persuasiveness, we do not here treat of this philosophy in detail. Furthermore, since this book is only incidentally concerned with religious thought, it seems more consistent to present the perennial philosophy in its most nearly secular version.

To characterize the Great Tradition as concerned with an intelligible world, with a realm beyond the physical, with a *metaphysical* realm, implies a further view, that the world is not merely intelligible but also meaningful. Traditional metaphysics, which has been called "the natural metaphysics of the human mind," is shot through and through with value; traditional metaphysics is a "value-charged scheme of thought."[63] Reality and value are conceived as being ultimately inseparable. Here the perennial philosophy stands in sharp contrast to philosophic modernism. For modernism nature is the whole of reality, and nature is morally neutral. For traditionalism, intelligibility is the whole of reality and is value-charged. We shall see now how this theme is elaborated in Wilbur Urban's version of perennial philosophy, selecting his thought because it is a solidly built and conscious attempt to adopt a standpoint which is "beyond realism and idealism."

This standpoint, to which Urban gave the name of the "axiological point of view," first emerged in his thinking out of the failure of the approach by way of psychology and biology to lead to an *understanding* of human values. One of his earlier works, *Valuation: Its Nature and Laws*, published in 1909, before he had reached the axiological standpoint, was a tentative exploration of all the different fields of value, with the intention of connecting fields which had previously been unrelated by the interpreters of value theory, to discover common principles or laws in these various fields, and to explain different levels of value and preferences among these levels. In this work Urban attempted to stand between the method of the descriptive sciences and that of the normative sciences. Although his book was well-received, Urban himself was not happy with it. In the course of writing the last chapters especially, he had become dissatisfied with the results achieved by the method he was using. Actually, in the light of more recent developments in value theory, Urban's book is more useful to the philosophic reader today than it was when it was written.

For the story we are telling here, what is important is to note that Urban's dissatisfaction with this book led him to reformulate his position, and to develop the fundamentals of the "axiological point of view" of his later writings, especially, *The Intelligible World: Metaphysics and Value*, published in 1929. He developed the view that value is ultimately indefinable, because it can not be understood through other things. "Value" is, rather, an ultimate category through which other things are to be understood. Thus the perplexing ambiguities and artificialities of value theory seemed to Urban to be the result of conceiving value as a quality. He came to believe that in reality there can be no separation between fact and value. "Reality, as we live it and know it, is our reality only as the stuff of experience is formed by the categories of value. We orient ourselves in the world by the relation of over and under, right and left, more and less, but not less necessarily by the relations of higher and lower, better and worse." [64]

The exploration of this conception led him to attempt a continuation of Immanuel Kant's work. Kant, in his *Critique of Pure Reason*, had maintained that our knowledge of nature is determined by certain forms of thought immanent in mind — the natural categories. In Kant's *Critique of Practical Reason*, however, the valuational categories, which Urban called "the equally necessary forms of interpretation of life and the world," [65] were differently conceived, not as immanent forms of thought, but as demands of our practical life. Urban tried to break down Kant's distinction between the categories of fact and those of value and to make both into categories of pure reason. The claim that fact and value are inseparable, and the inclusion of value among the ultimate categories, inevitably led him to the attempt to formulate a total world-view, a philosophic system, accounting in his terms for both fact and value. In this attempt, he found little difficulty in explaining the existence and nature of facts. There were, however, serious questions to be asked about the existence and nature of value. He found it almost impossible to give satisfactory answers to questions like, "What is value?" or, "Where is value?" He could not assert that value has a real existence like that of facts, nor could he content himself with the new realist assertion that values "subsist" (see Chapter 8, section I). He came to a sort of existentialist statement about value. Value, he said, is above all questions of being. The being of other things is explained by value, but about value itself one can say only that "Its being is its validity." [66]

This development had started when Urban became dissatisfied with the sort of psychologism and biologism which took possession of philosophic thinking in the wake of Darwin's evolutionary theory and William James' functional psychology. His most pointed and specific criticism was directed against the attempt to base our values upon the human biopsychic organism, which, he said, involves a vicious circle. We wish to understand values by carrying them back to life; but to wish to do this is already to assume that life and the continuance of life has value. That is, we acknowledge value as something known. To escape this circle, we must recognize that value is a logically primitive concept that can be neither defined nor validated in terms of anything else (for to attempt this is to assume that in terms of which we attempt to define or validate as having value). Urban insists that this recognition is the primary condition of any intelligible discourse about values. He finds this circle not only in discussing the non-logical values but also especially in discussing logical values. For, says he, "if knowledge and the logical values, upon the acknowledgment of which knowledge rests, get their significance solely from their teleological relation to life, surely life must get its significance from absolute values which it embodies, or knowledge itself loses all genuine significance." [67] As soon as we talk meaningfully about values, our talk presupposes that we acknowledge absolute value. Urban calls this the principle of philosophical intelligibility. We can not make meaningful judgments unless we assert a doctrine of absolute values.

When Urban had reached this point in his thought it was evident to him that the axiological standpoint was insecurely and precariously balanced. In its bare incompleteness it seems almost willful; absolute values must be affirmed, but they do not exist; yet their objectivity is their validity; they can only be acknowledged, not demonstrated, yet this very assertion is the condition of meaningful judgments of existence or truth. As it stood at this stage in the growth of Urban's position, something was lacking that would justify and prop up his weak doctrine of absolute values. Urban was led further, to develop a theory of knowledge which he describes as "beyond realism and idealism," and later to the statement of a metaphysical position based upon this theory of knowledge.

When his studies in value necessitated thinking through his approach to the problem of knowledge, "which, whether we like it or not we have been forced to make central in our thinking," [68] he rejected pragmatism, despite his sympathy for some of the positions James took, because of what he saw as a "curious process of denaturing" [69] that went on wherever "pragmatic value" touched. Everything touched by pragmatism seemed to him to lose its meaning. One of his articles was ironically entitled, "The Will to Make Believe," suggesting that Urban foresaw some of the later European developments of pragmatism. Similarly, though he wanted to be a realist, he had sharp criticisms of both new realism and critical realism, based upon his principle of philosophic intelligibility. By his account, the realist position boils down to this vicious circle: "First, various natural sciences are taken as premises for the conclusion that the objects or contents of consciousness occur within the organism as part of its response to stimulation by physical objects other than it. Then we are told that these intra-organic contents have a cognitive function. But how invest them with a function which by their very definition and characterization they do not have and are patently incapable of discharging?" [70]

Urban's dissatisfaction with the leading American schools of thought of his day drove him to study in Germany. As a result of these studies he arrived at the view that a multiplicity of conscious subjects communicating with each other is the ultimate fact to which all analysis of knowledge must come. This he calls the basis of a position beyond realism and idealism, because it makes the opposition between these two positions not a problem of knowledge at all, but a problem of dialectic, wholly within the realm of discourse. The arguments of either position can be accepted only by one who has already acknowledged the "ideal of genuine knowledge." The problem of knowledge is part of the problem of values, and from the axiological standpoint realists and idealists stand for compatible ideals of knowledge, and compatible values. The enterprise, therefore, becomes the formulation of an idealist theory of knowledge on realist lines.

In attempting to work out this type of position, Urban developed an "epistemological creed" of three articles: First, the activity of knowing can not itself be studied scientifically, because science, in any intelligible sense of that word, is grounded in an activity of knowing; second, for genuine knowledge to be at all possible the object of our knowledge must be different from our thinking, but there must also be communication from mind to mind, and such communication, to be intelligible, presupposes mutual acknowledgment of values; and third, the standpoint of a theory of knowledge is above the distinction of realism and idealism, for both realism and idealism are based upon communication and upon the realm of meanings and values, the acknowledgement of which alone makes communication possible.

Though this was as far as Urban's logic would take him, it did not satisfy his need for an inclusive and total world-view. He had to find a meaning behind the contradictions of modern culture, a contradiction he found mirrored not only in philosophy but also in art, religion, and science. He described the age in terms of its underlying contradiction — "It is doubtful whether there has ever been a period in which man has understood himself so little, in which man has at the same time been so knowing and so unaware, so burdened with purposes and yet at bottom so purposeless, so disillusioned and yet feeling himself so completely the victim of illusion." [71] The meaning of the contradictory character of the age he found in man's effort to decide whether human mind, intelligence, and reason, are merely biological adaptations, or whether they have also a transcendental meaning and status. To Urban, with his predisposition to formulate all problems in terms of values, the basic question seemed to be that of the status of values; "It does not do for the philosopher merely to assert that [values] are there; he must face the question of where they are and how they are there." [72]

Restoration of the status of values in philosophy seemed to him to demand a restatement of the perennial philosophy in which the meaning and value of things is connected in some determinate fashion with their origin and their end. So intimate is this connection that, as James suggested, "questions of origins and destiny are irrelevant and meaningless if abstracted from questions of value," [73] but also, as Urban added, "questions regarding the validity of values are meaningless if values are divorced from questions of origin and destiny." [74] Thus his axiological standpoint passes over into a metaphysics. "The entire body of traditional metaphysic was essentially a value-charged scheme of thought, and must be interpreted from this point of view." [75] If reality and value are separated in our thought, our view of the world lacks both intelligibility and meaning. We can not think of existence without value, and we can not think of value without existence. Since we can not *think* of existence and value in isolation from each other, they can not *be* in isolation from each other. Reality can not be either entirely mental or entirely material. It must be a realm in which existence and value are inseparable, an intelligible realm. But it is impossible to consider existence fully without considering its original cause and its ultimate end; where existence and value are inseparable, "value cannot be separated from origin and destiny." [76] No philosophic system can be complete or intelligible unless it satisfactorily accounts for first things and last things.

In the course of sketching this counter-reconstruction, we have mentioned Urban's belief that the approach he advocates is beyond realism and idealism. The time has come to spell out in more detail what Urban has meant by this statement. In 1917, he used the phrase as the title of an article in *The Philosophical Review*. In 1949, he used it as the title of a book. It is evidently one of the major pillars of his philosophic structure. His thesis is, in brief, that the conflict between realism and idealism which has loomed so large in recent centuries is an unnecessary one and that it may again be transcended as it was by earlier versions of the perennial philosophy. The point at which modern philosophers have erred, and thereby produced a stalemate, is in considering the basic issue between realism and idealism as one which can be solved by empirical or by rational methods. Urban suggests that the issue is not resolvable by these methods because neither realism nor idealism is knowledge. "Neither can refute the other and neither can prove his own position." [77] If the two positions were, as has so often been charged, contradictory, the fact that neither is factually or logically provable or disprovable would result in an impasse. The second phase of Urban's argument, therefore, is to show that the positions are complementary rather than contradictory.

Realism and idealism, Urban maintains, are varieties of a transcendental way of thinking about knowledge, which is opposed to a

310 Cross Currents of Realism

naturalistic way. For the naturalist, there is no problem of knowledge in general; knowledge is something we have in the same way as we have measles. Questions about particular bits of knowledge may be assigned by the naturalist to the special sciences. Urban contrasts this to the transcendental approach, shared by idealists and realists, which asks how knowledge is possible, how far it extends, and what its validity consists of. Realists and idealists ask and answer the same questions. What is fundamentally at issue between them is, he says, their differing evaluations of knowledge. Both agree that "man *must* know," and in admitting that he *must*, both accept and acknowledge truth as a value which is present before there is any activity of knowing. It is the nature of genuine knowledge that both realist and idealist seek to find out. Urban thinks it both tragic and humorous that each one believes that the other's theory makes genuine knowledge impossible. The realist can not conceive of genuine knowledge unless the object known is independent of the knower; the idealist can not see how genuine knowledge is possible unless the object known is in some sense dependent on the mind of the knower. It is this evaluation, this factually and logically unsupportable assumption in each case, which determines the theory of knowledge. It is the opposition of these value judgments which leads to the strife of these two systems. And it is this opposition which Urban describes as "dialectical."

Neither idealism nor realism is a term whose meaning can be fixed by logical definition, because they are not static positions. Idealism can not be defined in terms of any of the idealisms, nor can realism be defined in terms of any of the realisms. In order to achieve any sense of the meaning of these terms, we must consider them together. The changing forms of realism are reactions to changing forms of idealism; the changing forms of idealism are reactions to changing forms of realism. Realism and idealism are polar "life forms of the human reason." [78] Their great debate is not about facts or things. It takes place entirely on the level of discourse; it is a dispute about two meanings of knowledge. This is what Urban means by calling the dispute dialectical. But the essence of the use of dialectical method from Plato to Hegel is "the effort to eliminate false alternatives." [79] Dialectic is the process of discovering the unanalyzable presuppositions upon which conflicting analyses rest, and examining these presuppositions from various angles in order, finally, to discover some larger whole which includes all the conflicting views. Dialectic is, therefore, the proper method to apply in the conflict of realism and idealism.

The empirical method is applicable only to the resolution of conflicts about matters of fact. The rational method of logical demonstration can be applied only to conflicting propositions within the same logical system. When, as in this case, the statements are presuppositions which underlie alternative systems, dialectical resolution is the only way to deal with them. There is a recognized criterion for the accuracy of our use of empirical method, namely, empirical verification. Logical necessity is the criterion by which we determine the correctness of our rational demonstrations. The criterion of success in the application of dialectic method can not be either of these; if it were, then we were wrong to use dialectic method in the first place. Successful use of dialectic can be measured only by the principle of philosophical intelligibility.

What, then, are the irrefutable elements in idealism and realism about which the dialectic of generations of philosophers has played? The "driving force" of idealism is the principle that all genuine knowledge must be, in some sense, dependent on the mind. This principle Urban equates with the fundamental assumption of the perennial philosophy that there is a relation between reason and being such that being can be known. On the other hand, the "resistance" of realism is to be found in the principle that all genuine knowledge must be, in some sense, independent of the mind. Urban believes that this represents the other fundamental assumption of the perennial philosophy that there is being antecedent to thought. These two assumptions, thus interpreted, are not contradictory but complementary. Both are necessary to an intelligible theory of knowledge. No "sane philosophy," therefore, can be exclusively idealistic or exclusively realistic; it must make both assumptions.

This peace proposal is not completely ingenuous. What Urban has proposed in his various works, and stated most carefully in his book, *Beyond Realism and Idealism,* is not simply that realism and idealism should resolve their opposition by uniting on an axiological standpoint which transcends their differences. Urban comes nearer to saying that realism and idealism should become allies in opposition to naturalism. The alliance of realism and naturalism has been characteristic of modern American thought; in Urban's value-charged

language it is referred to as an "unholy alliance." [80] The very same
vicious circle which Urban, earlier in his career, ascribed to realistic
theories of knowledge, and which we have quoted above, is lifted
word for word out of its earlier context and used to describe the
"logical confusion characteristic of all naturalistic accounts of
knowledge." [81] The dialogue is the same, but the name of the villain
has been changed. The imprecise definition of nature in the work
of naturalists is referred to as a "fundamental ambiguity . . . fatal to
the formulation of any adequate philosophy." [82] Naturalism's theory
of knowledge is declared to be self-refuting. When the naturalist
derives "mind and knowledge from nature, as science conceives it,
he must assume that his own account of nature is true. But on his
premises, the truth of this account, like that of any other bit of
knowledge, is merely the function of the adjustment of the organism
to its environment, and thus has no more significance than any other
adjustment. Its sole value is its survival value." [83] Since Urban himself means something else by truth than survival value, the naturalists'
argument does not make sense to him.

Urban is trying, then, to wean realists away from the naturalist
camp by convincing them that they are not truly part of the modernist movement in philosophy, but rather a dialectically necessary
element in the perennial philosophy. He would willingly welcome
the prodigal son back into the ranks of those for whom the principle
of philosophical intelligibility is the heart of the speculative enterprise. In order to combat naturalism, Urban is ready now to make
common cause with his erstwhile enemies and to found his idealistic
metaphysics on a theory of knowledge which is "beyond realism
and idealism."

9

THE EMERGENCE OF NATURALISM

1. THE NATURALISTIC TEMPER

Philosophy since the time of Descartes, so-called "modern" philosophy, has characteristically been concerned especially with problems of knowledge. Most of these have arisen because a separation or division of some sort has been conceived to exist between the knower and the known. The antitheses that can lead to a problem of knowledge are many. "Man" can be opposed to "nature"; the "supernatural" to the "natural"; "spirit" to "matter"; "mind" to "body"; "self" to "not-self." All of these dualisms, however they are expressed, have one feature in common. They all place the knowing mind into one compartment — perhaps with its states of mind for company — and the world to be known into another compartment. Then they explain that the mind can know only that which is in the same compartment; the mind is shut off from the world it would like to know, and sometimes has the presumption to declare that it does know. If the mind and its contents, man's "experience," are conceived as spiritual and therefore of a different order of being from the natural world of matter, the problem of knowledge becomes both important and basically insoluble. In the light of an impassable gap between spirit and matter, it is difficult to explain how man's mind (a spiritual being), can know the world of nature (a material being). If the "self," as a knowing mind, is placed in one compartment, and the "not-self," including the material world and other minds as well, if there are any, is placed in a separate compartment, how can the self know anything beyond its own ideas, its own states? Furthermore, if the principle of explanation of the changes in natural events is conceived as lying outside of nature, in some nonnatural or supernatural realm, the problem is still more complicated.

It may be possible for the mind of man to know the principles governing natural changes without being able to know the natural changes themselves.

Some modern philosophies have remained frankly dualistic, and have explained the connection between the knowing mind and the material world on an assumption of parallelism between mind and nature. We have seen this in John Fiske. Others, like Francis Wayland, have assumed a benevolent creation which gave mind the power of knowing matter and matter the power of being known by mind; while retaining a distinction between the two, these relatively naive thinkers have by-passed the problem created by the distinction. Others have ended in a scepticism which denied the possibility of man's knowledge of the external world. Many philosophers, however, have attempted to find a solution to the problem set up in the separation of knower and known by reducing matter to some form of mind, or mind to some form of matter. Accepting this so-called "reductionist" solution amounts to a denial that there was any problem in the beginning. If what we know as matter is really some form of mind, the problem of knowledge reduces to the question of the ability of minds to know each other. If what we call the knowing mind is really some form of matter — or, in more sophisticated versions, some form of physical energy — the question arises how matter can know itself. Charles Sanders Peirce, we have seen, declared that matter is mind hidebound by habits; he illustrates the idealistic version of reductionism, making matter "nothing but" a form of mind. Jonathan Edwards (like Berkeley in England), worked out an immaterialistic view of a similar character, making man's experience of nature an exclusively mental event. Alternatively, Cadwallader Colden and Benjamin Rush in the eighteenth century, and such physiological psychologists as Oliver Wendell Holmes in the nineteenth, followed the materialistic pattern of reducing mind to "nothing but" a sort of matter. In writers of this sort man's thinking process is conceived of as a more or less refined example of matter in motion.

Especially in the first half of the twentieth century a great many American thinkers have come to be impatient with both dualism and the reductionist answers to dualism. As proponents of a revised approach to philosophic problems, these thinkers call themselves Naturalists, but they insist that their naturalism is neither a doctrine nor a system, but only an attitude, a temper, a program, a mood. This modern version of naturalism is distinguished from the philosophies in reaction to which it has arisen by the view that whatever man encounters in any area of human experience is natural. Nature is the whole of reality. In the sense in which a transcendental realm of ideas and beings has traditionally been viewed, as a supernatural realm of superior reality which is a dominant and directive force superimposed upon nature and human life, naturalism stands committed to opposition to all philosophies which maintain that such a realm exists. Individual naturalists differ in the degree to which they use traditional terms like "God" in their philosophies, but those who do use terms of this sort use them in a totally untraditional fashion to refer to something natural, or at least to something within the area of human experience. They do not mean a non-natural force whose operations explain changes which go on in the natural world, nor do they mean any transcendent source of knowledge of a reality which is by definition beyond the scope of human experience. In this respect, naturalism eliminates one of the dualisms which has been the source of much confusion and difficulty throughout the history of modern philosophy.

Again, naturalism sees the dualism of mind and matter and the problem of knowledge which this dualism creates as unnecessary. It is the product of a tendency on the part of men to assume that there must be a thing to correspond to each substantive word that we use in our language. Traditional philosophy was not satisfied with a human being who performed certain actions and behaved in certain ways — sometimes reflectively, sometimes emotionally, sometimes physically. It broke the whole human being to pieces and assumed that these pieces acted separately, each after its own fashion. Then each piece was given a name — mind, feelings, body — and assumed to be an entity with a life of its own. Finally it was so far forgotten that there was a whole man that the relations between one piece and another came to be a problem. If we reverse this process and recall to our thought that mind is a name for the whole human being acting reflectively, that feelings are a name for the whole human being acting emotionally, that body is a name for the whole human being acting physically, that, in short, there are not now and never were entities corresponding to the substantive words that we use, there is no longer a mind-body dualism. There is a human being acting as

316 The Emergence of Naturalism

a totality in various fashions. The hard and fast dualisms of earlier philosophic generations become, at most, convenient expedients in the analysis of philosophic problems. If we do make a separation between elements in order to analyze each in isolation, we must be careful to rejoin what we have discriminated, and not assume that what we can separate in thought is therefore necessarily separate in fact.

No less basic to naturalistic philosophy than the opposition to dualism is the opposition to reductionism. If man experiences anything as material, this materiality is inalienably an aspect of that thing. The thing need not be exclusively material, and may very well be more than it is experienced as being. But it can never be less. Later, as we study the thing more carefully, we may discover in it many aspects whose existence we never suspected in our first experience with it. But that first experience is not reducible to any later knowledge of the nature of the thing. The physical hypothesis that matter is in ultimate terms not "solid," while it may affect the superstructure of our experience, does not transform or invalidate our earlier experience, and does not take away the thing. Matter can not be reduced to a form of mind, nor mind to a form of matter. Sterling Lamprecht of Amherst College summed up the naturalistic objection to reductionism thus: "The nature of anything may of course be, and probably always is, much more than it is empirically found to be. But the point of the argument is that everything is at least what it is given as in experience." [1] What we experience as material or as mental may have other constituents, but despite these additions it remains ineluctably material or mental. Clearly the distinction between appearance and reality which has loomed so large in various modern philosophies is of little account to the naturalists.

Despite the suggestion implicit in the name of naturalism, this newer form of an old world-view does not take its start from any strict, systematic definition of nature. There may be found to be as many different accounts of nature as there are naturalists. Underlying these different descriptions, however, there is an assumption which is common to all the naturalists. This assumption, fed by a consideration, though not necessarily a detailed study, of the work of physical and biological science, is that there are observable orders in the universe which can be explained without going outside of nature itself. Nature includes not only things, but also relations.

Decay, or the passing out of existence of a natural object, is as much of a natural relation as growth. Death is as natural as birth. Change is as natural as permanence. The elementary forms of natural life are born and grow, decay and die, according to a regular pattern. The pattern is as much a part of nature as the relations, the relations as much a part of nature as the elements. The system of nature is self-contained, self-sufficient, and self-explanatory. Nature includes both the changeless and the changing — permanent elements, permanent relations, and permanent patterns, and changing things, changing events, and changing forms. And nature includes man, altogether and entirely and in all phases of his being. His birth is a natural event, his life a natural process, his death and disintegration a recombination of the natural elements of which he was made. There is no aspect of man which is outside of nature, call that aspect what you will. You may talk of soul or spirit only on the condition that you mean thereby some aspect of man's natural behavior; but you may not describe the "soul" of man as immortal, for to do so would be to remove it outside of nature. It is thus that naturalism, without paradox and without distortion of human experience, accounts for the intelligible character of the existing universe.

Again, the new naturalism has no doctrinaire account of nature It is, rather, naturalistic by virtue of its insistence that there is no realm to which the methods of science which have been so successful in achieving control of nature can not be applied. Only knowledge arrived at by methods resembling those of the scientist is acceptable to the naturalist. Just as the methods of science have radically transformed our understanding and our use of our external environment and in that way affected our relations with our fellow men, so naturalists believe that the direct application of similar methods to areas in which they have not yet been fully tried, chiefly areas concerned with human relations, will be productive of rapid advance.

Part of the polemic of naturalism against various forms of supernaturalism is based on the opposition of organized and institutionalized "anti-naturalism," as John Dewey calls it, to the entrance of scientific methods of inquiry into these areas. Dewey said "Anti-naturalism has prevented science from completing its career and fulfilling its constructive potentialities." [2] The science that Dewey is talking about has no necessary connection with any scientific subject matter or content. The content of the sciences has no privileged position among naturalists; it is merely one aspect of human experience among many others. At most science as subject matter is exemplary; it is the best available illustration of the application of the intellectual method to which naturalists attribute so much. The subject matter of philosophic naturalism is all that is natural, and that is all that can be experienced by human beings. Men can experience hatred and they can experience falling bodies; they can experience delusion and they can experience nuclear fission; they can experience dreams and they can experience certain colloids. Since men can experience all these things and many more, all of these are relevant to the philosophic naturalist. What distinguishes his consideration of, say, hatred is his method of studying it.

The primary quality which distinguishes the method which the naturalist calls scientific from other methods which have been used by philosophers is that method becomes a public affair. Regardless of what specific description of the procedures of philosophic investigation are given by any naturalist, his method will always require that the activities of inquiry must be open to public inspection and verification. Thus the naturalist would deny that the results of any purely mystical, subjective, or intuitive method would be knowledge. So, too, would statements offered on the basis of faith or authority, without credentials of verifiability. Some part of the current controversy about the status of value-judgments hinges on a debate about the application of this criterion of public verifiability. One group of naturalists maintains that value-judgments are essentially expressions of private preference, and therefore, have no philosophic significance; another group holds that such judgments are much open to public inspection as the propositions of any other aspect of philosophy.

Furthermore, for the naturalist we have noted that what is called "mind" is not a special, non-physical organ or instrument within the physical body. It is, rather, a name for certain types of behavior of the human organism. To the extent that we consider mind in these terms, we can not assert any total difference of kind between mental, biological, and physical behavior. This does not mean that mental operations can be reduced to biological or physical behavior, and that there is no difference whatever between them. It does mean that there is some sort of continuity between these different ways of acting. The mental way of behaving grows out of earlier types of behavior; this is part of the evolutionary heritage in naturalism. As life emerges evolutionally from non-life under certain conditions, so mind emerges evolutionally from non-mind. Just as the exact point of division between the living and the non-living is impossible to determine, so the exact point at which mental behavior starts is undeterminable. George Ellett Coghill, the zoologist, discovered evidences of a type of mind-like behavior, which he called "mentation," in the embryo of the salamander.[3] What is characteristic of mental behavior in its developed form is that it is a response to stimuli as signs rather than as things. It is a response then, as Professor Yervant Krikorian of the College of the City of New York has pointed out, to the meanings of stimuli. That is to say, mental behavior is a response in which the possible consequences of stimuli are anticipated. In mental operations, the future consequences of stimuli function as if they were present. The general characteristic of mind is that its objects are meanings. But we find in our reading of John Dewey that meaning is a natural character of natural events. Both mind and matter are "different characters of natural events, in which matter expresses their sequential order, and mind the order of their meanings in their logical connections and dependencies."[4] Mind, then, for Dewey, is in some sense objective and external; and the processes of thought, or logic, lead men to an objectively existing realm of meanings and logical connections.

This, however, is farther than many of the naturalists will go. Those who are most familiar with modern logical theory especially dispute any suggestion that logic is more than a methodology. The principles of logic, said Professor Ernest Nagel of Columbia University, are not "descriptive of an intrinsic and pervasive structure of things."[5] It does not do to consider specific logical processes as in any sense representative of specific physical or biological processes, even though the general principle of continuity is accepted. Furthermore, logical principles are not to be regarded as necessary truths except in reference to the use of language. The various logics are alternative systems for prescribing the way in which language is to be used, if it is to be used with clarity and precision, rather than with the looseness of everyday speech. Assuming that language is used as specified within a particular system, there are certain inferences which that system allows. Which of the alternative systems one accepts for a particular investigation depends upon the ends proposed for that investigation. Thus acceptance of one logic or another in a given situation is not an arbitrary matter, even though logic has no necessary truth. The objective basis on which one system is chosen over another is its success in the particular work at hand. This interpretation of the function of logical systems in philosophic analysis is a far better approximation to the methods of the scientist than is the more usual vague reference to scientific method or experimental method.

On one view, overlapping that of the group of naturalists just discussed, the entire enterprise of philosophy is concerned exclusively with the analysis of the conditions of intelligible discourse. Philosophy does not make statements about the most general characteristics of nature, but it does determine the meaning of such statements in terms of some over-all pattern of intelligibility. The most general characteristics of nature are usually called "categories," and the discovery of categories has always been regarded as a significant part of philosophy. Here the analysis rather than the discovery of categories is claimed as philosophy's proper task. Again, as in the variety of naturalism discussed above, philosophy is the study not of existence itself but of the language in which men talk about existence. Most of the naturalists, however, while recognizing the importance of linguistic analysis, insist that it is but a part of the total philosophic enterprise — that, in the case of the categories, for example, it is as much part of philosophy to discover the most general traits of existence by a study of existence as it is to analyze the meaning of the terms in which we express these traits.

One conclusion which can not be avoided when we examine the categories of naturalistic philosophy is that there is a partially healed breach between those naturalists who are akin in temper to the materialists of an earlier period, and those others for whom materialism is a reductionism. So, among the more materialistic of the school, the categories of interpretation still tend to be those of matter, motion, and energy, and the explanations which are given in these terms exclude from existence or from consideration the highest and most cherished of human values. On the other hand, many of the naturalists, like William R. Dennes of the University of California, find the significant interpretive categories in "events," "qualities," and "relations."[6] One way in which this difference has been explained is as the outgrowth of the differing emphases of those among the naturalists whose interests and background include special concern for the "structural" sciences, like physics and mathematics, and those whose scientific background is in the "functional" sciences, like biology or the social sciences. There is no doubt that this was an important distinction among the older generation of naturalists; in the sections which follow we shall see in Morris Raphael Cohen and John Dewey examples of structural and functional naturalistic philosophy. Among younger naturalists, however, this issue has become far less important because changes in physical theory have made it necessary for those who in earlier terms would have emphasized the categories of structure to accept dynamic and functional categories. Certainly the most important result of the discussion of categorial systems in naturalism has been to make clear that we accept one or another of these systems on the basis of its usefulness in interpreting our beliefs. We do not develop our beliefs by logical derivation from our categorial system.

Despite this increasingly evident shift from materialistic to dynamic categories, and despite the concern for qualitative differences which has been a large influence in motivating the shift, the opponents of naturalism insist upon classing it as materialistic. They maintain that moral and esthetic standards can not be justified in a naturalistic philosophy because such a philosophy is oriented toward the merely physical and material, and away from spirit. To this the naturalist might well reply that his whole philosophy is an attempt to give just consideration to the "spiritual" as well as the "physical," to values as well as facts. For men experience values as well as facts; the standards, ends, and goals of events are as natural as their causes, their spatio-temporal relations, or the events themselves. It is the anti-naturalist who creates an impossible situation by drawing a sharp line of demarcation between facts and values. As long as purposes occur in human experiences, purposes are natural. However we regard purpose, we must recognize that to say a purpose is achievable is to say that it is experienceable, and therefore natural. To say a purpose is achievable is to say that by the use of certain means it can be brought to realization. To be "means" they must themselves be intelligible in the same way as purposes are. In brief, purpose is a natural quality of natural events. By a similar examination, it is shown that standards of truth, goodness, and beauty occur in a natural context, and are aspects of human experience. It is important, however, to remember that the assertion of the naturalistic philosopher that purposes and values are natural contains no hint that external nature is moral or that nature consciously forwards human purposes. One can, by an extension of the term, say that the purpose of the seed is to become the flower; one can not say that the purpose of the seed is to adorn the debutante's gown. Nature as such is indifferent to human concerns or to human judgments, or to the use that men may make of it. No volcano erupts because the folk living on its slopes are wicked; famine does not come to a land to punish its inhabitants for revolution; rain falls on the just and unjust alike. To believe otherwise we would have to disregard the evidence of our experience. There is room in naturalistic philosophy for purposes and for values, but they are to have no preferential status.

The attitude which has been described has features in common with older philosophies. Its advocates like to point to Aristotle and Spinoza, in particular, as precursors of modern naturalism, while its antagonists invariably emphasize its kinship with materialism. Actually there have been incipient naturalistic ideas in the work of many earlier philosophers. Some of the naturalists of today are among the foremost historians of philosophy. They have drawn on the richness of the philosophic heritage for insights, but have restated these insights in the idiom of naturalism. The evolutionary naturalism of Chauncey Wright, Francis Ellingwood Abbot, and their less well-known contemporaries, Edmund Montgomery and Edward Drinker Cope, hovered on the edge of the type of naturalism which we have described here. It is clear, also, that some of the "new realists" and "critical realists" were verging on the new naturalism, and that the pragmatic movement also made its contribution. This is to say that in the new naturalism many of the inchoate and nascent tendencies of revolt against the completely academic systems of idealistic philosophy have found a home. Three different forms of philosophic naturalism are discussed in the balance of this chapter — the reluctant and poetic naturalism of George Santayana, who loved the realm of the spirit, though he recognized nature; the rationalistic naturalism of Morris Raphael Cohen, and the experimental naturalism of John Dewey. Many of the younger American naturalists were taught by these three men, and to them we now turn to trace their various distinctive versions of naturalism as a self-conscious philosophic attitude.

II. POETIC NATURALISM:
GEORGE SANTAYANA

In some of the thinkers whose philosophical ideas were developed during the years when the debate over evolutionary theory was at its height there was a fundamental inner conflict, frequently on the emotional level. They were constrained by studies of compelling force to reject the philosophic idealisms for which they felt a temperamental kinship, and to accept a naturalistic position by which they were emotionally repelled. In some cases these reluctant naturalists embraced their evolutionary naturalism with excessive zeal and intensity as if to compensate for their inability to feel as naturalistically as they thought.

George Santayana was a member of this group by virtue not only of temperament but also of the accident of biography. He was a Spaniard, educated, after his earliest childhood years, in Boston. By both nature and heritage he was a Roman Catholic; yet his father and his maternal grandfather were agnostics, his mother's piety was merely formal, and the American relatives with whom he spent many years were Protestants. Though he was indifferent to American education, Santayana's active years were spent teaching at Harvard. He thought of himself as a poet, and, indeed, some of his lyrics are among the more beautiful of American poems; yet it has been the philosophic side of his genius which has won the greatest admiration.

Santayana has always been concerned with man's highest ideals of the good, the true, and the beautiful. His primary interest lies in moral philosophy, by which he means the survey of all excellences as defined by a reflective spirit, by a life which understands its own conditions. He realized, however, very early in his career, that these ideals could not be discussed in abstraction from their context. And as he considered this context, he came to see that it could be only a natural one. He felt compelled to base his views of the good, the true, and the beautiful on a naturalistic account of being and a realistic account of knowing. Nature itself generates human ideals, and men try to control nature in order to adapt it to these naturally generated ideals. Santayana's view of the relation between nature and ideals can be summarized in his description of Aristotle's view; Santayana is firmly convinced that all ideals are natural in their origin, and all nature ideal in its possibilities. Moral philosophy for Santayana, then, is an evaluation of all human enterprises, including philosophy itself, in terms of the extent to which these enterprises realize the excellences, or values, which nature both suggests and sustains. Despite this concern for moral philosophy and the recognition that ideals are rooted in nature, no American philosopher has insisted more clearly and explicitly than Santayana that nature itself is morally neutral.

Naturalism, for Santayana, provides the only tenable view of the background of human values, "the true and safe foundation for human courage, human reason, and human imagination." [7] But the poet in him recognized that once this naturalistic background has been painted in so that courage, reason, and imagination can function, their functioning can be free. These human traits can paint what they will into the foreground. It was in the Greek philosophers and in Spinoza, Santayana has told us in his autobiography, that he found a combination of the two insights, necessary for his thought: "naturalism as to the origin and history of mankind, and fidelity in moral sentiment, to the inspiration of reason." [8] In the concern of the Greek philosophers and Spinoza for both nature and reason Santayana found a basis for describing what he thought philosophy ought to be, the free play of a reflective mind over all time and all existence. Philosophy is by no means either a science among other sciences, or an art among other arts; it is the attempt of a balanced mind to utilize all the sciences and all the arts in the composition of "as true a picture as possible of nature and human nature." [9] This is essentially a detached view, possible only to one who was *in* his time but not *of* it, and one, consequently, who was not involved in the pressures and counter-pressures of his age. Santayana by his own confession is and was such a detached spectator. He was intellectually repelled by the intellectual world in which he lived. He called it a "zoological garden of the mind." [10] In this zoological garden he preferred to be a visitor outside the cages looking in, not one of the specimens inside the cages looking out. This was in part why he preferred reading the books of his contemporaries to meeting with them.

From this detached and utterly unsentimental standpoint, Santayana came to the view that life, as human beings lead it, is "at once the quintessence and the sum of madness." [11] Madness is not unnatural; in fact there is a sort of madness to which Santayana gave the name of "normal madness." Before we can understand what he meant by this unusual combination of words, we must examine more closely what Santayana meant by conceiving madness as natural. We frequently confuse our speech, he said, by using the same word for things as they really are and things as they seem to humans to be. In the case of the word "madness" there are at least three ways in which we use it. We may use it to refer to a certain type of behavior. We may call certain mental illusions madness. We may use it to refer directly to neither of these, but simply to express an unwarranted and over-censorious comment on the behavior or the mentality of someone with whom we disagree, or of whom we do not approve. In any of these cases, the judgment which we make on behavior or delusion is that it is out of the usual and conventional pattern of our society. Because we fail to make the proper distinction between what is natural and what is merely conventional, we call "madness" an unnatural thing, though it is really nothing more than unconventional. Indeed, nothing that actually happens can be unnatural, and among the things that occur are maniacal actions, illusions, and delusions of all sorts, and even homicidal frenzy. They are, then, "not contrary to nature, but only to the habit of the majority." [12] Disease is as natural as health; death is as natural as life. It is human imagination which attributes sublimity and beauty, or gruesomeness and horror, to any natural event. None of these qualities is felt by nature; nature is indifferent to them all.

If there is one illusion which is most widespread and yet, as we have seen, most baseless, it is the view that nature is moral. Santayana would have had no patience with Ralph Waldo Emerson's assertion that "every animal function from the sponge up to Hercules hints or thunders to man the laws of right and wrong." [13] This is to assert that "one collocation of atoms or one conjunction of feelings" [14] is better or worse than another. It is to assert the objectivity of values in nature, and to believe that nature is moral. This unjustified opinion is held by every living creature – and this it is madness to believe. It is a madness so commonplace that it can be called "normal," so that the rare philosopher who freed himself from this illusion would be sane and, at the same time, abnormal. We come, then, to the view that nature is indifferent to human values, yet these values are grounded in nature and inspired by nature.

Furthermore, it is a matter of complete indifference to nature how men approach it. Human values may be developed in the scientific study of nature; they may be developed in a poetic appreciation of nature. Nature does not care whether men seek for truth or for beauty. Both can feed on nature and it is not concerned with their feeding or with their failure to find sustenance. Since Santayana believes that either method can reach its goal, and since the method he prefers is the poetic, it is this that he has used, especially in his later writings.

We must never forget, however, in considering Santayana's thought, that he takes his start from "the facts before every man's eyes." [15] He conceives the common sense realism of ordinary human experience as a sounder answer to the problems of knowledge than any of the answers given by particular philosophic schools, "each of which squints and overlooks half the facts and half the difficulties in its eagerness to find in some detail the key to the whole." [16] This is to say that Santayana considered the various philosophic theories of knowledge as reductionist, while common sense esteems all of experience as natural. At no point does Santayana attempt to dismiss or explain away as illusion or appearance any of the familiar facts of everyday experience. He accepts as ultimate not only the collocations of atoms but also the conjunctions of feelings. Ideas, ideals, and beliefs are as much facts of nature as stones, stars, and seasons. It is with the givenness of this natural world that we start; the only problem of knowledge is to get to know more about it. "Every deeper investigation presupposes ordinary perception and uses some at least of its data." [17] Scientific method he thought of as a refined and extended common sense, "developed perception, interpreted intent, common-sense rounded out and minutely articulated." [18]

Santayana's *Life of Reason*, published in five volumes in 1905-1906, represents most adequately the naturalistic aspect of its author's thought, and was the bible of naturalism for a generation of American students. In these volumes Santayana's philosophy of civilization is set forth, partly in terms of a moral evaluation of the past, partly in terms of an analysis of the functions of society, religion, science, and art in the institutional structure of a culture founded on reason, and partly in terms of a prophetic foreshadowing of rationality as a goal of all human activity. Thus it is both an historical study and a moral treatise. Santayana begins his discussion of each theme with a presention of historical information, which in each case consists of the given factual materials, the natural base. When this material has been presented, it is critically considered to determine its ideal potential. The fuller implications of this ideal development are then worked out in rational, philosophic analysis. The full statement of the ideal may then be used as an ethical norm, against which the actual progress of man toward the life of reason can be appraised. We may say that Santayana is illustrating in these books what he conceived at the time of their writing to be the proper method for a naturalistic study of institutions. He avoided the merely descriptive, merely genetic, and merely historical approach which was usual in evolutionary accounts. At the same time, he avoided the idealistic pitfall of making the ideal potential into the blueprint and therefore, in some sense, the cause, of historical development. Finally, it is important, in the light of what we have previously seen, to point out that here, too, the moral ideal has a natural rather than a moral ground.

The *Life of Reason* opens with a categorically naturalistic assertion that the forces which rule human life "must betray themselves in human experience," [19] if they are to be known at all. Progress, like the rest, whether in science or in religion, in morals or in art, is not an absolute and transcendent force, but is, rather, change relative to a human ideal, an ideal which human reason discovers in nature. With the introduction of critical reflection or reason, man moves away from a mere immersion in the flux of present sensations and develops a view of the past and of the future. From the life of impulse man moves into the life of reason. Reason is continuous with vital impulse; impulse itself is called reason "when it is modified by reflection and veers in sympathy with judgments pronounced on the past." [20] Rationality, whether it reflects the past in memory or the future in anticipation, is the absent working effectively in the present. The life of the prehuman animal is based upon unconscious impulse; it is not rational. A life of reverie, fantasy, vision, and dream, though it represents an intense consciousness, is not rational or human. "Reason and humanity begin with the union of instinct and ideation." [21] Instinct becomes aware of its goals, becomes self-conscious, and consciousness becomes concerned with its roots. Reason is not merely speculative; it is also "efficacious reflection." [22]

The life of reason, then, is not only reflection on progress; it is itself the embodiment of progress.

The rational life, Santayana found, could be attached to no modern school of philosophy at the beginning of the twentieth century, and neither Christian philosophy, which misrepresents facts and conditions, nor liberal theology, which enshrines a superstitious attitude towards the natural world, would serve the purpose either. To find straight thinkers in both natural and moral realms one must go behind modern thought and Christian thought to the Greeks. Among Greek philosophers, though Heraclitus, Democritus, and Socrates made important preliminary contributions, the ideal of reason found its full statement in Plato; and Aristotle made the fullest and broadest expression of the life of reason in his ethics. Although these classical sources are the philosophic inspiration of any modern attempt to survey the life of reason, the moral inspiration of any such rewriting must be the facts and conditions of modern life. The starting point of any such attempt must be the "immediate flux" of modern existence, including whatever objects and impulses are given. The program of the attempt is to interpret the ideals which are sustained by our modern situation.

Throughout the four volumes of the *Life of Reason* in which Santayana examines the particular institutions — society, religion, art, and science — in which the rational life is expressed, he presents an account of the historical development of these institutions. They develop, he said, through three stages. There is a first, pre-rational stage in which impulse, habit, and desire are the controlling factors in life. In the second, rational stage, the ideals supported by the natural impulses are recognized and clarified and consciously adapted to the control of life. The third, post-rational stage is "the form in which imagination clothes a rational and humane reason." [23] So, for example, there is a pre-rational morality which Santayana characterizes by the attributes "non-dialectical, casual, impulsive, polyglot." [24] It is morality unaware of the relation between a chosen course of conduct and the goal for the achievement of which that course was chosen. There must be some degree of reason in it, for a choice has been made; but it is unconscious reason. Pre-rational morality can be found in "the judgments of Mrs. Grundy, the aims of political parties and their maxims, the principles of war, the appreciation of art, the commandments of religious authorities, special revelations of duty to individuals, and all systems of intuitive ethics." [25] Pre-rational morality has a great deal of practical and emotional power, and may be said to be "morality proper." It is essentially part of anthropology rather than of science or philosophy.

Rational ethics, on the other hand, involves the logic of practice rather than practice itself. It requires the answering of a good many questions, some of which are physical and may therefore be answered by the natural sciences, and some of which are dialectical, involved in ascertaining philosophically the implications of the terms we use and the judgments we make. Because a rational practice is not attainable, Santayana is careful not to use the term "rational morality," but only "rational ethics." Rational practice is not to be reached because it would imply perfection of self-knowledge, a perfectly clear definition of moral purpose, and a perfect sympathy with the needs of all other beings. A rational morality is therefore a limited ideal. In its stead we have rational ethics which "sets forth the method of judgment and estimation which a rational morality would apply universally and express in practice." [26]

Post-rational morality is developed by men who are for one or another reason dissatisfied with the life of reason which they have tried; post-rational systems, he asserts, "are essentially religions." They are "experiments in redemption." [27] In a post-rational morality there is an effort to select one precept, pointing to some future blessing, and to make that precept the primary guide to practice. Because this saving precept is made a guide to action, in the post-rational stage we return from ethics to morality, even though philosophic and institutional structures may be reared upon it. Post-rational morality is not a real advance, and furnishes no real solution. It is merely the leap of "moral ambition" into a non-natural realm. In such a realm, Santayana insists, morality has neither meaning nor force. Only when "nature is suffered to bloom in the sanctuary" [28] does a post-rational morality have any value. When a supernaturalistic vocabulary and supernaturalistic forms become the poetic garments of experience and reason, and when they are but a symbolism to bring man back to nature, then post-rational morality has a real value in the life of reason.

Santayana's discussion of religion is extremely interesting, for it represents a comprehensive attempt to discover the rational worth of religion in a natural world. Historically religion has made the

attempt to explain natural causes by means of superstitious mythologies and to substitute magical procedures for technologies. Insofar as religion has historically misunderstood its ideal function, it has
attempted to replace science and technology by myth, magic, and
miracle. Rational religion still utilizes the mythologies which superstitious and primitive religions take as literal accounts of the origin
and destiny of man and the universe, but it utilizes them as poetic
renderings of the moral ideals of piety toward the sources of our
being and spirituality toward our ideal ends, rooted as they are in
nature. Thus Santayana was able to include the idea of God as a
symbol for human ideals. More than this, he found that he could
justify the introduction of an entire realm of the supernatural, provided that he could find some way to naturalize the supernatural.
The first step in his argument is a recapitulation of what we have
just noted. Science and religion are different aspects of man's relation to the real world of nature which surrounds him. Science is the
expression of the dynamic relations of man and nature. Religion
must not invade this area, for religion may not contradict or com-
pete with science; if it does it will "misrepresent" the dynamic
relations properly expressed by science. The function of religion is
to "express destiny in moral dimensions, in obviously mythical and
poetical images. . . . Religions are the great fairy-tales of the
conscience." [29] The second foundational point in this argument is
that somehow supernaturalism must be made to depend upon naturalism. Naturalism is not sacrosanct or beyond criticism. Santayana
himself was predisposed to criticize it. He recognized, however, that
without a naturalistic base there could be no human knowledge at
all, and that "if naturalism was condemned, supernaturalism itself
could have no point of application in the world of fact." [30]

Once these points were presented, Santayana asked what a supernatural realm in these terms would be. His question, as he went on
to explain, was not what the contents of the supernatural realm
would be. He sought to define, rather, what relation such a realm
must have to the realm of natural fact if it is to be really both supernatural and existent. By insisting on the reality of supernature,
Santayana intended to distinguish it from a purely conceptual realm
like mathematics. The relation on which he insisted is a dynamic
one. There must, he said, be a connection between the realm of
nature and that of supernature so that the two together would

"compose the total reality with which human knowledge, morality, and sentiment must reckon." [31] Supernaturalism, on this account, would be a completed naturalism; it would not be a dualism in which nature and supernature were opposed, as appearance and reality, but a dynamic continuity of nature and supernature, taking account of facts and forces which are "hidden from our near-sighted and imperfect science." [32] In the sense in which the term "nature" was used in our preceding section, Santayana means that dynamic continuity between nature and supernature is simply nature conceived in fullness and richness, unlimited by the attempt to deal solely with matter, motion, and energy. He seems to recognize this himself when he says "This almost tangible supernatural world is only the rest of nature, nature in her true depths and in her true infinity." [33] Yet the different language in which Santayana speaks of this supernatural nature introduces a possibility which many other naturalists would deny, and which contradicts his own earlier insistence on the moral neutrality of nature. For, in spite of his claim that nature and supernature are continuous, Santayana speculates on the possibility that the extension of nature may be "more sympathetic to our moral nature than this particular part to which we are native." [34]

With speculations of this sort we come to a final stage in Santayana's thought, in which, free from the exigencies of earning a living, he has been able, without abandoning his naturalistic foundation, to enter into the consideration of themes which seem far less naturalistic. He has been able, for nearly forty years, to be the detached spectator he always wanted to be. In his major work produced in this extended period of reflection, *Realms of Being*, he has distinguished four such realms, Matter, Essence, Truth, and Spirit. Each of these realms, which he conceives as distinct in being, and not merely in thought, reflects a different aspect of Santayana's portrait of the world in which we live. Matter is the realm of the biologically primary substance or stuff which is the unknowable yet ever-present basis of action. Matter, as Santayana conceives it, is the dominant factor in the activity of all being, even spiritual or immaterial being. "Matter is the principle of distribution for spirit as for every other feature of the existing world." [35]

Thus, in a word, Santayana, in his assertion of the dominance of matter in spiritual beings, is reaffirming his earlier view of nature as the source of ideals. If Matter is biologically primary, Essence is logically primary. An event or a fact in the realm of matter is known to human beings by an incomplete set of signals. The signals or indications are terms of discourse, not facts, and are, therefore, qualitatively distinct from the facts they designate. These terms are "essences existing nowhere." It is "the infinite multitude of distinguishable ideal terms (whether revealed to anybody or not)" [36] to which Santayana gave the name of the Realm of Essence. As the realm in which all mental discourse takes place it is a realm of freedom and of poetry. There is a particular part of the Realm of Essence which is composed of those essences which do occur in existence, which exist somewhere. This Santayana calls the Realm of Truth. Experience yields partial, fragmentary and relative truth, beliefs which are more or less correct. The only ground on which we can assert that they are relative, and that the beliefs of different people supplement rather than contradict each other is that "they refer to the same system of nature, the complete description of which, covering the whole past and the whole future, would be the absolute truth." Finally, the Realm of Spirit is Santayana's name for the play of fancy among ideas.

It is in the Realm of Spirit that the speculative philosopher is happiest. Spirit takes the matter and energy at hand in the world and reshapes it into an imaginative structure, orderly and harmonious. Spirit is not without relation to matter; it is, rather, the final and finest development of the life of the body. If it were ever to be divorced from its sustaining connection with facts and its attachment to "animal life," spirit would lose all the qualities of excitement and intensity which make it "a focus of knowledge." The great enemy of spirit is distraction; distraction tears the spirit away from its hard and rarely won harmony, spontaneity, and freedom. The ills and lusts of the Flesh, the cares of the World, and the temptations of the Devil fill the mind of the distracted philosopher. When there is no distraction, when the spirit is functioning well, "meaning, objects, ideas, remote reported events will alone fill your imagination." [37] Distraction produces conflict in the philosopher, who has come to realize by his study of nature that the "ant-hill" of human society has no particular authority. It is this realization which has liberated his spirit, so that his mind is free to range beyond the rigidities and constraints of those "pompous institutions by which the world carries on its merciless business." [38] Yet, however liberated the philosopher may be in mind, the world still has power over him; "in his life and person he is hardly less subject than other men to every worldly requirement, vice and affectation." [39] If the philosopher did not take himself so seriously, he might regard this dominance of the world and its distractions as "a part of the comedy of existence." [40] He would recognize that the whole enterprise of spirit is but the glint of the sun on the waves, a passing "surface phenomenon in the psyche." [41] Spirit is unwilling to see itself as merely play; it borrows tenacity from the animal part of our being. Then spirit becomes a regular and methodical routine. When definiteness has thus been introduced into the life of the free mind, "distraction becomes a conscious evil." [42]

Much of the speculation of the *Realms of Being* seems on the surface to be a merely fanciful construct, and it has been so regarded by certain critics of Santayana. In his final comments, however, Santayana reaffirmed the fundamental naturalism of his theory of existence, however much he tempered it by revelling in the world of imagination. His discussions of the realms of being, he insisted, are not metaphysical because, although he talks of "immaterial things," he talks of only some of them as existent and true. Those which exist or are true are "qualities, products, or ideal implications of the physical world." The foundations of things are revealed to man's knowledge by way of physical science, not metaphysical speculation. Discussion of the nature of various kinds of being "is a subsequent excursus of the mind . . . over all that the facts may suggest to the fancy," [43] but it can never desert the facts.

Santayana has been highly critical of Dewey's version of naturalism (see this chapter, section IV), and if we identify the "new" naturalism with Deweyan philosophy it would be unfair to consider Santayana as a member of that "school of thought." In this chapter (despite the author's own philosophic sympathies), there is an attempt to consider the new naturalism as broader than Deweyan thought, and to present it as a broad, modernist current in philosophy. In this more inclusive use of the term, it is hard to deny the importance of Santayana's contribution, especially in *The Life of Reason*, to the development of a naturalistic temper in recent American philosophy. Santayana has been more than merely a naturalist. But he has recently again avowed his naturalistic faith in uncompromising terms: "Naturalism . . . is something to which I am so thoroughly wedded that I like to call it materialism, so as to prevent all confusion from *romantic* naturalism like Goethe's, for instance, or that of Bergson. Mine is the hard, non-humanistic naturalism of the Ionian philosophers, of Democritus, Lucretius, and Spinoza. . . . My naturalism is fundamental and includes man, his mind, and all his works, products of the generative order of Nature." [44] However reluctantly Santayana may have been a naturalist in his earlier work, however poetically he has expounded his naturalism in his later work, he has never deserted his own form of naturalism.

III. RATIONALISTIC NATURALISM: MORRIS R. COHEN

Morris Raphael Cohen, professor of philosophy in the College of the City of New York, represented himself in his earlier years as "a stray dog unchained to any metaphysical kennel." [45] His fine critical sense saw readily the flaws in the philosophies current in his time, preventing his unqualified acceptance of any. His independent mind could not be boxed into any closed system. He had too much regard for the intellectual adventure of philosophy to be satisfied with anything less than perfection in his colleagues, in his students, and in himself. And perfection is rare in any field of human effort. Cohen's quest for perfection led to dissatisfaction with most of his own attempts to put on paper the ideas which made his philosophy. He was not a prolific writer, but what he did write was full of suggestions. Cohen's philosophy, like that of Chauncey Wright (see Chapter 5, section III), in whose thought he was very deeply interested, is incomplete, tentative, and unfinished.

For the present generation of naturalists, however, Cohen's influence, exerted largely in the classroom and through personal contact, is an important factor in the formation of their views. His published works are by no means a full measure of his impact on American thought. It is noteworthy that the collective volume, *Naturalism and the Human Spirit*, which was written chiefly by younger naturalists, was dedicated to Cohen.

The main outlines of Cohen's thought are clear. It was his conviction that recent philosophy in its attempt to found its ideas exclusively on observation and experiment, and to emphasize the similarity between philosophic method and scientific method, had conceived scientific method too narrowly. Science, it is true, has dramatized the importance of particular experiences, but it has not depended solely upon the particular or upon experience. That aspect of scientific method which recent philosophy has consistently underestimated is the contribution of deductive, rational technique to the development of scientific thought. The function in science of the techniques of deduction is to establish the universal validity of the results of particular experiences. The function in philosophy of the techniques of logic is to universalize the truths supplied by philosophic insight or vision.

Cohen's presidential address in 1929 before the Eastern division of the American Philosophical Association was significantly entitled, "Vision and Technique in Philosophy." Here he urged the need for the supplementation of insight by "laborious and thoroughgoing technique," [46] indispensable to any art or science or to philosophy. Vision without technique tends to be private, arbitrary, and irresponsible. It stands outside of "humanity's organized search for universally ascertainable truth." [47] Truth must be public, unaffected by partisan considerations; it must be open to criticism and doubt, and be able to withstand critical doubt. "Not only must the truth of a proposition be tested by its consequences, but its very meaning, if it is universal, is constituted by its implications or logical consequences." [48] The insight of the philosopher can not be justified by any sense of personal certainty. It can be justified only by its usefulness to other truth-seekers; it must be universalized before it can be verified. This universalization is the work of rational techniques of logic. Without technical development and verification in many fields, philosophic vision "may rightly be condemned as unsubstantial and visionary." [49] Logical universalization of particular insights is necessary to prevent vision from being visionary.

Cohen's criticism of the usual account of scientific method stresses the absence of insistence on universalization. He shows how it relies upon the sense impressions of the individual thinker and cannot, therefore, reach results which are universal. Its results must be fragmentary, partial, limited, and particular. A significant scientific method can not be developed on the theory, proposed by John Locke and his followers, that the human mind is passive, but has a capacity for receiving sense impressions. Our sensations are not the starting points of scientific investigation. They are part of the content of our knowledge and, therefore, "elements in a logical analysis of what we know." [50] Scientific investigation begins when reflection finds intellectual difficulties in common knowledge; these difficulties yield problems which "wonder or active curiosity" leads us to try to answer. Science is born out of the criticism of the common knowledge of any age.

Cohen regarded it as both curious and significant that our age, which has emphasized the claims of the "social" in so many areas of life, should hold an individualistic theory of knowledge and should consider that the intellectual salvation of man can be reached by reverting to individual sensations. The personal opinions developed by "our fragmentary partial experience" fall into the interpretational pattern of common knowledge, not rational science. Results which are tragically inadequate, and full of error and illusion, leading to the failure of human effort and aspiration, follow from the interpretation of individual experience in terms of common knowledge, which, in any age, "is funded out of traditional teachings, superstitions, and ancient metaphysics." [51]

To offset the current emphasis on the individual, Cohen pointed out with Aristotle that, while individuals occur only in experience, knowledge, even knowledge of particulars, can be expressed only in terms of universals. One can point to an individual object or grasp it; but as soon as there is any attempt to place the object in a meaningful context, to make any significant assertion about it, one must use abstract terms which are universal because they are applicable to individuals other than the one being talked about. Science is not concerned with *this* falling body, or *that* falling body, but with general principles, and universal assertions about the behavior of all falling bodies. All our particular experience with particular falling bodies will not yield a universal assertion about all falling bodies; only rational logical techniques can generalize or universalize our particular experiences.

This is not to equate science with the "rationality" of nineteenth-century idealism. Cohen maintained that this type of rationality was "at bottom hostile to strictly rational procedure." [52] Nineteenth-century idealism used superficially rationalistic methods as a ground for asserting the reality of a universe which existed only in the mind of the thinker. This is precisely the result which true rationalism seeks to avoid by insisting on "laborious methods to check or prevent the facile confusion between the fanciful world of our heart's desire and the more sober world of actual existence." [53] Only in relatively recent times has the description of scientific method been given in terms which excluded rationalism. Prior to the nineteenth century, with its strange and romantic perversion of reason, rationalism was the great and necessary ally of naturalism in the "war of emancipation from . . . the view that nature is sin and intellect the devil." [54] The great enemy of rationalism was authoritarianism, usually either itself supernaturalistic or justified by supernatural sanction. "It was the intimate union of rationalism and naturalism which . . . liberated science from the tutelage of theology, overthrew the Inquisition, prepared the way for a notable humanization of our treatment of the criminal, the sick, and the insane, and liberalized civil and international law." [55]

Although Cohen emphasizes the importance of rationality, he is careful to point out that "rationality does not exhaust existence." [56] He contends only that the intelligibility of things, not their existence, is constituted by their logical relations. In fact, the relational, rational pattern itself indicates the presence in existence of a non-rational factor. Mind is not all of life, but only the order in life. This distinction accounts for much of Cohen's dissatisfaction with the emphasis placed on change by anti-rational, biologized philosophy. The generalization that only change is real he regards as a "snap judgment resting on no proof of logic or fact," [57] and he points out that only with reference to some constant can there be said to be any change. Motion is specifiable only by indicating an object which has a continuous identity, a fixed point from which the distance of the object changes by some definite unit of measurement, and a definite direction in which the change takes place. If these constants are eliminated, "nothing is left of the fact of motion." [58]

It is historically possible to understand how the attempt to describe the world entirely in terms of change came about. Many of the traditional constancies had to be abandoned under the pressure of advancing physical and biological science, and the dramatic dissolution of these older constancies obscured the fact that new identities and new constancies are being discovered by the very sciences which are destroying the old. "If the growth of science dis-

solves the eternity of the hills or the fixity of species, it is also discovering constant relations and order in changes which previously
seemed chaotic and arbitrary." [59]   What science discovers is not a
constant which is isolated from the flux of experience, not some transcendent, unchanging, eternal permanency, but what the mathematician calls the "invariant," that which maintains its identity in the
midst of change. Only the discovery of identities of this sort enables
us to talk about change in any meaningful way; it is the "repetition
of identical patterns in different material " [60] which gives change a
definite character.

   Thus Cohen is able to assert that the nature of anything, its permanent character, is the group of invariant properties of which it
is made. From this point of view he makes the metaphysical distinction between the nature of a thing and its manifestations. The manifestations are the phenomena of experience. They are changing and
inconstant. Science is never satisfied with the data of experience, but
seeks, rather, to find the nature of anything by way of its manifestations, "the invariant properties amidst the flux." [61]   Science tries to
explain why things behave in a certain way. Its explanation involves
putting the data to be explained into a system whose nature we know.
When we know the nature, or invariant properties, of the system we
can arrive deductively and rationally at the explanation for which
we are seeking. The concrete particular fact of our experience is
not intelligible because it is isolated and because it is changing. By
identifying the unintelligible fact as a particular case of an abstract
law, thus breaking down its isolation and determining its constant
properties, the fact becomes intelligible. The fact, changing and impermanent, is real; the law, permanent and unchanging, is for Cohen
no less real than the fact.

   It is important to remember that neither Cohen nor any other
responsible thinker today believes that science can achieve demon-
stratively certain proof of the truth of its factual content. "All our
factual knowledge (that is, all except purely formal or mathematical
considerations) is only probable in the sense that we cannot *prove*
the contrary to be absolutely impossible." [62]   Cohen's claim for
science is more moderate; he asserts that "in constantly increasing
the relative probabilities of its results, science is essentially a self-
corrective system." [63]   It is because of this view that Cohen's rationalistic position can be identified with naturalism, for if science is a

self-corrective system, there is no need to refer to principles outside the system of science for the correction of any inaccuracies or false steps. Thus Cohen emphasizes the opposition to transcendental principles which we have found to be characteristic of naturalistic thought.

Though Cohen finds transcendental explanations unnecessary, and though, therefore, one traditional aspect of metaphysical speculation has no place in his thought, he does not seek the complete elimination of metaphysics, but rather its restriction to proper concerns. He described what he found to be the proper concerns of a metaphysic of scientific method, and showed how, according to this metaphysic, a recognition of a universe is involved in any true knowledge of particulars. Such a metaphysic is concerned to define the nature of the sort of world in which the kind of science we have described is possible. That type of world is one in which there is always a possibility of error and never any necessary truth in the results of scientific investigation. That sort of science is one in which there is a constant process of revision and self-correction according to an invariable ideal. Increased adequacy and correctness as the result of scientific study can not come by the application of principles and ideals external to science itself; they can come only from the invariable ideal which is internal to science.

The universe which emerged to Cohen's view from these considerations was one whose parts are "closely interconnected in certain ways and yet in some degree independent of each other." [64] Each part has an area in which it is individual, particular, and unique; it also has an area in which its "true existence" lies beyond itself, in the whole of which it is a part. Thus the eyes of human beings have a uniqueness as eyes, but a description of their existence would demand that they be described also as related to the whole human body, the system of which the eyes are a part. So with the universe as a whole. Each moment of time in its particularity yields an experience which is not a complete account of nature; but the meaning of the particular moment includes the whole of time, the system of which the moment is a part. A particular moment is not only "now;" it is also "here." It is its "nowness" in which the whole of time is involved; in its "hereness" the whole of space is involved. The whole of time and space, which is called the universe, is not actually present in the single moment, but is involved in the meaning of the moment. "In knowing the meaning of any fragment as a fragment we know the direction of completion." [65] In each moment, then, the universe is entailed as the system of which the moment is a part. Thus we find ourselves with "a point of view to which the whole of time and space has a meaning," [66] and this Cohen called the eternal. Eternity thus described is the "ordering principle" or "limit" toward which our experience of particular moments tends. This limit of our "expanding vistas" of the universe is ideal, it is true, but not merely mental. It is the internal ideal and "genuine condition of the series of stages in the self-corrective system of natural science." [67]

Cohen asserted the dependence of scientific method on the principle of causality, but he maintained that this principle is itself the application to events in time of the broader principle of sufficient reason: "Everything is connected in definite ways with definite other things, so that its full nature is not revealed except by its position and relations with a system." [68] It was on the basis of this broad principle and of what he called "the uneliminable character of contingency" in our thought that Cohen attacked the various doctrines of which he disapproved. In particular, he said that the attempt to characterize the universe as a whole in any determinate fashion — "as one (not many), continuous (not discontinuous), conscious or purposive, and the like" [69]—produces confusion by requiring that the way in which we ordinarily use words be stretched. This is not the way in which the principle of sufficient reason is actually used in science. To the scientific view, the total universe is never regarded as the cause of any of the particular facts which constitute the universe. This is so because the cause ascribed to anything must be something determinate if it is to be adequate to the purposes of science. The meaning of the principle of causality is that "something occupying a given position in time and space can be determined only by something else also occupying a definite position in space and enduring over a definite time-interval." [70] The totality of the universe can never occupy such a definite position or endure over a definite time-interval; in the sense in which the words are used here, the total universe, "the absolute collective whole," is not determinate. To be determinate, it would have to be determined by something outside itself. From the standpoint of scientific method, it can not be so determined.

The belief that the universe as a whole can not have a character so definite that we can infer from it the particular character traits of individuals in the universe suggested to Cohen that the character of the universe must be inclusive of all opposites. This, in turn, led him to hold to a very broad principle to which he assigned the name "the principle of polarity." By this principle he meant that all opposites "involve each other when applied to any significant entity." [71] There can be no action without reaction; life is a continuous process of dying. We cannot define motion save in terms of rest. The principle of polarity preserved in Cohen's thought all that he found worthy of preservation in the Hegelian dialectic.

Then, too, if every significant ascription of a quality or property to anything involves an ascription of its opposite, a large part of the vagueness and inconclusiveness of metaphysical and sociological discussion may well be the result of disregarding the principle of polarity and uncritically accepting one or the other of the alternatives, without recognizing its implication of the other. If substance and function are, as Cohen suggested, opposites, then a metaphysics which disregards either would be incomplete, partial, and inadequate. Somehow both must be taken into account in formulating our metaphysics. We must avoid "adhering to simple alternatives instead of resorting to the laborious process of integrating opposite assertions by finding the proper distinctions and qualifications." [72]

The field of ethics provided Cohen with an opportunity to apply the principle of polarity. For him the central question was whether science can be applied to the whole field of human conduct, and whether there can be an ethical science. He recognized that there are difficulties in the way of developing ethical science. Our moral judgments, more than any other judgments we make, are deeply rooted in our personal and habitual emotional attitudes and are similarly tied to the emotional attitudes of our society. The fabric of social order as it exists in our age is thought to depend upon the preservation of habitual morality, and there is the consequent fear that ethical science will discover that certain views destructive of the social fabric are true. Moral theory as it has been carried on by philosophers of the past has largely concerned itself with finding justifications for institutions which happen to exist, thus bolstering the *status quo*. In order to build an ethical science despite these difficulties, the moral philosopher must borrow the neutrality of the scientist. He must study propositions about the conduct of individuals in the same detached fashion as the physical scientist studies propositions about the behavior of gases. He must have no concern for the attainment of any preconceived result; his only effort must be to follow carefully and precisely "the rules of the scientific game." [73] Only when the ethical philosopher becomes the scientist of morals can we hope for the development of an ethical science.

As we look at the history of moral theory, we find that there have been two general and opposed patterns into which the theorists fall. One is the pattern of moral absolutism, which asserts that there are eternally valid and binding rules which ought to determine our choice in each actual decision we have to make. The other is the pattern of moral antinomianism, which argues that we are to be guided in each decision by our impressions of the actual situation in which the decision is to be made. Here is our opportunity to apply the principle of polarity by recognizing that both of these opposed assertions are properly included in any description of the process of moral decision, and, at the same time, that the adherents of each alternative go too far in insisting upon the exclusive value of their own approach. As a very minimum, "the absolutist is right in insisting that each such choice logically involves a principle of decision, and the empiricist is right in insisting on the primacy of the feeling or perception of the demands in the actual case before us." [74] We must reject the extreme claims for moral rules, but recognize in these rules useful generalizations of the fruits of human experience, in need of careful refinement and logical development and presentation. The content of our moral rules comes to us out of particular situations; absolutism contributes the rational method of developing and refining these empirically derived rules.

An adequate science of ethics must be grounded in what men actually do, and in a psychological study of what men believe they ought to do. But these studies are not the primary concern of ethical science. It is primarily "a logical study of the validity of judgments of right or wrong, good or evil, implied in our expressed or tacit choices." [75] The primary concern of this logical study of moral judgments is to see how far these judgments can be refined and presented as a system. Thus we see how Cohen found a place for ethical science within the rationalistic pattern of his thinking, especially by his emphasis on the principle of polarity.

Philosophers have made much of the alternative of means and ends, and in non-naturalistic systems have introduced difficulties by considering the ends as transcending nature. Cohen's rationalistic naturalism freed him from these difficulties by enabling him to demonstrate logically that the ends of rational conduct are not outside of human activity, but are a part of the characteristic pattern of life itself. The end is a whole within nature and includes as parts the necessary means. Thus, in the moral realm ends have the status which the ideal of eternity has in Cohen's metaphysics. We might paraphrase his statement about eternity by asserting that the end is the internal ideal and genuine condition of the series of stages in the self-corrective system of ethical science.

Morris Cohen's universe was a difficult one; there were no short-cuts in it. The road to knowledge, to rational science, was always laborious and toilsome. Mere vision, insight, and impression, however essential as a foundation, was never enough; techniques, precision, elaboration, and refinement had to be painstakingly added to form a superstructure. He had, however, a deep and abiding faith which justified this labor. When all that can be said of the difficulties of the course has been said, in the end we must also add that the universe in which we exist has "the particular character which it has, and not some other," and this particular character permits "the scientific pursuit of rational connection." [76] One of the characteristics of our universe is intelligibility in its own terms, without introducing explanatory principles from outside itself. This is the faith of a rationalistic naturalist.

IV. EXPERIMENTAL NATURALISM: JOHN DEWEY

The experimental naturalism of John Dewey is in many ways in contrast with the naturalistic philosophies of Santayana and Cohen. To anyone who reads the book in which the younger naturalists tell their story, *Naturalism and the Human Spirit* (edited by Professor Krikorian), it becomes clear that the contrast is less fundamental than the philosophers themselves would allow. These differing emphases in naturalism tend to reinforce each other. Professor Sidney Hook of New York University, one of the many naturalists who studied under both Cohen and Dewey, finds that these two varieties of the naturalistic temper are closely akin to each other. The difference between the two complementary emphases was exaggerated in discussion.

A similar point might be made about Dewey and Santayana. Like true philosophers, they have argued about their disagreements, and left their basic agreements for less controversial situations. Santayana attacked Dewey's empirical metaphysics. Cohen emphasized the structure, pattern, or universal, and asserted with scorn that the only way in which we can deal with particulars is to point to them. We can not even talk about particulars, for in talking we use words which are themselves universals, not particulars. Dewey agreed with Cohen that the only way of dealing with particulars is pointing, but did not share Cohen's scorn for this kind of experience. In fact, Dewey may be said to glorify this type of experience. Conceiving of experience in this fashion is of value to philosophy, because it makes clear that, in the final analysis, we depend upon the method of pointing; we are led by considering experience in these terms to recognize "the necessity of seeing what is pointed to and accepting what is found in good faith and without discount."[77] Thus our thought is directed toward the formulation of a theory of reality in which the real is not limited by any arbitrary or temperamental preferences of the thinker or his society. Reality, rather, is thought of as including "whatever is denotatively found." This would mean not only matter and motion, though it would surely include them. It would also include among the real aspects of our experience "devotion, piety, love, beauty, and mystery." [78] These human experiences, because they are experienced, must be regarded as just as real as anything else.

Dewey has frequently been called an anti-intellectualist. The reason for this is that he has completely discarded from his thought the understandable but unjustifiable prejudice of philosophers in favor of the superior reality of the objects of thought, of what is known. He rejects the dualistic view that there are two kinds of knowledge, knowledge of things and knowledge of ideas, and that the task of philosophy is to reconcile in some manner or other the different sorts of objects of knowledge. There are, instead, "two dimensions of experienced things." One of these dimensions is that of enjoying things, or simply having them unreflectively, as one might immediately and unreflectively have and enjoy a cup of coffee. This way of having things exists, and is not at all the same as knowing things. But it is a precondition for knowing things; it supplies the materials of reflection and knowledge. Knowing about things is the other dimension of experienced things. It is a purposive dimension; we get to know about things "so that we can again have them in more meaningful and secure ways." [79] All knowledge about things is instrumental.

Instrumentalism, as we have already noted (Chapter 7, section I), is the form that Dewey gave to pragmatism. It is a form of pragmatism which is closer in spirit to Peirce's version of pragmatism than to James'. Peirce had found that general ideas are bodied forth in habits, and serve as the ideas which control, govern, and regulate action. Dewey made all ideas regulative or instrumental. The meaning of any idea whatsoever always contains a plan of action, a specification of certain operations to be performed. The performance of these operations is the experimental testing of the validity of any idea. Thus an idea is tested in its functioning within a context. If, within that context, the idea proves instrumental in eliminating conflicts of experience and in bringing about a relative integration, it has been verified. Thus, to say that ideas are instrumental is, for Dewey, to say that they have an active, mediatory role to play in experience. Knowledge, thinking, and intelligence — in general, theory — can not be treated apart from action, and existence — in general, practice. Thought and action are continuous with each other. The context in which thought takes place is never a purely psychic one; thought exists in a context of both psychic and physical events.

Reflection, thinking, does not occur except when there is an obstacle to activity, when the expression of some impulse is blocked. The germ of thinking, then, is the problem set up by some conflict in experience. We do not, however, consciously present ourselves with a problem and deliberately sit down to think about it until we have reached a rather advanced stage in education. In the beginning, Dewey says, "the having of ideas is not so much something we do, as it is something that happens to us." [80] It is the problem, the situation of confusion or doubt which G. H. Mead (see Chapter 7, section IV) called "the blocking of an impulse," that starts the thinking. The gradual clarification of the problem by the integration of the confusion or the resolution of the doubt is, at one and the same time, both the operation and the verification of the thinking. "Intellectual organization originates and for a time grows as an accompaniment of the organization of the acts required to realize an end, not as the results of a direct appeal to thinking power." [81] Effective thinking requires an object toward which it moves. It intends to "accomplish something beyond thinking." The pattern which reflective thinking follows is what Dewey means by the eulogistic term "scientific method." In this method he makes a place for both inductive and deductive reasoning, for the formation of hypotheses on the basis of observed particulars, and for the development by reason of the bearings of the hypotheses suggested. Inasmuch as the entire process originates in a problem, the hypotheses are proposed solutions to the problem. It is the final step in the process of reflective thinking which Dewey insists upon. This is the testing of proposed solutions by experimentation, approaching as closely as the context permits to the conditions under which testing experiments are performed in a scientific laboratory. Dewey never considers that a solution is established until it has been tested by application to the resolution of the difficulty in which the thinking process originated.

Within this process, Dewey uses the word "idea" to mean an as yet untested hypothesis, a possible solution or meaning that is held in suspense, tentatively used to see whether the solution it proposes will actually resolve the perplexity. An idea is "a meaning used as a tool of judgment." [82] When an idea has been verified and is, therefore, fully accepted, it is no longer to be called an idea. To explain, in terms of such an account of ideas, what we mean when we say an idea is true, Dewey proposes a pragmatic test similar to James' interpretation of verification. An idea is a plan to act in a certain way in order to clarify some particular confused situation. When the idea is put into operation, either it resolves the situation to some extent or it does not. If it does, it is true; if it does not, it is false. "That which guides us truly is true — demonstrated capacity for such guidance is precisely what is meant by truth." [83] Thus it is the adverb "truly" which is fundamental; both the adjective "true" and the noun "truth" are derivative. An adverb, however, is dynamic; it expresses a quality of an action. Dewey's adverbial view of truth contradicts the traditional view of philosophy that truth is a property of Being rather than of activity. It upsets the notion that a fixed truth has existence prior to human experience and human reflection. Truth is the ever-growing body of warranted assertions. The traditional view supported the claims of authority and the maintenance of the *status quo*. The Deweyan view places a heavy responsibility on each individual to do his part in the discovery of ideas that guide men truly. "To generalize the recognition that the true means the verified and means nothing else places upon men the responsibility of surrendering political and moral dogmas, and subjecting to the test of consequences their most cherished prejudices. Such a change involves a great change in the seat of authority and the methods of decision in society." [84] Although this view is similar to that of William James, there is one significant difference. Truth for both James and Dewey is a form of satisfaction. For James, however, the satisfaction may be a matter of meeting some private need of an individual. For Dewey, such personal satisfaction is not involved. What is required is that the proposed idea must satisfy the needs of the problem in the solution of which it arose. Thus, satisfaction for Dewey is a far more public and objective matter than it was for James.

Throughout his philosophy, Dewey emphasizes the factor of chance and contingency quite as strongly as did Cohen. In his Carus lectures, published under the title *Experience and Nature*, Dewey suggests that the entire history of philosophy may be regarded as the record of variant methods of denying the contingent character which is an integral part of the universe, and embarking upon what the title of another of his books called "The Quest for Certainty." But, just as Santayana pointed out that disregard of the natural basis left the ideal no point of application, so Dewey insists that the denial of natural contingency leaves the philosopher with no hint of the real character of the universe about which he is reflecting. Dewey's view that thinking is originated in a problematic situation within experience gives him a very strong argument for contingency in nature. Thinking itself is the evidence that nature is subject to chance. Since thinking arises in the world of actual existences, and, moreover, arises in an uncertain, conflicting, unresolved situation in that world, the world must be the sort of world which produces uncertainty and conflict, "ignorance and inquiry, doubt and hypothesis, trial and temporal conclusions." [85] Eventually there is a mental reorganization of the elements of real existence into a more satisfactory pattern. Thus the very occurrence of thinking and the fact that by thinking we can discover a pattern into which the elements of nature may be reorganized proves that nature is not completely necessitated, but that there is a character of "genuine hazard, contingency, irregularity, and indeterminateness" to be found in nature.[86]

Nature, then, is not exclusively the highly structured and determinate body of static things in fixed relations, which it was described as being in the popular versions of mechanistic physics and among materialistic philosophers. Nature is instead a pattern of events and interrelations, in which even the pattern itself is an event, modified by its interaction with other events and processes. For Dewey there is no fixed and absolute distinction between structure and process. He has learned thoroughly the lesson of evolutionary biology; that his views are still relevant is, in part, the result of newer developments in physics with which Dewey's notion that all existence is existence in time is consistent. For Dewey, "every existence is an event."[87] There is no absolutely permanent and fixed structure. There are, however, two types of change. Some change is relatively slow and rhythmic. Dewey allows the name "structure" to be used for this long-term change. Structure is the relatively fixed, stable and permanent event which is the pattern of other events. Other change is more rapid and irregular, and it is to this that he gives the name "process." Thus Dewey develops a naturalistic metaphysics which recognizes both structure and process, both matter and mind, as aspects of a mixed world which has much of the character of polarity on which Cohen insisted.

Reality, he says, is commonly identified in philosophy with what is "sure, regular, and finished."[88] Yet the evidence of naive experience, of the sort which Dewey glories in, as we pointed out earlier, furnishes us with an entirely different picture of the world and theory of reality. The world in which we live is a mixed world, in which both regularities and irregularities, both completeness and incompleteness are actually found. "We live in a world which is an impressive and irresistible mixture of sufficiencies, tight completenesses, order, recurrences which make possible prediction and control, and singularities, ambiguities, uncertain possibilities, processes going on to consequences as yet indeterminate."[89] The regularities and irregularities, however they may be separated in discourse, can not be divided in life. They are vitally mixed as growths from the same root. This is where the polarity enters, and this is the basis for a naturalistic metaphysics. Polarity enters because "qualities have defects as necessary conditions of their excellencies; the instrumentalities of truth are the causes of error; change gives meaning to permanence and recurrence makes novelty possible . . . only a living world can include death." [90] Metaphysics is the recognition of the most general traits of existence, of existence and not of thought. But, as we have seen, contingency is precisely one of the most general characteristics of existence and must, therefore, be given an important place in a metaphysics. It is true that man's chief task as an intelligent being is "the striving to make stability of meaning prevail over the instability of events" [91] — an enterprise we have met in Santayana's thought under the name of "The life of reason." But we can not, legitimately, convert meaning into existence; nor can we transform "a moral insight to be made good in action into an antecedent metaphysics of existence." [92] It is this conversion and transformation to which Dewey refers as "*the* philosophic fallacy."[93]

We have seen that for Dewey thinking is instrumental; it takes place within nature as experience, starting from the "actually problematic" and confused situation and ending in the satisfactory resolution of the problem or confusion. In some types of human behavior, natural materials and natural energies are employed to reorganize an unsatisfactory situation into a satisfactory one, as when stones, wind, and water are used to grind wheat into flour. Thinking is an equally natural type of human behavior. "Thought and reason are not specific powers." [94] Reflection is a natural event, taking place within nature, "a continuous process of temporal reorganization within one and the same world of experienced things." [95] There is no gap between the real world of actual things and a world consisting entirely of objects of thought. The characteristics of thinking are of the same order of existence as the characteristics of other events in the real world. To the same degree, then, and in the same way as the sciences draw inferences about the world of nature from the characteristics of other natural events, the philosopher may draw inferences about the world of nature from the characteristics of thinking. Such inferences, made in the way Dewey indicates, constitute his naturalistic metaphysics.

From the standpoint of his experimental naturalism, Dewey regards as the weakness of most moral theories, except the utilitarian, their refusal to admit that moral values grow out of specific empirical facts. Most moralists find it necessary to introduce moral themes from outside of nature, and usually from above nature, because they insist upon treating nature as merely "a display of physical forces incapable of generating moral values." [96] Not that nature is itself to be described as moral, or to be morally judged; to do so would be to patronize nature. It is, rather, that moral science is, like the other sciences, empirically grounded. Dewey insists that morals, the most humane of all subjects and that which is closest to human nature, is "ineradicably empirical, not theological, nor metaphysical nor mathematical." [97] Furthermore, there is no breach or discontinuity between moral science and the other sciences of man. Human nature is the object of direct and primary concern to the moralist. All the sciences which are attempting to find out about human nature, therefore, are directly pertinent, and their results directly relevant, to the study of morals. On this ground, there is no question in Dewey's mind of the continuity between moral science and such sciences as physiology, medicine, anthropology, and psychology. Furthermore, in a moral science, our concern is not entirely with human nature in the abstract; it is, rather, with human nature existing and operating in an environment, "not as coins are in a box, but as a plant is in the sunlight and soil." [98] The relation of human nature to its environment is not mechanical, but organic. Consequently, the sciences descriptive of the environment of human nature are as germane to moral science as those which deal directly with human nature. The discipline of one who would study morals, therefore, must include the physical and social sciences as well as the biological, and the applied sciences as well as the pure. All of these sciences are part of the background the moralist needs in order "to understand the conditions and agencies through which man lives, and on account of which he forms and executes his plans." [99] In moral science all the other sciences are brought into the context of human life in order to cast light upon the activities of human life.

This does not mean that moral science is nothing but biological, physical, and social science. In illuminating the activities of men by the aid of the light cast by these sciences, we are trying to perceive the facts of human nature. Perception of facts is not the end for the moral scientist; it is only a halfway house, a stage in changing the facts. "Morality resides not in perception of fact, but in the use made of its perception." [100] Since morality is practiced not only to describe the way things are, but also to suggest how things can be changed, and perhaps improved, it does not have to be (as it so often has, in fact, been), merely a retrospective sanctioning of things as they are. Morality is intelligence applied to human life. Intelligence tells us whether, in a particular case, the present situation is desirable or undesirable. If it is desirable, we use the facts to preserve and conserve the present situation. If it is undesirable, we use the facts as a lever to change the conditions and thereby to change the results, to create a new situation. Dewey denies that the alternative is between denial of the facts in the interest of some completely non-natural moral ideal, and complete subservience to the facts, accepted as final and unalterable. There is a third possibility, that maintained by the naturalist in morals, and that is to recognize the facts, but to use them "as a challenge to intelligence to modify the environment and change habits." [101]

Dewey calls this possible third alternative the experimental method in morals. He asserts that a reflective morality of this sort demands the observation of particular situations in their fullness, rather than a rigid adherence to fixed moral principles which exist in the structure of the universe prior to human experience. Insofar as it is to be truly an experimental method, it requires freedom as its major condition, so that there may be experimental verification of its hypotheses. At different times and places there must be a chance to try out different methods of solution, to observe and to compare their effects. It is for this reason that he equates the experimental theory of morals with democracy, which, in his view, includes both regard for others and scientific inquiry into facts and the testing of ideas. In this experimental view, precedent is not discarded; it is, however, transformed from a guide into an instrument for the analysis of things as they are. By the use of precedent as an analytic tool, points for consideration are to be raised and possible solutions are to be tried. In general, Dewey finds that there is a presumption in favor of long-standing principles, but that newly-discovered facts or newly-created institutions may lead to the discarding of even the most time-hallowed of moral principles. "More fundamental than any particular principle held or decision reached is the attitude of willingness to re-examine and if necessary to revise current conditions, even if that course entails the effort to change by concerted effort existing institutions, and to direct existing tendencies to new ends." 102

The experimental method in morals is readily extended from the field of individual ethics to that of social philosophy. In the social area, experimental method is called "liberalism" or "democracy." Liberalism is not a single doctrine; there is no continuing program for liberalism. It is, rather, a continuing political and social trend which is recurrently reaffirmed in particular struggles against particular oppressive institutions. At any given time and place, the demand of liberalism is not for a general liberty, but for the release of particular energies which are dammed by a particular social situation. The release demanded in any age is the practical meaning of the liberal ideal in that context, and so this meaning is fixed in different ways in various cultural contexts. As we have seen, men in general and philosophers in particular tend to establish their specific ideals as eternal verities, as aspects of the structure of the universe. This has happened to older "liberalisms." In their day, they were clarion calls to particular, and probably necessary, reforms. Today they still hang tenaciously to life, remaining as stumbling blocks in the path of later liberty. In order to make provision for the differences between the liberalism of one age and that of another, Dewey formulated his theory of liberalism in terms of an emphasis upon a method of social action patterned after the experimental method in the sciences. He expressed a concern for the generalized method of liberalism rather than its specific content, the conclusions of any one generation.

This emphasis on the method of social action leads Dewey to attach great importance to "experimental" thinking as a central factor in making democracy work. "Fraternity," the third of the ideals of democracy, he interprets as cooperation, the ideal of the laboratory scientist. He considers this fraternal cooperation essential to the achievement of liberty and equality. Liberty and equality are not "natural rights" of man, retained from a pre-social state, but are instead the fruits in the life of the individual of fraternal cooperation in a democratic society. In the final analysis, democracy can be justified only by its similarity to the experimental method and by its ability to assimilate that method to the everyday problems of society. For the realization of democratic ideals, Dewey places far less reliance on government than on voluntary associations. A

government is democratic to the extent that it remains the servant
of various voluntary groups, with their diversified interests, "regulating" them only in preventing them from frustrating each other.
Men's living together is regulated by certain values which are fixed
within a society. When every mature person takes part in fixing
and formulating the values by which he is to live as a member of
his group, the society is following a democratic way of life. "All
those who are affected by social institutions must have a share in
producing and managing them." [103] Criticism has forced the discarding of some of the theories Thomas Jefferson accepted, like the
social contract theory of the origin of society. But, by and large,
Dewey shares the Jeffersonian ideal of democracy, the belief that
democracy is founded on faith in the capacities of human nature
and human intelligence, and faith that men thinking and working
together, sharing and pooling their experience like laboratory scientists, can build a better world.

The scientific laboratory is readily generalized into the world-
wide community of scientists, sharing an ideal and a moral code as
well as a method, and communicating through barriers of class and
nation which are otherwise impassable. The successful application
of intelligence to the solution of a special set of problems, and the
successful funding of the experience shared by scientists, has led
Dewey to a faith in the universal possibilities of shared experience.
It is his belief that, by extending the method of the community of
scientists to the solution of all the problems of men, advances in
human relations comparable to our advances in the control of nature
can take place. The principle of "cooperative association" or "shared
experience" is the heart of Dewey's religious attitude. He has declared that "Faith in the continued disclosing of truth through
directed cooperative human endeavor is more religious in quality
than is any faith in a completed revelation." [104] To be able to make
such a statement, Dewey first had to separate two concepts more
usually found in conjunction; and only then could he join the two
concepts of human effort and religion more usually found in opposition. Dewey first had to break down the widely-held view that a
religious quality is to be found only in association with a formal set
of beliefs and practices, institutionalized in a church and usually
associated with supernaturalism. Consistent with his other thinking,
but in opposition to many other twentieth-century thinkers, Dewey

maintains that experience is all of a piece, with various qualities discriminable in it. That is to say, there is no separate esthetic experience or ethical experience or religious experience, each to be judged by a special set of criteria. All experience is to be judged by the same criteria, and analysis of the same experience will reveal esthetic, ethical, religious, and scientific qualities. "The actual religious quality in the experience . . . is the *effect* produced, . . . not the manner and cause of its production." [105]

Dewey did use the term "God" in discussing these effects. However, the misinterpretation given to his words by many traditional theists has led him to express regret for having ever used the term. Tradition makes God the supernatural beginning and cause of all that men can experience. Dewey would make of God the name of a natural and *"active* relation between ideal and actual." [106] Dewey says repeatedly that this is what he intends by his use of the word "God." In fact, he goes much farther; it is only to such a usage that he is ready to grant the attribute "ideal." For if God has existence antecedent to experience, by the very fact of being *realized* existence, God must be non-ideal existence. Dewey goes on to assert the possibility that "the power and significance in life of the traditional conceptions of God are . . . due to the ideal qualities referred to by them." [107] The conversion of these ideal ends into antecedent reality — and the consequent loss, for Dewey, of their ideal character — is another example of the psychological quirk we have mentioned in other connections. The great advantage that Dewey claims for his usage is that the authority over us of ideal ends and values becomes clearer as the term "God" is no longer used for their guarantor by force.

If we accept Dewey's views, we find it impossible to talk of "religious experience" or "religious truth" as if these were special areas of experience and truth set apart from all others, subject to special methods of investigation, verification, and validation. All experience generates ideals. Commitment to these ideals in their broadest reach is the religious attitude. Religion is a quality of all experience, which is strongest where experience is democratically pooled so that men together may reach a goal which is the ideal fulfillment of their natural experience.

In these three brief sketches of three different yet related types of naturalism we have met the chief ideas of the major teachers of a generation of American naturalists. Though their differences led them to debate, sometimes half-humorously, and sometimes acrimoniously, a survey of their major themes indicates that on these their attitudes were very similar. The poetic naturalism of Santayana, the rationalistic naturalism of Cohen, and the experimental naturalism of Dewey, different though they may be in detail, and different though their authors are in temperament, together form a solid basis for the further speculations of their students and disciples. We have here seen enough to know that naturalism can not be dismissed as merely a materialism. It is a philosophic temper which, firmly grounded in nature, human nature, and human experience, yet finds room for ideal values in morals, art, and religion. The naturalists attempt in various ways, the success of which must be judged by the future, to walk philosophically with their heads in the clouds and their feet firmly on the ground.

FOOTNOTES AND SUGGESTED READING

There are full "Guides to the Literature" following each chapter of Herbert W. Schneider, *A History of American Philosophy*. Columbia University Press, 1946. Since these lists are available, the suggestions here have been kept to a minimum.

PRELUDE

Cotton Mather, *Magnalia Christi Americana*. Silas Andrus, 1820, reprints in full the text of such documents as the Cambridge Platform of 1649. The best selection of source materials for the intellectual life of the Puritans is Perry Miller and Thomas H. Johnson, *The Puritans*. American Book Co., 1938. Useful discussions of Puritan thought can be found in Perry Miller, *The New England Mind: the Seventeenth Century*. The Macmillan Co., 1939, and Ralph Barton Perry, *Puritanism and Democracy*. The Vanguard Press, 1944.

[1] Cotton Mather, *The Christian Philosopher*, especially Essay XXXII, "Of Man," in *Selections from Cotton Mather*. (Kenneth B. Murdock, editor) Harcourt, Brace and Co., 1926, pp. 349-362.

[2] Excerpts from Robinson's speech are quoted by Perry Miller, *Orthodoxy in Massachusetts*. Harvard University Press, 1933, p. 101n.

[3] Cotton Mather, *Magnalia*, Vol. II. Silas Andrus, 1820, pp. 184-185 reproduces the discussion of the saint in The Cambridge Platform, chap. III.

[4] The phrase is from The Cambridge Platform, and is quoted here from Mather's *Magnalia*, Vol. II, p. 193.

[5] Cotton's remarks from *The Keyes of the Kingdom of Heaven and Power Thereof According to the Word of God*. Thomas Goodwin, Philip Nye, London, 1644, p. 23.

[6] Samuel Stone's aphorism is quoted in Mather, *Magnalia*, Vol. I, p. 437.

[7] The fullest discussion of the Ramist basis of Puritan thought is to be found in Miller, *The New England Mind.*

[8] Willard's remark quoted in Miller, *op. cit.*, p. 167.

[9] Winthrop quoted in Miller and Johnson, *op. cit.*, p. 203.

[10] Winthrop quoted in Miller and Johnson, *ibid.*, p. 207.

[11] Cotton quoted in Miller and Johnson, *ibid.*, pp. 209-210.

[12] Davenport, *A Discourse about Civil Government.* Samuel Green and Marmaduke Johnson, Cambridge, 1663, pp. 8-9.

[13] Mather, *Magnalia*, Vol. II, p. 174.

[14] Hubbard's sermon is presented in abridged form in Miller and Johnson, *op. cit.*, pp. 247-250. The quotation is from p. 247.

[15] Willard, in Miller and Johnson, *ibid.*, p. 254.

[16] Selections from Wise's *Vindication* are printed in Anderson and Fisch, *Philosophy in America.* D. Appleton-Century Co., 1939, pp. 33-39, and in Miller and Johnson, *op. cit.*, 257-269.

CHAPTER 1

I. Bernard Cohen, *Some Early Tools of American Science.* Harvard University Press, 1950, contains a great deal of useful background material on the acceptance of Newton in the American colonies. Perry Miller, *Jonathan Edwards.* Wm. Sloane Associates, 1950, a biography in the American Men of Letters series, overstates the case for Edwards' uniqueness, but is otherwise good. The best brief account of Edwards' philosophy is to be found in the introduction to C. H. Faust and Thomas H. Johnson, *Jonathan Edwards: Representative Selections.* The American Book Co., 1935. Herbert W. Schneider, "The Mind of Samuel Johnson," is prefaced to the second volume of H. W. Schneider and C. Schneider, *Samuel Johnson, President of King's College, His Career and Writings.* Columbia University Press, 1929. There is no good study of Colden's philosophy, nor are most of his philosophic works available. Colden's brief "Introduction to Phylosophy" is printed in its entirety in *American Philosophic Addresses, 1700-1900.* (Joseph L. Blau, editor) Columbia University Press, 1946.

[1] See I. B. Cohen, *Some Early Tools of American Science.* Harvard University Press, 1950, *passim.*

[2] From the Preface to Book III of Newton's *Principia*, quoted in *Introduction to Contemporary Civilization in the West*. Vol. I, Columbia University Press, 1946, p. 630.

[3] See Merle Curti, "The Great Mr. Locke, America's Philosopher, 1783-1861," *The Huntington Library Bulletin*, No. 11, April, 1937, pp. 107-151; and F. E. Brasch, "The Newtonian Epoch in the American Colonies," *Proceedings of the American Antiquarian Society*, October, 1939, pp. 3-21.

[4] Sereno E. Dwight, "The Life of President Edwards," in Edwards, *Works*. Vol. I. Converse, 1829, p. 30.

[5] Faust and Johnson, *op. cit.*, pp. 27-28.

[6] *Ibid.*, p. 28.

[7] Quoted in *ibid.*, p. xxvii.

[8] Edwards, *Works* (1829 ed.), I, 706.

[9] Faust and Johnson, *op. cit.*, p. 30.

[10] Jonathan Edwards, *Images or Shadows of Divine Things*. (Perry Miller, editor) Yale University Press, 1948, Image No. 147.

[11] Faust and Johnson, *op. cit.*, p. 29.

[12] Quoted in Schneider, *op. cit.*, Vol. II, p. 14.

[13] *Ibid.*, II, 290.

[14] See Faust and Johnson, *op. cit.*, pp. 58-60.

[15] Quoted in Edwards, *Images*, p. 21.

[16] Faust and Johnson, *op. cit.*, p. 225.

[17] *Ibid.*

[18] *Ibid.*, p. 235.

[19] *Ibid.*, pp. 249-250.

[20] See *ibid.*, pp. 338-339.

[21] *Ibid.*, pp. 324-325.

[22] *Ibid.*, p. 349.

[23] *Ibid.*

[24] Quoted in *ibid.*, p. xcv.

[25] Quoted in *ibid.*, p. l.

[26] Quoted in *ibid.*, pp. xlvii-xlvix.

[27] Colden, "An Introduction to Phylosophy," in Blau, *op. cit.*, p. 298.

[28] *Ibid.*, pp. 294-295.

[29] In Colden's unpublished "The First Principles of Morality or the Actions of Intelligent Beings." Mr. Cornelius Fay has transcribed and introduced this manuscript; his typewritten transcription is on file in the Columbia University Library.

[30] Anderson and Fisch, *Philosophy in America*. D. Appleton-Century Co., 1939, p. 102.

[31] *Ibid.*, p. 103.

[32] *Ibid.*, p. 121.

CHAPTER 2

The best general introduction to the intellectual life of the Enlightenment in America is the "Introduction" to Frank L. Mott and Chester E. Jorgenson, *Benjamin Franklin: Representative Selections*. The American Book Co., 1936. Woolman's *Journal* is available in The Everyman Library. A. Koch and W. Peden edited a good collection of Jefferson's writings, *The Life and Selected Writings of Thomas Jefferson*, for the Modern Library. A more pointed collection of material is Saul K. Padover, *Thomas Jefferson on Democracy*. Penguin Books, Inc., 1946. H. H. Clark, *Thomas Paine: Representative Selections*. The American Book Co., 1944, has a brilliant introduction. W. E. Woodward, *Thomas Paine, America's Godfather*. E. P. Dutton and Co., 1945, is a good recent biography with comparatively few axes to grind. Dagobert Runes has edited *The Selected Writings of Benjamin Rush*. The Philosophical Library, 1947.

[1] Cotton Mather, *Essays to Do Good*. 1808, p. 19.

[2] Schneider, *Samuel Johnson*, II, Columbia University Press, 1929, p. 448.

[3] Mott and Jorgenson, *op. cit.*, pp. 114-128.

[4] In his *Autobiography*. See *ibid.*, p. 42.

[5] Frederick C. Prescott, *Alexander Hamilton and Thomas Jefferson: Representative Selections*. The American Book Co., 1934, pp. 6; 185-189.

[6] *The Selected Writings of John and John Quincy Adams*. (A. Koch and W. Peden, editors) Alfred A. Knopf, 1946, p. 25.

[7] Quoted in Charles E. Merriam, *A History of American Political Theories*. The Macmillan Co., 1924, p. 45.

[8] Quoted in *ibid.*, p. 49.

[9] John Adams, *Works*. Vol. IV, Little, Brown and Co., 1856, p. 28.

[10] To T. Law, 1814.

[11] *Ibid.*

[12] To William S. Smith, 1787.

[13] To Kosciusko, 1810; see also his letter to Van der Kemp, 1812.

[14] "Opinion . . . whether the seat of government shall be transferred to the Potomac," July 15, 1790.

[15] To Dupont de Nemours, 1816.

[16] To J. W. Eppes, 1813.

[17] To T. Earle, 1823.

[18] To Hartley, 1787.

[19] To J. H. Tiffany, 1816.

[20] *Ibid.*

[21] To James Madison,1787.

[22] To Hawkins, 1787.

[23] To Benjamin Rush, 1800.

[24] *Notes on Virginia*, Query XVII, in *Cornerstones of Religious Freedom in America*. (Joseph L. Blau, editor) The Beacon Press, 1949, p. 78.

[25] "An Act Establishing Religious Freedom in Virginia," in *ibid.*, p. 75.

[26] To De Meunier, 1786.

[27] To H. G. Spofford, 1814.

[28] *Notes on Virginia*, Query XIX, in Padover, *op. cit.*, pp. 69-70. See also, To Hagendorp, 1785, and To John Jay, 1785.

[29] Clark, *op. cit.*, p. 287.

[30] *Ibid.*, pp. 228-290.

[31] *Ibid.*, p. 85.

[32] *Ibid.*

[33] *Ibid.*, p. 86.

[34] *Ibid.*, p. 87.

[35] *Ibid.*, p. 88.

[36] *Ibid.*, p. 89.

[37] *Ibid.*, p. 5.

[38] *Ibid.*, p. 18.

[39] *Ibid.*, p. 65.

[40] *Ibid.*, p. 135.

[41] *Ibid.*, p. 188.

[42] *Ibid.*, p. 225.

[43] *Ibid.*, p. 226.

[44] *Ibid.*, p. 337.

[45] *Ibid.*, p. 338.

[46] *Ibid.*, p. 341.

[47] *Ibid.*, p. 369.

[48] *Ibid.*, p. 106.

[49] *Ibid.*, p. 235.

[50] *Ibid.*

[51] *Ibid.*, p. 241.

[52] *Ibid.*, p. 262.

53 *Ibid.*, p. 266.
54 *Ibid.*, p. 283.
55 Runes, *op. cit.*, pp. 247-248.
56 *Ibid.*, pp. 135-137.
57 *Ibid.*, p. 137.
58 *Ibid.*, p. 182.
59 *Ibid.*, p. 191.
60 *Ibid.*, pp. 97-100.
61 *Ibid.*, p. 321.

CHAPTER 3

Carl Becker, *The Declaration of Independence*. Alfred A. Knopf, 1948, presents a summary of the reaction against the ideas of the Declaration. William Sumner Jenkins, *Pro-Slavery Thought in the Old South*. University of North Carolina Press, 1935, is the most complete account of the defense of slavery. Jay W. Fay, *American Psychologies Before William James*. Rutgers University Press, 1939, discusses some aspects of the academic philosophy of the period. There is an unpublished doctoral dissertation by Walter T. James on "The Philosophy of Noah Porter" on file in the Columbia University Library. H. A. Larrabee, H. W. Schneider, and J. S. Bixler wrote brief essays on Hickok which are included in a pamphlet, *Laurens Perseus Hickok*. Union College, 1947. Francis Wayland, "The Philosophy of Analogy," and Noah Porter, "The Sciences of Nature *versus* the Science of Man," are reprinted in full in *American Philosophic Addresses, 1700-1900*. (Joseph L. Blau, editor) Columbia University Press, 1946.

1 F. C. Prescott, *Alexander Hamilton and Thomas Jefferson: Representative Selections*. The American Book Co., 1934, pp. 33-34.

2 *Ibid.*, p. 179.

3 Koch and Peden, *The Selected Writings of John and John Quincy Adams*. Alfred A. Knopf, 1946, pp. 109-111.

4 Adams, *Works*, Vol. VI. Little, Brown and Co., 1856, p. 392.

5 Koch and Peden, *op. cit.*, p. 177.

6 David Daggett, *Sunbeams may be extracted from cucumbers, but the process is tedious* . . . (New Haven, 1799), reprinted in *The Magazine of History, with Notes and Queries*. Extra number, no. 76 (Tarrytown, 1922), p. 206.

[7] Edward Hitchcock, *Religious Truth Illustrated from Science.* Phillips, Sampson and Co., 1857, p. 422.

[8] Tayler Lewis, *Faith, the Life of Science.* Hoffman and White, 1838, p. 34.

[9] *Ibid.*, p. 4.

[10] Wayland, *Elements of Intellectual Philosophy.* Phillips, Sampson and Co., 1854, p. iii.

[11] Samuel S. Smith, *The Lectures . . . on the Subjects of Moral and Political Philosophy.* Vol. I. Daniel Fenton, 1812, p.9.

[12] F. W. Seward, *Reminiscences of a War-Time Statesman and Diplomat.* G. P. Putnam's Sons, 1916, p. 65.

[13] Wayland, *The Elements of Moral Science.* Cooke and Co., 1835, p. x.

[14] *Ibid.*, p. 220.

[15] *Ibid.*, p. 227.

[16] *Ibid.*, p. 228.

[17] *Ibid.*, p. 229.

[18] J. Lewis Diman, "The Late President Wayland," *The Atlantic Monthly,* XXI (1868), p. 69.

[19] Wayland, *The Elements of Moral Science, op. cit.*, p. 12.

[20] *Ibid.*, p. 13.

[21] *Ibid.*, p. 12.

[22] *Ibid.*, p. 13.

[23] *Ibid.*, p. 14.

[24] *Ibid.*, p. 13.

[25] Wayland, "Philosophy of Analogy," in Blau, *American Philosophic Addresses, op. cit.*, p. 348.

[26] *Ibid.*, p. 348.

[27] *Ibid.*

[28] *Ibid.*

[29] *Ibid.*, p. 349.

[30] *Ibid.*

[31] *Ibid.*, p. 353.

[32] *Ibid.*

[33] *Ibid.*, p. 354.

[34] *Ibid.*, p. 362.

[35] Laurens P. Hickok, *Empirical Psychology.* (Revised by Seelye) Ginn, Heath, and Co., 1882, p. 272.

[36] Hickok, *Rational Psychology.* (Rev. ed.) Ivison, Blakeman, Taylor and Co., 1870, p. iii.

[37] Hickok, *Empirical Psychology, op. cit.*, pp. 279-280.

38 *Ibid.*, p. 281.
39 *Ibid.*, p. 290.
40 *Ibid.*, p. 274.
41 *Ibid.*, p. 48.
42 Hickok, *Rational Psychology, op. cit.*, p. 13.
43 *Ibid.*, p. 19.
44 Noah Porter, *The Human Intellect.* C. Scribner and Co., 1868, p. 60.
45 Noah Porter, *Science and Sentiment.* Charles Scribner's Sons, 1882, pp. 130-131.
46 *Ibid.*, p. 130.
47 *Ibid.*
48 *Ibid.*, pp. 306-307.
49 *Ibid.*, p. 306.
50 Porter, *The Human Intellect, op. cit.*, p. 95.
51 *Ibid.*, p. 594.
52 *Ibid.*, p. 662.

CHAPTER 4

The works of Emerson and Thoreau are available in many editions. Brief selections from the lesser transcendentalists may be found in Perry Miller, *The Transcendentalists.* Harvard University Press, 1950. H. S. Commager, *Theodore Parker: Yankee Crusader.* Little, Brown and Co., 1936, is a spirited biography emphasizing Parker's reform activities. J. E. Dirks, *The Critical Theology of Theodore Parker.* Columbia University Press, 1948, stresses the distinction between Parker and Emerson. Ronald V. Wells, *Three Christian Transcendentalists.* Columbia University Press, 1943, studies the philosophies of Marsh, Hedge, and Henry. Ralph L. Rusk, *Life of Ralph Waldo Emerson.* Charles Scribner's Sons, 1949, is a definitive biographical study. There is no adequate treatment of Emerson's philosophy, although an older work, Henry D. Gray, *Emerson; a Statement of New England Transcendentalism . . .* Leland Stanford Junior University, 1917, has some value. Joseph Wood Krutch, *Henry David Thoreau.* Wm. Sloane Associates, 1948, is a good biography. Very little of the work of Henry James the Elder is available; his 1861 address, "The Social Significance of our Institutions," is reprinted in *American Philosophic Addresses.* (Joseph L. Blau, editor) Columbia University Press, 1946. A recent critical study of merit is Frederic H. Young, *The Philosophy of Henry James, Sr.* Bookman Associates, 1951. Odell Shepard, *Pedlar's Progress: the Life of Bronson Alcott.* Little, Brown and Co., 1937, gives sympathetic treatment to its subject.

[1] Gray, *Emerson.* Leland Stanford Junior University, 1917, p. 12n.

[2] Frederic Henry Hedge, in J. W. Cabot, *A Memoir of Ralph Waldo Emerson.* Vol. I. Houghton Mifflin Co.,1888, p. 244.

[3] Parker, "Transcendentalism," in Muelder and Sears, *The Development of American Philosophy.* Houghton Mifflin Co., 1940, p. 138.

[4] Thoreau, *A Week on the Concord and Merrimack Rivers.* Houghton Mifflin Co., 1893, p. 85

[5] Channing, "Likeness to God," in Blau, *American Philosophic Addresses,* p. 568.

[6] S. T. Coleridge, *Aids to Reflection.* (James Marsh, ed.) Chauncey Goodrich, Burlington, Vt., 1829, "Preliminary Essay," p. xli.

[7] Frederic Henry Hedge, *Ways of the Spirit and Other Essays.* Roberts Brothers, 1878, p. 355.

[8] *Ibid.,* p. 356.

[9] C. S. Henry, *Satan as a Moral Philosopher, with Other Essays.* T. Whittaker, 1877, p. 4.

[10] Parker, "Letter to the Progressive Friends, 1853." Quoted in Blau, *American Philosophic Addresses,* p. 660.

[11] Theodore Parker, *West Roxbury Sermons, 1837-1848.* Roberts Brothers, 1892, p. xi.

[12] See her charming sketch "Transcendental Wild Oats," in Clara E. Sears, *Bronson Alcott's Fruitlands.* Houghton Mifflin Co., 1915, pp. 145-174.

[13] Quoted by Stuart P. Sherman, *Essays and Poems of Emerson.* Harcourt, Brace and Co., 1921, p. xx.

[14] Emerson, "Self Reliance," in *Essays, First Series.* Houghton Mifflin Co., 1895, p. 58.

[15] Cabot, *Memoir.* Vol. I, p. 339.

[16] Emerson, "Politics," in *Essays, Second Series.* Houghton Mifflin Co., 1895, p. 204.

[17] "Experience," in *ibid.,* p. 71.

[18] "History," in *Essays, First Series,* p. 10.

[19] Emerson, *Nature.* (Joseph L. Blau, editor) Liberal Arts Press, 1948, p. 4.

[20] Emerson, "American Civilization," in *Miscellanies.* Houghton Mifflin Co., 1895, p. 282.

[21] Emerson, "Culture," in *Conduct of Life*. Houghton Mifflin Co., 1894, p. 128.

[22] Emerson, *Nature*, p. 1.

[23] *Ibid.*, p. 1.

[24] *Ibid.*, p. 5.

[25] *Ibid.*, pp. 6-7.

[26] *Ibid.*, p. 10.

[27] *Ibid.*, p. 12.

[28] *Ibid.*, p. 14.

[29] *Ibid.*, pp. 14-15.

[30] *Ibid.*, p. 18.

[31] *Ibid.*

[32] *Ibid.*, p. 15.

[33] *Ibid.*, p. 19.

[34] Emerson, "Progress of Culture," in *Letters and Social Aims*. Houghton Mifflin Co., 1897, p. 212.

[35] Emerson, *Nature*, p. 19.

[36] *Ibid.*, p. 21.

[37] *Ibid.*, p. 23.

[38] *Ibid.*, p. 25.

[39] *Ibid.*, p. 28.

[40] *Ibid.*, p. 30.

[41] *Ibid.*, p. 32.

[42] *Ibid.*, p. 34.

[43] *Ibid.*, p. 37.

[44] Emerson, "Divinity School Address," in *American Philosophic Addresses*, p. 602.

[45] Emerson, "Man the Reformer," in *Nature, Address and Lectures*. Houghton Mifflin Co., 1895, p. 235.

[46] Emerson, *Uncollected Lectures*. (Clarence Gohdes, ed.) W. E. Rudge, 1932, p. 55.

[47] Thoreau, *Week*, p. 94.

[48] *Ibid.*, p. 68.

[49] *Ibid.*, pp. 81-82.

[50] *Ibid.*, p. 82.

[51] *Ibid.*, pp. 94-95.

[52] Thoreau, "Civil Disobedience," *Miscellanies*. Houghton Mifflin Co., 1893, p. 149.

[53] *Ibid.*, p. 131.

[54] *Ibid.*, p. 132.

[55] *Ibid.,* p. 134.

[56] *Ibid.*

[57] *Ibid.*

[58] *Ibid.,* p. 149.

[59] *Ibid.,* p. 137.

[60] *Ibid.,* p. 147.

[61] *Ibid.,* p. 170.

[62] *Collected Poems of Henry Thoreau.* (Carl Bode, ed.) Packard and Co., 1943, p. 10.

[63] *Ibid.,* p. 133.

[64] *Ibid.,* pp. 198-199.

[65] Thoreau, *Walden; or Life in the Woods.* Houghton Mifflin Co., 1893, p. 211.

[66] *Ibid.,* pp. 211-212.

[67] *Ibid.,* p. 155.

[68] *Ibid.,* p. 26.

[69] Thoreau, *Week,* p. 84.

[70] *Ibid.,* p. 91.

[71] *Ibid.,* p. 96.

[72] *Ibid.*

[73] *Ibid.,* p. 92.

[74] Emerson, "Divinity School Address," in *American Philosophic Addresses,* p. 601.

[75] Wilkinson to Henry James, Sr., May 20, 1879. In Ralph Barton Perry, *The Thought and Character of William James.* Vol. I. Little, Brown and Co., 1936, p. 26.

[76] James, *Christianity the Logic of Creation.* D. Appleton & Co., 1857, p. 133.

[77] James, *Society the Redeemed Form of Man.* Houghton, Osgood, and Co., 1879, p. 185.

[78] *The Literary Remains of Henry James.* (William James, ed.) James R. Osgood and Co., 1885, p. 25n.

[79] James, *The Social Significance of Our Institutions.* Ticknor and Fields, 1861, p. 44.

[80] *Ibid.,* p. 44.

[81] *Ibid.,* pp. 44-45.

[82] *Ibid.,* p. 45.

[83] James, *Lectures and Miscellanies.* Redfield, 1852, p. 38.

[84] *Ibid.,* p. 4.

[85] *Ibid.,* p. 18.

[86] *Ibid.*, p. 9.

[87] *Ibid.*, p. 15.

[88] *Ibid.*, p. 11.

[89] *Ibid.*, p. 44.

[90] *Ibid.*, p. 11.

CHAPTER 5

Stow Persons has edited an illuminating series of lectures under the title *Evolutionary Thought in America*. Yale University Press, 1950. Richard Hofstadter, *Social Darwinism in American Thought, 1860-1915*. University of Pennsylvania Press, 1944, is an excellent historical survey. Philip P. Wiener, *Evolution and the Founders of Pragmatism*. Harvard University Press, 1949, makes available a series of careful studies conducted by the author over a period of years. Fiske is a relatively neglected figure; one of Wiener's essays considers his cosmic philosophy as a philosophy of history. An earlier account that shows keen insight into Fiske's thought was written by Josiah Royce; it can be found as an introduction to the 1903 edition of Fiske's *Outlines of Cosmic Philosophy*. Wright has been discussed in Wiener's book. His *Letters*, edited by James B. Thayer (privately printed, 1878), and *Philosophical Discussions*, edited by Charles E. Norton (Henry Holt and Co., 1877), are both rewarding. The latter includes the complete text of Wright's "Evolution of Self-Consciousness." Stow Persons, *Free Religion — An American Faith*. Yale University Press, 1947, has considerable material on Abbot; Abbot's "The Genius of Christianity and of Free Religion" is included in *American Philosophic Addresses*. (Joseph Blau, editor) Columbia University Press, 1946. Abbot's *Scientific Theism*. Little, Brown and Co., 1885, is the most readable account of his philosophy, but his thought can not be mastered without study of his *Syllogistic Philosophy*. Little Brown and Co., 1906.

[1] Alexander Winchell, *Walks and Talks in the Geological Field*. Chautauqua Press, 1886, p.33.

[2] *Ibid.*, p. 308.

[3] *Ibid.*, p. 311.

[4] James McCosh, *The Religious Aspect of Evolution*. G. P. Putnam's Sons, 1888, p. x.

[5] *Ibid.*, pp. x-xi.

[6] Charles Hodge, *What is Darwinism?* Scribner, Armstrong and Co., 1874, p. 74.

[7] Minot J. Savage, *The Irrespressible Conflict Between Two World-Theories.* Arena Publishing Co., 1892.

[8] *Ibid.*, p. 20.

[9] George Harris, *Moral Evolution.* Houghton Mifflin Co., 1896, p. 3.

[10] *Ibid.*, p. 7.

[11] John Fiske, *Darwinism, and Other Essays.* Houghton Mifflin Co., 1885, p. 144.

[12] *Ibid.*, p. 146.

[13] John Fiske, *Outlines of Cosmic Philosophy.* Vol. I. Houghton Mifflin Co., 1903, p. 268.

[14] *Ibid.*, p. xiv.

[15] *Ibid.*

[16] John Fiske, *The Idea of God as Affected by Modern Knowledge.* Houghton Mifflin Co., 1885, p. 109.

[17] *Outlines of Cosmic Philosophy*, Vol. IV, p. 257.

[18] *The Idea of God*, p. 110.

[19] *Ibid.*

[20] *Outlines of Cosmic Philosophy*, Vol. II, p. 338.

[21] *Ibid.*, Vol. II, p. 334-335.

[22] *Letters of Chauncey Wright.* (J. B. Thayer, editor)Privately printed, 1878, p. 227.

[23] Chauncey Wright, *Philosophical Discussions.* Henry Holt and Co., 1877, pp. 237, 239.

[24] *Ibid.*, p. 237.

[25] *Ibid.*, p. 248.

[26] *Ibid.*, p. 56.

[27] William James, *Collected Essays and Reviews.* Longmans, Green and Co., 1920, pp. 23-24.

[28] Wright, *Letters*, p. 133.

[29] *Ibid.*, p. 248.

[30] Wright, *Philosophical Discussions*, p. 201.

[31] *Ibid.*, p. 219.

[32] *Ibid.*, p. 223.

[33] *Ibid.*

[34] *Ibid.*, p. 217.

[35] *Ibid.*, pp. 251-252.

[36] *Ibid.*, p. 255.

[37] *Ibid.*, p. 257.
[38] Abbot, *The Syllogistic Philosophy*. Vol. I. Little, Brown and Co., 1906, p.ix.
[39] *Ibid.*, Vol. II, p. 234.
[40] *Ibid.*, Vol. I, p. vii.
[41] *Ibid.*
[42] *Ibid.*
[43] *Ibid.*, Vol. II, p. 286.
[44] *Ibid.*, Vol. II. p. 104.
[45] *Ibid.*, Vol. I, p. viii.
[46] *Ibid.*
[47] *Ibid.*
[48] *Ibid.*, Vol. I, p. 2.
[49] *Ibid.*
[50] *Ibid.*, Vol. I, p. 6.
[51] *Ibid.*, Vol. I, p. 8.
[52] *Ibid.*, Vol. I, p. 60.
[53] *Ibid.*, Vol. I, p. 34.
[54] *Ibid.*, Vol. I, p. 70.
[55] *Ibid.*, Vol. I, p. 175.
[56] *Ibid.*
[57] *Ibid.*, Vol. II, p. 148.
[58] *Ibid.*, Vol. II, p. 297.
[59] *Ibid.*
[60] *Ibid.*, Vol. II, pp. 297-298.
[61] *Ibid.*, Vol. II, p. 287.

CHAPTER 6

J. H. Muirhead, *The Platonic Tradition in Anglo-Saxon Philosophy*. G. Allen and Unwin, 1931, despite its title, contains in Part III an interesting treatment of "Idealism in America," with particular emphasis upon the thought of Josiah Royce. G. Watts Cunningham, *The Idealistic Argument in Recent British and American Philosophy*. The Century Co., 1933, includes an excellent discussion of the argument for metaphysical idealism in Royce, Creighton, Howison and Bowne. *Contemporary Idealism in America*. (Clifford Barrett, editor) The Macmillan Co., 1932, is a series of studies in various aspects of idealism as a philosophy, dedicated to the memory of Josiah Royce. H. G. Townsend, *Philosophical Ideas in the United States*. The American Book Co., 1934, has good statements on Creighton and Royce. Philosophic autobiographies of then-living American idealists were included in G. P. Adams and W. P. Montague, *Contemporary American Philosophy*. The Macmillan Co., 1930. Individual studies of the major idealists are numerous; of recent additions, special mention should be made of John E. Smith, *Royce's Social Infinite*. Liberal Arts Press, 1950, which analyzes carefully the theory of community of Royce's later works; Marc E. Jones, *George Sylvester Morris: His Philosophic Career and Theistic Idealism*. David McKay Co., 1948, which includes as an appendix some of the less readily available of Morris' articles; and Evelyn Shirk, *Adventurous Idealism*. University of Michigan Press, 1952, a pioneering reconstruction of the philosophy of Alfred H. Lloyd.

[1] Emerson, *Nature*. (J. Blau, editor) Liberal Arts Press, 1948, p. 34.

[2] G. H. Howison, *The Limits of Evolution and other Essays*. The Macmillan Co., 1901, pp. xiii-xiv.

[3] *Ibid.*, p. xv.

[4] Felix Adler, *The Reconstruction of the Spiritual Ideal*. D. Appleton and Co., 1924, pp. 30-31.

[5] *Ibid.*, p. 31.

[6] *Ibid.*

[7] Felix Adler, *An Ethical Philosophy of Life*. D. Appleton and Co., 1918, p. 116.

[8] *Ibid.*, p. 117.

[9] Lloyd, *Dynamic Idealism*. A. C. McClurg and Co., 1898, p. 19.

[10] *Ibid.*, p. 21.

[11] *Ibid.*, p. 24.

[12] *Ibid.*, p. 45.

[13] Edgar A. Singer, Jr., "Thoughts on a Translation of Schelling's *Weltalter*," *The Review of Religion*. VIII (1943), p. 53.

[14] C. I. Lewis, *Mind and the World-Order*. Charles Scribner's Sons, 1929, p. 25.

[15] *Ibid.*, p. 30.

[16] F. J. E. Woodbridge, *The Realm of Mind*. Columbia University Press, 1926, p. 1.

[17] *Ibid.*, p. 37.

[18] *Ibid.*, p. vi.

[19] W. E. Hocking, *Types of Philosophy*. Charles Scribner's Sons, 1929, p. 437.

[20] *Ibid.*, p. 440.

[21] Hocking, *The Self; Its Body and Freedom*. Yale University Press, 1928, p. 136.

[22] Borden Parker Bowne, *Metaphysics*. Boston University Press, 1943, p. 44.

[23] *Ibid.*, p. 64.

[24] *Ibid.*, p. 65.

[25] Quoted in Francis J. McConnell, *Borden Parker Bowne*. The Abingdon Press, 1929, pp. 118-119.

[26] Bowne, *Metaphysics*. Harper and Brothers, 1882, p. 100.

[27] *Ibid.*, p. 114.

[28] *Ibid.*, p. 126.

[29] *Ibid.*, p. 169.

[30] *Metaphysics*, 1943 edition, p. 294.

[31] The familiar passage in Kant's *Critique of Pure Reason*, "Transcendental Doctrine of Method," Chapter II, Section II, lists only the first three of these questions. The fourth, leading to philosophical anthropology, is added in the *Handbook* to Kant's Lectures on Logic.

[32] Josiah Royce, *The Religious Aspect of Philosophy*. Houghton Mifflin Co., 1885, p. 13.

[33] *Ibid.*, p. 14.

[34] *Ibid.*, p. 149.

[35] *Ibid.*, p. 148.

[36] *Ibid.*, p. 169.

[37] *Ibid.*, p. 170.

[38] *Ibid.*, pp. 215-218.

[39] *Ibid.*, p. 385.

[40] *Ibid.*, p. 372.

[41] *Ibid.*, p. 375.

[42] *Ibid.*

[43] *Ibid.*, p. 376.

[44] Josiah Royce, *The Spirit of Modern Philosophy*. Houghton Mifflin Co., 1892, p. 368.

[45] *Ibid.*

[46] *Ibid.*, p. 372.

[47] *Ibid.*, p. 373.

[48] Josiah Royce, et. al., *The Conception of God*. The Macmillan Co., 1898, p. 43.

[49] Josiah Royce, *The World and the Individual.* Vol. I. The Macmillan Co., 1912, p. 339.

[50] *Ibid.*, p. 400.

[51] Josiah Royce, *The Philosophy of Loyalty.* The Macmillan Co., 1908, especially pp. 101-146.

[52] Josiah Royce, *War and Insurance.* The Macmillan Co., 1914, p. 51.

[53] James Edwin Creighton, *Studies in Speculative Philosophy.* The Macmillan Co., 1925, p. 13. Used with permission of The Macmillan Co.

[54] *Ibid.*

[55] Jacob G. Schurman, "Prefatory Note," *The Philosophical Review.* I (1892), p. 5.

[56] Creighton, *Studies in Speculative Philosophy.* The Macmillan Co., 1925, p. 259.

[57] *Ibid.*, p. 258.

[58] *Ibid.*

[59] *Ibid.*, pp. 259-260.

[60] *Ibid.*, pp. 260-261.

[61] *Ibid.*, p. 262.

[62] *Ibid.*, p. 114.

[63] *Ibid.*, p. 266.

[64] *Ibid.*, p. 267.

[65] *Ibid.*, p. 115.

[66] *Ibid.*

[67] *Ibid.*, p. 114.

[68] *Ibid.*, p. 115.

[69] *Ibid.*

[70] *Ibid.*, p. 270.

[71] *Ibid.*, p. 46.

[72] *Ibid.*, p. 51.

[73] *Ibid.*, pp. 49-50

[74] *Ibid.*, p. 61.

[75] *Ibid.*, p. 65.

[76] *Ibid.*, p. 70.

[77] *Ibid.*, p. 6.

[78] *Ibid.*

[79] *Ibid.*, p. 7.

[80] *Ibid.*, p. 14.

[81] *Ibid.*, p. 116.

[82] *Ibid.*, p. 117.

[83] *Ibid.*, p. 118.

374 Footnotes and Suggested Reading

CHAPTER 7

There have been a number of premature attempts to write definitive accounts of pragmatism; the most useful is John Dewey's historical article "The Development of American Pragmatism," originally published as a supplement to *Studies in the History of Ideas*, by the Department of Philosophy of Columbia University. Vol. II. Columbia University Press, 1925. This article was reprinted in Dewey's *Philosophy and Civilization*. Minton, Balch and Co., 1931. Philip P. Wiener, *Evolution and the Founders of Pragmatism*. Harvard University Press, 1949, has added greatly to our detailed knowledge of the background of pragmatism, especially in Peirce. Justus Buchler, *Charles Peirce's Empiricism*. Harcourt, Brace and Co., 1939, is an excellent study of the methodological side of Peirce's thoughts; Thomas A. Goudge, *The Thought of C. S. Peirce*. University of Toronto Press, 1950, is a sensitive treatment of the conflict in Peirce's thought between scientific and transcendental motivations. Some of Peirce's manuscripts, edited by C. Hartshorne and P. Weiss, have been published in six volumes under the title *Collected Papers*. Harvard University Press, 1931-35. *Chance, Love and Logic*. (M. R. Cohen, editor) Harcourt, Brace and Co., New York, 1923, and *The Philosophy of Peirce: Selected Writings*. (Justus Buchler, editor) Harcourt, Brace and Co., 1940, contain useful selections. Ralph Barton Perry, *The Thought and Character of William James*. 2 volumes, Little, Brown and Co., 1935, is a monumental study which should be read by everyone interested in James. All of James' works are readily available. The best analytic studies of the philosophy of Mead are the introductions to his works, *Mind, Self and Society*. (C. W. Morris, editor) University of Chicago Press, 1934, and *The Philosophy of the Present*. (A. E. Murphy, editor) Open Court Publishing Co., 1932. John Dewey, et al., *Creative Intelligence*. Henry Holt and Co., 1917, brings together many of Dewey's colleagues and former students at the University of Chicago in a collective (and not merely aggregative), statement of instrumentalism.

[1] H. Heath Bawden, *The Principles of Pragmatism*. Houghton Mifflin Co., 1910, pp. 4-5.

[2] Joseph Le Conte, *Evolution and its Relation to Religious Thought*. D. Appleton and Co., 1888, p. 259.

[3] This was the subtitle of James' book, *Pragmatism*.

[4] Addison W. Moore, *Pragmatism and its Critics.* University of Chicago Press, 1910, p. 3.

[5] Quoted in Peirce, *Chance, Love and Logic.* (M. R. Cohen, editor) Harcourt, Brace and Co., 1923, p. xixn.

[6] *Ibid.*

[7] Moore, *op.cit.,* p. 77.

[8] Bawden, *op. cit.,* p. 198.

[9] Quoted in *ibid.,* p. 258.

[10] John Dewey, et al., *op. cit.,* p. 47.

[11] *Ibid.,* p. 65.

[12] John Dewey, *Experience and Education.* 1938, p. 8.

[13] *Ibid.,* p. 16.

[14] *Holmes-Pollock Letters.* Vol. I. (Mark DeWolfe Howe, editor) Harvard University Press, 1941, p. 138.

[15] O. W. Holmes, Jr., *The Common Law.* Little, Brown and Co., 1881, p. 1.

[16] *Ibid.,* p. 149.

[17] O. W. Holmes, Jr., *Collected Legal Papers.* Harcourt, Brace and Howe, 1920, p. 167.

[18] Roscoe Pound, *The Spirit of the Common Law.* Marshall Jones Co., 1921, p. 176.

[19] Arthur F. Bentley, *The Process of Government.* Privately printed, 1935.

[20] *Ibid.,* p. 189.

[21] Ralph Barton Perry, *The Thought and Character of William James.* Vol. II. Little, Brown and Co., 1936, p. 419.

[22] Justus Buchler, ed., *The Philosophy of Peirce: Selected Writings.* Harcourt, Brace and Co., 1940, p. 253.

[23] *Ibid.,* p. 321.

[24] *Ibid.,* p. 129.

[25] *Ibid.,* pp. 129-130.

[26] *Ibid.,* p. 350.

[27] *Ibid.,* p. 31.

[28] *Ibid.,* p. 290.

[29] *Ibid.,* p. 252.

[30] *Ibid.,* p. 261.

[31] *Ibid.*

[32] *Ibid.,* p. 31.

[33] *Ibid.,* p. 30.

[34] *Ibid.,* p. 8.

[35] *Ibid.*, p. 9.

[36] *Ibid.*, p. 10.

[37] *Ibid.*

[38] *Ibid.*, p. 11.

[39] *Ibid.*, p. 13.

[40] *Ibid.*, p. 14.

[41] *Ibid.*, p. 188.

[42] *Ibid.*, p. 304.

[43] Peirce, *Collected Papers.* Vol. II. Harvard University Press, 1931-35, p. 385 (2.640).

[44] *Ibid.*, p. 153 (2.270).

[45] William James, *Pragmatism . . . with Four Related Essays selected from The Meaning of Truth.* Longmans, Green and Co., 1943, p. 310.

[46] *Ibid.*

[47] *Ibid.*, p. 311.

[48] William James, *Philosophical Conceptions and Practical Results.* University of California, 1898, p. 7.

[49] James, *Pragmatism*, p. 68.

[50] *Ibid.*, pp. 54-55.

[51] *Ibid.*, p. 201.

[52] *Ibid.*

[53] *Ibid.*, p. 204.

[54] *Ibid.*, p. 200.

[55] *Ibid.*, p. 207.

[56] *Ibid.*, p. 215.

[57] *Ibid.*, p. 222.

[58] Royce, *The Philosophy of Loyalty.* The Macmillan Co., 1908, p. 332.

[59] James, *Pragmatism*, p. 7.

[60] James, *Essays on Faith and Morals.* Longmans, Green and Co., 1943, p. 103.

[61] Quoted in Perry, *op. cit.*, p. 212.

[62] *Ibid.*, Vol. I, p. 817.

[63] James, *A Pluralistic Universe.* Longmans, Green and Co., 1943, p. 322.

[64] *Ibid.*, p. 279.

[65] *Ibid.*, p. 323-324.

[66] *Ibid.*, p. 325.

[67] *Ibid.*, p. 324.

[68] *Ibid.*

[69] *Ibid.*, p. 326.

[70] Mead, *Mind, Self and Society*. The University of Chicago Press, 1934, p. 130.

[71] *Ibid.*, p. xxi n.

[72] *Ibid.*, p. 386.

[73] Mead, *The Philosophy of the Act*. The University of Chicago Press, 1938, p. xiii n.

[74] Mead, *Mind, Self and Society*, p. 88.

[75] *Ibid.*, p. 89.

[76] *Ibid.*

[77] *Ibid.*, p. 90.

[78] Mead, *The Philosophy of the Present*. Open Court Publishing Co., 1932, p. 30.

[79] *Ibid.*, p. 23.

[80] *Ibid.*, p. 146.

[81] *Ibid.*, p. 79.

[82] *Ibid.*, p. 85.

[83] *Ibid.*, p. 90.

CHAPTER 8

William Pepperell Montague, "The Story of American Realism," is included in *The Ways of Things: A Philosophy of Knowledge, Nature, and Value*. Prentice-Hall, Inc., 1940, pp. 230-261. Arthur O. Lovejoy, *The Revolt Against Dualism*. Open Court Publishing Co., 1930, offers many insights into the varieties of American realism as well as a clear statement of Lovejoy's position. *Contemporary American Philosophy*. (G. P. Adams and W. P. Montague, editors) The Macmillan Co., 1930, contains personal statements by some of the realists. Philosophic journals between 1910 and 1925 are filled with polemical articles dealing with one or another aspect of realism; these may be consulted profitably only by the most dogged of students.

[1] W. P. Montague, *The Ways of Things*. Prentice-Hall, Inc., 1940, p. 237.

[2] *Ibid.*, p. 238.

[3] *Ibid.*, p. 246.

[4] *Ibid.*, p. 247.

[5] *The New Realism*. The Macmillan Co., 1912, pp. 482-483.

[6] *Ibid.*, pp. 480-481.

7 *Ibid.*, p. 481.

8 *Essays in Critical Realism.* The Macmillan Co., 1920, p. 98.

9 *Ibid.*, p. 110.

10 Montague, *op. cit.*, p. 260.

11 Adams and Montague, *Contemporary American Philosophy.* Vol. II. The Macmillan Co., 1930, p. 188. Used with permission of the Macmillan Co. and George Allen Unwin Ltd., London.

12 *Ibid.*, p. 191.

13 Perry, *Present Philosophical Tendencies.* Longmans, Green and Co., 1925, p. 131.

14 Adams and Montague, *op. cit.*, p. 192.

15 Perry, *op. cit.*, p. 155.

16 *Ibid.*, pp. 126-128.

17 *Ibid.*, p. 218.

18 *Ibid.*, p. 221.

19 *Ibid.*, p. 273.

20 *Ibid.*, pp. 273-275.

21 *Ibid.*, p. 277.

22 *Ibid.*, p. 304.

23 *Ibid.*

24 *Ibid.*, p. 311.

25 *Ibid.*, p. 312.

26 *Ibid.*, p. 313.

27 Adams and Montague, *op. cit.*, p. 203.

28 *Ibid.*

29 *Ibid.*, p. 208.

30 Perry, *The Moral Economy.* Charles Scribner's Sons, 1909, p. 10.

31 *Ibid.*, p. 13.

32 *Ibid.*, p. 14.

33 Perry, *Present Philosophical Tendencies*, p. 334.

34 Perry, *The Moral Economy*, p. 54.

35 *Ibid.*, p. 2.

36 *Ibid.*, p. 73.

37 Perry, *Puritanism and Democracy.* The Vanguard Press, 1944, p. 627.

38 *Ibid.*, p. 650.

39 *Ibid.*, p. 631.

40 Perry, *One World in the Making.* A. A. Wyn, 1945, p. 55.

41 *Ibid.*, p. 66.

42 R. W. Sellars, *Critical Realism.* Rand, McNally and Co., 1916, p. 5.

43 R. W. Sellars, *The Philosophy of Physical Realism.* The Macmillan Co. 1932, p. v. Used with permission of The Macmillan Co.

44 Sellars, *Critical Realism*, p. 12.

45 Sellars, *The Philosophy of Physical Realism*, p. 64.

46 *Ibid.*, p. 69.

47 *Ibid.*, p. 87.

48 *Ibid.*

49 *Ibid.*, p. 91.

50 *Ibid.*, p. 3.

51 *Ibid.*

52 *Ibid.*, p. 6.

53 *Ibid.*, p. 276.

54 Adams and Montague, *op. cit.*, p. 276.

55 *Ibid.*, p. 281.

56 *Ibid.*, p. 282.

57 Sellars, *The Philosophy of Physical Realism*, p. 444.

58 *Ibid.*, p. 445.

59 Adams and Montague, *op. cit.*, p. 283.

60 Sellars, *The Philosophy of Physical Realism*, p. 462.

61 *Ibid.*, p. 468.

62 W. M. Urban, *The Intelligible World. Metaphysics and Value.* G. Allen and Unwin, 1929, p. 1.

63 Adams and Montague, *op. cit.*, pp. 373, 374.

64 *Ibid.*, p. 362.

65 *Ibid.*

66 *Ibid.*

67 *Ibid.*, p. 363.

68 *Ibid.*, p. 364.

69 *Ibid.*, p. 366.

70 *Ibid.*, p. 367.

71 *Ibid.*, p. 371.

72 *Ibid.*, p. 372.

73 *Ibid.*, p. 374.

74 *Ibid.*

75 *Ibid.*

76 *Ibid.*, p. 375.

77 Urban, *Beyond Realism and Idealism*. G. Allen and Unwin, 1949, p. 7.

78 *Ibid.*, p. 25.

79 *Ibid.*, p. 30.

80 *Ibid.*, p. 237.

81 *Ibid.*, p. 236.

[82] *Ibid.*, p. 233.

[83] *Ibid.*, p. 236.

CHAPTER 9

There has been no systematic attempt to expound the history of the naturalistic temper in recent American thought. Perhaps naturalism is still too much alive to qualify for an obituary. The collective volume, *Naturalism and the Human Spirit*. (Yervant H. Krikorian, editor) Columbia University Press, 1944, includes articles by many of the students of Dewey and Cohen as well as a reprinting of one of Dewey's polemical articles. There are some satisfactory studies of special aspects of the thought of Santayana; e.g., Milton Munitz, *The Moral Philosophy of Santayana*. Columbia University Press, 1939. Paul A. Schilpp has edited *The Philosophy of George Santayana*. Northwestern University, 1940, and *The Philosophy of John Dewey*. Northwestern University, 1939, in The Library of Living Philosophers. Jerome Nathanson's *John Dewey*. Charles Scribner's Sons, 1951, is a competent non-technical exposition of the major themes of Dewey's thought. An excellent technical discussion of Dewey's instrumentalism is to be found in Morton G. White, *The Origin of Dewey's Instrumentalism*. Columbia University Pres, 1943. There are critical studies of particular aspects of Cohen's thought in *Freedom and Reason. Studies . . . in Memory of Morris Raphael Cohen*. (S. W. Baron, E. Nagel and K. Pinson, editors) The Conference on Jewish Relations, 1951. On the whole, however, the best introduction to the varieties of naturalism is to read the works of Santayana, especially *The Life of Reason*, of Cohen, especially *Reason and Nature*, and of Dewey, especially *Experience and Nature*.

[1] Yervant H. Krikorian, editor, *Naturalism and the Human Spirit*. Columbia University Press, 1944, p. 19n.

[2] *Ibid.*, p. 3.

[3] See C. Judson Herrick, *George Ellett Coghill, Naturalist and Philosopher*. The University of Chicago Press, 1949, *passim*.

[4] John Dewey, *Experience and Nature*. Open Court Publishing Co., 1925, p. 74.

[5] Krikorian, *op. cit.*, p. 232.

[6] *Ibid.,* p. 270.

[7] George Santayana, *The Middle Span.* Charles Scribner's Sons, 1945, p. 6.

[8] *Ibid.,* p. 6.

[9] *Ibid.,* p. 9.

[10] *Ibid.,* p. 35.

[11] George Santayana, *Dialogues in Limbo.* Charles Scribner's Sons, 1926, p. 37.

[12] *Ibid.,* p. 38.

[13] Emerson, *Nature.* (J. Blau, editor) Liberal Arts Press, 1948, p. 23.

[14] Santayana, *op. cit.,* p. 44.

[15] Santayana, *Scepticism and Animal Faith.* Charles Scribner's Sons, 1923, p. x.

[16] *Ibid.,* p. v.

[17] Santayana, *The Life of Reason: Reason in Science.* Charles Scribner's Sons, 1933, p. 36.

[18] *Ibid.,* p. 307.

[19] Santayana, *The Life of Reason: Reason in Common Sense.* Charles Scribner's Sons, 1922, p. 1.

[20] *Ibid.,* p. 2.

[21] *Ibid.,* p. 5.

[22] *Ibid.,* p. 2.

[23] Santayana, *Reason in Science,* p. 299.

[24] *Ibid.,* p. 211.

[25] *Ibid.,* p. 212.

[26] *Ibid.,* p. 240.

[27] *Ibid.,* p. 266.

[28] *Ibid.,* p. 298.

[29] Adams and Montague, *Contemporary American Philosophy.* Vol II. The Macmillan Co., 1930, p. 244.

[30] *Ibid.,* p. 245.

[31] Santayana, *The Genteel Tradition.* Charles Scribner's Sons, 1931, p. 30.

[32] *Ibid.,* p. 30.

[33] *Ibid.,* p. 32.

[34] *Ibid.*

[35] Santayana, *The Realm of Spirit.* Charles Scribner's Sons, 1940, p. 2ʊ.

[36] Santayana, *Realms of Being,* I. Triton Edition, Charles Scribner's Sons, 1937, p. xiv.

[37] Santayana, *The Realm of Spirit,* p. 120.

[38] *Ibid.*, p. 158.

[39] *Ibid.*, p. 159.

[40] *Ibid.*

[41] *Ibid.*

[42] *Ibid.*

[43] *Ibid.*, p. 274.

[44] *The Humanist*, XI (1951), p. 199. This statement was made by Santayana on February 9, 1951, in reply to a questionnaire addressed to him by Warren Allen Smith.

[45] Morris R. Cohen, *The Faith of a Liberal*. Henry Holt and Co., 1946, p. 3.

[46] *Ibid.*, p. 366.

[47] *Ibid.*, p. 367.

[48] *Ibid.*

[49] *Ibid.*

[50] Cohen, *Reason and Nature*. Harcourt, Brace and Co., 1931, p. 78.

[51] *Ibid.*, p. 79.

[52] *Ibid.*, p. 10.

[53] *Ibid.*

[54] *Ibid.*, p. 5.

[55] *Ibid.*, p. 6.

[56] *Ibid.*, p. 164.

[57] *Ibid.*, p. 18.

[58] *Ibid.*, p. 19.

[59] *Ibid.*, p. 157.

[60] *Ibid.*

[61] *Ibid.*

[62] Cohen, *A Preface to Logic*. Henry Holt and Co., 1944, p. 100.

[63] Cohen, *Reason and Nature*, p. 155.

[64] *Ibid.*

[65] *Ibid.*, p. 156.

[66] *Ibid.*

[67] *Ibid.*

[68] *Ibid.*, p. 150.

[69] *Ibid.*, p. 153.

[70] *Ibid.*, p. 152.

[71] *Ibid.*, p. 165.

[72] *Ibid.*, p. 166.

[73] *Ibid.*, p. 429.

74 *Ibid.*, pp. 437-438.

75 *Ibid.*, pp. 438-439.

76 *Ibid.*, pp. 152-153.

77 John Dewey, *Experience and Nature.* Open Court Publishing Co.. 1925, p. 11.

78 *Ibid.*, p.17.

79 *Ibid.*, p. 21.

80 Dewey, *How We Think.* D. C. Heath and Co., 1933, pp. 41-42.

81 *Ibid.*, pp. 48-49.

82 Dewey, *How We Think.* D. C. Heath and Co., 1910, p. 108.

83 Dewey, *Reconstruction in Philosophy.* Henry Holt and Co., 1920, p. 156.

84 *Ibid.*, p. 160.

85 Dewey, *Experience and Nature*, p. 69.

86 *Ibid.*

87 *Ibid.*, p. 71.

88 *Ibid.*, p. 47.

89 *Ibid.*

90 *Ibid.*, pp. 47-48.

91 *Ibid.*, p. 50.

92 *Ibid.*

93 *Ibid.*, p. 35.

94 *Ibid.*, p. 67.

95 *Ibid.*, pp. 67-68.

96 Dewey, *Human Nature and Conduct.* Modern Library, 1930, p. 295.

97 *Ibid.*

98 *Ibid.*, p. 296.

99 *Ibid.*

100 *Ibid.*, p. 298.

101 *Ibid.*, p. 302.

102 Dewey and Tufts, *Ethics.* Rev. ed., Henry Holt and Co., 1932, p. 366.

103 *Intelligence in the Modern World; John Dewey's Philosophy.* (J. Ratner, editor) Modern Library Giant, 1939, p. 401.

104 Dewey, *A Common Faith.* Yale University Press, 1934, p. 26.

105 *Ibid.*, p. 14.

106 *Ibid.*, p. 51.

107 *Ibid.*, p. 43.

INDEX

A

Abbot, Francis Ellingwood, 159, 165, 175-186, 218, 232, 322
  "The Conditioned and the Unconditioned," 176
  "The Philosophy of Space and Time," 176
  The Syllogistic Philosophy, 179
Abduction, 251
Abolition, 85
Abolitionism, 120
Abolitionists, 137
Absolute, Hegelian, 191
Absolute Being, 215
Absolute Experience, 214
Absolute Idea, 214
Absolute Idealism, 199
Absolute Mind, 212
Absolute moral person, 210
Absolute Person, 207, 215
Absolute Self, 213
Absolute Truth, 212
Absolute Will, 211
Absolutism, Royce's, 260
Acquired characteristics, inheritance of, 152
Act:
  Mead's theory of, 266
  stages of, 266
  universality of, 268
"Act Establishing Religious Freedom," 46, 54-55
Action, mental, 287
Active powers, in matter, 29
Activity, in education, 237
Adam, federal head of human race, 22
Adams, Jasper, *The Elements of Moral Philosophy*, 86
Adams, John, 42, 43, 44, 45, 56, 72, 75
  Defense of the Constitutions of Government of the United States, 75

Adams, John *(cont.)*
  Discourses on Davila, 75
  Letters to John Taylor of Caroline, 75
Adams, Samuel, 43
Adjustment, 253
Adler, Felix, 193, 194
Affections, gracious, 230
Agassiz, Louis, 167
Agency:
  material, 31, 32
  spiritual, 31, 32
Agnosticism, 182
"Agrarian justice," Paine's view of, 61-63
Agrarianism, 54, 61
Agreeable leadings, 255
Aitkin, Robert, 56
Alcott, A. Bronson, 120, 131, 132, 142, 164, 190
Alcott, Louisa May, 120
American life, spiritual interpretation of, 150
American Philosophical Association, 218, 219, 225, 226, 335
American Philosophic Society, 46
Ames, Fisher, 75, 76
  "On the Dangers of American Liberty," 76
Analogy:
  science of, 90
  the science of sciences, 91
Anarchism, in Thoreau, 134, 137, 141
Andover Theological Seminary, 83
Appearance, reality and, 112, 316
Aristocracy, 60
  natural vs. hereditary, 53
Aristotle, 184, 191, 322, 323, 328, 336
Associationism, 105
Authoritarianism, foe of rationalism, 337

385

Church:
Invisible, 4
Visible, 4
Church and State, separation of, 55
Church Covenant, 4
Churches:
Christianity of, 141
Paine's attack on, 64
Cincinnati, Society of, 53
Cities, Jefferson's scorn of, 54
Civil rights, 49
Clarke, James Freeman, 110
Clarke, Samuel, 42
Coghill, George Ellett, 319
Cohen, Morris Raphael, 191, 321, 322, *334-343*, 344, 347, 348, 355
"Vision and Technique in Philosophy," 335
Colden, Cadwallader, 16, 17, *27-35*, 69, 314
An Explication of the First Causes of Action in Matter, 29
"An Introduction to Phylosophy," 30
"First Principles of Morality," 32
hedonistic ethics, 32-34
History of the Five Indian Nations, 29
The Principles of Action in Matter, 29
Coleridge, Samuel Taylor, 92, 102, 110, 115, 116, 117, 120, 121, 154
Aids to Reflection, 115
Columbia Law School, 238
Columbia University, 12
Commerce, 61
Common sense:
in Hickok, 100
inverted by culture, 129
Communication, 174, 263, 267, 308
social, 265
Community, 198, 224, 250, 266, 272
international, 216-217
of interests, 290
of interpretation, 216, 217
of minds, 192
of scientists, 353
Royce's theory of, 215
theory of, 227
Communities, Comtean, 155
Compulsion, 148

Comte Auguste, 155, 161, 169
Positive Philosophy, 161
Concord Summer School of Philosophy, 164, 190, 191
Concurrent majorities, 78
Conditioned, Hamilton's law of, 175
Condorcet, Jean Antoine Nicholas de, 160
Conduct, relation to belief, 244
Congregationalism, 3
Conscience, 48, 68
in Thoreau, 132
Puritan, 131
Transcendental, 131
world-wide, 293
Consciousness, 195, 227, 264
animal, 172
elementary forms of, 173
human, 172
reflective use of, 173
stream of, 200, 261
Consent, 60
doctrine of, 45
of the governed, 137
Consequences, particular, 254
Consistency, 123
Constitution of the United States, 74, 180
Content, of mind, 287
Contingency, 340, 347, 349
Control, 266
Cooper, Thomas, 71
Cooperation, 224, 225, 226, 290, 352
Cope, Edward Drinker, 322
Copernican astronomy, 9
Cornell University, 219, 220
Correspondence, doctrine of, in Emerson, 127
Cosmic Theism, 164, 186
Cotton, John, 5, 6
Cousin, Victor, 92, 118
Covenant Theology, 2
Creation, 156
doubleness of, 144
in Henry James, 143
philosophical, in Henry James, 147
plan of, 5
the true revelation, 64
Creativity, in nature, 300
Creator, 145
Creed, of Paine, 64

Experience *(cont.)*
  in education, 237
  law and, 238
  of particulars, 336
  unity of, 354
Experimentalism, of Jefferson, 47, 51
Experimental method, in morals, 351, 352
Explanation, in science, 338
External world, 187, 200

F

Fabian Society, 191
Fact, an interaction, 234
Faculties:
  of the mind, in Hickok, 98
  trustworthiness of, 200
Fall of Adam, nature of, 23
Fallacy of the universal, 202, 203
Farmers, superiority of as citizens, 54
Federalist, The, 74
Fellowship of the New Life, 191
Fermentation, 35
First Cause, in Fiske, 164
Fichte, J. G., 116, 117, 189
Fiske, John, *159-167,* 168, 186, 232, 263, 314
  Outlines of Cosmic Philosophy, 161, 166
  "The Meaning of Infancy," 166
  Through Nature to God, 164
Fluxions, 28
Formation, the first movement of creation, 144
Fossils, study of, 152
Fourier, Charles, 120, 150
Franklin, Benjamin, 16, 40, 41, 56, 65, 66, 71, 230
  A Dissertation on Libery and Necessity, Pleasure and Pain, 40
  "Busybody Papers," 40
  "Dogood Papers," 40
Fraternity, as cooperation, 352
Freedom, 300, 351
  of religion, 63
  of scientist, 169
  of speculative thought, 218
  of thought, 63
  of will, 259
Freethought, Christian, 140

Free thought, in Paine, 64
Free trade, 85
Free will, 15, 16, 26
  theories, 300
French revolution, 73
Friends, Society of *(see* Quakers)
Fruitlands, 120
Fugitive slave law, 136
Fuller, Margaret, 131, 142
Fuller, Richard (and Wayland, Francis), *Domestic Slavery* . . . , 86
Function, 321, 341
Fundamental truths, intuition of, 107

G

Gandhi, Mahatma Mohandas K., 134
Gelasius I, Pope, 6
Generalization, 231, 241, 242, 244, 251
Generalizations, consequences of, 230
  origin of, 230
  Wright's rejection of, 171
Generalized other, 266, 268, 271
Genetic theory of reality, 159
Genteel tradition, 142
Geology, 79, 152
German idealistic philosophy, 189
Germany, American students in, 189
Gestures, internalized, 264
  significant, 265
God, 207, 214
  a designer, 34
  an almighty lecturer, 65
  as constitutional ruler, 2
  benevolence of, 34
  Bowne's view of, 205
  Calvinist concept of, 1
  Dewey's use of term, 354
  goodness of, in Mayhew, 42
  influence of evolution on belief in, 156
  in Henry James, 142
  in naturalist usage, 315
  in Santayana, 330
  man's knowledge of, in Porter, 108
  not author of sin, 23
  the spirit of community, 215
  Thoreau's views of, 133
Godliness, 20
Goethe, J. W. von, 334
Gorges, Thomas, 8

James, William *(cont.)*
  Principles of Psychology, 252, 253, 261
  The Meaning of Truth, 247, 253
  "The Will to Believe," 259
  Varieties of the Religious Experience, 262
Jefferson, Thomas, 8, 43, *46-55*, 56, 59, 60, 61, 65, 70, 71, 72, 75, 76, 77, 134, 151, 152, 353
  "Act for Establishing Religious Freedom in Virginia," 52
  "Summary View of the Rights of British America," 43
Jeffersonians, attack on, 75
Jesus, 64
Jones, Dr. Hiram K., 190, 191
Johns Hopkins University, 228
Johnson, Samuel, 12, 15-17, 35, 39
  Ethica, 40
  Noetica, 16
Journal of Philosophy, The, 218
Journal of Speculative Philosophy, The, 190, 218
Judgment, 227
Judgments:
  cognitional, 301
  valuational, 301

K

Kames, (Henry Home) Lord, *Elements of Criticism*, 81
Kant, Immanuel, 88, 92, 93, 99, 100, 103, 105, 106, 108, 113, 116, 117, 176, 185, 189, 192, 193, 200, 201, 207, 208, 219, 222, 230, 274, 280, 281, 282
  Critique of Practical Reason, 305
  Critique of Pure Reason, 112, 305
King's College, 12
Knowability, 223
Knowing, constitutive of self, 205
Knowledge, 101, 197, 231, 251
  Abbot's early view, 176
  acquisition of, 89
  an activity of the self, 200
  Colden's theory of, 31
  critical realist theory of, 280
  critique of, 274
  explicit, 296
  implicit, 296
  instrumental, 235, 282, 345

Knowledge *(cont.)*
  levels of, 297
  limitations of, 163
  limits of, in Hamilton, 176
  nature of, 233, 310
  object of, 147
  of universals, 336
  of value, possibility of, 289
  Perry's theory of, 285
  pragmatic theory of, 241
  problem of, 280
  reach of, in Porter, 107
  realists' exclusive concern with, 276
  Sellars' theory of, 295
  theory of, 326
  Urban's theory of, 308
  Virtue and, 33
Knudson, A.C., 202
Krikorian, Yervant, 319
  (ed.), *Naturalism and the Human Spirit*, 334, 343

L

Laissez-faire, 38
Lamarck, Jean, 151
Lamarckism, 151-152
Lamprecht, Sterling, 316
Lange, C., 258
Language, 245, 265
  evolutionary account of, 174
  nature and, 126
  the social dimension of thought, 267
  vocal gesture, 264
  systems, 319
Larger self, 213
Law, 240
  divine, 165
  Holmes' pragmatic definition of, 238
  in Henry James, 148
  in Thoreau, 136
  moral, 58
  natural, 165
  sociological view of, 238
Laws, 242
  negative character of, 149
  of social change, 160
  statute, 60
Learning by experience, 237
Le Comte, Joseph, 229
Legal realism, 238
Legal theory, 237

Supernaturalism, 317
a completed naturalism, 331
Supreme Person, 206
Survival of the fittest, 158
Swedenborg, Emanuel, 124, 143, 144, 145, 150
Syllogism:
Abbot's interpretation of, 178
of Being, 185
of Doing, 186
of Knowing, 185
traditional, 178
Syllogism of Syllogisms, 186
Symbol, 269
meaning of, 244

T

Taste, 250
standard of, in Hickok, 95
Taxation without representation, 44
Taylor, Dr. John, 22
Taylor, John, of Caroline, 76, 78
Arator, 77
Taylor, Nathaniel W., 102
Temperament:
James' theory of, 257
pragmatism as a, 229
Tenacity, method of, 248
"Tender-minded" philosophy, 257
Term, universality of, 268
Terms, of value judgments, 300
Textbooks, production of, 80
Theism, personal, 204
Theocracy, 6
Theology:
Colden's optimistic, 34
philosophy and, 115, 117
Theory, and practice, 229, 235, 345
Theory of knowledge, 200, 207, 262
Fiske's, 162
Hickok's, 96
importance of, in Porter, 103
Theory of value, 262
Thinking, 347
a means of survival, 233
a plan, 265
a type of behavior, 349
social nature of, 225
Thomas Aquinas, 275, 304
Thoreau, Henry David, 51, 121, 114, *131-141*, 142, 150

Thoreau, Henry David *(cont.)*
A Week on the Concord and Merrimac Rivers, 140
"Essay on Civil Disobedience," 134, 137
Walden, 139
Thought:
act of, 225
biologically functional, 234
dynamic view of, 194
existence and, 178
laws of, 179
Time, 339
Mead's theory of, 269
Toleration, 63
Total depravity, 21
"Tough-minded" philosophy, 257
Tradition, limits of, 50
Transcendence, Mead's denial of, 263
Transcendental Club, 116-117, 122
Transcendental empiricism, Bowne's, 201-202
Transcendentalism, 102
a philosophic mood, 111
Cohen's opposition to, 339
Wright's opposition to, 168, 169
Transcendentalists, 92, 154, 189
rebellion of, 142
use of Oriental materials, 110
Transcendental method, 122, 133
Transylvania University, 78
Trendelenburg, Adolf, 102, 106, 194
Triad, the basic harmonious relation, 216
Tripersonality of God, in Hickok, 96
True Theology, 65
Truth, 93-94, 206, 208, 212, 214, 236, 247, 248, 250, 255, 256, 285, 312, 335, 346, 347
absolute, 231
factors in, 297
in mathematics, 100
James' theory of, 254
law of, in Hickok, 95
necessary, 181
pragmatic theory, 213
realm of, 331, 332
relative and absolute, 163
systematic coherence of, 128
verification of, 224
Truth-value, 256
Tyranny, Jefferson's opposition to, 52